PR...

GUARDIANS...

"Captivating . . . Muir's adventures in an almost virginal Yosemite will entrance park lovers, outdoor enthusiasts, and California history buffs, the narrative swept along by Muir's shimmering, deftly excerpted prose."

—*Los Angeles Times*

"*Guardians of the Valley* is propulsive, revelatory, and immensely readable. Summoning new research and fresh insights into the extraordinary character of John Muir, Dean King has written an absorbing paean to a deep friendship that rescued one of the planet's most magical landscapes from the jaws of mammon."

—Hampton Sides, #1 *New York Times* bestselling author of *Blood and Thunder* and *In the Kingdom of Ice*

"A well-researched story . . . King's tribute to Muir and Johnson is exemplary and, reading his book, Americans will understand the great debt we owe to these men."

—*The Explorers Journal*

"Like an experienced trail guide, Mr. King takes time to linger over remarkable landscapes, recount revealing anecdotes, and take worthwhile detours."

—*The Wall Street Journal*

"Compelling . . . a book about the power of storytelling . . . To effectively draw strength from Muir's writing, as King suggests we do, we might reconsider which stories are told around the campfire."

—*The New York Times Book Review*

"*Guardians of the Valley* is both timely and timeless, a sweeping narrative that's also a deeply personal story. Its hero is John Muir, the great sage and protector of the natural world. Its theme is urgent: without the wild things, we're lost. With a mastery of small details that accrue into grand vistas, Dean King summons the majesty of the Yosemite Valley and the souls who recognized it. King has written an epic."

—Susan Casey, author of *The Wave* and *The Devil's Teeth*

"*Guardians of the Valley* brings to life two compelling figures whose flaws are more apparent in our time than they were in theirs: a reminder that history is the final editor. It's also a poignant portrait of an era when mere words could change the world."

—*San Francisco Chronicle*

"Just when I thought we had heard all we could read and hear about the miraculous John Muir, this wonderful book on Muir's lifelong battle to save wild lands came into my hands. Deeply thoughtful, precisely researched, it is testimony to our ongoing obligation to protect the natural world. Muir is our inspiration and our teacher."

—Gretel Ehrlich, author of *The Solace of Open Spaces*

"This comprehensively researched and compellingly readable history offers an intimate yet sweeping portrait of an inspirational friendship that literally altered the American landscape and enshrined the modern-day conservation movement."

—*Booklist* (starred review)

"King, drawing extensively on the Muir–Johnson letters, tells the story of the work they did together and the admiration they bore for each other, crafting prose as absorbing as one of Muir's articles in the *Century*."

—*Natural History* magazine

"Lively . . . comprehensive . . . [King turns] up small but meaningful moments of history. . . . The author is particularly adept at recounting the complex politics surrounding frontier resources in a time when official policy was utilitarian. . . . A welcome study of environmental politics in action."

—*Kirkus Reviews*

"In the long arc of Muir's life, no place was more sacred to him than Yosemite—and in the fight to protect that space and its many wonders from the ravages of commercial loggers, rapacious tourism developers, and municipal water thieves, no alliance mattered more than his friendship with Robert Underwood Johnson, the gifted magazine editor who first helped Muir to find his voice, later goaded him to hone it to a keen edge, and eventually gave him the means to draw that sword and begin swinging it on behalf of nature. In *Guardians of the Valley*, Dean King has forged a flaming tribute to perhaps the greatest knight of American conservation, and to the extraordinary landscape that was his paramount source of inspiration."

—Kevin Fedarko, author of *The Emerald Mile*

"King probes the transformative partnership between a writer and an editor in this sparkling history. . . . [He] vividly chronicles Muir's evolution from 'self-styled hobo' to forceful activist, goaded and nurtured by the 'urbane' Johnson, and weaves in intriguing vignettes of Theodore Roosevelt, *Poetry* magazine founder Harriet Monroe, and others, as well as rhapsodic descriptions of the Sierra Nevada landscape. Fans of Ken Burns's *The National Parks* documentary will cherish this inspired account of how an American treasure was saved."

—*Publishers Weekly*

"A library of books has been written about John Muir, many of which mention Robert Underwood Johnson, but not many adequately describe his long collaboration with Muir. In this book, Dean King remedies that oversight. . . . Very worth reading."

—*National Parks Traveler*

"King tells the rousing tale of how muscular outdoorsman John Muir and the bookish Robert Underwood Johnson, Muir's editor at the *Century Magazine*, forged a friendship that marshaled the nascent forces of conservation, created the modern environmental movement, and, against all odds, saved Yosemite from the maw of industrialization and birthed the national parks—the best idea we've ever had."

—Gregory Crouch, author of *The Bonanza King*

"There have been many books written about John Muir, but no one has so keenly identified the transformational nature of the faithful friendship between Muir and Robert Underwood Johnson. . . . King has written a stirring tribute to the power of an alliance that transformed environmentalism in the US, a psalm to the radiant beauty of Yosemite, and an homage to John Muir, whom, as King assiduously sands away the polish of legend, emerges as a visionary, a mystic, and a reluctant but surprisingly accomplished political brawler dedicated to preserving the 'temples of Nature' for all Americans to cherish."

—James Campbell, author of *The Final Frontiersman* and *Braving It*

"Dean King's account of Muir and Johnson's 'unlikely partnership' makes for an enjoyable joint biography."

—*Nature*

"Read *Guardians of the Valley* and get swept up in the rousing and inspiring story of John Muir. In these challenging times, this riveting book reminds us of the importance of life beyond the human, and gives us a template for the climate fight ahead in the marriage of Muir's passion and Robert Johnson's political savvy. It also puts the lie to the recent clumsy attempts to cancel Muir, who, while flawed like all of us, lived a life filled with courage, passion, humor, and love. A fascinating chronicle of the man who changed the way we think about nature."

—David Gessner, author of *All the Wild That Remains*

"From the heights of Yosemite to the halls of Congress, Dean King vividly illuminates the bond formed between John Muir and Robert Johnson on their quest to save endangered American landscapes. A haunting forerunner of today's planetary crisis, *Guardians of the Valley* brings to life the battles won, then lost and fought again, with irreplaceable ecological treasures at stake."

—Andrea Pitzer, author of *Icebound*

"In *Guardians of the Valley*, Dean King chooses Robert Underwood Johnson as the perfect cornerstone to trace John Muir's passion to preserve natural spaces. Much like Muir found paths among the giant sequoias, King found a path among these late nineteenth-century literary giants' archives to trace their relationship and the early American conservation movement. King starts with their historic campfire in 1889, which prompted the preservation of Yosemite and the birth of the Sierra Club, and concludes with the damming of Hetch Hetchy. He tells the story so well that the reader may think that *this time* the valley will be preserved."

—Mike Wurtz, head of the University of the Pacific
Special Collections and the John Muir Papers and editor of
John Muir's Grand Yosemite: Musings & Sketches

"*Guardians of the Valley* propels Dean King to the first rank of writers on nature, letting us discover as if for the first time the beauty and majesty of Yosemite. And in his equally enthralling parallel story of John Muir's partnership with editor and power broker Robert Underwood Johnson, King demonstrates how passion and politics, in support of noble causes, can unite rather than divide a nation. In that sense, this extraordinary book is more than great history. It just might be a blueprint for our own times."

—Charles Slack, author of *Liberty's First Crisis*

Robert Underwood Johnson   *John Muir*

GUARDIANS
OF THE
VALLEY

JOHN MUIR AND THE
FRIENDSHIP THAT SAVED
YOSEMITE

DEAN KING

SCRIBNER

NEW YORK LONDON TORONTO SYDNEY NEW DELHI

Scribner

An Imprint of Simon & Schuster, LLC

1230 Avenue of the Americas

New York, NY 10020

First Scribner trade paperback edition March 2024

SCRIBNER and design are trademarks of Simon & Schuster, LLC

Simon & Schuster: Celebrating 100 Years of Publishing in 2024

For information about special discounts for bulk purchases, please contact
Simon & Schuster Special Sales at 1-866-506-1949 or business@simonandschuster.com.

The Simon & Schuster Speakers Bureau can bring authors to your live event.
For more information or to book an event, contact the Simon & Schuster Speakers Bureau
at 1-866-248-3049 or visit our website at www.simonspeakers.com.

Interior design by Kyle Kabel

Manufactured in the United States of America

1   3   5   7   9   10   8   6   4   2

Library of Congress Cataloging-in-Publication Data

Names: King, Dean, 1962– author.
Title: Guardians of the valley : John Muir and the friendship that saved Yosemite / Dean King.
Other titles: John Muir and the friendship that saved Yosemite
Description: First Scribner hardcover edition. | New York : Scribner, 2023. |
Includes bibliographical references and index.
Identifiers: LCCN 2022044155 (print) | LCCN 2022044156 (ebook) |
ISBN 9781982144463 (hardcover) | ISBN 9781982144487 (ebook)
Subjects: LCSH: Yosemite National Park (Calif.)—History. |
Muir, John, 1838–1914—Friends and associates. |
Johnson, Robert Underwood, 1853–1937—Friends and associates. |
Nature conservation—Government policy—United States—History—19th century. |
National parks and reserves—Government policy—United States—History—19th century. |
Yosemite Valley (Calif.)—History. | Sierra Club—Biography. |
Conservationists—United States—Biography. | Periodical editors—United States—Biography. |
Naturalists—United States—Biography.
Classification: LCC F868.Y6 K495 2023 (print) | LCC F868.Y6 (ebook) |
DDC 333.7209794/47—dc23/eng/20220922
LC record available at https://lccn.loc.gov/2022044155
LC ebook record available at https://lccn.loc.gov/2022044156

ISBN 978-1-9821-4446-3
ISBN 978-1-9821-4447-0 (pbk)
ISBN 978-1-9821-4448-7 (ebook)

For Jessica and for our daughters, Hazel, Grace, Willa, and Nora, who are collectively ablaze with creativity, empathy, wanderlust, and curiosity. May the mindfulness, spirit, and friendship of Muir and Johnson inspire your efforts and innovations in protecting the globe we live on and cherish.

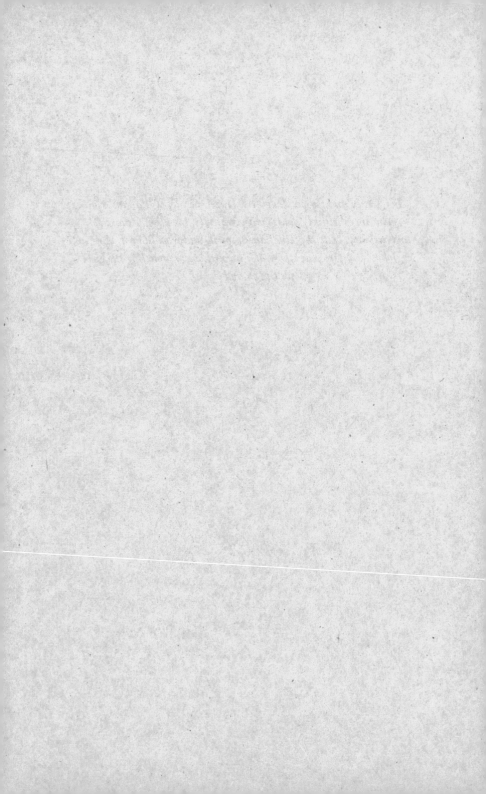

My dear Mr. Johnson,

I began that confounded letter a dozen times & could never make anything satisfactory out of it. It now lies & has lain on my table for more than a month, a scrawny orderless mass of fragments. You would have written such a letter in half an hour & no doubt would like to see me hanged for not being able to write it in a month. But I will send that letter yet & when you see it you will agree with me that it is worthless.

—John Muir, October 29, 1889

My dear Muir,

Why don't you start an association for preserving California's monuments & natural wonders—or at least Yosemite? It would be a good influence. How timid you Californians are, anyhow!

—R. U. Johnson, November 21, 1889

Dear Mr. Johnson,

All the world is indebted to you for your work in saving so fine a section of the Sierra from cheap vulgar ruin.

—John Muir, September 12, 1890

My dear Mr. Muir,

When can you come East? Your Yosemite articles have made you many new friends in this region, and I wish you could come East and deliver a few lectures before geographical societies or Columbia College—or we could let you give an open-air reading in Central Park, which is now looking its best.

—R. U. Johnson, October 24, 1890

Dear Muir,

Hurray for you! Yosemite is saved, and the Lord must be happier. I congratulate you with all my heart, my dear Muir, for you have been the heart—the fons et origo—of this movement.

—R. U. Johnson, February 24, 1905

Dear Mr. Johnson,

I want everybody to know that in particular you invented Yosemite Park.

—John Muir, January 26, 1911

Contents

PART II MAKING THE MOUNTAINS GLAD

PART III THE WATER STEALERS

PART IV A CALIFORNIA WATER WAR

JOHN MUIR'S CALIFORNIA

Note: NM, NP, and NF indicate a present-day National Monument, National Park, or National Forest

MUIR'S 1868 ROUTE

North Fork American River

Sacramento Valley

American River

Sacramento

Mokelumne River

Suisun Bay

Carquinez Strait

Martinez

Stockton

San Rafael

Mount Tamalpais

Muir Woods NM

Berkeley

Oakland

Alameda

San Francisco

CONTRA COSTA COUNTY

LA GRANGE DAM

Tuolumne River

Hayward

San Mateo

Fremont

Milpitas

STANFORD UNIVERSITY

Snelling

Hopeton

CALAVERAS DAM

Santa Clara

San Jose

Hill's Ferry

Merced River

Merced

San Joaquin Valley

Pacific Ocean

Morgan Hill

Pacheco Pass

Santa Cruz

Gilroy

CALIFORNIA

0 Miles 25 50

0 Kilometers 50

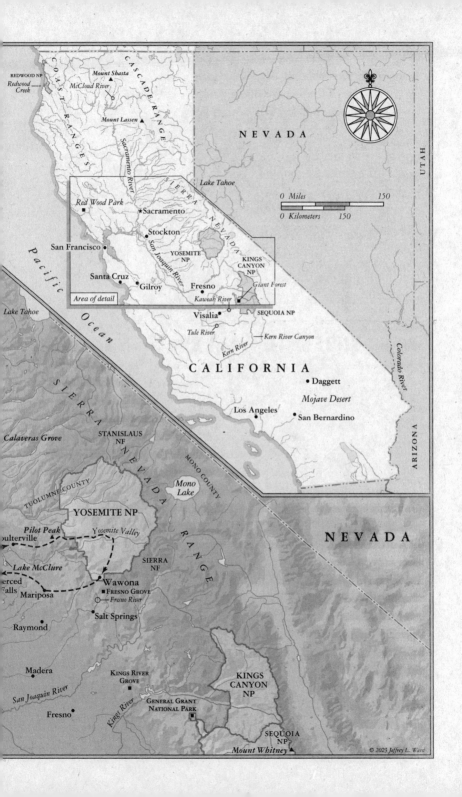

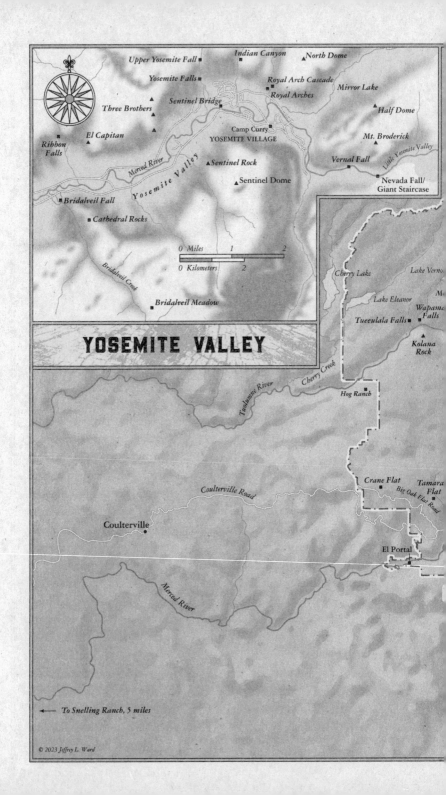

Upper Yosemite Fall ▪   Indian Canyon ▪   North Dome ▪

Yosemite Falls ▪   Royal Arch Cascade   Mirror Lake

Three Brothers ▲   Sentinel Bridge   Royal Arches

El Capitan   Camp Curry   Half Dome
                    YOSEMITE VILLAGE
Ribbon   Mt. Broderick ▲
Falls   Little Yosemite Valley

     Merced River   ▲Sentinel Rock   Vernal Fall ▪

          Yosemite Valley   ▲ Sentinel Dome   Nevada Fall/
                                                       Giant Staircase
▪ Bridalveil Fall

   ▪ Cathedral Rocks

                                                       Cherry Lake   Lake Verno

                    0 Miles   1   2
                                                            Lake Eleanor   M
                    0 Kilometers   2   Wapama
     Bridalveil Creek   Tueeulala Falls ▪   Falls ▪

          ▪ Bridalveil Meadow   ▲ Kolana
                                                                 Rock

YOSEMITE VALLEY

                              Tuolumne River   Cherry Creek

                                        Hog Ranch ▪

                    Coulterville Road   Crane Flat   Tamara
                                                           ▪   Flat
                                                              Big Oak Flat Road
          Coulterville
          ●
                                                           El Portal
                                                           ▪

          Merced River

← To Snelling Ranch, 5 miles

YOSEMITE NATIONAL PARK AND REGION, CIRCA 1895

Sierra Nevada

Keyes Peak ▲

Acker Peak ▲

Mono Lake

Gibson ▲

Rancheria Mountain

Tuolumne Canyon

Tuolumne River

Muir Gorge

Waterwheel Falls

Hetch Hetchy Valley

Soda Springs

Dana Fork

Mount Dana

Bloody Canyon

YOSEMITE PARK

Tuolumne Meadows

Lyell Fork

Mount Hoffmann ▲

Cathedral Lakes

Porcupine Flat ▪

Yosemite Creek

Merced River

Mount Maclure ▲

Mount Lyell

Washburn Lake

Inspiration Point ▪

Area of detail

Mount Ritter ▲

Wawona Road

Empire Meadow ▪

| 0 Miles | | 10 | | 20 |
| 0 Kilometers | | | 20 | |

Wawona/Clarks Station ▪

Wawona Hotel ▪

Mariposa Grove, Wawona Tree, Grizzly Giant ▪

To Mount Gabb, 12 miles ➤

Sugar Pine ▪

Nelder Grove ▪

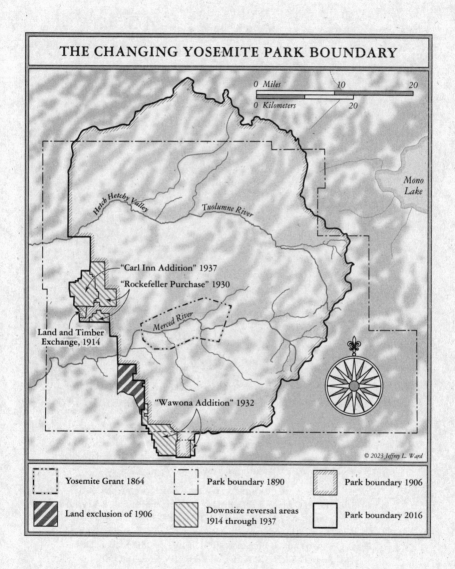

THE CHANGING YOSEMITE PARK BOUNDARY

0 Miles 10 20
0 Kilometers 20

Mono Lake

Hetch Hetchy Valley

Tuolumne River

"Carl Inn Addition" 1937

"Rockefeller Purchase" 1930

Merced River

Land and Timber
Exchange, 1914

"Wawona Addition" 1932

© 2023 Jeffrey L. Ward

Yosemite Grant 1864

Park boundary 1890

Park boundary 1906

Land exclusion of 1906

Downsize reversal areas
1914 through 1937

Park boundary 2016

A diagram of Yosemite Valley from "The Story of the Yosemite Valley (Guide Leaflet No. 60)," by François E. Matthews, produced by the American Museum of Natural History in 1901. Entering the valley from the southwest along the Merced River (**MR**) and leading to Yosemite Village (**YV**), Mirror Lake (**ML**), and Tenaya Canyon (**TC**).

VALLEY FEATURES, CLOCKWISE FROM THE SOUTHWEST, INCLUDE:
RF Ribbon Falls **EC** El Capitan **EP** Eagle Peak **YF** Yosemite Falls **R** Royal Arches
W Washington Column **ND** North Dome **BD** Basket Dome **MW** Mount Watkins
C Cloud's Rest **HD** Half (or South) Dome **LY** Little Yosemite Valley
G Glacier Point **B** Mount Broderick **LC** Liberty Cap **SD** Sentinel Dome
SR Sentinel Rock **CR** Cathedral Rock **BV** Bridalveil Fall

Author's Note

When the California nature savant John Muir and his urbane *Century Magazine* editor Robert Underwood Johnson, based in New York City, decided in 1889 to take their case for the formation of a national park not just to the pages of one of the nation's most influential magazines but to the corridors of Capitol Hill, they ignited a quarter century of legislation and environmental activism that would change the shape of the nation and of stewardship of nature everywhere.

Guardians of the Valley is the true story of the unlikely partnership of two men who helped shape the way we perceive and appreciate nature to this day. Not only did Muir and Johnson create, improve, and fight to preserve Yosemite National Park, but they also helped found and guide the Sierra Club, enlightened and vastly broadened the base of citizens concerned for the country's natural grandeur, and ran herd on the nation's most powerful change agent and friend of the wilds, President Theodore Roosevelt.

This book traces the central vein of Muir's rich and varied career as he became America's greatest mountaineer and nature bard and eventually its principal wilderness advocate, earning him the sobriquet "father of the national parks." But without the instigation, cunning, and cajoling of the author-whisperer Johnson, himself a notable poet and man of letters, Muir would never have made the impact that he did.

Relying on the power of the press and on their own grit, Muir and Johnson waged an epic battle against the headlong rush of the globe's most ambitious, yet still formative, nation. Muir, a rugged explorer who thrived on hardship, deployed wisdom, faith, and an uncanny ability to observe nature and inspire reverence for it. The refined Johnson, who would later become the US ambassador to Italy, brought both moxie and diplomacy. Their campaign for nature and the environment navigated the administrations of seven presidents (with their changing personalities, policies, and secretaries of the interior) and ten mayors of San Francisco, their adversary in the fight to keep a reservoir out of Yosemite National Park and thus to establish the sanctity and permanence of all national parks—the nation's first great environmental war.

Even as we grapple with the global environmental crisis today, the founders of the modern conservation movement are rightly being scrutinized for their racial views and the implications of those views, leading to much thoughtful commentary both critical and supportive of Muir. He and Johnson operated in a world tinged with racism, and they themselves occasionally failed to transcend negative stereotypes. But they were both socially progressive, and Muir would ultimately reveal that he believed in the equality of all people. Like all of us, he was a person of his time and place—and yet he was dramatically ahead of his time. It is my hope that this book will provide a framework for understanding Muir's life of service and the powerful message of his passion for nature.

And if it encourages some readers to visit Yosemite National Park, particularly Tuolomne Meadows, where 133 years ago Muir and Johnson hatched their partnership for nature, it will attest to Muir's legacy once again.

—Dean King
Savage's Trading Post, California
October 2022

A Note on the Text

The tale of these two men takes place across the latter half of the nineteenth century and into the early twentieth, and I have quoted from many sources, including letters—handwritten and typed—newspapers, magazines, and hearing transcripts, which employed a wide range of punctuation and spelling. I have taken certain small liberties with these texts for the convenience of the modern reader in regularizing spellings, editing punctuation, correcting obvious errors, and compressing (but never inventing) dialogue in quoted material. For example, Muir wrote *grip* for *grippe*; I have used the latter, more common, spelling throughout. I have eliminated the diacritic in the word *cañon*, which Muir and Johnson used, opting for the current spelling, *canyon*. Since 1890 the US Board on Geographic Names has discouraged the use of apostrophes in geographical names. Muir spelled Kings Canyon with an apostrophe (King's), but I have used the modern standard spelling. The disputed valley in Yosemite National Park, Hetch Hetchy, was often hyphenated (Hetch-Hetchy); I have standardized this too. I have also regularized and italicized publication titles for ease of reading and occasionally filled out shorthand that appears in Muir's letters.

The Photo

— May 17, 1903 —

Whether the photographer, who would forever remain anonymous, felt the conceivably immense pressure we will never know. But with the head of the nation and the soul of the nation's preservation movement, both rugged, demanding, and outspoken men, paired together for a brief time, posed against arguably the nation's most transcendent and iconic landscape, a long journey by train, horseback, and boot from any major city, the stakes in making a good image were high.

The photo—the official portrait of John Muir, age sixty-five, and Theodore Roosevelt, age forty-four, at Overhanging Rock—would come to symbolize the young president's love of nature and serve as a memorial to the meeting of the two indomitable men who had camped there together the night before. Yet all might not have been as copacetic as it appeared, or as Roosevelt, who was laying the groundwork for election to a second term, would later lead us to believe. Were these two pillars of American conservation, these two headstrong men, truly in accord that day, or had they, representing two very different and irreconcilable visions, clashed? Did they themselves even know?

The Roosevelt-Muir photo op took place five decades after the California Gold Rush, when the first white men to enter the magnificent valley, the Mariposa Battalion—a volunteer army of prospectors, ranchers, and roughnecks—led by the trader James Savage, who had quarreled with the Miwuk, went there in the spring of 1851 to rout the tribe from its stronghold, a remote valley and bear den they called Yosemite. Reaching what became known as Inspiration Point, at least one of them, the gold miner L. H. Bunnell, realized the specialness of the place. "Haze hung over the valley—light as gossamer—and clouds partially dimmed the higher cliffs and mountains," he later wrote. "This obscurity of vision but increased the awe with which I beheld it, and as I looked, a peculiar exalted sensation seemed to fill my whole being, and I found my eyes in tears with emotion."[1]

Four decades had passed since President Abraham Lincoln had signed a bill granting Yosemite (Miwuk for "those who kill") Valley and the Mariposa Grove of Big Trees to the State of California to preserve and protect "for public use, recreation and enjoyment, inalienable for all time." Lincoln's Yosemite grant—preceding the creation of Yellowstone National Park by eight years—was the first to establish government protection of any land. This little-observed act, in the midst of the Civil War, would become the fountainhead of the nation's conservation movement, and Muir, its champion, the embodiment of the nation's passion for its wilderness. It was not by accident that Roosevelt, on a two-month, twenty-five-state, two-hundred-speech whistle-stop tour of the West that was meant to boost the electoral viability of the youngest president ever, came to meet Muir at this time and in this place.[2]

One can almost imagine the pulse of the still inchoate nation beating in the veins of the two men—the backcountry immigrant and the Ivy League president—in this moment. Theirs was a country enthralled with itself and its unknowable potential even after thirteen decades of independence on top of seventeen of colonial expansion. It lacked introspection or remorse at brutally driving the native peoples off their lands—from Jamestown in 1607 to Manhattan to the Black Hills and to this valley before the Civil War—in part because in the wake of the war, it was simultaneously redefining its borders and relationships and struggling with its complexities and paradoxes while dizzyingly hurtling into the future; it lacked hindsight because it had not yet arrived to look back. That reckoning lay in the distant future. But these two men, for very different reasons, at least had the insight to know that they must put a stop to the devastation that white men had brought to the land.

That was their fight. This was their summit. There was a real sense that Yosemite Valley, where they now met, represented the nation's natural beauty and that its fate would somehow define the nation's future.

The night before the photo was taken, Muir and Roosevelt camped with their guides near the upper end of the valley, a couple miles from Glacier Point, where Overhanging Rock juts out and gives a spectacular view of the mile-deep Yosemite Valley and the panoramic Sierra Nevada. Roosevelt was already well into his cross-country tour and eager to escape the coffin-like luxury of his plush Pullman railcar, the ever-present phalanx of reporters, and the pressure to perform and please at every stop. Since his years as a Dakotas rancher and lieutenant colonel leading the Rough Riders cavalry regiment in the Spanish-American War, Roosevelt preferred horseback to a reclining cushioned seat. After a satisfying day of riding their mounts through deep snowdrifts, the men lay beside the campfire on beds made from the bent boughs of a fir tree and, both being capital storytellers, rattled away at each other, neither afraid to speak his mind.[3]

Muir found much to like in the "interesting, hearty, and manly" Roosevelt, but he mistrusted his motivations for preserving nature and his interpretation of what might constitute "the greatest good for the greatest number," the mantra of his forestry chief. When Roosevelt bragged about his hunting, Muir, angered by America's heedless eradication of the passenger pigeon and the American buffalo, chastised him for killing animals for sport: "Mr. Roosevelt, when are you going to get beyond the boyishness of killing things?" he blurted out. "It is all very well for a young fellow who has not formed his standards to rush out in the heat of youth and slaughter animals, but are you not getting far enough along to leave that off?"

Though Roosevelt lacked any remorse when it came to slaying animals, he was a consummate diplomat when he wanted to be, and he considered the point. "Muir," he responded at last, "I guess you are right."[4]

It was a dubious concession. Roosevelt had collected and stuffed more than a thousand birds by the time he went off to college. He had left his pregnant wife to rush out to the Badlands to shoot a buffalo, a species on the brink of extinction, before it was too late to bag one, and on this train tour, he was barely persuaded by his handlers not to dog-hunt cougars in Yellowstone, where hunting was forbidden, for fear of a public outcry. While Roosevelt would never escape his chest-thumping glee of the kill, Muir, a hunter in his youth in Wisconsin, had long ago rejected the notion that wild animals were created solely for food, recreation, and "other uses not yet discovered," and had once declared in his journal that if a war broke out "between the wild beasts and Lord Man, I would be tempted to sympathize with the bears."[5]

Perhaps they would not see eye to eye on hunting, but Muir had trees and whole ecosystems to save. Blinded by its own hubris, the nation was grotesquely cannibalizing itself, felling giant sequoias, some of the planet's oldest and largest living organisms, thousands of years old, and even shipping them off to be exhibited in monstrous fashion, like circus spectacles. The irony was that they would have to undo Lincoln's grant in substance to save it in spirit. Muir and his coconspirator, his editor at the *Century Magazine*, Robert Underwood Johnson, felt in their hearts that this bold, and in many circles unpopular, maneuver was necessary.

Muir took a torch from the fire and with his face and his shaggy salt-and-pepper beard flickering in chiaroscuro ignited a brown pine tree nearby. He loved the drama of fire at night, how it brought the trees to life and drew them into the conversation. He had built bonfires for such eminent naturalists as Asa Gray and Sir Joseph Hooker and had once attempted to build one for Ralph Waldo Emerson. The glow of Muir's immense fires transformed the surrounding firs into "enormous pagodas of silver," recounted his friend Annie Bidwell, while Muir would wave his arms ecstatically, shouting, "Look at the glory!"

Now as Muir and Roosevelt watched in awe, like tenderfooted boys, the dead tree roared to life, shooting stars into the sky. "Hurrah!" Roosevelt shouted, the exclamation leaping from his gut. "That's a candle it took five hundred years to make. Hurrah for Yosemite!"

With its spectacular scenery and well-heeled tourists, Yosemite had attracted some of the country's most skilled photographers. Though this one—a hired hand sent by Underwood & Underwood, the world's largest publisher of stereoviews—would go unnamed, perhaps it was Arthur Pillsbury, a company stringer, who had taken a shot of them two days before in front of the immense sequoia Grizzly Giant. Whoever it was clearly knew the precise place and time to produce a memorable image. "Sunrise from Glacier Point!" Muir's late friend and geologist Joseph LeConte had once exclaimed. "No one can appreciate it who has not seen it. . . . I had never imagined the grandeur of the reality."[6]

Before breakfast, in the soft morning light, Roosevelt and Muir took their places by the cliff's edge at Glacier Point, with a view across the valley as a backdrop. Though neither cared much for sartorial splendor, they both looked kempt in their hats and jackets. Roosevelt wore jodhpurs and boots, Rough Rider–fashion, with a kerchief around his neck. Muir wore a simple broadcloth suit.

A photograph for the ages: Theodore Roosevelt and John Muir at Glacier Point, Yosemite Valley, one of the most enduring images of the early conservation movement in the United States. Underwood & Underwood.

In the photograph, there's no hint that they had refused tents to sleep by the campfire and that five inches of snow had dropped on them overnight, a Sierra Nevada baptism verifying that the President had indeed escaped pampered civilization and the claws of his handlers to be immersed in the bosom of nature. At dawn, he had emerged from a thicket of forty army blankets, shaken off the additional blanket of snow, and shaved by the light of the campfire.

Overhanging Rock jutted out precipitously and from certain angles looked only a footstep away from Yosemite Falls all the way across the valley. Half Dome stood stark against the sky. To Muir, it looked "down the valley like the most living being of all the rocks and mountains," such that one could "fancy that there were brains in that lofty brow." The promontory provided just the right perspective on the Giant Staircase, the impressive drop of the Merced River into the valley over the 594-foot Nevada Fall (Wowywe, or "twisted current," to the Miwuk) and just downstream the 317-foot Vernal Fall (Yanopah, "little cloud"). The view stirred the President. On his tour he had seen the Grand Canyon for the first time and declared it "beautiful and terrible and unearthly." Casting his eyes now on what many believed was the most spectacular panorama in the nation, the nation that he led, Roosevelt felt a welling of emotion. Not only was it a sight of awesome beauty and grandeur, it was an immense responsibility. Though if tears streaked his face, as was reported, you would never know it from the photo. The photographer, who took two shots of the pair and two of Roosevelt alone, made sure of that.[7]

The photographer oriented the distant Yosemite Falls—a flowing white streak—on the left-hand side of the frame, below the President's right shoulder. Nature was the great equalizer, but he placed Roosevelt, who was five feet, eight inches tall, on the higher part of the boulder with his broad shoulders square to the camera. He positioned Muir, who was a few inches taller (and with his thin build looked even more so), at an angle a little lower on the right. The men were thus as evenly matched in height as in stature, each being master of his own realm.

Roosevelt looked boldly into the lens, as if daring the viewer to question him. Muir, lithe and erect of posture even in his seventh decade, bushy bearded, gazed pensively, hands deferentially clasped behind his back, as if he were pausing in the middle of a conversation with the President. He had embellished himself, as he liked to do, with a botanical spray as a boutonniere. (A perhaps not altogether innocent gesture: "There is that in the glance of a flower which may at times control the greatest of creation's braggart lords," he had written.) The sun cast his shadow onto the President. Roosevelt was the last best hope to prevent the American wilderness from being swallowed whole by a voracious nation whose appetites and aspirations were fueled by its natural resources.[8]

Muir, who believed that not everything was put on earth to save man, had one more night in the majestic valley to bring the President around.

PART I

COMING TO CALIFORNIA

•

I often wonder what man will do with the mountains—that is, with their utilizable, destructible garments. Will he cut down all the trees to make ships and houses? If so, what will be the final and far upshot? Will human destructions like those of Nature—fire and flood and avalanche—work out a higher good, a finer beauty? Will a better civilization come in accord with obvious nature, and all this wild beauty be set to human poetry and song? Another universal outpouring of lava or the coming of a glacial period could scarce wipe out the flowers and shrubs more efficiently than do the sheep. And what then is coming? What is the human part of the mountains' destiny?

—John Muir, August 1875

300.

Yosemite Valley from Inspiration Point, with El Capitan on the left, Bridalveil Fall on the right, and Half Dome in the distance. George Fiske, ca. 1883.

CHAPTER 1

Discovering the Range of Light

Most of the men who arrived in San Francisco during the 1849 Gold Rush, eager to get rich, stayed in town for only a few nights before pushing on to Oakland and the journey east toward the Sierra Nevada mines. And most soon learned that searching for gold was a largely futile and frequently treacherous pursuit in such a lawless land. While a few of the forty-niners would get rich, the majority came a long way only to find hardship and despair, as well as to see the city of their arrival burn to the ground seven times in eighteen months. John Muir, who that same year had migrated with his father and several siblings (his mother and the rest would follow) from Scotland to southern Wisconsin, where they plowed the earth for crops, not gold, landed in San Francisco two decades later at the age of twenty-nine and did not give the place even a single night.

When the Muirs settled in Wisconsin, the country, under President James K. Polk, was just finishing up a massive expansion, adding California, the Oregon Territory, and Texas. Now the nation had just expanded again with the purchase of Alaska from the Russians for $7.2 million. Muir seemed intent on exploring it all. Before reaching the West Coast, he had trekked through the Midwest and across the Deep South, finding ample opportunity to indulge his passion for nature, but it was California and Alaska that would ignite his soul, drive his intense curiosity, and compel him to fight to save nature from man.[1]

Like San Francisco, Muir was well acquainted with fire—not to mention brimstone. While carving a farm out of the Wisconsin wilderness, his father, Daniel, had used bonfires to clear the land. One day while Muir stood before a fire so hot he could not approach it to toss on more branches, Daniel bade his son to study the flames: "Now, John, just think what an awful thing it'd be to be thrown into that fire," he said, "and then think of hellfire, which is so many times hotter. Into that fire all bad boys, sinners of every sort who disobey God, will be cast just as we're casting branches into this bonfire, and although suffering so much, their sufferings will never, never end because neither the fire nor the sinners can die." As a Disciples of Christ evangelist, Daniel believed in the literal truth of the Bible—the only book welcome in his house—and austere living. Muir learned his Bible verses at the threat of the whip, worked in the fields from dawn to dusk, and for a time, like the rest of the family, survived on gruel dished out once a day, thanks to his father's interpretation of the "wholesome" and trendy Graham Diet, the brainchild of the evangelist Sylvester Graham, who believed that a sparse, meatless, and bland diet of whole grains, fruits, and vegetables would lower sexual desire and thus improve morality and health.[2]

Intensely smart and curious, the boy, who loathed bullies, caught glimpses of Wisconsin's fleeting native peoples in the woods and felt the injustice of their being "robbed of their lands and pushed ruthlessly back . . . by alien races," in a cruel case of "the rule of might with but little or no thought for the right or welfare of the other fellow if he were the weaker." The teenager smuggled books of poetry and adventure into the house and read them in the wee hours of the morning, awakened when his early-rising machine—a clock-based invention that he had whittled out of wood—collapsed the foot of his bed and dumped him feetfirst into a pan of cold water. A series of clashes with his father propelled young Muir from the nest in 1860, at the age of twenty-two. By then he was a devout but restless spiritual seeker with a fierce independent streak, a stout work ethic, a knack for innovation, a photographic recall of Scripture, and a wry sense of humor. His knowledge of Wisconsin's plants and animals was encyclopedic, and his uncanny ability to endure peril and hardship, as well as to scamper over mountain terrain, would become legendary.

Fire played a role in the next chapter of Muir's life too. During a furious blizzard, a freak gust of wind shot down the chimney and sucked smoldering embers up onto the roof of the factory deep in the Canadian woods where he and his younger brother Dan worked during the Civil War. Thirty thousand broom handles and six thousand rake handles went up in smoke. It was a crushing blow, as Muir had not only reengineered the factory, greatly improving its efficiency and profitability, but had also found a new family of sorts among its owners, who were devout and nature loving and who had offered him a partnership in the business.[3]

The blaze cost Muir his savings and his hopes of returning to the University of Wisconsin, which he had attended for two years before running out of funds. In Madison he had met his soul mate and muse, Jeanne Carr, a botanist and the wife of Ezra Carr, a medical doctor and professor of natural sciences. Jeanne would serve as a mentor to Muir and introduce him to a number of the brilliant minds of their day, along with the woman who would become his wife. Muir, sporting a neat beard and mustache below piercing gray-blue eyes, had been an outsize personality at Madison, where his room full of plant specimens and his mechanical clock-based inventions, including his early-rising machine and a hand-carved desk with a rotating book carousel, were a campus attraction. He had gained recognition for both his creative genius and his folksy vernacular. He was a shy but outspoken self-taught nature zealot with big hands powerful from farmwork and a penchant for moralizing.

Penniless after the fire, he took a job in a wagon factory in Indianapolis, where he invented a state-of-the-art process for making wagon wheels. But one day as he was repairing a machine belt, a wayward spike punctured his right eye and left him temporarily blind in both eyes due to a sympathetic reaction. Confined to a dark room, he lapsed into melancholy. "I have often in my heart wondered what God was training you for," Carr wrote him while he was recuperating. She had been amazed by Muir's handmade inventions, his Scots-inflected poetic observations and insights, and his knowledge of and devotion to the natural world, and now she reassured her young friend with Emersonian verve: "He gave you the eye within the eye, to see in all natural objects the realized ideas of His mind. He gave you pure tastes, and the sturdy preference of whatsoever is most lovely and excellent. He has made you a more individualized existence than is common, and by your very nature, removed you from common temptations. . . . He will surely place you where your work is."⁴

While convalescing for a month, as his eyesight gradually recovered, Muir reflected on his purpose in life and decided to return to his most cherished pursuit—the study of nature. He resolved to travel to South America to follow in the footsteps of the German explorer and naturalist Alexander von Humboldt, whose writings about the interconnectedness of nature he admired. In the fall of 1867, Muir took a train from Indianapolis to Jeffersonville, Kentucky, then set out on foot through the Southern wilderness to the Gulf Coast of Florida, carrying little more in his rubber travel bag than a change of undergarments, his plant press, and copies of the New Testament, *Paradise Lost*, and Robert Burns's *Poems*. In the course of a thousand miles, he met people even more isolated from the rest of the nation than he and his siblings had been on their remote Wisconsin farm and narrowly escaped a confrontation with a band of ex-Confederate marauders. He was mauled by mosquitoes, chased by an alligator, and suffered the fever spasms of malaria. By the end, in Cuba, he was delirious from hunger and disease, but his walk in the wilderness had provided some clarity. He had seen life rugged and raw, nature broad and powerful. He had been reduced, stripped bare, and separated from a world ruled by the desire for material success.⁵

Haunted by malarial fevers, Muir postponed retracing Humboldt's route. He decided instead to pursue nature in the American West and booked passage from New York to California, via the Isthmus of Panama. By the time he had disembarked from the steamship *Nebraska* in San Francisco, in March 1868, he was already eager to escape the brawl of humanity—the whiskey, gambling, and prostitution dens of the city's notorious Barbary Coast—and to head for the vast forests, mountains, and wilderness that he had heard so much about. He stopped a man on the street carrying a carpenter's kit on his shoulders and asked him for "the nearest way out of town to the wild part of the State." Surprised, the man set down his kit and inquired, "Where do you wish to go?" "Anywhere that's wild," Muir responded. He and another passenger from the voyage, Joseph Chilwell, a world-wandering cockney, who called Muir "Scottie," took the ferry to Oakland, as directed, and set out for Yosemite Valley, not by the usual route— a river steamer to the town of Stockton and then on by stage and horseback—but on foot, "drifting leisurely," as Muir proposed, paying little heed to roads or time and camping in their blankets wherever nightfall overtook them.[6]

Muir was soon smitten by California's sun-drenched lowlands and coastal ranges, where larks sang amid hills so blanketed with flowers "they seemed to be painted." Happy and relaxed, he wanted only to take his time crossing the 250 miles to Yosemite in the Sierra Nevada. "Cattle and cultivation were making few scars as yet," he later wrote, "and I wandered enchanted in long, wavering curves, aware now and then that Yosemite lay to the eastward, and that some time, I should find it." Muir and Chilwell walked down the Santa Clara Valley, and on a bright morning at the head of the remote fourteen-mile Pacheco Pass through the Diablo Mountains of the Coast Ranges—a place once known as Robber's Pass—Muir was stunned by his first view of the Sierra. In the foreground, at his feet, lay the San Joaquin and Sacramento Valleys, "the great central plain of California, level as a lake thirty or forty miles wide, four hundred long, one rich furred bed of golden Compositae," some of them taller than he was, a floral landscape that he called "the most divinely beautiful and sublime I have ever beheld."

In the distance, on the eastern edge of this "lake of gold," the "mighty" Sierra rose "in massive, tranquil grandeur":

. . . so gloriously colored and so radiant that it seemed not clothed with light, but wholly composed of it, like the wall of some celestial city. Along the top . . . was a rich pearl-gray belt of snow; then a belt of blue and dark purple, marking the extension of the forests; and stretching along the base of the range a broad belt of rose-purple, where lay the miners' gold and the open foothill gardens—all the colors smoothly blending, making a wall of light clear as crystal and ineffably fine, yet firm as adamant. Then it seemed to me the Sierra should be called, not the Nevada or Snowy Range, but the Range of Light.

Muir had not come to the Gold Rush hills looking for gold, but he had found it anyway. "It was all one sea of golden and purple bloom, so deep and dense that in walking through it you would press more than a hundred flowers at every stop," he recounted. At sunset each day, he and Chilwell threw down their blankets "and the flowers closed over me as if I had sunk beneath the waters of a lake." When he opened his eyes in the morning, his gaze fell on plants he had never before encountered, and his botanical studies began before he got up. "Not even in Florida or Cuba had I seen anything half so glorious," he said.

Change was about to come fast to Central California amid rampant farm expansion and the consequent water wars. "I have always thanked the Lord that I came here before the dust and smoke of civilization had dimmed the sky and before the wild bloom had vanished from the plain," he would tell an audience almost three decades later. But in that moment, he and Chilwell felt enthralled and awakened by the fresh and varied scents in the air—the sweetest air there is to breathe, Muir hailed it. "The atmosphere was spicy and exhilarating," he recalled. "This San Jose sky was not simply pure and bright, and mixed with plenty of well-tempered sunshine, but it possessed a positive flavor, a *taste* that thrilled throughout every tissue of the body." Muir and Chilwell, having lived only on "common air" all their lives, now discovered "multitudes of palates" and a much vaster "capacity for happiness" than they knew existed. "We were . . . born again; and truly not until this time were we fairly conscious that we were born at all," Muir enthused. "Never more, thought I as we strode forward at faster speed, never more shall I sentimentalize about getting free from the flesh, for it is steeped like a sponge in immortal pleasure."[7]

They crossed the San Joaquin River at Hill's Ferry, then headed east along the Merced River toward Yosemite Valley, a former Ahwahnechee stronghold and sanctuary. After ascending the foothills from Snelling Ranch, the Merced County seat, which simplified its named to Snelling two years later, to the gold mining town of Coulterville, nearly fifteen hundred feet higher in elevation, they bought supplies—flour, tea, and a shotgun—and asked the Italian storekeeper about the route into the valley. He described forests of pines up to ten feet in diameter but warned that it had been a severe winter and the Yosemite Trail was still buried in snow up to ten feet deep. He advised them to wait a month to avoid getting lost in the snowdrifts. "It would be delightful to see snow ten feet deep and trees ten feet thick, even if lost," Muir replied, "but I never get lost in wild woods."

Surviving on tea and unleavened flour cakes toasted on coals—though he had been a crack shot as a youth, Muir had given up hunting—the pair followed a rough wagon road, shunning lodging of any sort. The road ended at a trail that climbed up the side of a ridge dividing the Merced and the Tuolumne to Crane Flat, at six thousand feet. Here they found the promised great pines, towering firs, and six feet of snow. Muir considered it "a fine change from the burning foothills and plains." Coming to an abandoned cabin, they decided against wading on through the snow. Although Muir preferred to sleep under the stars, regardless of the snow, Chilwell, who was eager for even a semblance of a roof overhead, swept away the snow on the cabin floor and made a bed out of silver-fir boughs. He had asked Muir to teach him how to shoot and had pinned a target to the outside of the cabin for Muir to test the gun. As Muir prepared to shoot at it from thirty yards away, Chilwell disappeared. Muir, unaware that he had gone back inside the cabin, fired, and Chilwell came running out, hollering, "You've shot me! You've shot me, Scottie!" The lead shot had penetrated the soft pine wall and Chilwell's several layers of clothing and embedded in his shoulder. Muir had to pick out the pellets with a penknife.

They set out again the following day through the snow, Muir guiding them by the topography. Just as they reached a trail on the Yosemite Valley rim, Bridalveil Fall came into sight. "See that dainty little fall over there, Joe?" Muir said. "I should like to camp at the foot of it to see the ferns and lilies that may be there. It looks small from here, only about fifteen or twenty feet, but it may be sixty or seventy." Later, after observing the six-hundred-foot fall up close, he laughed. "So little did we then know of Yosemite magnitudes!" As they camped in the Bridalveil Meadow, a grizzly bear approached to within thirty feet, though on the other side of their fire. Muir added buckshot to the bird shot in the gun and waited silently, hoping the bear would not come closer, as Chilwell trembled beside him. Fortunately, the grizzly finally ambled off.[8]

Bridalveil Fall by Herve Friend, ca. 1906.

For ten days the two explored the falls and the views from the valley walls, sketching and collecting ferns and flowers. Muir had seen enough to know he had to return. In the meantime, although low on provisions, the pair headed down the south fork of the Merced River to see the famous trees. After a few days, they reached Wawona—"big tree" in the Miwuk language, derived from the sound of the hoot of an owl, the guardian spirit of the sequoias—and the nearby Mariposa sequoia grove. Here they met a woodsman who more than a dozen years earlier had built his cabin at a river ford near the trail that led to the sequoia grove and to the valley. Galen Clark, a Canadian-born former gold miner, who had been made the Guardian of the Valley by the park commissioners in May 1866, gave them a supply of flour and fresh meat. They reached the grove after dark, built a great fire from the fallen brush buried beneath the snow, and roasted the meat, neither having ever tasted bear before. Chilwell, famished, gobbled his down (he would later also eat owl soup), but Muir, as deprived as he was, found the pungent, oily meat inedible. He would prove on this and many occasions to have an unusual ability to thrive on the most minimal intake. Camping in the Mariposa Grove, amid "the greatest of trees, the greatest of living things," was nourishment enough for him.

Galen Clark in front of the Grizzly Giant in Mariposa Grove.
Carleton Watkins, ca. 1858–60.

Little could Muir know that he and Clark would eventually spend much time together. Four years after this first meeting, in 1872, Clark would assist Muir in setting stakes in a Mount Maclure glacier as Muir tested his hypothesis that glacier motion shaped Yosemite Valley and all the Sierra Nevada. They were two of a kind. Muir, known for his swift pace over steep and rough terrain and his unconcern for hardship, admired Clark's ease in passing through the dense chaparral and his ability to sleep "anywhere on any ground, rough or smooth, without taking pains even to remove cobbles or sharp-angled rocks." These two single-minded men would later find themselves essential companions in the fight to save Yosemite.[9]

After their adventure Muir and Chilwell headed west to Snelling Ranch, on the San Joaquin plain, and took jobs as hired hands on a farm. While Muir had found farming under his father grim and debasing at times, he now discovered a renewed appreciation for agricultural pursuits and decided to stay on after Chilwell left and help the other hands—a mixture of Spaniards, Britons, and Native Americans—harvest wheat, shear sheep, and break Arabian mustangs. As the summer of 1868 gave way to fall, he abandoned his idea of traveling in the footsteps of Humboldt to stay in California for another year, or perhaps two. The beauty of the Sierra Nevada had surpassed his expectations, and he wanted to explore it.

In the spring, he found an undulating flower-filled depression between the Merced and Tuolumne Rivers, which he dubbed Twenty Hill Hollow. He calculated that every square yard of the hollow held from a thousand to ten thousand flowers. "The earth has indeed become a sky," he enthused, "and the two cloudless skies, raying toward each other flower-beams and sun-beams, are fused and congolded into one glowing heaven." From one of the surrounding hills, he could see Mount Diablo and Pacheco Peak, far away but not distant. "Their spiritual power and the goodness of the sky make them near, as a circle of friends," he wrote. "Plain, sky, and mountains ray beauty, as if warming at a camp-fire. Presently you lose consciousness of your own separate existence; you blend with the landscape, and become part and parcel of nature."

Before long, an Irish sheepherder named John Connel, who liked the inquisitive, poetic, hardworking Wisconsin Scot, approached Muir and asked him to watch his flock. Once a shepherd with only a couple dozen scruffy ewes, Connel, who went by the name Smoky Jack, was a

well-known success story, now "sheep rich," with a flock of thousands
in three bands. Smoky Jack offered Muir $30 a month plus room and
board and assured him the sheep would show him the range and "all
would go smooth and aisy." For that lie, Muir would skewer Smoky
Jack with a Twain-worthy humorous description:

> [Smoky Jack] lived mostly on beans. In the morning after his bean
> breakfast he filled his pockets from the pot with dripping beans for
> luncheon, which he ate in handfuls as he followed the flock. His
> overalls and boots soon, of course, became thoroughly saturated, and
> instead of wearing thin, wore thicker and stouter, and by sitting down
> to rest from time to time, parts of all the vegetation, leaves, petals,
> etc., were embedded in them, together with wool fibres, butterfly
> wings, mica crystals, fragments of nearly everything that part of the
> world contained—rubbed in, embedded and coarsely stratified, so
> that these wonderful garments grew to have a rich geological and
> biological significance.

All Muir had to do was find his way to the shepherd's cabin, about
five miles away on Dry Creek. "You'd better go right over tonight, for
the man that is there wants to quit," Smoky Jack said. "You'll have no
trouble in finding the way. Just take the Snelling road, and the first
shanty you see on a hill to the right—that's the place."

As Old World traditions and British Romantic poetry still colored
Muir's notion of shepherding, Smoky Jack's offer seemed to provide an
ideal opportunity to observe and explore nature on the wild hillsides.
Although Muir had grown up around beasts of all sorts, he had no idea
what he was getting into. He arrived at the Dry Creek cabin at dusk
the next day to find Smoky Jack's young shepherd fixing his supper. A
quick look around the defiled place hinted at a long, slow descent to its
hellish state. "I've tried many kinds of work," the shepherd wasted no
time in informing him, "but this of chasing a band of starving sheep is
the worst of all." He then launched into a recitation of his grievances
and admonitions, liberally cursing sheep in general and this flock in
particular, while preparing to depart. Taken aback, Muir begged the
brusque shepherd to stay the night and show him the ropes in the
morning.

"Oh, no need for that!" the shepherd chided. "It'd do you no good. I'm going away tonight. All you have to do is open the corral in the morning and run after them like a coyote all day and try to keep in sight of them. They'll soon show you the range." With that, he departed, leaving Muir to explore his new home for himself. A closer look did not reassure. The layers of filth and detritus showed that previous shepherds had left the place in shambles and the most recent had merely augmented it. Among the Boschian heaps of ashes, rancid old shoes, and other rubbish strewn around the dirt floor were sheep jaws and skulls, some with ram horns, skeletons with attached tendons, and "other dead evils." Though pervious to rain, wind, and light, the hut reeked of charred grease, mold, and sweat. It took little imagination to picture small demons dancing here with fiendish glee. Inclined to sleep outside under the stars, Muir discovered that, despite the two sheepdogs he had inherited, aggressive wild hogs rooted and ruled at night. He opted for the rickety bed-shelf in the corner of the shack, its mattress a wool sack stuffed with straw and old overalls, and gazed at the stars through the gaps in the roof while drifting off.[10]

It was a cloudless morning, and when he opened the corral gate, eighteen hundred sheep burst out, "like water escaping from a broken flume," as he put it, trampling through Dry Creek and scattering across a dozen hills and rocky banks. He went in pursuit, not quite sure what to do and feeling "that like spilt water they would hardly be gathered into one flock again." While the old and lean soon tuckered out, a thousand or so pushed on until they at last homed in on their own suitable grazing patch. But five hundred or thereabouts, whom Muir dubbed "secessionists," bolted off, halting only occasionally to pluck green shoots, seemingly more interested in escape and adventure or quite possibly in testing and hazing their new sitter. Muir dashed ahead to try to cut them off, and they soon discovered that he was even more fleet-footed and stubborn than they were. With the hot afternoon helping to tire out the runners, he slowly managed to turn them back toward the herd and create a semblance of order. About two hours before sunset, he started driving the flock the two miles back to the corral. They reached Dry Creek at dusk, where to his surprise his charges obediently formed parallel columns and streamed back into the pen.[11]

It turned out to be an unusually bitter winter. Through the solitary months, Muir came to understand the previous shepherd's desperate need to leave the place. With California's free pasturage and favorable climate, sheep owners might double their wealth every other year, but while the owners got rich, their shepherds toiled away in harsh isolation and rarely managed to become owners themselves. In Scotland, a shepherd usually came from a line of shepherds, inheriting a love and aptitude for the life. He had only a small flock to tend, supported by his collies, saw family and neighbors regularly, and often had time to read books in the field and thus "to converse with kings." But the California shepherd, alone in his dingy hovel, stupidly weary, had no balance in his life, leading to dejection, poor health, and in a few cases even insanity.

For five months Muir observed the life cycle of sheep with all its complications and pleasures. He participated in the arrival and departure of life over and again. Hundreds of ewes lambed that spring, only for the newborns to be exposed to the unseasonably frigid weather. He carried many of them into the hut to keep them warm by the fire and bottle-fed more than two hundred. But he could not protect the entire flock, and one icy morning he woke to find that about a hundred sheep, huddled together against the cold, had frozen to death overnight. One day out on the open plain, he discovered two little black piglets, "lying dead in a small bed which they had dug in the sand just the length of their bodies. They had died without a struggle side by side in the same position. Poor unfriended creatures." And it dawned on him: "Man has injured every animal he has touched."

Indeed, Muir had recently been wrestling with the hypocrisy of "civilized man," as he recorded in his journal, in no uncertain terms, while walking across the South:

> Let a Christian hunter go to the Lord's woods and kill his well-kept beasts, or wild Indians, and it is well; but let an enterprising specimen of these proper, predestined victims go to houses and fields and kill the most worthless person of the vertical godlike killers,—oh! that is horribly unorthodox, and on the part of the Indians atrocious murder! Well, I have precious little sympathy for the selfish propriety of civilized man.

Muir saw how the shepherds preceding him had had their spirits crushed, living like hapless beasts themselves. He seethed at the greed and cruelty of California's industrial sheep farming, where as long as resources were unlimited and cheap, animal life was taken for granted. Despite the hardships, Muir later valued his time tending Smoky Jack's flock, some of the most trying work he ever did.[12]

Yosemite, First Blush, Summer 1869

At the beginning of June, after seeing some of Muir's sketches and hearing that he wanted to study the higher regions of the Sierra, Smoky Jack's neighbor Pat Delaney offered him a job overseeing his shepherd. Delaney, whom Muir described as "bony and tall, with a sharply hacked profile like Don Quixote," assured Muir that his main duty would be to keep an eye on the shepherd, Billy Simms, who would do the actual herding, and that Muir would be otherwise free to collect plants, sketch, explore, and observe the wildlife. Delaney, or "the Don," as Muir called him, said he would travel with them to the first mountain camp and then periodically return with mail and provisions as they moved higher up the mountains. Muir would only be needed in case of accidents or other emergencies. Eager to return to the highlands, he agreed.

He would not be alone this time. The traveling party included a Chinese workman, a Native American herder, and a new companion: Carlo, a Saint Bernard whose owner had asked Muir to take him along for fear that the valley's summer heat might be too much for the shaggy creature. As the group began the climb, Muir gazed at the snowy peaks above them and prayed that he would get to explore them.[13]

Delaney and the others left Muir and Simms, the shepherd, in a place that could not have been more unlike Smoky Jack's hut. Muir found enchantment and peace in the camp grove. He was now acquainted with the art of tending sheep, and Simms, an experienced hand, was responsible for them, allowing Muir to explore the wilderness, making keen observations on ferns, black ants, and sugar pines. "Life seems neither long nor short," he observed, "and we take no more heed to save time or make haste than do the trees and stars. This is true freedom, a good practical sort of immortality."

One morning while Muir was absorbed in his journal, he looked up and was surprised to see a Miwuk man only steps away. The moment resonated with Muir. "All Indians seem to have learned this wonderful way of walking unseen," he would write. He thought this skill had probably been acquired over generations of hunting and fighting and survival against enemies. Muir admired how Native Americans had long lived in harmony with nature. "Indians walk softly and hurt the landscape hardly more than the birds and squirrels," he wrote. Their trails were barely noticeable and their brush and bark huts ephemeral. Their most lasting impact was caused by the fires they made in the forests to improve their hunting grounds. In contrast, white men blasted roads in the solid rock, dammed and tamed wild streams, and washed away hills and the "skin of the mountain face" while searching for gold. Even worse, the white man had debased the Native Americans, until they were no more harmonious with nature than he was.

"This June seems the greatest of all the months of my life," Muir wrote in his journal, "the most truly divinely free, boundless like eternity, immortal." But in early July his and Simms's rations dwindled until the only thing they had to eat was mutton, which was soon almost inedible to Muir. They began to feel weak and lethargic. Muir's stomach ached to a degree he found difficult to bear. "We dream of bread, a sure sign we need it," he wrote. "Like the Indians, we ought to know how to get the starch out of fern and saxifrage stalks, lily bulbs, pine bark, etc." He admired their ability to live off the land on berries, roots, birds' eggs, bee larvae, and ants. "Our education has been sadly neglected for many generations." Finally, Delaney returned with fresh supplies, and Muir and Simms quickly recovered. It was time to move the sheep higher into the mountains, and while they did, Muir noted that the Native American who worked for Delaney was calm and alert and "silently watched for wanderers likely to be overlooked." At night he needed neither fire nor blanket to stay warm. "A fine thing," thought Muir, who would push the bounds of wilderness survival, always striving to do more and stay longer with less, "to be independent of clothing where it is so hard to carry."[14]

On July 11, they camped at seven thousand feet beside ice-cold Tamarack Creek, which flowed swiftly through a high green meadow. Only a few hundred yards below them, the ground was rocky with sporadic stunted trees growing from seams and fissures. Here and there were massive boulders that had somehow traveled from afar—as their color and composition showed—and been left in this spot eons ago. Muir wondered how they had gotten here. He examined them closely and found the answer written on the stone itself. The most resistant and unweathered surfaces showed parallel scoring and striation, suggesting that the region had been swept by a glacier, grinding down the mountains, wrenching and scraping and carrying great fragments of the landscape with it. When the ice melted, it deposited the boulders where Muir now found them.

With Chilwell, Muir had only whetted his appetite for Yosemite Valley, a place of enchantment considered sacred by the now displaced Ahwahnechee, and he was eager to experience it more deeply. He was granted his wish after only a few days, when snow in the high mountains forced Simms to move the flock to lower elevations. As they approached the great valley—which had in the two decades since its "discovery" and the brutal expulsion of the Ahwahnechee achieved an almost mythical status across the nation—a party of tourists passed nearby on horses. They seemed to care little for the scenery, and Muir felt no need to talk to them. Though he had many close friends, male and female, he missed society little and looked forward to studying and sketching the plants and rocks in solitude and to scrambling with Carlo along the spectacular valley rim.[15]

As they pushed east over the rim into the Yosemite Creek basin, Muir marveled at the clear evidence of the former presence of ice in the glacier-polished granite. "How raw and young this region appears!" he wrote. "Had the ice sheet that swept over it vanished but yesterday, its traces . . . could hardly be more distinct than they are now." Horses, sheep, and men all slipped on the smooth stone.

They reached Yosemite Creek about two miles before it plummeted into the valley. Delaney and Simms and their helpers plunged into a slippery battle with the flock, which was determined not to cross the swift forty-foot-wide and four-foot-deep creek and responded like a force of nature. As each group was pushed into the stream, it returned at its soonest opportunity to the flock waiting on the creek bank. In vain Delaney heaved sheep after sheep into the current and even leaped in himself to lead a surge. The effort was not won until it was abandoned. The famished sheep then suddenly decided on their own to cross the stream and search for new forage, and their scramble to get to the other side created a new crisis. "The Don jumped into the thickest of the gasping, gurgling, drowning mass," Muir reported, "and shoved them right and left as if each sheep was a piece of floating timber." Although Muir "expected that hundreds would gain the romantic fate of being swept into Yosemite over the highest waterfall in the world," none did, and all were soon happily munching and baaing on the far bank, as if this tumultuous minor miracle—their safe crossing—had never happened. "A sheep can hardly be called an animal," he concluded, with rare disdain for the natural world. "An entire flock is required to make one foolish individual."

The next day Muir set out on his own with Carlo, climbing a fragrant steeply rising slope on the valley's east rim. Before they reached the top, they veered south into a shallow basin, and Muir set up a bivouac. After lunch, they explored Indian Canyon's western ridge and, as they gained the top, looked out on a stunning panorama of the upper basin of the Merced River—the mountains above Yosemite Valley—snowcapped peaks kissing a cobalt sky above domes, canyons, and upsweeping dark forests, windless and still, all radiant with sunshine. Overwhelmed by "so boundless an affluence of sublime mountain beauty," the likes of which he had never before seen, Muir felt himself swell with spirituality and joy. A spontaneous shout escaped his lips, and his core and limbs shook "in a wild burst of ecstasy."

He took several strides but was brought up short, as a massive grizzly rose from its hiding place. The bear shook free of a thicket of brush, sucked in wind, and roared off, trampling the twisted manzanita bushes in its desire, Muir imagined, to escape the human lunatic. Carlo, his ears pinned back in fear, shook feverishly, waiting for the command to hunt.

The glorious sight below him was what Muir had wandered so far— the distance hardly seemed possible—to discover. He was like a drop of blood propelled unwittingly through the circulatory system of the war-ravaged country to its very heart chamber: the valley of Yosemite. Before him he saw the grandeur that the nation, so recently smothered in its horrible bloodshed, possessed. The heights to which it could soar. He saw redemption. This was the place where his enthrallment with nature, which had caused him to spurn all reasonable and worldly pursuits—his belief in its worth, power, and sacredness—would crystallize. He felt the warmth of his friend Jeanne Carr's approving gaze, and a yearning for her presence.

Under this spell, with Carlo at his heels, Muir followed the ridge as it gradually fell to the south, and between Indian Canyon and Yosemite Falls, they made their way to the cliff's edge. Here, again, the view brought him up. They were on top of the world. The entire valley stretched out before them, and below, the majestic river of mercy, the Merced, sparkled as it swept through an Eden of sunlit meadows and oak and pine groves. At the upper end of the valley, Tissiack, or Half Dome (also known as South Dome), presided over this landscape, thrusting nearly a mile into the sky, so well proportioned that it drew the eye like a magnet away from the beauty around it, absorbing and magnifying the falls, the meadows, the cliffs, and the distant mountains.

Eager to see the long view right down to the valley floor, Muir jogged along the rim, but its sloping edge made it difficult to find a vantage point. He searched for a slot or a sheer ledge. When he finally found a jutting shelf, he shuffled to the very edge, set his feet, braced his legs, drew his body up tall, and craned into the air. Muir had no fear of heights, perhaps dangerously, and after four years on the move, roved over the terrain like a billy goat, trusting his legs absolutely. For a moment, though the rock was solid, the notion of its breaking off and sending him on a half-mile plummet gave him a frisson. But the feeling soon passed, and his nerves grew steady again. Over the next hour, in the grasp of something more powerful than his own will, he took yet more risks to see this spellbinding view, each time swearing not to venture so close to the edge again.[16]

Eventually, he and Carlo arrived at the now-narrow Yosemite Creek rushing over twinkling granite on its way to the precipice. Just before the drop, it gathered in a basin and relaxed, the boil of the rapids calmed, the water a somber gray. Then it slowly glided over the lip of the pool, onto the last slope, accelerating swiftly to the brink. Finally, with—as Muir saw it—"sublime, fateful confidence," it flew into the air, where it levitated momentarily, as if resisting gravity, before it escaped to another world. In its departure from the raw mountaintop to the green valley, it burst into particles, and a shimmering rainbow—a spray bow—marked this transformation from caterpillar to butterfly.

Yosemite Falls from a stereograph. Muir wrote that the fall was "crowned in glory above its fellows" and "comes to us as an endless revelation—mysterious, unreadable, immeasurable, yet holding its hearers spellbound with the divine majesty and loveliness of its forms and voices."

Wishing to be part of this God-work as nearly as possible, Muir took off his shoes and stockings and, pressing his feet and hands against the slick granite, worked his way down until his head was near the booming, rushing, energizing stream. Noticing that it leveled before its dive, he hoped he could lean out over the edge and see down into the falling water and through it to the bottom. But when he reached the edge, he discovered it to be false. Another, steeper, ledge lay below. It appeared too steep to allow him to reach the brink. However, once again, he could not convince himself to abandon the effort. He could see the cliff fully now and spied a narrow rim, just wide enough to hold his heels. Studying the polished surface of river wall, he noticed a rough seam on the steep rock face, a fault line that might provide him the needed fingerholds to reach the cliff's edge. His nerves tingled as he considered his next move. The reverberation of the water enveloped him, and he began to feel a part of it. A giddy mix of emotions—elation, wonder, fear—swam in his head. He decided again not to move forward. But then he did.

Some inner wildness had taken over. As he advanced, choosing his steps carefully, tufts of artemisia dangling from the clefts caught his eye. He plucked a few leaves, bit down on them, and soon felt the sedative effect of their bitter juice. Time slowed. The slope was not his enemy. He was a part of it. He crept forward and, when he reached the small ledge, about three inches wide, planted his heels on it. Then he shuffled sideways, like a crab, toward the precipice—thirty feet to go, twenty feet, the water beside him now white and agitated as it sped to its threshold, ten feet. At last the edge was right in front of him. Legs firm, body stiff, arching, he peered over. His eyes bored into the billowing free fall, and he watched the spill separate into streamers, comets of water whose tails refracted the sunlight.

As the creek flowed past him on its grand adventure, his body and soul seemed to hang there, somewhere in between terra firma and air infinitum. Another current—Emerson's words—he well knew: "In the woods, we return to reason and faith. There I feel nothing can befall me in life—no disgrace, no calamity (leaving me my eyes)—which nature cannot repair. Standing on the bare ground—my head bathed by the blithe air, and uplifted into infinite space—all mean egotism vanishes. I become a transparent eyeball." Muir was nothing; he saw all. He lost any sense of the passage of time and later could not remember his retreat from the ledge. Although a slip of the heel could have sent him over with the powerful creek, the magnificence of the fall—its ever-active and changing form, its rumble and sudden silence, its action and refraction, its immediacy and its distance—had him spellbound.

So many stimuli bombarded his senses that there was no room for fear. Instead, where earth and water met air and light, Muir, with the

religious fervor of his upbringing, saw God. He saw God in the frag-
mentation of the stream and in the rays of the sun passing through to
make vivid rainbow beads. He saw God in the rebirth of the stream
suddenly expelled from earth, as death and a new life, a new journey,
were simultaneously manifest.[17]

Around dark, Muir and Carlo returned to camp. The exhilaration of
the afternoon ebbed, and a deep exhaustion settled in. It had been "a
most memorable day of days." Muir had had "his first view of the High
Sierra, first view looking down into Yosemite, the death song of Yosemite
Creek, and its flight over the cliff," each a lifetime moment, and all in
all "enjoyment enough to kill if that were possible." He felt he had been
admitted to a place of divine beauty, and it was already reshaping the
way he perceived the world and existence, just as Emerson had said it
would in his essay "Nature." That night while Muir's tired body slept
soundly, his mind raced. The mountain he was on crumbled in his res-
tive dream, and an avalanche of water and stone swept him into the
sky. He tumbled and free-fell into the valley, not from the mountain
but with it. They were one.

In the days that followed, Muir's mind was ablaze with new sensations and thoughts. On July 27, he would write in his journal, "When
we try to pick out anything by itself we find that it is bound fast by a
thousand invisible cords that cannot be broken, to everything in the universe." It was a line echoing and perhaps inspired, whether consciously or
subconsciously, by his literary hero, Emerson, who had written, "Nothing is quite beautiful alone; nothing but is beautiful in the whole." And
Muir would later rewrite the line, as it appears, famously, in his book
My First Summer in the Sierra: "When we try to pick out anything by
itself, we find it hitched to everything else in the Universe."[18]

While Muir was getting "hitched to everything" in the metaphysical
sense, the nation was actually getting hitched. Just two months before
Muir peered into Yosemite Valley, Leland Stanford had hammered in a
golden spike at Promontory Summit in the Utah Territory, completing
the transcontinental railroad after a seven-year rail-laying frenzy ignited
by the 1862 Pacific Railroad Act, passed for that purpose. This feat
spawned the Gilded Age and its explosive economic growth, political

and market upheaval (including depressions following panics in 1873 and 1893), and unprecedented tourism. Now passengers, mail, and freight could zoom from coast to coast in six days, while the cost of crossing the country fell from $1,000 to $150. The railroads hyped the West to drum up traffic, and a new wave of settlers—farmers, ranchers, loggers, and miners—poured in from the East Coast and Europe to seek their fortunes.[19]

They came to be transformed. But they would do the transforming, and the quantum leap in the nation's ability to extract and transport natural resources would help them ravage the landscape at a record pace and on an industrial level—right before the eyes, so recently returned to sight, of John Muir.

CHAPTER 2

The Brag About the West

Ralph Waldo Emerson with his posse of Eastern intellectuals and socialites rode into Yosemite in the spring of 1871 like a prophet followed by his apostles. On their journey from San Francisco—where Emerson had delivered speeches to packed houses, wowed the socialites and cognoscenti in his usual way, and been urged to seek out a certain backwoods prodigy in the valley—they had suffered both unseasonable heat, over a hundred degrees, and shocking cold, on top of the nagging altitude fatigue and constant jolting. Riding in a buckboard, the Sage, as the poet's coterie sometimes called him, went from sweating profusely in the valley heat to shivering beneath buffalo skins in the mountains, all the while showering his fellow travelers with fulminations one minute and keen witticisms the next.

Before reaching San Francisco, the party had crossed the country on a sightseeing trip organized by railroad magnate John Murray Forbes, a close friend of Emerson's. They had traveled on Forbes's private train on the new transcontinental railroad. The excursion was meant to be a restorative journey for Emerson, who was about to turn sixty-eight and whose health and memory were said to be slipping. George Pullman himself had seen the party off from Chicago in his best car, *Huron*. The accommodations were lavish, but they had been disappointed by what they had seen from the windows and during their stopovers. Wild Bill Hickok's mythological West no longer existed, if it ever had. The plains were bereft of buffalo, except for a few sad specimens in pens. At one stop there was a miserable caged grizzly, and everywhere impoverished Native American mothers begged at the stations. Unimpressed in general, Emerson specifically deemed the Mormon leader Brigham Young, whom he met in Salt Lake City, "a sufficient ruler, & perhaps civilizer of his kingdom of blockheads."

From a voyage of utmost luxury and modernity, Forbes's party, accompanied by seventeen horses, three wranglers, two guides, and a cook, had then tumbled into the past. Whether on foot or horseback, the three-day journey through primitive mountain terrain to Yosemite was rugged, often precarious, and at times downright death-defying. At Crane Flat, which was six thousand feet high and sixteen miles from the valley, bullfrogs bellowed from the snow-rimmed pond in front of the hotel where they were to stay. The owners were absent, leaving service in the hands of one simple man, and at meals guests had to provide their own silverware. Still, once the party began the harrowing descent into the valley, all the discomforts that had preceded seemed as nothing. The trail was little short of terrifying. Leaving Tamarack Flat, about five miles from the valley and at sixty-three hundred feet the highest point on the trail, a stony defile formed a plunging stairway to another world, a drop of more than a mile over five miles, across loose boulders and scree. The ersatz path rounded points of shelving rock, where a misplaced step could send a horse over the edge. Even intrepid riders blanched here, before proceeding, nerves inflamed, muscles rigid, leaning into the mountain, ready to leap if the mount slipped or the ledge crumbled.

And then it got worse. Over a treacherous two-thousand-foot stretch, the trail plunged five hundred feet down an infamous stairway of stone. Riders had to dismount and rope their horses down. Some, hugging the cliff, refused to lead their animals for fear of being pulled over the side with them if they tumbled.

This passage was followed by a gentler slope, leading to a crystal-clear spring and a dense grove of trees. On his mount, Pegasus, a pied mustang, Emerson deliriously praised the landscape he had heard so much about, the nearly pristine wilderness before his eyes: alligator-skinned sugar pines thirty-feet around and soaring hundreds of feet into the sky, with pine cones as long as a man's arm; giant cedars covered in golden

moss, glowing as if lit by streetlamps; and clear rushing streams. Entering the nearly eight-mile valley, with its talus-free clean lines and vivid
waterfalls—so alien and otherworldly in appearance that the Easterners
half expected to see dinosaurs roaming there—he surrendered to the
grandeur, releasing the leather reins, trusting Pegasus to carry him the
rest of the way down the hair-raising path. If the horse was not up to
the task, God help them both.[1]

Ever since Professor James Butler had encouraged Muir and his fellow
University of Wisconsin students to keep a commonplace book, as Emerson did, and to collect trifles and ideas and put them down "stamped in
Nature's mint of ecstasy," Muir had maintained the practice. Emerson's
essays had in many ways defined nature for Muir, and his journals mim-
icked Emerson's writing as much as possible. Emerson's essay "Nature,"
which Muir had originally read under the guidance of Professor Carr
and studied by the fireside many nights since, was one of his dearest
possessions. It fed him when he was hungry, soothed him when he was
lonely, and directed him when he was lost. "Nothing can befall me . . .
which nature cannot repair." These were words, echoed by Thoreau—
"While I enjoy the friendship of the seasons I trust that nothing can
make life a burden to me"—that he lived by. But the prospect of meeting
Emerson in person was another matter. He had idealized the man for
so long that in some ways it was mortifying. What if Emerson found
him unworthy and despised him?

Wrestling with philosophical quandaries and conflicting interests,
Muir, now thirty-three, still lacked direction—or rather, was pulled
in too many. James Hutchings, a Yosemite Valley promoter and hotel
owner, owed him money and had reneged on a promise to lend him a
cabin—a cabin Muir himself had built the year before—but nonetheless
begged him to return to work for him because no one could keep his
sawmill buzzing like Muir, even if he insisted on cutting only fallen
wood. That winter, Muir had debated going with the Carrs' son Ned on
an expedition to the Amazon to check on land claims. While this would
have satisfied his long-held desire to travel in Humboldt's footsteps,
he had decided against it. ("We shall go, I am sure of it," Jeanne later
consoled Muir.) Hutchings owed him money but had none. The only

way to get his back wages was to run the sawmill so that Hutchings
could pay him out of the profits.

Ezra Carr was now at the newly established University of California,
where he had been one of the first professors hired, and from Berkeley,
Jeanne, who knew everybody who needed to be known, had written
Muir that she had been corresponding with Emerson. Emerson had sent
a letter suggesting that Ezra edit Thoreau's journals for publication, and
in her reply she had told him that he must find Muir when he reached
Yosemite. She also told Muir that his recent "*moonlight* letter was a beam
from the upper sky," which she had been taking "out into the dewy
moonlights—where the large oaks are looking their beautifulest"—to
sit on a root and mull over.

Muir had written Jeanne, who had taken a job teaching botany at
a girls' high school in San Mateo, to tell her about his perilous adventure on Fern Ledge. One afternoon in early April, he had gone to the
Middle Cascade of Yosemite Falls with a blanket and a piece of bread
to spend the night in prayer. As the creek soared over the cliff, its spray
levitated in the light of the moon to create a double prismatic lunar
spray bow—an immense arc reaching to the fall's base with glorious
colors as clear as those of a rainbow but softer—one of the evangels of
the place, he told Carr. This mesmerizing scene beckoned him onto Fern
Ledge, a shelf behind the fall. He edged out to a spot where he could
almost touch the fall's delicate moonlit outer veil, as ephemeral as spent
clouds. Eager to see the moon through the denser flow in the center,
he crept farther along behind the fall, then crept farther still, unaware
that the only reason he could do so was that the wind had swayed the
fall out and that it would inevitably swing back again. The effect was
enchanting. He was in an alcove of granite and water lit by the moon.
Sound and energy roared down the cliff and resonated inside as if he
were in the sound box of a mighty musical instrument, ferocious notes
playing above, beneath, and around him. The moon hovered over the
column of water, its beams dancing and flashing, and the space between
the rock face and the wild illumined fall was a fairyland.[2]

As Muir stared past the edge of the fall into the five-hundred-foot
precipice, the wind changed, and suddenly a torrent of frigid water
struck him like a club, knocking him down. The enchanting curtain
of water, harmless at a distance, was now upon him, hammering his

shoulders and filling his lungs with a choking spray. On his knees, he clung to the ledge and struggled for breath, frozen in the icy stream. He rolled into a ball, pummeled as if by cobblestones, his ears filled not with water music but a confusion of hissing, gurgling, and clashing. As his head exploded with pain, he weighed his chances. With the next blast of wind would the column sway away from him or hit him even harder? The fall was in flood, and its weight would not be budged lightly. His fate depended on the vagaries of the wind.

It moved out. The pounding mercifully ceased, and the moonlight returned. As feeling burned back to life in his skin, his muscles remained achingly dumb, and he teetered and nearly fell. Then his limbs too throbbed to life, and when the steadiness of light told him it was safe, he rose and scuttled off the ledge.[3]

He built a fire in a sheltered place and around midnight wrote the letter to Carr: "I am in the Upper Yosemite Falls and can hardly calm to write, but, from my first baptism an hour ago, you have been so present that I must try to fix you a written thought. . . ." He told her what had happened. "How little do we know of ourselves, of our profoundest attractions and repulsions, of our spiritual affinities! How interesting does man become, considered in his relations to the spirit of this rock and water! How significant does every atom of our world become amid the influences of those beings unseen, spiritual, angelic mountaineers that so throng these pure mansions of crystal foam and purple granite!"

"I suppose if you are gone over the fall, John," she responded, "some button or rag would have told the story, but I should have felt that you were safe and always to be found in those parts."[4]

Among Emerson's party of family and friends who had come to see the valley and—it was clear—to hover around him, were not only Forbes but his wife, three daughters, and son, Colonel William Forbes, along with his wife, Edith, Emerson's daughter. Emerson's cousin Sophia was on the trip with her husband, Jim Thayer, a Harvard-educated Boston attorney. Another member of the party was the twenty-six-year-old son of Henry James, Wilkie James, who as an officer in Shaw's Fifty-Fourth Massachusetts Regiment, the Civil War's first black regiment of a free state, had been shot during a charge in South Carolina and now walked with a limp.

The party much preferred Leidig's Hotel—the new and, for these parts, grand establishment with serviceable mattresses, palatable food prepared by the attractive, dark-eyed Mrs. Leidig herself, and porches facing Yosemite Falls—to their Crane Flat lodging. Still, several of them chose to camp, at least until the rain drove them inside. Emerson, meanwhile, puffed on cigars in the parlor, where despite the halo of smoke, his wit and habitual smile ensured that he was constantly surrounded by admirers. Hearing Leidig's staff whisper in reverent tones, "Emerson is here," Muir later said: "I was excited as I had never been excited before, and my heart throbbed as if an angel direct from heaven had alighted on the Sierran rocks. But so great was my awe and reverence, I did not dare to go to him." And despite Carr's efforts at making an introduction, he received no message. With his rough-hewn attire and calloused hands, he hesitated to penetrate the literary titan's assembly and instead "hovered on the outside of the crowd of people that were pressing forward to be introduced to him."

No one could blame Muir for being wary of the intrusion. The last celebrity to visit Yosemite, the previous November, was the English actress, author, and adventuress Theresa Yelverton, Viscountess Avonmore. Known worldwide for the sensational trials of her husband for bigamy, she had befriended Muir and fictionalized him (though barely) in a romance novel. "Kenmuir" first appears in the novel as a "singular creature" perched on the brim of Glacier Point. The heroine, Sylvia Brown, wonders, "Is it a man, or a tree, or a bird?" When Kenmuir later approaches, she observes the "rhythmic motion of his flexible form" and the "active grace which only trained muscles can assume." Kenmuir's "bright intelligent face" holds "open blue eyes of honest questioning," and his "glorious auburn hair might have stood as a portrait of the angel Raphael." Yelverton's sensual descriptions caused much speculation, if not scandal. When Muir left the valley alone to study the Merced River's formation, some spread what would turn out to be a stubborn rumor that it was to escape her attentions.[5]

During the day, Emerson and his party made minor excursions on horseback. They went to Mirror Lake to gaze up at Half Dome, whose extraordinary shape and scale they acclaimed. They believed that its other half had cracked and crumbled in an earthquake, as Josiah Whitney, a Harvard professor and chief of the California Geological Survey, had wrongly claimed, and that the surviving half was unclimbable. They were disappointed to arrive at Mirror Lake after the breeze rose, ruffling it and distorting the glassy reflection. Another day they went to the Emerald Pool, where the Merced rests at the bottom of Nevada Fall before completing its journey in Vernal Fall. They lauded Vernal Fall's "thick, milk-white, exquisite fleece of descending foam," as Thayer described it, which had prompted someone to quote from Longfellow's "Wreck of the Hesperus": "She struck where the white and fleecy waves / Looked soft as carded wool."[6]

Emerson, whose spirit and philosophy were said to have hardened owing to age and personal crises, was finally impressed, calling these mountains "perhaps unmatched on the Globe." "This valley," he declared, "is the only place that meets the brag about the West, and, in fact, exceeds it."

Not until May 8, when Muir received Carr's letter of May 1, telling him that she was about to send a note to Emerson about him, did Muir overcome his shyness. "I am feeling as glad for you as possible," she had written, "since Mr. Emerson will be in the Valley in a few days—and in your hands I hope and trust, the dear old singer in the places where we have sung his song." Muir could not let her down.

As Emerson's party prepared to leave the valley, Muir carefully crafted a note. "While the spirits of these rocks & waters hail you after long waiting as their kinsman & persuade you to closer communion . . . , I invite you to join me in a month's worship with Nature in the high temples of the great Sierra Crown beyond our holy Yosemite. It will cost you <u>nothing</u> save the time & very little of that for you will be mostly in Eternity." Suggesting a month's stay was audacious, but Muir had supreme confidence in the worthiness of Yosemite, if not of himself, and to his way of thinking, it took at least that long to know the place better than a passing tourist. He walked over to the hotel, where Emerson's party, having just returned from sightseeing, had retired to the veranda to watch the sunset. As always, a small crowd hovered around Emerson. Muir handed the note to a member of the entourage and left.

Nevada Fall. "With what deep enthusiasm it goes to its fate!" wrote Muir. Pillsbury Picture Co., ca. 1907.

Vernal Fall. "The Vernal is the greenest, most rectangular fall in the valley," wrote Muir. "It is a sheet composed of five or six united parallel falls." Pillsbury Picture Co., ca. 1908.

It concluded, "In the name of Mts Dana & Gabb, of the grand glacial hieroglyphics of Tuolumne Meadows & Bloody Canyon, in the name of a hundred glacial lakes, of a hundred glacial daisy-gentian meadows, in the name of a hundred cascades that barbarous visitors never see, in the name of the grand upper forests . . . and in the name of all the spirit creatures of these rocks & of this whole spiritual atmosphere: Do not leave us now." He had signed off, "I am yours in Nature."

The following morning, Muir was at work in Hutchings's mill cutting timber to build cottages when, above the whining of the saws, he heard a voice calling his name. He walked out, and there was Emerson, sitting on his horse, basking in the sunlight with Thayer by his side.[7]

"I am Mr. Muir."

Thayer took a closer look. "Then Mr. Muir must have brought his own letter."

"Yes, that was me."

Emerson looked Muir up and down but with a kindly smile that put him instantly at ease. "Why did you not make yourself known last evening? I should have been very glad to have seen you." His voice was softer than Muir had expected. The three men entered the mill, which was fragrant with fresh-sawn pine.

Since Hutchings's cabin had never materialized, Muir had built an unlikely aerial appendage onto the mill's upper level, a room jutting out fifty feet above the valley, which everyone called the Hang Nest. Reaching it required climbing a precarious series of henhouse ladders. "Fortunately the only people that I dislike," Muir had recently told his sister Sarah in a letter, "are afraid to enter it." Despite his age, Emerson boldly mounted the ladders. The views from Muir's observatory, Emerson soon found, were worth the trouble and somehow managed ingeniously to heighten the God-given drama of the place. They were like daguerreotypes, only live. One window framed the valley to the west. Another provided a pinhole view of Yosemite Falls. On clear nights the central skylight revealed a heaven full of the brightest stars visible to man. In "Nature," where Emerson had laid down the tenets of transcendentalism—the belief that God is found in nature and nature defines reality—he said that to truly experience nature, we must separate from the distractions of society and find solitude. "If a man would be alone, let him look at the stars," Emerson had written. "The rays that come from those heavenly worlds, will separate between him and vulgar things." Muir's Hang Nest, with its portal on the stars, was an astonishing embodiment of that.

From another hole in the roof, Half Dome loomed five thousand feet above. If Emerson had been there in winter, he might have seen "this grand gray dome" as alive as Muir once had, standing "like a god, a real living creature of power and glory, awful, incomprehensible," clad in "feathery pines . . . dazzled by snow"—a divine ornamental work "in its first winter mantle woven and jeweled in a night." But then that was Muir, who in his copy of Emerson's "Nature"—in the margin by the line "There is in the woods and waters . . . a failure to yield a present satisfaction, a disappointment . . . felt in every landscape"—would scrawl, "No, always we find more than we expect."[8]

Yosemite Valley in winter by George Fiske.

Muir showed the two men his plant specimens. Emerson began to fire questions at him, and Muir rattled off botanical names and details. Emerson's desire to know more about each one inspired Muir to produce more. Emerson showed such interest in Muir's pencil sketches of peaks, forests, and trees that Muir pulled out even more and begged him to take any he wanted. Emerson asked only that he be permitted to bring the others to see them.

Emerson had recently abandoned what he thought was to be his masterpiece due to the demands of a lecture series that he was giving at Harvard. Even here in the valley, his Harvard life loomed, with most of his caretakers being alumni and Thayer following him around noting everything he did and said. With essentially no independence, no escape from the intellectual world that had contributed to his stressful condition, Emerson was hemmed in and observed like the captive buffalo. Muir, if nothing else, was free in nature, fiercely free. For the next few days, Emerson visited Muir whenever he could and, when his party was preparing to depart, invited him to accompany them out to Clark's Station and the Mariposa Grove of Big Trees. By this time, they had achieved sufficient intimacy to be forthright. "I'll go, Mr. Emerson," Muir said, "if you promise to camp with me in the grove. I'll build a glorious campfire, and the great brown boles of the giant sequoias will be most impressively lighted up, and the night will be glorious."

Emerson beamed. "Yes, yes, we will camp out, camp out."

The next day they all rode off together, covering twenty-five miles through the stately Sierra forests to the Mariposa Grove. Emerson kept Muir talking as they rode, but it was different now among the Bostonians. The glee had vanished. Returned to his attendants, Emerson was subdued and testy. He sounded Muir out on his literary tastes, the au courant Easterners snickering at his preference for the prolific Ohio-born poet Alice Cary over Lord Byron, whom Emerson praised. But Muir was on sound footing here and objected to a certain infelicitous word in a remembered Byron passage. "Yes," Emerson conceded. "I hadn't thought of that particular word. I read it for the first time younger, perhaps, than you did. But he doesn't delay you on that. There is a certain scenic and general luck about him." Emerson also praised the nature poet William Cullen Bryant, saying, "He has a cold, clear eye and writes in a manner very different from our other rhymers. He has a right to talk of trees and nature."

It was apparent, however—and Muir was pleased to see—that the colossal silver and Douglas firs, cypresses, and sugar pines, the kings and priests of the conifers, delighted Emerson. On a ridge of sugar pines, Muir's favorite of all the trees, he drew the poet aside and quoted him, "'Come to me,'/ Quoth the pine-tree, / 'I am the giver of honor.'"[9]

"They spread their arms with majestic gestures," Muir continued, "addressing the surrounding trees like very priests of the woods."

Emerson, gazing long, said, "No other forest has so fine a preacher or so well-dressed and well-behaved and devout a congregation. . . . Oh, you Gentlemen Pines!" Muir had been put through the great man's paces, and he, like the trees, had passed the test.

That afternoon they reached Clark's Station, where the same woodsman who once shared his bear meat with Muir and Chilwell, Galen Clark, had built his cabin beside the South Fork of the Merced and the trail to the valley. Already the place had changed much since Muir's first arrival. Now known as Wawona Tavern, it doubled as the headquarters of Yosemite Stage & Turnpike and a guesthouse for tourists and travelers. Clark, who had been stunned by the beauty of Yosemite when he first saw it in 1855, at the age of forty-one, had discovered the Mariposa Grove of Big Trees eight miles from his cabin and then built a horse trail to it and devoted his life to studying and serving the valley and the trees. His letter to California senator John Conness and President Lincoln had spurred the former to introduce a bill to grant Yosemite Valley and the Mariposa Grove to the State of California to preserve and protect and the latter to sign it. Clark had been appointed one of the eight commissioners to oversee the park, and in 1866, the commission, chaired by Frederick Law Olmsted, the designer of New York City's Central Park, had wisely tapped Clark to serve as the official Guardian of the Valley and Big Tree Grove.[10]

Muir was surprised to see the party dismount here. He thought they would camp in the grove. "No," he was told, "it would never do to lie out in the night air. Mr. Emerson might take cold." Glancing at Emerson, he could see how it stood. Denied the group's permission to camp, he was incapable of arguing, like a deflated child before his parents. Muir merely needed to point to Clark to counter this misguided notion. Before settling here, Clark had been diagnosed with consumption and given just six months to live. But the rugged mountaineer, the best Muir ever met, who had forged close ties with the area's tribes and become an authority on the local geology, flora, and fauna, had recuperated outside in the mountain air—night and day.

Colds are caught only in homes and hotels, Muir argued, adding that no one ever caught a cold camping in these salubrious woods, there not being a single sneeze in all the Sierra. But neither his argument nor his jest did the trick. He described the bonfire he would build. The fragrance of the sequoia flame would protect them from any lurking vapors, and the purple firelight would transform the trees as the stars peered down from on high. He urged them to make an immortal Emerson night of it. But he was unable to overcome their dread of the pure night air, to convince them that it was just cooled day air with a little dew. They seemed to prefer the carpet dust and stuffiness of the interior.

It was a sad commentary on Boston culture, Muir felt, and on these professed disciples of transcendentalism. Their cavalier rejection of the simple act of camping and being exposed to nature stung him. Emerson's beliefs were the foundation of his own, and at that moment they rang hollow. You can say whatever you want, he thought, but what you do reveals the truth. Emerson-inspired ecstasy in nature was something that he had shared with Jeanne Carr and cherished, but he would not get to share it with Emerson himself.

He had to make the best of it. Despite his inclination to go up the mountain and camp alone, he decided, with Emerson leaving so soon, to stay with the party at the now-overflowing hotel. While Emerson, tired from the day's efforts, was restrained all evening, Muir still basked in the light of his smile and calm conversation. After the poet retired to the room he was sharing with five others, Muir joined the few Bostonians, including Thayer, who because of the crowding, and much to Muir's amusement, had no choice but to sleep on the porch in the cold night air.

The next morning, the party set out for the Mariposa Grove, riding with the affable Clark as guide on the trail that he had built. During the sunny and pleasant ride, Clark was quiet, however, while Muir talked of the trees, helping the Easterners to distinguish a sugar pine from a yellow pine and a silver fir from a sequoia. But the grove was Clark's. To him it was hallowed ground. Emerson's crew was suitably awed, gawking at the cinnamon-colored giants, measuring the biggest ones with a tape, riding through prostrate fire-bored trunks, examining the surprisingly tiny cones, whose size Clark compared to a hen's egg. He had studied the trees closely over time and could explain their growth mechanics. Each year the incremental increase in the size of the tree inside the bark pushed out the old bark in ridges, which gradually moved from dark purple to cinnamon in color and grew up to three feet thick in the oldest trees.

One of the sequoias, the first that Clark had seen when he discovered the grove, was named after Clark himself. But he had a particular fondness for the Grizzly Giant, beneath which Carleton Watkins had photographed him in 1865. Clark loved the rugged two-thousand-year-old tree not for its height or shape, but for its endurance. Centuries of wind and snow had shorn its upper carriage. Fires had ravaged and shrunk its base circumference from a hundred feet to ninety-three. Still the resilient tree, as Clark proudly pointed out, supported a branch more than six feet in diameter a hundred feet above the ground.[11]

Watkins was on his third visit to the area when he took the photo of Clark. Fascinated by the grand scale of the landscape, he used mammoth plates, eighteen-by-twenty-two-inch glass plates, to produce his images. His photos had impressed Oliver Wendell Holmes Sr., who called them "calm," "clear," and "distanced" in the *Atlantic Monthly*, and were so influential in the East that—along with the lobbying of Clark and others—they had persuaded Congress, in 1864, to take time out from the war to protect the valley and the trees, and thus to create the seed for what eventually was to become the National Park System.

The nation was changing rapidly and irrevocably. The controversial greenback dollar, paper currency not redeemable by gold or silver, had been made legal tender in 1862 so that the Union could pay for the war. Now only faith in the nation backed its currency. To many, and to the financial markets in particular, this was unsettling. Protecting the country's monumental trees and spectacular granite valley was, to some degree, an equal and opposite reaction, a subconscious balancing of the scales—saving and highlighting the solid natural assets that backed the nation, illuminating the better and more harmonious future that awaited a reunified land, and providing a glimmer of the West's ability to restore hope to a war-weary people.[12]

Wandering through the grove, Emerson and Muir had occasional moments alone. At one point among a fine group of trees, as if spellbound, Emerson quoted Genesis 6:4: "There were giants in the earth in those days." Afterward, the group sat down to eat lunch near a hut—Clark's Hospice, which Clark had built to shelter visitors. As they finished, he pointed out the finest still-unnamed tree and gave Emerson the honor of naming it. The Sage christened it Samoset, after the first Native American to make contact with the Plymouth colonists, and recorded in his journal with satisfaction that "the tree was a strong healthy one" and that he had given Clark money to have a plaque made for it.

Soon their time together was over. While Emerson was being helped into his saddle, Muir made a last bid for him to tarry. "You are yourself a sequoia," he sallied. "You should stop and get better acquainted with your big brethren."[13]

But Emerson, as Muir had already seen, was helpless in the hands of these urbane Easterners, who were unable to fully grasp the nature right in front of them, let alone to comprehend its ability to heal body and soul. While Thayer would go on to become a celebrated Harvard law professor, known for his constitutional expertise and defense of Native American rights, in the Western wilderness he and the others appeared to be book-learned ninnies and old-fashioned conformists, lacking in vision. Emerson was a comet, and they were the dust of his tail.

In his recent "Natural History of the Intellect" talk at Harvard, Emerson had presciently stated that the answer to life's big questions would not come from supercilious professors but from the remote purlieus of native genius. Now he had had a brush with that native genius. He urged Muir to come East, though he recognized the "awe & terror lying over this new garden" of the West, compared to which, Chicago and St. Louis were mere toys. "I should think no young man would come back from it."[14]

And Muir would never leave it, even to accept Emerson's invitation. Yet he felt lonely for the first time in the woods after Emerson departed. To restore his peace of mind, he built a bonfire and listened to the songs of the birds and the forest.

With this meeting, Jeanne Carr's deep belief in Muir was once again affirmed. Before leaving California, Emerson paid a surprise visit to the Oakland cottage where she and Ezra lived. She had never "heard him so delightful in conversation" than about Yosemite Valley and his visit with Muir. "His silver speech flowed on and on."

"If there is any joy of angels to be had in the flesh," she told Muir, "it is that of finding your soul confirmed in its faith through the soul of another.' And so, dear friend, my joy *in you* was full, and I laugh to think how they go up to the mountains, the beautiful ones, to find *you* in the confessional, the only soul I know whom the mountains fully own and bless." If there was a passing of Nature's poetic torch from one generation to the next, it had just gone from Emerson through Carr to Muir.[15]

Chapter 3

A Ramble in Hetch Hetchy

Inspired by Emerson's visit, his diminished state notwithstanding, Muir and Carr dreamed of again singing his song together, in a way that only the two of them seemed to do, finding God in nature—via spirit, flesh, and intellect. In a weaker moment Carr revealed her disdain for those who were not among the "initiated," privy to the manifestation of God through nature and able to receive God's communion there, in the holy temple of Yosemite Valley: "I pity you in my inmost heart, if you do make guiding a business," she wrote Muir, "for even here I feel as if some one were calling my mother bad names when I meet the returning squadrons and hear their comments upon the trip. If I were forced to hear her insulted to her face I should be pitching people over those cliffs."

"Amid all Yosemite things," Muir responded to Carr, "there is this constant thought—your early coming." He hoped for a month's rambling with her, "a month containing a greater number of days than was ever heard of in rhyme or reason. . . . Bring your Doctor and [son] Allie if you possibly can, and any of your other friends if you cannot possibly help it."[1]

Meanwhile Emerson's invitation to Muir to come East to the ivory towers lingered like a sweet but invasive scent to be sniffed with guilty pleasure and forsaken. Far more enticing was Muir's quest to explain the creation of the Sierra. While those who had previously investigated Yosemite believed that it had been formed by an earthquake, and this was widely accepted, his observations told him a different story. Ancient glaciers, he was convinced, had carved the canyons. Seeing it was the easy part. The hard part would be compiling the evidence and fashioning an elegant argument to convince the academics of the truth. To Muir, it was a holy mission. The closer he could get to telling the accurate story—through the use of scientific data—the closer humans would be to understanding their place in the natural world, and to God.

So, in early November 1871, he set out for Hetch Hetchy, the Yosemite-like valley at the mouth of the great Tuolumne Canyon, to seek more evidence for his theories. He had first glimpsed the valley two years before from the height of Tuolumne Meadows, where he had gone with the shepherd Billy Simms, and had first entered the valley the previous September while wandering in the mountains. He had found a spot on the rugged edge of the canyon's south wall where he could sit and look. While the sun glowed on the distant peaks, several miles of the Tuolumne River spangled below, curving past granite faces and through groves and meadows, sounding of rapids but not falls. Studying the canyon's far wall, Muir felt certain it had been made when the ridges that were once there were shorn off by the Tuolumne glacier that flowed past them.[2]

From where he sat, on the edge of the mighty wall, he could see the channels of five immense tributary glaciers that had entered the canyon from the summits to the northeast. Each of these ice rivers had been powerful enough to thrust its head down into the bottom of the main Tuolumne glacier. So clearly were they recorded here that, as he gazed, he could practically perceive the canyon below filled again with creeping ice, pocked with gray boulders and scarred by crevasses. Wide snowy basins below the summits glowed white in the sun, blue in the shadows of black peaks. He felt the world young. The last days of this glacial winter were not over. Humans were still experiencing the dawn of creation, the world growing more beautiful daily.

Muir had descended nearly a mile into the canyon the next day and found its features so similar to Yosemite's, yet still unspoiled, that he felt as if he had gone back in time. It gave him hope to know that Hetch Hetchy—this Yosemite twin—was so remote and so little altered by the men who put their commercial interests above the health of the land that provided them. Leaving again that same day, he knew he would come back as soon as he could. What he did not and could not know was that one day, it would fall to him to defend the valley from such men. A quarter of a century later, he would write incredulously:

> It is impossible to overestimate the value of wild mountains and mountain temples. They are the greatest of our natural resources, God's best gifts, but none, however high and holy, is beyond reach of the spoiler. . . . These temple destroyers, devotees of ravaging commercialism, seem to have a perfect contempt for Nature, and instead of lifting their eyes to the mountains, lift them to dams and town skyscrapers. Dam Hetch Hetchy! As well dam for water tanks the peoples' cathedrals and churches, for no holier temple has ever been consecrated by the heart of man![3]

Hetch Hetchy lay some twenty miles to the northwest of Yosemite as the crow flies, but on foot it was a winding forty miles, by road to Hardin's Mills, then by a path through rocks and chaparral. Muir did not follow trails when he could cross "living granite," so he set out by Yosemite's Indian Canyon heading straight across the mountains. This late in the year, he risked being caught in a blizzard, but with no companion to slow him down or to worry about, he feared nothing but grizzlies. As usual, he traveled light, carrying only a pair of wool blankets, three loaves of bread, a small sack of coffee, and a jar of Baron Liebig's Extract of Meat—a popular nutritional supplement. Two loaves of bread would be enough for four days. In a pinch, he could live on the third, a big round that he called his "storm loaf," for up to a week.

The first night he settled down on a bed of springy fir branches by a stream in a deep groove three miles back from the face of El Capitan. As his fire crackled, he imagined this groove as it was millennia ago, beneath the glacier that had so slowly ground and polished it. This did the trick, and as he put it, the pure, refreshing wildwood sleep swept over him. "To those who receive the mountains into their souls, as well as into their sight—living with them clean and free—sleep is a beautiful death," he later wrote, "from which we arise every dawn into a new-created world, to begin a new life in a new body."

Accordingly, he rose at dawn and with new vigor spent the day crossing the ice-polished canyons along Cascade Creek before camping in a grove of silver fir. He knew a challenging descent lay ahead. In September, he had been so excited to reach the valley floor that he had dashed shouting with elation through dense sedge and over the rim of a side canyon to near disaster. After dropping five hundred feet in a flash, he had come upon a small polished shelf and a pool of water in the canyon wall, which he recognized as evidence of glacial movement through the tributary canyon eons before; here the ice had met an immovable bar of granite, forcing it to rise, while the softer granite behind eroded, creating a basin. Below this, he had picked his way down the face of the canyon past beds of sharply angled rocks covered in willow tangles crushed and felted by the deep snow that sat on them half the year. Mixed in were small patches of lilies, columbines, and larkspurs up to eight feet high.

Halfway down, the canyon narrowed and grew steeper. Having been scoured by centuries of avalanches, its walls were slick. He crept forward, wetting his hands with his tongue and slapping them on the rock to make them stick. In this way he approached a seam that led to a climbable part of the main wall, studded with shrub oaks. He did not know if he would be able to reach it, but he trusted his body to tell him. He had often deemed a wall too steep and lacking in holds only to have his feet and hands set out and carry him forward almost against his will. But now all his senses warned him against risking the fall. He realized he had no choice but to backtrack five hundred feet up the face to reach a point where he could climb out to the main canyon wall.

Still, the attempt had not been futile. He had learned more about the ancient glaciers. The side canyon he had descended was only a niche in the south main wall. Those on the north wall were much larger, often connected to others that reached back to the high glaciers. Those on the south were local, the result of small glaciers lingering in the shade of the walls long after those of the sunnier north side, and were cut off high above the bottom of the trunk canyon as the glaciers that made them were swept round and carried away by the larger trunk glacier. This made it a challenge to reach the floor of the main canyon from the south.[4]

Now, in November, after spending a day climbing a long timbered slope and then crossing several more valleys the next morning, he reached the rim of the Tuolumne Canyon a mile or two above Hetch Hetchy. The view was a feast of mountains rising gradually higher, ridge over ridge, dome over dome, to the top of the range, and Muir thought it among the "very grandest" he had ever seen. He searched more than a mile of canyon wall and found a curve descending to the bottom. Several hundred yards down, he hit a trail and before long was startled by a sound that he feared was a mother grizzly but turned out to be a deer, which bounded up the mountain, kicking rocks down the slope, barely missing him. A little farther, he came to a cliff and, peering out over thousands of feet, spotted a thin ledge fringed with shrub oaks. Reaching the ledge, he discovered bear tracks going his way and crept forward until he came to a recess with a few trees. The bear had climbed to a slope above using a dead pine that leaned against it like a ladder. Empty-handed, he might have followed suit, but his blankets and provisions made such a climb too tricky. Instead, he backtracked and zigzagged down a fissure in the wall to a bushy seam, hoping to regain the bear trail by creeping along the rock face, but this shelf also ended abruptly. Again, he backtracked. Finding a stone cavity filled with a few quarts of water on a brushy ledge, he stopped, built a twig fire, and brewed a cup of coffee. When he set out again, the trail quickly improved. Now descending with relative ease through thickets of chaparral, he reached a lush valley full of black oaks and manzanita and discovered the reason for the path: it was a bear highway, as he described it, to the bear gardens, the valley's plentiful acorns and berries.

The next morning, he ate a hunk of bread and started down the riverbank to Hetch Hetchy. He reached it in about an hour, missing the early-rising bears, who had already stamped the hoarfrost with their massive paws. Regional tribes had visited the valley, cultivated it, and fought over it from time immemorial. Still, to his eyes it looked little disturbed. A hunter, Joe Screech, and his party, the first whites to come upon it, in 1850—a year before the Mariposa Battalion reached Yosemite—had failed to establish it for large-scale herding or mining. The valley was simply too remote. Muir found nothing but a few empty huts of the Paiute, who came for the abundant namesake grain and acorns, and a couple of deteriorating shepherd shacks, along with the inevitable sheep damage.

View of Hetch Hetchy Valley from Eleanor Road.

Hetch Hetchy, the last of a chain of lake basins in the Tuolumne Canyon, was about three miles long and up to a half mile wide, oriented east-west but, like Yosemite, bent north-south in the middle between precipitous granite walls. The Tuolumne flowed slowly through Hetch Hetchy, wider than the Merced in Yosemite; however, a narrow canyon pinched its west end enough to back up spring floods and create a seasonal lake. To the south, rocks towered like the Cathedral Rocks of Yosemite, and to the north, a wall soared like El Capitan. In spring a large stream free-fell a thousand feet over this wall. East of this, Hetch Hetchy Falls correlated to Yosemite Falls. A mile inside the east end of the canyon, to the south, a rock formation called Kolana by the Paiute resembled Half Dome. And in a position similar to that of Yosemite's North Dome stood a dome with the largest, most voluminous waterfall Muir had ever seen.[5]

He marveled anew at the realization that the world was so rich as to have two Yosemites instead of one. If a thousand people were magically transported from Yosemite to Hetch Hetchy, he imagined, fewer than ten would notice the difference. He would take to calling this valley the Tuolumne Yosemite.

"Hetch Hetchy Landscape Garden" by Muir's friend Herbert Gleason,
which was published in the June 1910 *Sierra Club Bulletin*.

By mid-November, Muir was back in Yosemite Valley, and the snow was coming down heavily. It fell for three days straight, mounting to four feet on the valley rim. That year a record 2,150 people had visited the valley, but by winter only 26 remained. "I am more lonely this winter than ever," he told his brother David in a letter. Jim Lamon, a farmer and the first Yosemite settler to overwinter there, had departed, and so had Elvira Hutchings, James Hutchings's wife, to whom Muir had grown close (later the cause of unwarranted speculation from her husband and others), "and there is not left one soul with whom I can exchange a thought."

"All days & seasons flow past in one unmeasured, undivided stream to me, a result of the kind of life which I live," he told David, but he did remember "that old fashioned holidays are near" and asked his brother to tell their siblings and their spouses, to whom he would always remain loyal, to buy at his expense any book they wanted in the stores in Portage or Madison or from the Eastern catalogs.[6]

While the proprietors of the various hotels and businesses were away, a skeleton crew of workers and caretakers remained behind. Muir was staying on as the off-season keeper of Black's Hotel, a pleasantly drafty pine-plank lodge, where he planned to write about his findings on the glacial formation of the Sierra Nevada. He had recently combined a series of his letters about his glacial studies—including his letters to John Runkle, president of the Massachusetts Institute of Technology, who had come West to learn firsthand about the glaciers—into an article, which he titled "The Death of a Glacier" and submitted to the *New-York Tribune.* The story ran in early December, and he received a check for his efforts and a request from the editors for more. Carr, Emerson, and Runkle had all urged him to write a book on the subject. Though he was a frequent correspondent and journalist and had few qualms about expressing his thoughts to those he knew were sympathetic, writing for the academic world intimidated him. He had no fancy degrees—no degree at all—and lived far from the scholars East and West, other than those in Carr's sphere. Why should anyone pay attention to him? But he felt he must try to set the record straight and describe the great glacial system that he knew had once covered and then formed Yosemite Valley and the entire Sierra Nevada.[7]

Naturally his thoughts turned to his family when news of staggering fires in the Midwest reached him. Although overshadowed by the Great Chicago Fire, an even deadlier one closer to home started that same day, October 8. Ferocious winds whipped a railroad clearing burn and other small fires into a firestorm near Peshtigo, Wisconsin, and in the Upper Peninsula of Michigan, wiping out more than a million acres of forest, destroying a number of rural communities, and killing fifteen hundred people. It was (and still is) the deadliest wildfire in US history. Muir wrote his mother, Ann, to say he was relieved to hear that the family was safe. He also told her about his mountain research:

> For the last two or three months I have worked incessantly among the most remote and undiscoverable of the deep Canyons of this Merced basin, finding many a mountain page glorious with the writing of God and in characters that any earnest eye could read. The few Scientific men who have written upon this region tell us that Yosemite Valley is unlike anything else, an exceptional creation, separate in all respects from all other valleys, but such is not true. Yosemite is one of <u>many</u>. One chapter of a great mountain book written by the same pen of ice which the Lord

long ago passed over every page of our great Sierra Nevada. I know how Yosemite and all the other valleys of these magnificent mountains were made and the next year or two of my life will be occupied chiefly in writing their history in a human book—a glorious subject, which God help me preach aright.

Although while researching he had been tired, hungry, and sleeping in the elements, he told her, the thrill of his investigation and his "Scottish pluck and perseverance" fueled him. "I never wander, am never lost," he assured her. "Providence guides through every danger and takes me to all the truths which I need to learn, and some day I hope to show you my sheaves, my big bound pages of mountain gospel."[8]

Though Muir did not know it, he was about to experience a unique display of nature's power. In December, after a cluster of golden balmy days, twenty inches of rain and forty of snow pelted the valley. On the afternoon of the sixteenth, while Muir was out walking, he saw a massive crimson, almost translucent, cloud forming over Cathedral Rocks, on the south rim across from El Capitan. Its smooth tapered base bulged like an old sequoia, rising to a bossy down-coiled crown. Although he was acutely alert to the nuances of clouds and weather, he had never seen anything like it.

The next day gray clouds, curly-grained like bird's-eye maple, heaped over the valley, and by the following morning a storm had unleashed nearly a foot of fresh snow and showed no signs of abating. Not only was fate intervening again to stall the writing of his scientific book, it was delivering him the most colossal, marvelous, and perilous natural phenomenon he would ever experience—the Flood of 1871—and as usual he would not be content to remain safely behind closed doors.[9]

CHAPTER 4

Johnson Becomes an Editor

R obert Underwood Johnson would eventually become one of America's most prominent magazine editors—at a time when that ilk held enormous sway over the nation—and an unsung hero on many fronts. At home in the halls of Congress, he would shepherd legislation on matters as diverse as international copyright law and the protection of nature. He would write critically acclaimed poetry, help found the American Academy of Arts and Letters, raise money for the Italian ambulance corps during World War I, become the US ambassador to Italy, and receive decorations from multiple European nations. Along the way, he would edit and befriend Mark Twain, Ulysses S. Grant, John Burroughs, Nikola Tesla, and many other literary and intellectual lights for the pages of the *Century Magazine*—including, for four decades, a raw and original talent out of California by the name of John Muir, a deep-thinking and painstaking writer who was somewhat eccentric, often pleasingly so, and needed a certain special touch.

But that future was a long way off in February 1873. After seventeen months working for Scribner Educational Books in Chicago, the strapping twenty-year-old graduate of Earlham College, in Indiana, took his first vacation and traveled to Washington, DC, where he had been born in his grandfather's house on Capitol Hill on January 12, 1853, and had spent many happy summers. For his vacation, he had arranged to stay with an aunt and uncle, and would use his time off to contemplate his next career step. Although he grew up in Indiana, the city was in his blood, and he planned to visit his childhood haunts on Capitol Hill. His grandfather and namesake, Robert Underwood, had made a strong impact on his grandson. After arriving in Washington from Ireland in 1800, Underwood had built his house where the rotunda of the Capitol would later rise and gone to work in the auditor's office of the Treasury Department. A devout Presbyterian of Calvinist leanings, he was an early riser, scrupulously exact in all matters, and liked to hunt, fish, botanize, and play the cello. He was both social and literary.[1]

When Johnson stepped off the train in DC, he discovered a vibrant and changed city. It was only eight years since the end of the Civil War, and he found a charged partisan atmosphere, in which President Grant and many other Union-officers-turned-politicians were hotly debating the issues of the day and modernizing the standards for governing. The city, Johnson found, was abuzz with the impeachment of two members of the House of Representatives—Massachusetts Republican Oakes Ames, a shovel and railroad magnate, and New York Democrat James Brooks, the founder and editor of the *New York Daily Express*—for corruption involving the Union Pacific Railroad. Ames, who had taken on control of the Union Pacific in 1865 at the request of President Lincoln to build tracks during the war, had employed his family's industrial know-how to get the job done, but he was now accused of bribing Congress with stock to win votes on legislation favorable to the railroad, abetted by Brooks, a government director of the railway, and bilking the government of tens of millions of dollars.

Johnson, whose father, Nimrod Johnson, was an Indiana judge, had practically grown up in a courtroom, and he now spent a chunk of his vacation in the Senate press gallery riveted by the dramatic testimony. Ames shed tears. Brooks appeared to be in shock. Ames's roguish attorney, Benjamin Butler, argued that the two representatives were being scapegoated by the bloodthirsty press. Raising his eyes upward, he opined, "I thank heaven that I am a man that God made, and not the newspapers." To which a reporter in the gallery, up to the occasion, riposted in a stage whisper, "Thank heaven he doesn't charge it upon us!" Johnson, who later observed that "the proceedings raised the standard of official scrupulousness in America to a higher plane," was hooked.

The halls of Congress and the upper echelons of the press were to be his chosen milieus.[2]

Since the war, Washington's streets had been repaved and trees had been planted. Compared to Chicago and its clogged traffic, the nation's capital now seemed appealingly modern, a clean and calm place, which Johnson began to think offered a better atmosphere for the reading and studies he hoped to pursue. Among the reforms going on, a merit system of exams for public service positions was being implemented. Before heading back to Chicago and his job at Scribner, he sat for an exam in the hopes of becoming a clerk in the Treasury Department, where his grandfather had worked.

Despite his ties to the city, Johnson had grown up five hundred miles away, in Centerville, Indiana, where his father, a Quaker and an Abe Lincoln Republican, had his court. In 1869, two years before Johnson graduated from Earlham in a class of four, his father, a kind and gentle man, though sometimes fiery in public life, had died. At his commencement ceremony, Hiram Hadley, a Quaker friend of his father's, offered the young graduate a job as a clerk at Scribner. At the age of eighteen, the idealistic Johnson, steeped in Earlham's Quaker emphasis on peace, community, and social justice, packed up and moved to Chicago.

His role was to support Hadley, the publisher and bookseller, as well as his two agents, who sold books to schools through superintendents and school boards in a territory of six states. One of his main duties was to dispatch sample textbooks. Hadley was kind to his new hire and gave him sage advice. "Robert, I want to tell thee something," he said shortly after Johnson started. "There are three kinds of employees: first, the one who shirks; second, the one who gives an exact equivalent, so far as he can calculate it, keeping his eye upon the clock; and third, the one who always does more than he has bargained for or than is expected of him. It is only the last who succeeds." Johnson never forgot these words.

After six weeks in Washington, Johnson returned to Chicago and soon learned that he had passed the exam and earned a job at the Treasury. Eager for a new opportunity, he decided to resign from Scribner. He told Hadley, who congratulated him and showed no disappointment or animosity; Hadley had anticipated the need for his talented young clerk to advance his station and also had news. He had just returned from New York City, where he had heard about a vacancy in the editorial department of the company's two-year-old general-interest magazine, *Scribner's Monthly,* which had recently absorbed *Putnam's Monthly Magazine,* founded in 1853 to focus on American literature, science, and art. He had taken the liberty of recommending Johnson for the position, which was being held for him until he could show up and prove that he was competent for the job.

Johnson had a tough decision to make. With few attachments in Chicago, he could leave in a matter of days, but would it be for New York or Washington? In either case, Chicago would always be important to him. It had been the place of his first job, of many life lessons, and where he had witnessed one of the most devastating spectacles ever seen in America. Just over a month after he arrived, he had been staying with relatives on the west side of town when he heard the urgent gongs of fire engines rushing to a blaze. It was the night of October 8, 1871. On the heels of a summer drought, a blaze had ignited near Catherine and Patrick O'Leary's barn in a muddle of wooden buildings. Johnson rushed outside to see the dramatic action of the firefighters battling flames. When it appeared that matters were under control, he headed off for another part of town, but by the time he reached the Madison Street Bridge, a furious gale had not only revived the fire but was sweeping burning rafters, planks, and embers across the sky into the business district. The entire city was soon erupting in flames.

As Johnson watched, buggies, carriages, and wagons filled with panicked citizens and their prized possessions clogged the streets. "It was like the rout of a great army," he later wrote. "And yet, with it all, I had a curious sense of satisfaction in being part of such a colossal event." Returning to the west side, he found the Washington Street tunnel dark and so choked with fleeing residents that he feared he might suffocate. He climbed onto a girder of the Madison Street Bridge, over the Chicago and Northwestern Railway track, to watch the proud commercial buildings succumb to the fire. The heat grew so hellish that it vaporized brick, iron, granite, and marble, "leaving nothing worthy of the name fireproof," as Johnson put it. During that long night Scribner Educational Books on East Madison Street ceased to exist. The next morning, even as firefighters exploded dynamite to try to prevent the spread of the fire, Hadley sent Johnson a message to report to the new headquarters being established on the South Side. He had already ordered a fresh stock of books by telegraph, and within twenty-four hours, it would be back to business as usual, supplying *Guyot's Geography*s and *Felter's Arithmetic*s to all in need.

The Great Fire destroyed more than three square miles of the city and gutted the central business district, killing three hundred people and leaving a hundred thousand homeless. It was followed by two brutal winters during which several feet of snow often shut down the city's streetcars, wagons, and messenger services. Johnson showed his own steely resolve, forged in the conflagration he had witnessed and its aftermath, as bold souls pushed on despite the catastrophe. When Hadley's field agents sent telegrams directing him to ship sample textbooks by the evening train "without fail," Johnson packed the books in bundles and with cords digging into his hands hauled them across the frozen city to the railroad station, never missing a deadline.[3]

In two decades Chicago, risen up from the wreckage, would reinvent itself as an industrial and banking powerhouse, a whole new modernist paradigm for the nation, but one that Johnson would find himself in conflict with.

With his Chicago experience and Hadley's no-nonsense training, Johnson opted not for a job in the government bureaucracy, which would offer the more secure career path, but for one as an editor, about which he knew little. Instead of heading to Washington, as he had originally intended, he boarded a train for New York. On May 10, he arrived in Manhattan for the first time. But he had already experienced another first that day that would have a profound influence on his life. On the ride from Chicago, he had asked a porter to wake him at dawn, when the train would be passing Niagara Falls. What he saw in the early-morning light—the vast tumult of water and billowing mist—took his breath away. Despite having spent much of his youth outdoors, he reckoned it was the first great natural scenery he had ever seen. In that moment, a passion for America's sublime natural beauty was born.

Johnson reported to Roswell Smith, the magazine's cofounder and publisher, whose wife, Annie Ellsworth Smith, had been a childhood friend of Johnson's mother in Washington. The two women shared the memory of witnessing Samuel Morse's first transmission of a telegraph, which was sent from Washington to Baltimore. Annie had even been asked to give the message, which her mother had come up with: "What hath God wrought!"

But even with the personal connection, Roswell Smith would not make it easy for Johnson to settle in place. "Mr. Johnson," Smith demanded, shortly after the young man began his new job, "everybody in the world is trying to do something he can't do and is more or less dissatisfied with what he is doing. What makes you think you might succeed in literary work?"[4]

CHAPTER 5

Ice and Fire

A t thirty-seven, Muir was uncommonly vigorous with an unyielding gait over the roughest terrain and a remarkable capacity for exposure to weather, hunger, and hardships. Not only was he one of the nation's most notable alpinists, but he was in the midst of publishing seven articles in the *Overland Monthly* on his observations regarding the glacial formation of Yosemite Valley and the Sierra Nevada, adding to his reputation as an expert on the region. While Josiah Whitney, the renowned Harvard professor and namesake of California's highest peak, would stubbornly cling to his view that a geological cataclysm has caused the Yosemite Valley floor to sink, purportedly deriding Muir as an "ignoramus" and "mere sheepherder," Muir's carefully observed conclusions were actually correct.

Muir had also recently cataloged the flora and fauna of the most prominent peak of the Sierra Nevada, Mount Shasta, in articles in the *San Francisco Daily Evening Bulletin*. But his talent for storytelling—so evident in his conversation and in his correspondence with his family, Carr, and others—had yet to fully emerge in print. This was about to change. His account of a flash blizzard on top of Shasta, in *Harper's New Monthly Magazine*, would rivet the nation.

In the fall of 1874, following three hundred days of city life in San Francisco, which Muir called a "season of fog and refinement," he had made his way through Shasta's foothills, inspecting the pines and rock formations and in a single day discovering a new species of woodpecker, three new species of wild buckwheat, and a wild grapevine he had never seen—or as he put it, "met"—before. He also stumbled upon a salmon hatchery on the McCloud River, from which 5 million eggs would be shipped that year around the nation. Fascinated, he described the artificial spawning process in the *Evening Bulletin* and expressed his growing concern for the environment: "When the New England pilgrims began to fish and build, it seemed incredible that any species of destruction could ever be made to tell upon forest and fisheries apparently so boundless in extent, but neither our 'illimitable' forests or ocean, lake or river fisheries are now regarded inexhaustible." He worried that the damage had made lakes and rivers "barren as deserts," as when the mud from gold mining drove the teeming salmon out of the Tuolumne. "Uncle Sam seldom manifests any disposition to look very far into the future," Muir noted, "nevertheless, Congress has at length been convinced that our stores of trees and fishes may be exhausted."[1]

Having recently returned from his Shasta wanderings, Muir was a natural choice to ascend the mountain to assist in Captain A. F. "Gus" Rodgers's US Coast Survey experiments in late April 1875. The fact that springtime, when the volcanic slopes are still covered in snow, is the season of capricious and potentially perilous weather at altitude meant that Muir, known to be resourceful and fearless, was even more certainly the best man for the job. Captain Rodgers, who was installing a fourteen-foot-tall geodetic monument on the summit of Shasta to be used in surveying Northern California, had a timetable to keep, and the spring had been temperate thus far, so Muir and Jerome Fay, a seasoned mountain guide, hunter, and wrangler, who had accompanied Muir up Shasta before, agreed to hike to the top to make barometric observations while Rodgers made comparable observations at the base—his loss, to Muir's way of thinking. To climb the immense volcano from the south, the usual plan was to ride the ten miles from Strawberry Valley, reachable by the Oregon and California stage road, to the upper timberline on the first day, then leave early the next morning for the summit. That is what Muir intended to do.[2]

At Sisson Tavern, an inn, restaurant, and hunting, fishing, and climbing outfitter established by Justin and Lydia Sisson in 1866, the forest opened up, revealing a sight that never failed to stop Muir in his tracks, though Fay appeared to be indifferent to it: the crooked stream behind

Sisson's cabin carried the eye through a smooth green meadow to a towering forest of fir and pine, and then aloft to Shasta's white cone of a summit, snowcapped year-round. At this distance and angle—the best anywhere to take in Shasta—meadow, forest, and mountain blended in a dreamscape, framed by the arching sky.

At just over fourteen thousand feet, Shasta is not the state's tallest mountain, but it is its most impressive, visible from up to a hundred miles away. While Mount Whitney's granite peak rises five hundred feet higher—an elevation quite familiar to Muir, who in 1873 was the first to ascend the mountain's difficult eastern face—it contends for visual impact with a stretch of high Southern Sierra peaks, and its base lies at eleven thousand feet. Shasta soars from a plain at four thousand feet, giving it nearly three times the rise of Whitney, and at seventy miles around, Shasta's lava base dwarfs Whitney's by a factor of seventeen.[3]

A little more than an hour after leaving Sisson's, Muir and Fay with their packhorses entered the second of Shasta's three botanic zones, a two-mile ring of silver firs at an elevation between six thousand and eight thousand feet. Muir knew the territory—and the telltale signs of primordial ice—well. Shasta's hulking shoulders had once been covered in a massive glacier. Over the millennia, the ice descended, pulverizing and sculpting and depositing rich moraine soil, which later spawned the forests. Lighter porous soil flooded down, creating smooth gray deltas at the base in striking contrast to the rough lava flows. Swaths of towering conifers—sugar pine, yellow pine, Douglas and silver fir, and incense cedar—many two hundred feet high and seven feet in diameter, streaked the chaparral.

As they rode through the dense thicket of manzanita, cherry, chinquapin, and buckthorn up to six feet tall—a glorious sight when in bloom and impressive even covered in snow—Fay related a few stories of bear hunts and Native American encounters. Among the firs, the snow had heaped to five feet or more. Breaking through it with the pack animals was hard work, and they soon realized that they would not reach the summer campground before dark. They trudged through the drifts until dusk, then bivouacked on a lava ridge protruding from the snow.

The next morning, they shouldered blankets and provisions and hiked over the snow to the timberline. At ninety-five hundred feet, the dwarf pines were only chest high. At the end of the day, they camped behind a block of gritty red trachyte, looking up on the snow-covered alpine zone, tufted by wort, spirea, and dwarf daisies. Above that it was just lichens and red snow. They rose beneath a star-filled sky. As they would be moving briskly, Muir dressed lightly, sure that he would stay warm. They drank coffee in tin cups and ate strips of smoky venison. By half past three, they were navigating the slope by starlight while the mountain brooded in deep predawn silence, broken only by the sound of the wind and occasional tumbling rocks. The wild beauty of the morning stirred Muir, as he loped forward with Fay in tow. They crossed the gorge between the two lava cones, then scrambled up sweeping slopes of snow around the broad mile-and-a-half Whitney Glacier. The summit, two extensive snow and névé fields bound by crumbling peaks and ridges, was about a mile and a half in diameter, skewed from southwest to northeast. The mountain's volcanic energy still exhibited itself in sulfuric gases hissing through the fumaroles that Muir and Fay skirted near the base of the narrow east ridge. Other vents in the lava spewed boiling hot spray, which rose and fell, cooling and reheating in a prickly mist.

At its base Shasta emerges from the plain in beguilingly gentle slopes, but the pitch near the top is severe, up to thirty-five degrees. Four hours after setting out, the pair reached the summit and looked down on the vast lava plain extending to Lassen Butte, shimmering in the sunlight sixty miles away. Rhett and Klamath Lakes, silvery disks, twinkled on the Oregon border beside the black lava beds where the bloody Modoc War, between the Modoc people and federal troops, had been fought two years before. The snowy peaks of Oregon, the Scott and Trinity Mountains in Idaho, and the blue Coast Range came in and out of focus—real, and then pretending to be mirages. The sky was of the thinnest, purest azure adorned with white cumuli; for Muir, spiritual life filled every rock and every cloud. The elation of being in such a spectacular place, where few had ever been, erased the effects of the lack of sleep. The weariness in his limbs melted away.

At first Muir and Fay saw no hint of the brewing storm. At nine in the morning, the temperature was thirty-four degrees in the shade, rising steadily. By one o'clock, with heat radiating from the sun-warmed cliffs, it was fifty degrees, and a lost bee, a mile or more above the nearest honey flower, buzzed around their heads. More cumulus clouds were piling up below and ringing the mountain. First the sprawling view— a relief map of the West Coast's notable features—faded from sight, then the coniferous forests below them vanished. They were isolated on the summit. The sun was doubly intense, hitting them not only from above but, reflecting off the clouds, from below too. "A man can go snow-blind," Fay said. "We might be the first to go cloud-blind."

The wind picked up, and after a while a vast master cloud bank, corresponding to Shasta, rose so near and so dense that it seemed as if they could leap onto it and scramble down its sides to the ground. Muir and Fay now took notice. Spring usually brought plenty of rain and light snow to the middle Sierra, but on the highest summits, such as Shasta's, spring storms could be as severe as those of winter. What they saw boded trouble. Muir considered abandoning the three o'clock observation and heading back to camp. Fay peered over the jagged ridge. Gesturing anxiously in the stiffening wind, he declared, "If we don't make a speedy escape, we'll have to pass the night on the summit." But Muir did not want to disappoint Captain Rodgers and was determined to complete the task. Pride was a shortcoming, he knew. Later, during the worst of it, he would reflect that he could accept the loss of his own life, if necessary, but to sacrifice Fay's for his pride was an iniquity. At this point, though, he dismissed Fay's warning: "Two mountaineers, such as us, can break through any storm likely to fall."

About half past one, fibrous clouds began blowing over the north side of the summit, spinning and spilling together in translucent gray rolls, like foam on a river. Produced by the chilling of the air during its upward deflection against the mountain, these higher clouds steadily amassed on the north rim. The sky darkened, and snow and hail began to fall. Just as Muir completed his observations and boxed the instruments, a fierce storm blasted them with hailstones that roared down the red and gray lava of the mountainside. Muir and Fay pushed their way down the eastern ridge. As they passed the hissing fumaroles, the sky turned black, and the temperature sank twenty degrees. Lightning flashed, accompanied by tremendous muffled cracks, so close they made their hair stand on end. The wind boomed, and a blizzard replaced the hail. All of a sudden, waves of snow bowled over them like ocean breakers. Even against this, if they had been able to immediately descend the snow-filled grooves leading down to the forests, they might have escaped the worst of it. However, before they could, they had to traverse a treacherous snow-covered ridge more than a mile long. On the way up, Muir had reflexively memorized the trickiest points, and he believed they could do it.

After passing the fumaroles, Muir stopped in the shelter of a lava block to wait for Fay, but when he caught up, he refused to proceed. "The ridge is too dangerous," he said. "The snow's blinding, and it's too cold. Even if it's possible to grope our way in the dark, the wind might hurl us over the cliffs." Muir disagreed but let him finish. "Our best hope," Fay said, "is to wait it out among the fumaroles, where we should at least avoid freezing."

"The wind's at our back," Muir countered. "West of the cone, we can slide down and make our way to camp. We can creep along the ridge and clear the ice and gaps on our hands and feet." But Fay refused to take on the storm in that direction. Feeling responsible, Muir fell silent. Leaving the shelter of the lava block, Fay backtracked against the wailing wind toward the fumaroles. Wavering and struggling as if caught in a torrent of water, it took all he had to cover the twenty or thirty yards. After waiting in vain for a lull in the storm that Fay might consider moving forward in, Muir joined him. "Here, we'll be safe from frost," said Fay.

"We can lie in this mud and gravel, hot at least on one side. But how do we protect our lungs from the gases?" responded Muir. "And after the storm, when our clothing's wet with snowmelt, how will we reach camp without freezing?" The volcanic patch, about a quarter of an acre, was flat, and at the moment, the scalding gas jets were neutralized, swept away by the frigid wind. Suddenly the storm began to rage with an intensity unlike anything Muir had ever seen. The flying crystals were so fine and densely packed that there seemed to be no space between them; it was like trying to breathe underwater. Even then, Muir took a minute to study the crystals on his sleeve. Some presented their rays exquisitely, but most were dinged from striking one another and rolling on the ground. They heaped up around the two men and clung to their clothes. In nothing but shirtsleeves, Muir was cold and soaked to the bone. Fay wore a snug coat. Yet he, like Muir, shivered violently.

Stranded without food, shelter, or firewood, they would have to endure the night almost entirely exposed. Muir tried to coax Fay into telling more stories as a distraction against the snow piling up, but the guide had grown somber. He said little, only occasionally indulging in calculations on how long they could survive under the circumstances, speculating that the storm might last all night and the next day, and pessimistically assessing the chances that Sisson might come rescue them. Only later would they learn that, from below, the summit appeared to be haloed in placid clouds and Sisson had no idea they were in the throes of a deadly storm. To cheer themselves up, Muir predicted the morning breaking sunny and clear. "Storms don't blow continuously from day to day this time of year," he ventured. "Out of all this frost and weariness, we'll yet escape to our friends and homes. All that'll be left of a trying night will be a clump of memories we'll tell our children."

They lay on the ground, both to give the wind as small a surface as possible to lash and to absorb the volcanic heat—their bane and salvation. The granular snow enshrouded them, drifting into the hollows of their clothing and dulling the wind but then freezing into a stiff cocoon.

"Last year," said Fay, at length, "I guided a minister up here. I wish he were here now to try some prayers. What do you really think, Muir—would they help a fellow in a time like this?"

"You're named for a saint, a translator of the Bible, and a penitent who beat his breast with a stone. That should count for something," Muir replied. "They help, sure enough. Maybe not so much at a time like this, though. Firewood would be better right now. You might try some prayers when you get back, though, for that we will."

Without the blessing of firewood, they endured the unusual torment of being simultaneously scalded and frostbitten. Even as Muir's back and hips blistered, his beard, watch chain, and two barometer guards he was carrying all froze together.[4]

As much as they suffered from the wind, Muir feared that if it fell off, the carbonic acid in the volcanic gases might concentrate to a lethal degree. This was not merely theoretical for him. He had once nearly succumbed to subterranean gases while digging a well for his family in Wisconsin. At ninety feet below ground, he had lost consciousness, and only with great effort had his father and brother saved him, using the pulley system they had rigged up for the work.

During the night, whenever either man roused suddenly from his agonizing stupor, he would shout out to make sure the other was not unconscious. Ordinary sensations of cold, even imagined in the extreme, Muir would later say, were an inadequate comparison to what they experienced.

Hallucinating, Muir saw dry pine logs smelling of resin and prime for a campfire, only to reach out and be jarred awake with disappointment. With strange clarity, lush valleys and fir woods invited him into their welcoming arms at the bottom of the mountain. Then the howling wind broke the blissful mirage.

"Muir," Fay uttered, pitifully faint, "are you suffering much?"

"Yes"—Muir forced his voice to be strong—"the pains of a Scandinavian hell, at once frozen and burned. But never mind, Jerome. The night'll wear away, and tomorrow we go a-maying. What campfires we'll make, and what sunbaths we shall take!"

Finally, a glimmer of hope: a faint lightening of the horizon suggested that dawn would indeed arrive on this extraordinary first day of May. Still, it felt like an eternity before the sun scaled the peak and with slow deliberation reduced the cold shadows beneath it. From where they lay looking up, the sky was cloudless. For several hours, hours that felt both infinite and nonexistent in the blur of pain, numbness, and delirium, the light crept toward them over the sparkling snow. Soon they would have to make an effort to reach camp, and they wondered if they would have the strength to rise, let alone to negotiate the miles of snowdrifts. Trapped in a shell of ice and frozen garments, Muir tried to feel his fingers and toes and to work his small joints back to life before busting out. At around eight in the morning, he and Fay rose from the ground, like ice creatures. They eased their stiff joints into motion and then started to wade through the deep snow. Muir's left arm, frozen stiff, hung like a deadweight from his side, but his legs moved surprisingly well. Determination propelled them back to camp, three thousand feet below, where, they found, it was sunny and warm, and where Sisson, worried since they had not returned, soon showed up to fix them coffee and lead them back to the tavern on horseback.

By mid-June Muir was already camping again in the High Sierra, and in August, he and a mule named Brownie set out from Yosemite on a journey to study the colossal southern Sierra sequoias. "The Big Tree . . . is nature's forest masterpiece, and, as far as I know the greatest of living things," he would write. To him, they were not just big trees, but were of an altogether different order, their scale and longevity something to be grappled with in humanity's continuing effort to understand its place in the universe:

> Who of all the dwellers of the plains and prairies and fertile home forests of round-headed oak and maple, hickory and elm, ever dreamed that earth could bear such growths?—trees that the familiar pines and firs seem to know nothing about, lonely, silent, serene, with a physiognomy almost god-like, and so old, thousands of them still living had already counted their years by tens of centuries when Columbus set sail from Spain, and were in the vigor of youth or middle age when the star led the Chaldean sages to the infant Saviour's cradle. As far as man is concerned, they are the same yesterday, today, and forever, emblems of permanence.[5]

Except, as Muir well knew, European Americans, who had only discovered the trees in 1852 in the Calaveras Grove, in the high Sierra Nevada sixty miles northwest of Yosemite, had almost immediately cut down the one they called the Mammoth Tree—a process that took the loggers three weeks—to exhibit for profit. The wood being too heavy to move, sections of bark were cut and sent to be reassembled for display on Broadway in New York City and eventually burned in a fire in 1855. A hotel for tourists, who flocked to the site where the tree had been hewn, was built near the gargantuan stump, which became a dance floor for thirty people at a time, while a building housing a two-lane bowling alley was built on its fallen trunk. The entrepreneurs soon stripped the lower bark off another nearby big tree—the Mother of the Forest, no less—to be displayed at London's Crystal Palace before perishing in a fire in 1866. It was "skinned alive . . . and the bark sent to London to show how fine and big that Calaveras tree was—as sensible a scheme as skinning our great men would be to prove their greatness," Muir later wrote. "This grand tree is, of course, dead, a ghastly disfigured ruin, but it still stands erect and holds forth its majestic arms, as if alive and saying, 'forgive them, they know not what they do.'"[6]

Brownie had been foisted upon him by a well-meaning friend, and Muir soon regretted it, as the mule, though spirited, had a hard time keeping up. They spent a week in the Mariposa Grove, where Muir searched the perimeter for evidence that it had once been bigger and was receding, then headed southwest to the Fresno Grove. Here they stayed with a retired forty-niner, John Nelder, a self-appointed keeper of the grove, which, Muir noted happily, was "betraying no sign of approach to extinction." However, he lamented, loggers were building a mill and flume nearby, "assuring widespread destruction."

Farther south, in a remote Kaweah River meadow, they encountered a horse wrangler. "What are you doing?" asked the surprised man, who had brought a band of horses into the mountains for pasturage. "How did you get here?" Muir explained that he had come across the canyons from Yosemite to look at the trees. "Oh, then I know you," the man responded. "You must be John Muir."

The Good Samaritan, as Muir referred to him, shared his camp in a burned-out sequoia trunk, which Muir, doing his best real-estate-agent imitation, described as "a spacious log house of one log, carbon-lined, centuries old, yet sweet and fresh, weather-proof, earthquake proof, likely to outlast the most durable stone castle, commanding views of garden and grove grander far than the richest king ever enjoyed."

On one of the four forks of the Kaweah, in what would later become part of Sequoia National Park, Muir and Brownie encountered a "grand" wildfire, the "master scourge" and shaper of the forests, which Muir was keen to observe, especially for its effect on the big trees. The fierce fire came roaring out of nowhere up the chaparral-covered slope of the East Fork canyon, a "cataract of flames," consuming acres of green bushes at a breath, "now towering high in the air, as if looking abroad to choose a way, then stooping to feed again" in a "terrible rushing and roaring" of lurid surges and choking smoke. Muir was unfazed and eager to study the action of the firestorm. He tethered Brownie a safe distance away, on the edge of a meadow beside a stream. Then he stowed his provisions and made his usual bed of ferns and boughs in a "big stout hollow trunk," which he believed would resist "the fall of burning trees." He would barely use his bed as he observed the fire for the next several days and nights, mesmerized by the otherworldly "wild fireworks."

The first night, he saw a dozen or more fires in the tops of the largest sequoias, flames flaring hundreds of feet in the dark sky, like signal beacons on watchtowers. He roamed about, watching in wonder as these giant candles repeatedly ignited, until he figured out how it was happening. When the fire met the forest, the chaotic flames calmed, "like a torrent entering a lake," now creeping through the cake of compressed needles, leaves, and ground cover beneath the trees in inch-high flames, a long, crooked, smoke-filled crimson line that in the dark looked like the fissure of hell. Periodically they would explode on small bushes, brome, dead branches, and fallen trees, sometimes in bursts that Muir described as "perfect storms of energy." The live sequoias, especially the ancient ones, persisted, their thick fibrous bark impervious to fire; however, flames sometimes raced up the bristles in the furrows of the bark, in "pale blue quivering, bickering rills . . . with a low, earnest, whispering sound." These ephemeral "lamp-lighting" rills, the "most beautiful fire streams" he had ever seen, vanished after a minute or two, but the lightning-shattered tops sometimes combusted into "big lamps," burning for days—sparks cascading like a fountain, red coals sifting through the branches, and then, startlingly, a "big burned-off chunk weighing perhaps half a ton" would plummet from on high.

On hillsides, fires "roaring and blooming like waterfalls" blazed on the upward sides of trees that had trapped limbs and debris, while branches high overhead, tossed and shaken by the ascending air currents, seemed to writhe in pain. Recurring fires over hundreds of years had burned such detritus against the gigantic trunks and formed shallow scars on the uphill sides of the trees. Eventually the wounds would deepen until, far beyond the center of gravity, the trees fell. Among the most impressive sights that Muir saw, at night especially, were great fallen trunks, some two hundred feet long and up to twenty feet thick, bark and sapwood removed by repeated burnings, their charred, cracked surfaces lit in a "pure rich furred ruby glow, almost flameless and smokeless," radiating "like colossal iron bars fresh from a furnace."

As the fire moved relatively slowly, it allowed Muir to observe the action up close, though when he was near the burning giants, he had to constantly watch for falling limbs and knots and shattered flaming tops. As always, he seemed tranquil in the face of danger, observing that the "immense bonfires" erupting beneath an old giant with fifty cords of "peeled, split, smashed wood" piled up around its base "illuminated the circle of onlooking trees magnificently" and so brightly that he could read print three hundred yards away. Most spectacular of all was the spontaneous combustion of the sequoia saplings (of a mere century or two), which exploded with a "heaving" boom into a roaring, throbbing tower of flame hundreds of feet high. To burn green trees in a flash, it took a tremendous updraft of scorching heat fueled by dead wood. These flash tree fires vanished almost as quickly as they happened, leaving the tree a "black dead mast, bristled and roughened with down-curling boughs."

After the fire, Muir and Brownie moved on to the Tule Basin forests, and Muir found that the array of majestic trees on the North Fork surpassed even the Giant Forest of the Kaweah. But south of that, the sequoia band tapered off, and the hills were so decimated by sheep that Brownie had trouble finding enough forage to survive and Muir had to share his bread with him.

Muir concluded that the sequoia was not a fading dinosaur of a tree, a relic of some larger past, as many then thought. Having scoured the outer edges of the forests and sequoia groves and the gaps of the sequoia belt, he found no traces of a former larger expanse of sequoias—no outlying fallen ancient trunks or ditches or root bowls, all common in the established groves. The area featuring the species, as far as he could tell, had not diminished in the last ten thousand years, and most likely not in postglacial times. In fact, he saw evidence that the sequoia was discreetly expanding its realm, with individual saplings occasionally thriving a mile or more from a grove.

But what nature had created over millennia, man could destroy in the blink of an eye, and to no good end. "The value of these forests in storing and dispensing the bounty of the mountain clouds is infinitely greater than lumber or sheep," he later argued in the *Atlantic Monthly*. "To the dwellers of the plain, dependent on irrigation, the Big Tree . . . is a tree of life, a never failing spring, sending living water to the lowlands all through the hot, rainless summer." The common currency in

California was water, and Muir well knew it. Forget for a moment the trees majesty and their beauty; destroying the sequoias was bad water management. That was something that both farmers and politicians could, perhaps, understand.[7]

In 1876 Muir had, at the age of thirty-eight, begun to publicly lobby for forest protection. He was so nervous before his first lecture, to the Sacramento Literary Institute, that, at Keith's suggestion, he placed Keith's painting *Headwaters of the Merced* in the church where he was lecturing to transport himself to the soothing mountains during his speech. It worked. "He forgot himself and his audience, only remembering that he was to make clear some wondrous mysteries, and to unfold to those who listened to the story of the six years he has spent in the mountains, reading their lives and tracing alike their growth and destruction," the *Daily Record* reported. "Mr. Muir was at once the most unartistic and refreshing, the most unconventional and positive lecturer we have yet had in Sacramento." It was just the boost he needed.

On the other side of the country, that September, a socially awkward asthmatic young man from Manhattan, who suffered from a nervous stomach among other ailments, headed off to Harvard. Though he also had poor eyesight, he was an obsessive and unrepentant shooter, skinner, and collector of birds. Well practiced in the art of taxidermy, he had collected hundreds of stuffed specimens of birds and other mostly small animals. He was seventeen and already had an exceptional ear for birdsong. His name was Theodore Roosevelt.[8]

CHAPTER 6

Mr. Muir and Mr. Johnson

In the fall of 1877, Muir traveled to Mount Shasta with two celebrated botanists: Asa Gray of Harvard and the Englishman Sir Joseph Hooker. Hooker had seen all the world's great forests and worked beside John Tyndall, T. H. Huxley, and Charles Darwin. At night Muir built bonfires, as he loved to do, illuminating the flowers and the trees. The three men exchanged stories and argued over plant species. Hooker acknowledged that the Sierra coniferous forests—its cedars, firs, pines, and sequoias—were the world's grandest. Gray asked Muir why he had yet to find *Linnaea borealis* in California, insisting that it must be there on the north boundary of the Sierra. Muir said he had not forgotten this favorite "fragrant little plant" that carpeted the cool woods of Canada and the Great Lakes and had seen many of its relations in the high mountain woods and glacier meadows. "The blessed fellow must be living hereabouts no great distance off," Gray insisted.

The next day, while Gray worked on Shasta's flanks, Muir and Hooker made a westerly excursion. After fording an ice-cold branch of the Sacramento River, they noticed a green carpet on the bank, not yet in bloom. Hooker plucked a specimen and said, "Isn't that *Linnaea*? It's awfully like it." Then he found some withered flowers and confirmed the first known sighting of the plant, commonly known as twinflower, in California. Muir considered the "little slender, creeping, trailing evergreen, with . . . a delicate, fragrant white and purple flower," to be the "wildest and the gentlest, the most beautiful and most loveful of all the inhabitants of the wilderness." In *Linnaean* woods, he declared, he would "encamp forever and forego even heaven."[1]

Muir's first story for *Scribner's Monthly* had not yet run in the fall of 1877—it would come out the following February—when Johnson, a twenty-four-year-old assistant editor, wrote to the outdoorsman from the magazine's editorial rooms at 743 Broadway, in New York City, to "beg" that he would tell them if he had more ideas. "In fact," Johnson wrote, "we should be glad to learn what are your enthusiasms and whether you have time to put them on paper." The editors were interested in a story on farm life in California but did not know if he "would write spontaneously of the subject." Muir, Johnson would soon discover, did not like writing on demand. "As our best work is unsolicited," he continued, "we hesitate about naming subjects, but trust that, if our overtures are welcome to you, you will frankly write us, suggesting the topics that are nearest your heart."

The editors' desire to cultivate Muir—then an emerging explorer and writer on nature and the West—might have had something to do with his most recent story being hot off the press in the pages of *Scribner's* rival and elder, *Harper's New Monthly Magazine*, the leading magazine in the land, founded in New York City in 1850. Called "Snow-Storm on Mount Shasta," the article was very different from Muir's upcoming story in *Scribner's* about a water-loving California bird—the ouzel. "Snow-Storm" was a wilderness thriller of defying death, a survival tale of extreme weather, unearthly landscapes, and superhuman grit, the type of story that kept eyeballs fused to pages and that any popular-magazine editor would kill for. Nonetheless, Muir had done wonders with the water ouzel, now better known as the American dipper, a kindred spirit with a penchant for daredevil acts over rapids, and one that, he argued, was more inseparably related to water than even a duck, which frequently makes long overland flights:

> Our ouzel, born on the very brink of a stream, seldom leaves it for a
> single moment. For, notwithstanding he is often on the wing, he never
> flies overland, but whirs with rapid, quail-like beat above the stream,

tracing all its winding modulations with great minuteness. . . . The vertical curves and angles of the most precipitous Alpine torrents he traces with the same rigid fidelity. Swooping adown the inclines of cascades, dropping sheer over dizzy falls amid the spray, and ascending with the same fearlessness and ease, seldom seeking to lessen the steepness of the acclivity by beginning to ascend before reaching the base of the fall. No matter how high it may be, he holds straight on as if about to dash headlong into the throng of booming rockets, then darts abruptly upward, and, after alighting at the top of the precipice to rest a moment, proceeds to feed and sing.

Like Muir himself, his intelligent ouzel had ceaseless energy, unbounded courage, and an imperviousness to hardship. "The ouzel never calls forth a single touch of pity," he wrote, "not because he is strong to endure, but rather because he seems to live a charmed life beyond the reach of every influence that makes endurance necessary."[2]

Johnson and Muir were in some ways an unlikely pairing, and some ways not. Recently wed to the love of his life, Katharine McMahon, a striking curly-haired blonde with soft blue eyes, Johnson was a proper and precocious editor and East Coast urbanite. His hero was his father, Nim, with whom he had had a close relationship, and who, along with his wife, Catherine, a devout Presbyterian, had created an idyllic small-town existence for Johnson and his older brother, Henry Underwood Johnson (later a four-term US congressman). The family house in Centerville was on the National Road, which ran from Cumberland, Maryland, to St. Louis. Nim, who was outgoing and talked to everyone he met, also read history and literature voraciously and published verse in the *Knickerbocker* magazine. Trees, specimens of which he frequently pointed out to Johnson, were one of his passions, and another was all things Scottish. Although Nim was never able to visit Scotland, he prevailed on a friend to bring him back a pot of heather. Unfortunately, he died young—"by accident" is all Johnson ever said—at the age of forty-eight, and "did not have the satisfaction he desired, for the heather arrived on the very day of his funeral! It was placed on his grave."[3]

As a boy, Johnson read everything from Beadle's dime novels, which he and his friends passed around, to Dickens, whose stories he "reveled in" and even cried over. Dickens, whom he would later credit with helping to inspire "the whole movement of social reformation that swept the English and American world in the last half of the nineteenth century," was, along with Earlham College, one of the forces that shaped Johnson's progressive thinking. Johnson was free to roam and frequently ran in and out of the courthouse when his father was there. He and his friends often gathered to watch the trains of canvas-covered wagons heading West, enjoying the inevitable dogfights between "the dogs of the town and the dogs of the road," and wondering what would become of the families in their new lives. The spring and fall were marked by the arrival of immense flocks of migratory pigeons as they darkened the sky in "wedge-shaped phalanxes." The boys would shoot at them with arrows and visit their roosting places to see the resulting "cyclonic havoc of broken branches."

In 1864, during the Civil War, Johnson, over his father's objections since he was only eleven, took a job with the station agent at the town's busy train depot, where he learned to operate the telegraph machine. He reveled in taking down the lightning-fast transmissions from an Indianapolis operator—the teenaged Thomas Edison—which were dreaded by the older operators, who could not keep up. Johnson would sometimes stay for the arrival of the midnight train and "chat" by telegraph with operator friends while he waited. His job and the hurly-burly of war exposed him to all sides of life, and he grew up fast, once having to ride a cart horse three miles to deliver a death message to a soldier's family and witnessing their grief. On April 15, 1865, he was at his machine when this message came through:

> President Lincoln was shot last night at Ford's Theatre by John Wilkes Booth, an actor, who escaped and is now being pursued. The President is unconscious and his death is expected at any moment.

Johnson rushed out to the train platform and announced the news to general disbelief.[4]

Both Johnson and Muir were heavily influenced by their fathers, albeit in very different ways. In addition to Nim's love of literature, civic engagement, and charm, Johnson had picked up another of his qualities: his love of trees.

Johnson and his winsome bride, Katharine, spent two weeks of their honeymoon in Philadelphia attending the Centennial Exhibition, where, Johnson later said, "we got our first bent toward the esthetic. . . . Progressive America may be said to date from that year, especially in interior decoration." They would eventually move into a Murray Hill brownstone, the Brown House, and decorate it in golden-brown tones with draperies of gold damask to hold the morning and afternoon light. They reveled in "beautifying the home" and hosting spirited dinner parties, where artists, actors, musicians, opera singers, and writers and poets commingled, celebrating the Gilded Age with bohemian flair. The Johnsons' idea of "an oasis of rest and tranquility" was quite different from John Muir's.

Muir, Scotland-born and Wisconsin-bred, was a wilderness savant, mystic, and self-styled hobo, one who had rejected the entreaties of Emerson and others to come East and teach at Harvard. He remained a determined bachelor with no fixed address and barely enough possessions to fill a rucksack. His preferred abode was a bivouac with a roof of stars and a bed of pine boughs, and he relished the company of birds and squirrels. In many regards, he and Johnson could not have been more different.[5]

At the same time, *Scribner's Monthly* offered a big tent. The magazine was cofounded in 1870 by Dr. Josiah Holland as editor and Roswell Smith as publisher—a pair of individualists of boundless curiosity and creativity. Over six feet tall, with long raven-black hair and dark eyes, Holland, a brooding medical doctor, poet, novelist, and essayist, was passionate about many things—freedom of speech and religion chief among them—and argued tenaciously and in, as Johnson later judged, "incisive, direct and forcible" prose. He set a tone of candor, open-minded debate, intellectual leadership, and public service and was much esteemed by his colleagues. Roswell Smith, also tall and vigorous, with shaggy graying hair and beard, was himself full of article and series ideas. Holland listened but drew the line when it came to editorial control, which rested with the editors, not the publisher. Still, according to Johnson, Smith "was always searching for a man 'big enough and broad enough' to carry out some enterprise he had in mind, and this phrase came to be one of the bywords of the office." Johnson, to whom three years earlier Smith had issued the rhetorical challenge—"What makes you think you might succeed in literary work?"—increasingly appeared to be that man.

Working at *Scribner's Monthly* was no picnic—the clock was always ticking with the next deadline, and the editing load seemed to expand to fill any void—but Johnson found it exciting and intellectually stimulating, and he appreciated the opportunity to be at the forefront of the national conversation. He had fit right in from the start. Indeed, his trial period had not lasted the suggested three months. He showed such promise and was so dedicated to his work that after three weeks Holland had come to his desk and said, "Johnson, if you like us as well as we like you, you may hang up your hat and call it a bargain."[6]

In April 1878, Johnson wrote to tell Muir that the editors had read and accepted his piece on the Douglas squirrel. "It is not necessary to repeat that we hold your work in high regard," he concluded, encouraging Muir to condense his farm-life observations, when he could, for another story. But farm life had been a trap of sorts for Muir, and he had mixed feelings about it. While it let you be out in nature, it also required that you tame and destroy it. His father had worked him and his siblings at their two successive properties near Portage, Wisconsin—Fountain Lake Farm and Hickory Hill Farm—from dawn to dusk for more than a decade. It was stultifying toil, and only his intense curiosity for the natural world, his imagination, and his genius for inventing machines that freed him up for intellectual pursuits had allowed him to rise above it. No, Muir had other ideas. Instead of delivering Johnson an encomium on farming, as the *Scribner's* editors had requested, he sent them a riveting account of a windstorm that he had experienced in a treetop. It was an ode to the wind, which carries with it the evidence of all its travels. In it he described an instance of the wind transporting him across the years, unlocking buried memories, and preceded Proust's famous madeleine as a trigger of involuntary memory by three decades:

I breathed sea-air on the Firth of Forth, in Scotland, while a boy; then was taken to Wisconsin, where I remained nineteen years; then, without in all this time having breathed one breath of the sea, I walked quietly, alone, from the middle of the Mississippi Valley to the Gulf of Mexico, on a botanical excursion, and while in Florida, far from the coast, my attention wholly bent on the splendid tropical vegetation about me, I suddenly recognized a sea-breeze, as it came sifting through the palmettos and blooming vine-tangles, which at once awakened and set free a thousand dormant associations, and made me a boy again in Scotland.

In the story, he asserted that a storm, far from being merely destructive, is an essential force in the cycle of life: "We hear much nowadays concerning the universal struggle for existence, but no struggle in the common meaning of the word was manifest here, no recognition of danger by any tree; no deprecation; but rather an invincible gladness as remote from exultation as from fear." Then in one ninety-four-word sentence he offered an insight that was well before its time:

When the storm is over, and we behold the same forests tranquil again, towering fresh and unscathed in erect majesty, and consider what centuries of storms have fallen upon them since they were first planted—hail to break the tender seedlings; lightning to scorch and shatter; snow, winds, and avalanches to crush and overwhelm—while the manifest result of all this wild storm-culture is the glorious perfection we behold; then faith in Nature's forestry is established, and we cease to deplore the violence of her most destructive gales, or of any other storm-implement whatsoever.

The story came out in November, becoming the first of a series by Muir that ran in the next four issues. Blair and Charles Scribner, owners of the magazine's recently rechristened parent company, Charles Scribner's Sons, liked the series so much that they wrote him to say that they would be interested in publishing the stories in a book, along with those published in *Harper's* (of which there were by now several, dating back to 1875). But Muir's path, even when it appeared to be straightforward, was generally circuitous. His first book would not come out for more than fifteen years.

In fact, his life was about to take a dramatic turn. Over the years, Muir had had many close female friends, including Emily Pelton, the niece of the family he boarded with and worked for in Prairie du Chien, Wisconsin, when he first left home; Catharine Merrill, an author and pioneering educator in Indianapolis, who had taken care of him when he temporarily lost his eyesight in an industrial accident; and first and foremost, his particular friend, Jeanne Carr. As a handsome and rugged Yosemite guide, always quick with an entertaining tale from the wilderness, he had charmed many women but had pursued none with the passion he had shown for nature. In 1874, however, Carr had found a worthy match for her protégé and introduced them. Five years later, in the spring of 1879, Muir finally got around to proposing to Louisa "Louie" Strentzel, the Texas-born daughter of a Polish doctor, John Strentzel, and his wife, Louisiana, who had brought their family to California in a covered wagon in 1849. They eventually established a prosperous fruit ranch in what they called Alhambra Valley, near the Suisun Bay town of Martinez, twenty-three miles northeast of San Francisco as the crow flies. Louie, who had curly dark hair, a round face, and a penetrating gaze, had attended the Miss Atkins Ladies Seminary, where she had excelled in English, entomology, and especially piano. She had learned about growing and hybridizing fruits and flowers from her father and was devoted to the family business.

Louie Wanda Strentzel, ca. 1880, around the time of her marriage to John Muir.

In 1880, the week before he turned forty-two, Muir married Louie, who was thirty-two, at the Strentzel ranch. He took up farm life, partnering with Dr. Strentzel in managing the family's sprawling twenty-six-hundred-acre ranch, an all-consuming year-round job, but a lucrative one. Two years later, the Strentzels built a seventeen-room Italianate mansion with twelve-foot ceilings and a cupola on the peaked roof. On a knoll overlooking the valley, the Big House, as they called it, had six bedrooms, seven imported Italian marble fireplaces, a bathroom, and two water closets. It was state-of-the-art, with gas lighting and indoor plumbing, using rainwater collected from the roof and groundwater pumped from wells and stored in redwood tanks in the attic. The newlyweds lived in a farmhouse a mile away. The first of their two daughters, Wanda, was born in 1881. Their second, Helen, would arrive in 1886.

The Muir family at their early home in Alhambra Valley, near Martinez.
The farmhouse was later lost in a fire.

Muir devoted his time and energy to the fruit ranch. His visits to Yosemite ground to a halt, yet he managed to take several expeditions to Alaska and write about them. His only narration of a harrowing experience he had with a brave little dog in a storm on a glacier was, however, verbal, driving Johnson nearly apoplectic with Muir's inability to put perhaps his best—and certainly his most heartrending—adventure into writing.[7]

In one of his last articles before turning his focus to Alaska, Muir had struck a serious note that in hindsight resonates like a clarion call and testifies to his ecological foresight. Not in a national magazine but in the *San Francisco Real Estate Circular*, he articulated his frustration at humanity's disregard for trees, which he saw being destroyed all around him. "Our coniferous forests growing so luxuriantly along our mountain ranges are by far the most precious and indispensable, and at the same time the most destructible, of the three main divisions of our natural wealth," he wrote, "and were the real value at all appreciated and understood—how they affect climate, act as barriers against destructive floods, protect and hold in store the fertilizing rain and snow, and form foundations for the irrigating rivers—they would be guarded by the government with most jealous care." He advocated restrictions on the fires set by timbering and railroad companies, sheep grazing, and tree cutting and called for the formation of a forestry commission similar to those in parts of Europe. "Barn-burning and the firing of grain fields," he concluded, pulling no punches, "should not be considered so criminal as the firing of forests." It was his last word. For now.

In New York's November 1881 election, Theodore Roosevelt, who had transformed himself during his Harvard years from an introspective oddball into a weight lifter, woodsman, and dapper man-about-campus, won a seat as a Republican in the state assembly. Roosevelt's life had changed in many ways. He had lost his role-model father, found direction in wilderness adventure and hunting in Maine and the Midwestern prairies, and married the cousin of a college friend. More recently he had abandoned his boyhood dream of being a naturalist, dispersed his collection of specimens to the Smithsonian and the Museum of Natural History in New York City, and taken up legal studies at Columbia. None of this dampened his passion for trophy hunting.[8]

In October, as *Scribner's* was changing its name to the *Century*, after a transition in ownership, its larger-than-life founding editor, Josiah Holland, a close friend and correspondent of Emily Dickinson's and a biographer of Lincoln, had died at the age of sixty-two. Associate editor Richard Watson Gilder, who under Holland's watch had become a force in public affairs, assumed the reins. Gilder, a poet, and his wife, Helena de Kay Gilder, an artist, model for Winslow Homer, and founder of the Art Students League and the Society of American Artists, hosted an influential literary salon at their home on East Fifteenth Street, known to habitués as the Studio.

One day, Theodore Roosevelt came into the *Century* offices to visit Gilder. "He was in his usual volatile spirits and was full of humorous anecdotes of the New York Assembly," Johnson, by this point an associate editor, would later recall. "He won us all by his humor and his democratic spirit." At the time, Johnson was living with Katharine and their toddler, Owen, on the outskirts of the city, near the East River Park, which ran from Eighty-Fourth to Eighty-Sixth Streets (and later became part of Carl Schurz Park). The city was growing rapidly, and Johnson believed that the park should be expanded. With some like-minded neighbors, in 1884 he presented the idea to Roosevelt and to Hampden Robb, a state senator who would become a notable advocate for Niagara Falls. Together they crafted a bill to condemn the private property to the north of the park and enlarge its boundary. "After a stiff fight in the legislature," as Johnson characterized it, the bill passed and the park was extended. A resulting law would lead to more small parks, transforming the New York City landscape. Johnson had notched his first legislative victory, a win for nature.[9]

In the summer of 1883 Johnson began to steer what would become the *Century*'s multiyear series of Civil War battle accounts told by the commanders of both sides. He and another editor had conceived the project but had had to convince Roswell Smith, who was skeptical despite the success of the magazine's postwar Great South series that spotlighted the region's potential and gave it a sense of optimism. It had been the *Century*'s "first high note of nationalism," according to Johnson, who hoped that the new series would likewise promote understanding and healing.[10]

Although Smith, whom Johnson called a man of "large conceptions and Napoleonic boldness," did not see the potential to increase circulation much beyond its current level of 125,000, he authorized the venture based on the editors' enthusiasm. They did not let him down. The project transformed the magazine. As the nation's all-consuming war played out again—this time in the poignant words of its commanders—the *Century* became the talk of the land.

The task of wrangling the most important contributor—former president Ulysses S. Grant—fell to the persuasive Johnson, who despite his powers of charm and tact, would twice be challenged to duels during the making of the fraught series, by officers on either side. Busy with his affairs and a reluctant writer, Grant initially rejected the idea, but in need of income after falling prey to a business scam, he finally yielded to the determined editor. Johnson would eventually crown the series with Grant's personal insights, but first he had to coax the general away from what he later called his "deadly official report," noting that "the general, of course, did not realize the requirements of a popular publication on the war, and it was for me to help him turn this new disaster of Shiloh into a signal success." Over the course of four articles, Johnson ingratiated himself with the former president, and the two became close. Grant's son Fred would call Johnson his father's "literary tutor." By the conclusion of the series, Johnson had helped double the magazine's circulation, bringing it all the political clout that that implied, and had also convinced Grant to write his memoirs to be published by the Century Company. Johnson's status was on the rise.[11]

At the same time, one of his jobs was to stay on top of John Muir, who was now busy with the fruit ranch and his family. It would be five years before Muir wrote for the *Century* again, but Johnson, who would be distracted by a grand tour of Europe in 1885 and 1886, wanted him back in the fold. And what Johnson wanted, he usually got.

CHAPTER 7

Rebirth on Mount Rainier

America's ability to harness and manipulate natural resources—and to consume them—was accelerating near the turn of the century; at the same time the nation was beginning to understand the need to preserve and cultivate its bountiful resources, instead of merely using and depleting them. In 1887, California, where water was already increasingly coveted, had passed the Wright Act, authorizing the formation of irrigation districts, public entities that could tax landowners and issue public bonds. These entities along with the federal Bureau of Reclamation would reshape the waterways of California. The following year, in Washington, DC, a group of thirty-three visionary explorers, naturalists, educators, and conservationists—including the influential C. Hart Merriam, chief of the Office of Economic Ornithology, and John Wesley Powell, who two decades before had made the first documented descent of the Colorado River—founded the National Geographic Society to increase and spread geographic knowledge. This knowledge was growing at an unprecedented rate, even as the United States was waking up to its status as the industrial and innovative leader of the Western world.[1]

On August 14, 1888, on the other side of the country, eight climbers huddled on a slope of Washington's Mount Rainier, the most glaciated peak in the continental United States, for much the same reason—to better understand the nation's geographical extremes. After a five-and-a-half-hour climb, they had taken refuge for the night in a small windhole on a narrow ridge at just above ten thousand feet on the divide between the snowfield they had ascended and a glacier. Major Ed Ingraham, the superintendent of Seattle's public schools, dubbed it Camp Muir.

Muir, who had engaged Ingraham to lead the climb, had discovered and suggested the bivouac. Here they would spend a short night before departing by starlight to the top. After roughing out sleeping spaces in the lava and hastily building a low rock wall as a windbreak, they ate hardtack and then hunkered down, burying their faces in their jackets against the swirling grit. Shivering in the cold, which photographer Art Warner compared to a December night in Minnesota, they dozed off in short spasms of nervous exhaustion.[2]

It would have taken even worse conditions to dampen Muir's joy. The stress of running the ranch for eight years had turned him pale and sickly. He had yearned for the elements. As he withdrew from nature advocacy, letters had poured in from East and West, urging him to write. Feeling the need to reengage, Muir had agreed to edit and write six articles for the illustrated anthology *Picturesque California*, which would unroll in a thirty-month subscription series and promote the natural wonders of the state and the Pacific Northwest.

While the subject was in Muir's wheelhouse, he struggled to meet the deadlines and had to hole up in a hotel for several weeks to focus. Around the same time, he and Louie had a fright when Helen fell so ill that they thought she might not survive. "We now know what the agony of the loss a child is for we had lost hope for a time of her recovery," he wrote David, in August 1887. "I am all nerve-shaken, and lean as a crow, loaded with care, work, and worry." By November he had written four pieces for the book and assigned others to Jeanne Carr and John P. Irish, a newspaper editor, gadfly, and future nemesis. Irish wrote about the Sacramento Valley, where, he gloated, a tract of irrigated wheat fields less than twice the size of Rhode Island was now worth more than Mexico had been paid for all of California and several other states ($15 million, in 1848).[3]

"Have to write Alaska, Sierra Lakes, Shasta, San Rafael Redwoods, etc. (*and run the ranch*)," Muir reported to Carr, "and edit the whole compound business." When Carr struggled with her piece on Southern

California, Muir urged her to shake her academic stiffness: "Look at the landscapes as the sun looks at them. Strike right out into the midst of your pictures." But Muir himself felt drained of inspiration. "One cannot remain on speaking terms with anything wild after being away so long," he wrote. Louie encouraged him to take a break, and in June, he had gone on a research trip to Lake Tahoe with the botanist Charles Parry, discoverer of the Torrey pine. As Louie had hoped, the trip boosted Muir's spirits. Next, he headed north to write about his beloved Mount Shasta, and then it was on to Mount Rainier.[4]

Muir's friend and fellow Scot William Keith, a landscape painter, manned their base camp on the southern approach to Rainier. Since they had first met in Yosemite in 1872—on Carr's recommendation—Muir and Keith had become close friends, gathered often in San Francisco, and traveled together on many Yosemite outings, including a trek through the Tuolumne Canyon with Carr. The two spoke each other's language and engaged in an incessant banter that—though sprinkled with snippets of Tennyson, Keats, Shelley, Burns, and the Bible—often sounded like arguing. Among their skirmishes, Keith decried Muir's lack of culinary taste, as Muir could happily live off bread and tea or coffee and provisioned his treks accordingly, while Muir chastised Keith for taking liberties with mountain scenery by loosening paint strokes and occasionally inserting imagined features for effect.[5]

"You never saw a sunrise like that, Keith," Muir might carp. "Why in the deuce don't you imitate nature? You'll never paint a decent picture till you can do that."

"Look here now, John, if you'll go out early tomorrow morning and look toward the [east], you'll see nature imitating my sunrise." At which point, as Keith once told a reporter, "Muir will go off growling looking exactly like Carlyle in a fit of dyspepsia."[6]

On this trip, the two had agreed to meet near Shasta, which like Yosemite and Tuolumne Canyon, was one of Muir's holy places, despite its nearly taking his life in 1875. Now he hoped it had the power to restore a jaded soul. Long ago, alone, weary, and on foot, when he first glimpsed the mountain, from fifty miles away and across the Sacramento

Valley, he had felt its healing power, writing, "My blood turned to wine and I have not been weary since." Removed from the wilds, however, he had eventually found himself depleted. And what he and Keith saw now was even more demoralizing. The woods had been clear-cut, leaving fields of stumps and farmland. Muir realized that he was once again caught on the wrong side of the equation: formerly a factory worker turning lumber into at various times broom handles or wagon wheels, he was now part of an agricultural industry that was likewise consuming the wildlands that he loved. Dispirited, he and Keith soon set out for Seattle to regroup before tackling Rainier.[7]

In Seattle, Muir hired Ingraham, thirty-six, and Warner, a twenty-four-year-old Northern Pacific Railway photographer, and prepared for their attempt to climb the 14,400-foot, snowcapped Rainier, a feat that had been accomplished only a handful of times because of its treacherous ice cliffs and crevasse-ridden glaciers. On August 9, Muir, Keith, Ingraham, Warner, and a small band of recruits took a train to Tacoma and then Yelm, where they met the celebrated climber Philemon Beecher Van Trump, the storekeeper and postmaster at Yelm, whom they persuaded to be their guide. They were outfitted with mounts and packhorses and then rode to the farm of Sutelik, better known as Indian Henry, a local farmer and guide who also joined the team. As they traveled the hundred or so winding miles over untarnished Yellow Jacket Pass, where they were accosted by said insects, to the meadows at Rainier's base, belting out Scottish songs all the while, Muir's spirits soared. Unsure when they had set out whether he would be strong enough to reach the summit, he was determined to do so now.[8]

Ascending along the Nisqually River, they set up camp above Paradise Valley at fifty-nine hundred feet, declaring it Camp of the Clouds. On the afternoon of the fourteenth, the summit party set off on foot while Keith stayed behind to mind the horses and make sketches of the Tatoosh Range. Indian Henry would guide to a point but considered Tacoma, as members of the local Puyallup tribe called the mountain, sacred and avoided venturing onto the glaciers protecting its summit for fear that he would be cursed. In 1870, Van Trump had led the Rhode Island Civil War general Hazard Stevens on the first documented ascent of the volcanic Rainier, which had last erupted before the Civil War, and had guided Muir's friend George Bayley on a harrowing summit in 1883.[9]

Camp of the Clouds, August 13, 1888. From left to right,
Indian Henry, John Muir, Henry Loomis, Philemon Beecher Van Trump,
Ed Ingraham, William Keith, and Norman Booth.

After a protracted campaign, Muir, Van Trump, and the US Geological
Survey engineer and geologist Bailey Willis, who called Rainier, with its
contrasting icy heights and vibrant wildflower valleys, "an arctic island
in a temperate sea," would eventually be hailed as the driving forces in
making Rainier the fifth national park. Muir considered Rainier's environs "the most luxuriant and the most extravagantly beautiful of all the
alpine gardens" he had ever seen. Early on the morning of August 15,
1888, however, those alpine gardens were merely the monochromatic
backdrop to an epic climb. Muir and the crew, which also included
a young botanist named Charles Piper, who would later write about
the flora of Mount Rainier, rose in the thin, turbulent, starlit air and
began to climb the ridge above their camp. It was only the seventh
known ascent of Rainier, then believed to be the highest mountain in
the United States.

In 1936, a large section of the Gibraltar Trail, used since 1870,
was destroyed by a rockslide, leaving nothing there but a scar on the
mountain. Today a more southerly route, via the Gibraltar Ledge, carries a warning from the Mountaineers, a Pacific Northwest outdoors
organization founded in 1906: "This climb can only be recommended

during winter months due to extreme rockfall and icefall on the ledges," and climbers must wear hard hats. Even then, "mid-day warming" could be dangerous. Muir's party, however, did not have the benefit of this advice.[10]

Sometimes on top of the ridge and sometimes on either side, they worked their way around canted mounds of ice, crawling past massive walls and steep faces. Below the ledge, a fifteen-hundred-foot drop ended in a chaos of ice blocks and crevasses. Adding to the other threats, falling rocks, at first unseen faint echoes, careened off projections above and roared by, like rubble-tailed comets.

The ridge at last disappeared beneath a steep and severe ice cap. The toughest part now lay before them. "Danger increasing is met with increasing power," Muir would observe, "and when thus successfully met, produces an exaltation joined with an increase of power over every muscle." As the morning dawned in pink hues, they searched for ledges, shelves, pillars, and pinnacles, the only footholds and grips on the ice-covered lava flow. The sight of their goal—Rainier's sparkling peak—breaking through the clouds drove them on. Six hours later, after narrowly avoiding calamity in several instances, they came to a resting place, at about twelve thousand feet, and prepared for the summit. "The surface almost everywhere was bare, hard, snowless ice, extremely slippery," Muir later noted, "and though smooth in general, it was interrupted by a network of yawning crevasses."[11]

Every member of the party removed his shoes and hammered half-inch steel calks into the soles. They secured scarves and sunglasses against the glaring sun. Equipped with crude alpenstocks, made of a rake handle with a spike in the end, and an ax for chopping footholds, recounted Muir, "we stepped forth afresh, slowly groping our way through tangled lines of crevasses, crossing on snow bridges . . . after cautiously testing them, jumping at narrow places, or crawling around the ends of the largest." Muir, feeling focused and strong, rallied the slower climbers through the critical maneuvers of their ascent.

As the team approached the mountain's highest point, between two fuming ice-covered craters, hundreds of feet deep, around noon, wind pummeled them and a sulfuric rime coated their exposed skin. Cold, hungry, and exhausted, they were nevertheless exhilarated. "For the first time I could see that the world was round," Warner, who had lugged up fifty pounds of photographic equipment, including an Eastman Dry Plate camera and glass plates needed to make the images, later said. Muir made his way to a jutting shelf to collect his thoughts. He gazed out on the sprawling landscape below, on the Cascade Range for hundreds of miles into Oregon and as far as the eastern plains of Washington, on the summits of St. Helen's, Adams, and Hood. The view was grand and sublime. "The keenness of perception induced by danger brought a far richer vision than otherwise possible," he would recall. The mountains were speaking to him again, and there, on high, far from the ranch, he could hear them.[12]

On the summit of Mount Rainier, Muir, seated, and flanked by members of the climbing party, including the Rainier guide Philemon Beecher Van Trump, holding a walking stick, and Major Ed Ingraham, waving his hat. Photograph by Arthur C. Warner, August 14, 1888.

The descent was even more perilous than the climb. On the icy dome, where their spiked boots barely gripped, Muir watched helplessly as his newfound friend Van Trump sped past him on his back. Fortunately, at the last second, the experienced guide managed to flip himself over, jam his alpenstock into snow, and skid to a stop. Piper nearly plunged into a crevasse and, losing his alpenstock, had to be roped down by the team. Farther down, to avoid a deadly cascade of rocks and ice caused by the midafternoon heat, they had to cross a stone face on a two-foot-wide ledge above a fifteen-hundred-foot dive onto a glacier. Finally, past the worst of it, they glissaded down snow-covered slopes on their backsides. Muir and his fellow climbers returned to Seattle several days later with swollen and blistered faces, battered but euphoric from their climb. Warner's photos—the first ones taken from Rainier's summit—would run in Muir's *Picturesque California*. To make them, Warner had mounted the camera, a foot square and eighteen inches long, on a tripod, draped his coat over it, and, since it lacked a mechanical shutter, removed and replaced the lens cap to capture the exposure. "I . . . nearly froze my arms," he said.[13]

The mountains had reawakened Muir. Before leaving Rainier, he had hammered stakes into the Nisqually Glacier to measure its flow rate. But his greatest accomplishment from the excursion would be the first description of the mountain and its alpine beauty to captivate a broad American audience, building the base of those who would see the purpose of protecting and preserving such rare places of natural splendor. And in Van Trump, Muir had gained a friend and influential environmental ally in the Pacific Northwest, who would later back Muir's efforts to keep sheep out of the northwest forest reserves and off Mount Rainier. Muir, in turn, would support Van Trump's efforts to change the name of Mount Rainier, to what Van Trump called its "original, rightful and euphonious native name," Tahoma, a variation on Tacoma.

Muir found a letter from Louie waiting for him in Seattle. From Martinez, just as he had set out to visit Rainier, she had written him regarding a decision she had made about the ranch, and him.

John Muir's impact on the nation's landscape might have amounted to little if at this juncture Louie had not realized what a burden farm life had become to him. It not only separated him from the wilds he cherished, it also hampered his ability to evoke them for others, his greatest talent. He was an able farmer and a loving husband and father, but Louie understood well enough that he had much more to offer, gifts that could benefit all of humanity, and she would not let these be smothered any longer by the stress of running the ranch.

Louie enjoyed nothing more than to be at Alhambra, reading poetry and articles about world affairs, playing the Steinway grand piano her father had bought for her when she was young, attending to her family and the ranch, and being a sounding board and editor for her husband.

She did not like to travel and was most content in the garden among the fragrant flowers they cultivated—roses, jasmine, honeysuckle, lavender, lilies, magnolias, and wisteria—where she could bird-watch and point out the constellations to her daughters at night. But she understood that her husband was compelled to explore nature; for him, daunting heights, extreme weather, hunger, and solitude were merely invigorating. But it was all meaningless if he was unable to find the time and space to express in words what he observed and felt there and what that meant. Louie knew this. "A ranch that needs and takes the sacrifice of a noble life, or work, ought to be flung away beyond all reach and power for harm," she wrote. "The Alaska book and the Yosemite book, dear John, must be written, and you need to be your own self, well and strong, to make them worthy of you."[14]

Muir's sketch of pushing Louie uphill in Yosemite
in the summer of 1884, drawn for three-year-old Wanda,
who was at home in Martinez with her grandparents.

PART II

MAKING THE MOUNTAINS GLAD

•

It seems incredible that Government should have abandoned so much of the forest cover of the mountains to destruction. As well sell the rain-clouds, and the fountain-snow, and the rivers, to be cut up and carried away, if that were possible.

—John Muir, May 30, 1891

Half Dome from the Yosemite Valley floor, by P. M. Brusser, ca. 1923.

Presidents: Benjamin Harrison, Republican, 1889–93; Grover Cleveland, Democrat, 1893–97; William McKinley, Republican, 1897–1901

Secretaries of the Interior: John Noble, 1889–93; Hoke Smith, 1893–96; David Francis, 1896–97; Cornelius Bliss, 1897–99; Ethan Hitchcock, 1899–1907

CHAPTER 8

Shaken and Stirred

Within two months of Benjamin Harrison's inauguration as the nation's twenty-third president, the Oklahoma Land Rush, starting at noon on April 22, 1889, sent tens of thousands of homesteaders racing to stake claims on 2 million acres of the former Indian Territory. Cheaters who took an early start were called Sooners. Grover Cleveland, the outgoing president, had signed the latest of a series of Indian Appropriations Acts just days before leaving office, opening the nation to further settlement while disenfranchising Native Americans and harnessing wildlands to the yoke. By the end of the year, four new states—the two Dakotas, Montana, and Washington—would be admitted to the Union, fueling more growth.

A little more than a month after the Oklahoma Land Rush, on the last day of May, an earthen dam in western Pennsylvania burst, unleashing a biblical deluge on Johnstown. Twenty million tons of water—a roiling forty-foot wall of trees, rock, and soil—crashed into the steel town of thirty thousand people (makers of the barbed wire that tamed the West) with the force of Niagara Falls. The catastrophe, a result of greedy deforestation, heavy rains, and an unstable dam built to create a fishing pond for Pittsburgh steel and coal barons—including Andrew Carnegie, Andrew Mellon, and Henry Frick—killed more than two thousand people. One body washed to Cincinnati and another went missing until 1911. Clara Barton and fifty Red Cross volunteers rushed to the scene of one of the worst man-made environmental disasters in

American history, and public indignation soon erupted over the failure to hold anyone accountable.[1]

In June, Muir warned that even as the great forests of Maine, Michigan, and Wisconsin were being denuded for lumber, mills were also proliferating in the West. "The magnificent redwood belt of the coast is fast disappearing, and the only other sequoia to be found in the world—our far-famed big tree—is also being cut for lumber." The logs too large for the mills were "blasted with gunpowder" and their massive tops left in smashed heaps, "food for tremendous fires."[2]

That May, Johnson was in San Francisco working on the *Century*'s series on the Gold Rush and eager to finally meet Muir. When Muir arrived at Johnson's invitation at the ornate reception desk of the Palace Hotel on Market Street, San Francisco's wide main artery in the Financial District, he was told that Johnson was dressing for dinner and had suggested Muir come up to his room. Muir was soon lost in the sprawling Palace, which was the largest, most ostentatious hotel on the West Coast and even had an intercom system, allowing the desk captain to speak directly to guests in their rooms, and four redwood-paneled elevators, or "hydraulic lifting rooms." Two earthquake tremors had shaken San Francisco that day, and Johnson would not soon forget the strange sensation of the quivering city. Still, nothing seemed amiss in this mighty building, with its steel-banded brick walls and underground support columns, advertised as fireproof and earthquake-proof. Finally reaching what he believed to be the right floor but unsure where to go from there, Muir cried out, "Johnson, Johnson! Where are you?"[3]

Johnson had been expecting Muir for some minutes now and was about to call down and inquire about him when he heard his name shouted in the hallway. He opened the door to his room. "Mr. Muir?" he called. "This way."

A wiry, weathered man of upper-medium height, with a shaggy light-brown beard just beginning to gray, soon arrived and fixed him with intense gray eyes. "I can't find my way in these confounded city canyons," he said with a touch of his native Scottish brogue and a mischievous gleam in his eye. "There is nothing here to tell you where to go. Now, if you were up in the Sierra, every tree and mound and scratch on the cliff would give you your direction. Everything there is as plain as a signpost, but here, how is one to know?"

Though Johnson had been acquainted with Muir via correspondence for more than a decade and had seen his image in photographs, this was the first time the tall, dignified, and, to some, imposing editor, whose whiskers, unlike Muir's, were neatly cropped and fastidiously groomed, had laid eyes on his writer.[4]

It had been Johnson's job as far back as 1877 to wrangle stories out of Muir—and he had, starting with a dozen in the first four years. Now it was his job again. As had often been the case in Johnson's career, his timing was good. Muir's recent visit to Mount Shasta and climbing of Mount Rainier had opened his creative floodgates. In late June and early July 1889, he would see no fewer than half a dozen of his stories published in two of the San Francisco newspapers—the *Daily Evening Bulletin* and the *Daily Examiner*—and in the *Oakland Ledger*, in which he devoted many column inches to condemning the rampant commercialism destroying Tahoe and Shasta. Johnson had several weeks of work to do on the *Century*'s Gold Hunters series, a follow-up to its blockbuster Civil War series. Muir, having lived in the San Francisco area for three decades, had useful contacts for him. But their conversation soon turned to Yosemite, a place Johnson had heard much about through Muir and others but had never had a chance to visit. He convinced Muir to lead him on an excursion there when he was done—or nearly done—with his interviews. Muir had been so consumed by the ranch, domestic life, and recently writing and editing *Picturesque California* that he had not been there in seven years.[5]

Muir, Johnson, and their party set off from San Francisco by stagecoach on the second of June. Muir gazed out as they passed Martinez, at around eleven o'clock. "It seemed strange I should ever go past that renowned town," he later wrote Louie. "I thought of you all as sleeping and safe." He had earlier that year spent several weeks nursing Wanda through scarlet fever while Louie had taken Helen to stay at the Big House. "Whatever more of travel I am to do must be done soon as it grows ever harder to leave my Mrs + young," he added. Otherwise, all on board were in high spirits for the outing. The Republican governor,

Robert "Old Honesty" Waterman, a silver and gold miner and rancher who had ascended from lieutenant governor to governor somewhat reluctantly after the sudden death of his predecessor, a Democrat, in the fall of 1887, was along for the expedition, "big burly and somewhat childishly jolly," as Muir described him to Louie. "Also some other jolly fellows & fellowesses."

They stayed the night at Wawona, visiting the nearby grove of big trees, at which point Johnson declared the trip already a success. "The imagination is staggered," he later wrote, "in the endeavor to realize the antiquity of these primeval structures, that have grown with the centuried growth of the human race while dynasties have risen and fallen and out of the wreck of civilizations nothing worthwhile has survived but Literature and Art."[6]

He was not even in the valley yet.

They called on the English painter Thomas Hill, who had gone with Muir two years earlier to Alaska and had a studio at the Wawona Hotel, a clapboard Victorian with stacked verandas four miles inside the park's south entrance. Hill was most famous for his 1881 painting *The Driving of the Last Spike*, celebrating the transcontinental railroad. Muir saw a "large Yosemite" that, he reported to Louie, "I fancy you would all like." It was sold, but he thought that Hill, whose paintings were collected by the likes of Leland Stanford and William Ralston, the builder of the Palace Hotel, would paint another if he asked him to.

They arrived in Yosemite Valley the next day, Monday, the third of June, at about one o'clock "after a fine glorious ride thru the forests, not much dust, not very hot—the entire trip very delightful & restful and exhilarating," according to Muir. "Johnson was charming all the way," he wrote to Louie later that day. "The foothills and all the woods and the valley are flowery far beyond what I could have looked for, and the sugar pines seemed nobler than ever. Indeed all seems so new I fancy I could take up the study of these mountain glories with fresh enthusiasm as if I were getting into a sort of second youth or dotage."

But it would be different this time. Muir was a devoted family man, and though he would travel for extended periods, his close-knit family was never far from his mind. Even as he recorded these thoughts, Wanda, now a precocious eight-year-old, wrote him, "O dear Papa when will

I be strong enoufe to climb the mountains with you? Don't you think in a year or two I might?" Young Helen, whom Wanda called simply "baby" most of the time, was wondering where Papa was. Louie and the girls stayed in the Big House at night, carrying Muir's much-prized journals there with them to keep his words safe. Louie had read to the girls Muir's musings on the water ouzel, and Wanda, a budding naturalist, reported that they had found another "sweet and gentle" goldfinch nesting in the roses and that it had let them approach very near.

"The next morning took us to the Valley of Valleys, no view of which is more thrilling than the first from Inspiration Point, though wonder follows wonder as one proceeds," wrote Johnson in his memoirs. "I shall not attempt anything so banal as a description. Only the pen of John Muir has ever approached an adequate reflection of the feeling of a sensitive person in that Holy of Holies."[7]

However, even before they entered the valley, signs of the abuse of the land had begun to mount. New roads led straight to the heart of the biggest stands of sequoias to funnel tourists there. They were littered with rusty tin cans and rotting garbage. "The trees themselves," Muir said, "seem withdrawn, as if trying their hardest to remain unnoticed." More than a thousand guests had already registered that season at the Stoneman House, where he and Johnson would briefly stay. Families of campers from the Central Valley were rolling in, in stout wagons, filled with tents, bedding, and provisions. Muir estimated that up to five thousand people would visit the valley that season.[8]

The valley commissioners, the managers of park affairs appointed to four-year terms, had clearly prioritized profits for the hotels and stables, despite early guidance by one of the first commissioners, Frederick Law Olmsted, who in 1865 had penned a visionary study on Yosemite and the Mariposa Grove, elucidating man's need for contact with wilderness, the practical benefits of beautiful natural scenery, and the necessity to preserve it. His document—the first ever to express such principles— also suggested ways to manage the park to provide the most access to the scenery while doing the least harm to it. Later considered profound, it was initially ignored. After Olmsted read it at a meeting, his fellow commissioners suppressed it. Olmsted left the state for good that year, and the commission fell into a pattern of bad habits.[9]

A decade later, in 1875, local mountaineer George Anderson had roped his way up Half Dome, nearly a thousand feet, by drilling holes in the granite, plugging the holes with pine, and screwing eyebolts into the plugs. As far as anyone knew, he was the first person to stand on its summit, though many would follow.

In the valley, the residents had set fires and plowed up meadows to make hayfields for the livestock, reducing some of the oldest trees to charred stumps. Buildings, pigpens, corrals, and tourist attractions cluttered the landscape. Livestock devoured the vegetation. In 1875 the old hotels—Black's and Leidig's—had been replaced by the Stoneman House, a "first-class" hotel with peaked roofs and covered porches in a midvalley meadow. It could hold 150 guests, Muir told Louie, but looked "silly . . . amid surroundings so massive & sublime." In the pages of the *Century*, Johnson would dismiss the "cheap summer-resort type" building and "repellent" grounds, featuring a saloon, a marshy field of stumps, a fetid pigsty, and trees hacked up so guests could see and be seen by approaching stages. As a result, some Californians would ridicule him for being an effete Easterner with no business commenting on the West. Bernard's Hotel, a small inn nearby, had mowed down a wide lane of the valley's finest old-growth oak trees to give its bar and porches a view of Yosemite Falls. "The great trees thus slaughtered had been left lying where they fell," observed Johnson.[10]

The valley commissioners, including the ex officio president, Governor Waterman, who had vowed to run a businesslike state intolerant of dishonesty, inebriation, and lavish spending, were there for their annual meeting that Wednesday, June 5. "Everybody is good to us—Frank Pixley is here and Ben C. Truman," Muir reported to Louie, referring to two of the commissioners. "I found old Galen Clark also. He looks well—and is earning a living by carrying passengers about the valley." Now seventy-five, Clark, who had held the Guardian of the Valley position from inception until he was replaced by Muir's old employer, the testy and self-serving James Hutchings, in 1880, was being restored to the role after nine troublesome years during which Hutchings and his two successors had failed to live up to expectations. Clark alone seemed eminently suited to the post.[11]

Muir gave Johnson a thorough tour of the valley floor. The editor was awed by the "many colossal features . . . any one of which would be worth a trip across the continent." He later wrote in the *Century* letter:

> What most impresses one in the valley is the close congregation of its wonders. Here, indeed, Ossa is piled upon Pelion. Along a winding gorge, less than ten miles in length and from half a mile to two miles in width, between walls rising almost sheer to the height of three thousand feet, is a series of wonders. . . . Lake, river, forests, waterfalls, headlands—there is nothing that is not unique, nothing that is not great.

But Muir was appalled at its mistreatment. He and Johnson heard much talk about schemes to project colored lights onto the falls and further reduce the valley's understory so that the approach of the stagecoach could be better seen. Eager to escape and to show Johnson the high country above the state park, Muir hired three burros and a wrangler named Pike, who doubled as a cook. They left the valley, climbing a steep three and a half miles to the top of Yosemite Falls, the plowed meadows weighing heavily on Muir. While farming for profit was distressing him at home, it was likewise wreaking havoc on his Yosemite. Before setting out, he had written Louie to tell her that they were heading into the wilds. "But how much we will be able to accomplish," he said, "will depend upon the snow & the legs & resolution of *The Century*." He had no idea how prescient that would prove to be.[12]

Along the way to Tuolumne Meadows, about fifteen miles, Muir chatted gregariously. Johnson learned about his "meagre, hardy, rigid boyhood" in Dunbar, on the east coast of Scotland; his "awakening" to mechanics, books, and nature on the remote Wisconsin farm where the family had moved when he was eleven; and his university life in Madison. If there was more than a hint of Scottish inflection to Muir's voice as he regaled Johnson with the tales of his youth, it doubtlessly reminded Johnson of his own boyhood, when his mother liked to strum the guitar and sing Scottish folk songs.

There was less snow on the ground than usual for this time of year. April had been warm, Muir observed, and the June snow line was high. At between eight thousand and ninety-five hundred feet, where normally five feet of snow would cover the ground, only small patches lurked in the shadows. "Everywhere throughout the middle region is heard the happy rush and dance of rejoicing water," he reported. "But the supply will not last through the dry summer in anything like its present fullness." As a fruit farmer, Muir knew this spelled trouble for the coast, where by late summer rivers would run low and farms would lack water for irrigation.[13]

Muir talked joyously about how his interest in plants and trees had grown and how, inspired by Humboldt, he had set out on foot for Florida en route to the Amazon. He had walked a thousand miles before his journey was disrupted by malaria and fate carried him to California. Then there were his explorations of Yosemite, living at times off nothing but bread, coffee, and berries. Muir was a superb raconteur, beyond even what his writing might indicate, discovered Johnson, who compared him to Twain in the "piquancy of his gradual approach to the point." They proceeded all day across the divide through open forests north to the Tuolumne watershed. Muir was on a balky burro, having given the better one to Johnson, and the guide, Pike, who had a raw throat and could only speak in a hoarse croak, encouraged him in a fervent stage whisper, "Wallop 'im, John. Wallop 'im!"

In the evening, they reached Soda Springs in Tuolumne Meadows, at about seven thousand feet, and set up their camp by the river. Here Johnson discovered that Pike was much more of a wrangler than a chef while Muir, who was notoriously indifferent to the quality of the food he ate, as Keith often attested, did not seem to notice. Muir and Johnson talked at length by the fire under a ceiling of stars until Muir tucked Johnson in with his feet toward the fire.

The next morning after sunrise—Johnson would call it a "revelation of glory as the clear sun came bounding over the solemn glacial peaks"—they set out to explore, heading through the open evergreen forests into Tuolumne Canyon, which Johnson later described as "the wildest region ever haunted by the God of Silence." One dense brake of low-slung birch saplings nearly demoralized the editor, but he managed to squeeze through it into an open gorge at the base of a waterfall descending from a thousand-foot wall of granite. All along, Muir, who "leaped from rock to rock as surely as a mountain goat," according to

Johnson, "or skimmed along the surface of the ground—a trick of easy locomotion learned from Indians," chatted away, often ribbing Johnson for his lack of outdoors skills and inability to keep up. Now that he could see Muir in his element, Johnson was in awe of him: "In the wilderness, Muir looked like John the Baptist, as portrayed in bronze by Donatello. . . . He was spare of frame, full-bearded, hardy, keen of eye and visage, and on the march eager of movement."

Johnson was not the only one to find Muir divinely transformed by nature. Theresa Yelverton had not only invoked Raphael when describing her Muir-inspired character, Kenmuir, she had also depicted his face as "shining with a pure and holy enthusiasm" that reminded her of "the face of a Christ I had seen years ago in some little old Italian village."[14]

Farther into the canyon, a talus scramble was complicated by stubborn manzanita. While Muir crossed the tricky boulders with deft certainty and magically avoided being jabbed by the shrub, which concealed rigid trunks and branches beneath canopies of soft leaves, Johnson "fell and floundered like a bad swimmer," as he described it, so that Muir had to give him "many a helpful hand and cheering word." Johnson suffered multiple wounds from the manzanita and spitefully dubbed it an "objectionable shrub." But the painful journey was not in vain. When he finally called it quits, he thought the resting place that Muir found him was one of the most beautiful spots he had ever seen, "where the rushing river, striking potholes in its granite bed, was thrown up into a dozen water wheels twenty feet high!" Muir left him in peace for another hour's exploration on his own.

After a full day, they made it back to camp, where Muir, who would prove to be a doting caregiver to his family over the years, particularly to his sickly younger daughter, Helen, looked after his exhausted and scratched-up editor with great care. At nightfall Muir, like some benevolent woods creature, again tucked Johnson into his blankets with the same "tenderness that he gave to children and animals," though in later years he often kidded Johnson about his "adventure with the manzanita." They lay by the fire and, according to Johnson, "revealed our innermost selves (as one does only by the fireside) until we were overcome by sleep." No doubt, the name of Emerson, whom both revered, was invoked. Muir had wanted to guide Emerson on a similar outing. Johnson had sought out his inspiration on two occasions, once when Emerson spoke at a church in Chicago as the city was still recovering from the Great Fire and again at the Concord Centennial in 1875. He considered Emerson (now gone seven years) the nation's greatest, most imaginative man of letters and foremost poet and believed that "the influence of Emerson's sane mind and pure spirit" would "do much to save America from the destructive mania that is threatening the stability of the world."

By this campfire at Soda Springs, Muir and Johnson began a conversation that would profoundly impact the way America preserved its most precious landscapes. Whereas Muir was a philosopher and a man of action in the outdoors, he felt hopeless at swaying policy makers. Johnson, on the other hand, was an activist, shaping the nation's conversation, whether at his Brown House dinner table with the likes of Twain, Burroughs, Kipling, and Tesla; in the pages of the *Century Magazine*; or in the halls of Congress. Having heard Muir and having now experienced for himself the simultaneous beauty and degradation of Yosemite, he felt an urge to do something about it, and he thought the two of them could make a powerful case for stronger protections. Now all he had to do was overcome Muir's skepticism that politicians would have the foresight and courage to protect the environment. So far, Muir had seen no such inclination. He feared that the decimation of Yosemite was inevitable: "The people of California are blinded by moneymaking and are indifferent to the destruction of their natural resources."

While coming over the divide, Johnson had commented that they had not encountered any of the remarkable mountain meadows that Muir had written about in his magazine articles, where flowers grew "luxuriantly up to the breast of one's horse."[15]

"No," Muir had said, "we do not see any more of those now. Their extinction is due to the hooved locusts." Massive flocks of sheep, he explained, were brought up every summer to the foot of the glaciers and not only devoured all the plants but yanked out their roots as well. Without underbrush to hold the snow, it melted faster in the spring, which in turn caused the falls to dry up during the summer. The forest floor was "as bare as the streets of San Francisco," Muir would write, looking "as if it had not only been trampled over, but had been used as a corral, until no trace of life remained."[16]

The point, as Muir would later articulate in Johnson's magazine, was this: "The branching canyons and valleys of the basins of the streams that pour into Yosemite are as closely related to it as are the fingers to the palm of the hand—as the branches, foliage, and flowers of a tree to the trunk. Therefore, very naturally, all the fountain region above Yosemite, with its peaks, canyons, snow fields, glaciers, forests, and streams, should be included in the park to make it an harmonious unit instead of a fragment."[17]

"Obviously the thing to do is to make a Yosemite National Park around the Valley on the plan of Yellowstone," Johnson declared. Had there been any movement in that direction? he asked. Many years back, Senator Newton Booth of California had introduced some such project in Congress, Muir told him, but nobody took an interest in it. He added that his own attempt, in 1881, to establish a reserve in the Kings-Kaweah region had been a waste of time.[18]

Johnson, however, insisted that creating a national park was imperative. He was confident in their ability to pull it off and began to formulate a plan. He would be in Washington soon to advocate for an international copyright agreement, he told Muir, and he could use the opportunity to lobby the Public Lands Committees, where he had connections. Judge Holman of Indiana, a friend of his father's, was on the House committee, and Preston Plumb of Kansas, a former Union officer whom Johnson knew and felt would be well disposed to the idea, was chairman of the Senate committee. In their enthusiasm in the mountain air, Muir and Johnson talked of creating a federal reserve so well managed that California would be eager to merge Yosemite Valley into it.

Still, Muir was dubious. Up to this point, even his modest efforts at preserving treasured places had failed. His own brother-in-law had refused to sell him forty acres of meadows beside Fountain Lake, his boyhood home, to be fenced against cattle and hogs to preserve its ferns and flowers. Muir had explained, "Even if I should never see it again, the beauty of its lilies and orchids are so pressed into my mind I shall always enjoy looking back to them in imagination, even across seas and continents, and perhaps after I am dead." But his brother-in-law had dismissed the idea as a "sentimental dream wholly impracticable." Later, Muir's efforts to save a flowery quarter section of the San Joaquin plain had failed when interlopers repeatedly ripped down his fence.[19]

But Johnson assured him that the measure would pass. All Muir had to do was to write two articles for the *Century* to fire up the public and give Johnson the facts and the narrative he would need to win political support. With *Century* subscribers rallying to the cause, he would put the articles in the hands of the legislators and have a bill introduced in Congress. If Muir agreed, Johnson would telegraph Gilder as soon as they returned from Yosemite to confirm the assignments.

And if he did agree, this budding partnership between Muir and Johnson, writer and editor, Westerner and Easterner, might just change the landscape of America.

CHAPTER 9

Treasures of the Yosemite

By the time they arrived back in San Francisco, Muir, despite his doubts, had agreed to Johnson's plan. Muir would be poet, heart, and soul of their two-man preservation movement, and Johnson the ringmaster. Muir wrote a trio of stories about the trip, which ran on consecutive days in San Francisco's *Daily Evening Bulletin*. In "Yosemite Valley" he celebrated that visitors were pouring into Yosemite "in search of rest and health, and wild reviving beauty" and that roads, trails, bridges, and vistas provided "more than hasty glimpses" to even the hurried and infirm. However, he complained, haphazard cutting of flowering shrubs and trees, including the felling of old oaks and pines, and the trampling of flowers and grasses had done much to "break the charm of wildness." Fenced hayfields and vegetable gardens had replaced meadows and swaths of wild lilies and roses; grazing horses had turned the valley floor into "a dusty, exhausted wayside pasture"; tin cans and kitchen rubbish were inescapable; and one pigsty stank to the top of the domes.[1]

The commissioners, who had once allocated money to build a dam to "repair" Nevada Fall by diverting Liberty Cap Cascades, a splinter of the river, back into its main channel, to Muir's mirth and scorn, lacked a comprehensive plan and—Muir and Johnson agreed—needed to hire a master landscape gardener. The idea was to create one harmonious plan that would prevent the various parties from not only detracting from the natural beauty but also from working haphazardly and often at cross-purposes in an effort to enhance it. They favored the celebrated Frederick Law Olmsted, now sixty-seven, for the job.

In his second essay from the trip, "The Snow," Muir, who had surely weathered more snowstorms at altitude than any other writer, waxed lyrical about his favorite element, water, in the form in which he loved it best. And in his third, "Forests of the Sierra," he warned that the trees of the Sierra were "being rapidly and ruthlessly destroyed," as if they were considered "pernicious weeds," and "nobody in power . . . seems to care." The sheep, he insisted, were worse than the mills, for reasons that went back to the snow: eventually the pines and conifers would recover from the cutting and rise again to retain the snowpack and deliver water in a timely way to the farmers' fields at lower elevations. Only the hordes of sheep, which trampled and devoured the young pine and fir seedlings each summer, would permanently prevent the forests from regrowth. These three articles were a good warm-up for his promised stories to Johnson.

Before even returning to New York, Johnson told Muir that he needed the first Yosemite article soon and passed on his kindest regards to Mrs. Muir, adding, "Tell her to give you no rest till you get back into the literary harness." Johnson's jocularity appealed to Muir's own wry sense of humor, but fulfilling this request would turn out to be no laughing matter.[2]

He was already behind. To knock out one of his articles for *Picturesque California,* Muir stole away from the ranch again, in early July, to the Grand Hotel in San Francisco, an eclectic mash-up of Italianate, Second Empire, and neoclassical architecture and the Palace's elder neighbor. Even as he ensconced himself there to write about trees, the forests near Yosemite began to burn, and before the end of the month, false rumors would fly through the press that Yosemite Valley itself was on fire. The commissioners said that a blaze surrounding the Mariposa Grove had scorched and scarred many of the big trees and blamed it on "forest arson," although they could not say whether this "most despicable" crime was caused by careless campers or deliberate sheepherders. The blaze did not reach the valley, but ten miles to the southeast, on a branch of the Fresno River, where Madera Flume and Trading Company had recently built a mill and loggers would drop hundreds of giant sequoias over the next four years, fire also raged. John Nelder, the unofficial watchman of the grove—whom Muir dubbed "the good hermit" after staying with him for a week in 1875—and his cabin, which was so fresh it was "still redolent of gum and balsam," both perished in the flames.[3]

At the Grand, Muir was dealing with matters far more inane. Having become a celebrity of sorts—famous for championing Yosemite and for his recent discovery of a glacier in Alaska that now bore his name— he was stalked by the press. Distracted by his work one evening, he allowed a young reporter from the *Examiner* to come to his room. Muir protested that he was in town on personal business and did not care to be disturbed, but the reporter hooked him with a quick question about snakes, a subject that, he doubtless knew, Muir found irresistible.

"Mr. Muir," he said, "I would like to know the highest altitude at which a snake will live?" On a later trip in the Tuolumne Canyon, Muir would coolly face four rattlesnakes in two days. In the brush and rocks at the head of Muir Gorge (the name another token of his fame), he tossed his traveling bundle forward onto the third that day, which "coiled and thundered" and lashed out at him as he scraped by. The next day beside the river, he stepped within five inches of the head of another, which, he bore no grudge, as he reckoned it had come, like him, simply to get a drink of water. Muir had not always been so understanding. His mind had changed in 1869 while he was tending sheep and came upon a rattler coiled in the grass. Knowing that it could not strike when it was on the move, he dislodged it by throwing dirt at it and then—as he had seen the deer do—jumped on it, dodging a strike and landing a deadly blow. "He defended himself bravely, and I ought to have been bitten," he wrote remorsefully in his journal. "He was innocent and deserved life."

To the reporter, Muir offered that the snake line in the Sierra was up to eighty-five hundred feet; that left alone the Nevada rattler was generally friendly; and that rattlesnakes could kill hogs but would not eat them, or so the reporter later wrote. "It makes a good deal of difference how thick a hog's skin is," he quoted Muir. "Probably a little rattlesnake, if it tackled a big swine, wouldn't have much effect on it, but take an average-sized hog and a medium-sized snake, and the . . . hog dies." Muir, having often slept on the ground and never been disturbed, did not fear snakes. "There are far more reptiles down here in the city," he told the reporter.

Muir allowed to Louie that he had "talked carelessly for a few minutes," but he was shocked the next morning to see the "villainous" story "The Snakes of Fresno" in the *Examiner*. "'John Muir says they kill hogs and eat rabbits, but don't eat hogs because too big, etc.,'" he quoted in a letter to Louie. "What poetry! It's so perfectly ridiculous, I have at least had a good laugh out of it. 'The toughness of the skin makes a difference,' etc.—should think it would!"

The next morning Muir went down for breakfast and discovered that the *Call* had amplified the snake story. "The curly, crooked things have fairly gained the papers and bid fair to crawl through them all, leaving a track never, I fear, to be obliterated," he wrote Louie. More stories followed hard on their heels. "When, oh, when is that fatal interview to end?" he lamented to Louie. "How many more idiotic articles are to grow out of it? 'Muir's Strange Story,' 'Elephants' bones are sticking in the Yukon River, says geologist John Muir'! 'Bering Straits may be bridged because Bering Sea is shallow!' Oh! Oh! If the *Examiner* would only examine its logic!!! . . . What is to become of this nation and the *Examiner*?"[4]

The *Examiner* was the newly muscled and sensationalist daily of the ambitious twenty-six-year-old William Randolph Hearst, who had hired his own editors, changed it from evening to morning publication, and christened it with its Hearst Eagle masthead "the Monarch of the Dailies." Before leaving the Grand, on July 18, Muir wrote Johnson that the *Examiner* had run an article claiming to report "your saying on the Yosemite question." The piece "seems to have been very carefully prepared, & expresses your views very fairly," he said. But the *Argonaut*, Frank Pixley's politically influential journal, had published a "bitter" reply "in Pixley's style" but signed by P. Irish.

That same day, Johnson, having just returned from his trip West, found Muir's June 28 letter. The two had tried to reconnect in San Francisco but missed each other repeatedly while Johnson polished off his Gold Rush research and lobbied Pixley and such luminaries as Southern Pacific president Leland Stanford and Sam Miller, an influential railroad and stagecoach agent based at the Grand, about hiring Olmsted. "Stanford gave no response but to express confidence in Olmsted, but I fancy I made some impression on him," Johnson wrote to Muir. "I

didn't get to see his darned university. Miller tackled me, and I told
him I was working in his interest," added Johnson, who deemed Miller
"a poor stick." Pixley "fenced and pretended he had no confidence in
Olmsted" and, when Johnson asked why, claimed Olmsted had failed
to save the dunes in Golden Gate Park from wind erosion, so Pixley
had had to do it himself. Johnson made it clear to Pixley that he and
Muir considered Olmsted the best in his field.[5]

In mid-September, Muir, not yet relieved of his ranch duties, told Johnson he was hearing "little sound from the dashings of my inkstand." At
Johnson's "urgent request," Muir was now trying to write an open letter
on Yosemite but was feeling "awkwardly anxious to say too much &
therefore may likely say too little." He promised to deliver something
soon, which, if useless, Johnson should send "on a flying excursion to the
wastebasket." He had recently run into the well-known landscape and
marine painter Charles Robinson, who lived in Yosemite in the summer. Robinson had "held forth on the wickedness & woe of the Yoe &
its affairs" and declared that the cure was "a band of lovely disinterested
commissioners made up of He Me & Hutch. He, the artist with the
eye, Hutch with the long love & me the poetico-trampo-geologist-bot
& ornith-natural etc etc !-!-!-!"

Ten days later, Johnson reminded Muir that the *Century* printed
six weeks in advance of an issue and that he hoped to run the letter by
December. He wanted "direct and vigorous," not comprehensive. Muir
flailed away at what he called his "poor dull Yosemite growl," expressing
to Johnson at the end of October just how deep his self-doubt—albeit
tinged with humor—could go:

> I am very sorry to learn that my dullness & stupidity has occasioned so
> much trouble. I have not failed however through carelessness. I began
> that confounded letter a dozen times & could never make anything
> satisfactory out of it. It now lies & has lain on my table for more than a
> month, a scrawny orderless mass of fragments. You would have written
> such a letter in half an hour & no doubt would like to see me hanged
> for not being able to write it in a month. But I will send that letter
> yet & when you see it you will agree with me that it is worthless.[6]

By late November, Johnson had still not seen it and sent Muir motivation, for his eyes only: the Yosemite letters scheduled for January. Johnson's observations from his eight-day trek with "the well-known California naturalist" made a case for better oversight of the area, especially the Tuolumne. While the wonders of Yosemite are "supreme in American scenery," he argued, they are "hardly more unique and marvelous than the little-known cataracts of the Tuolumne River." The journey up the rugged canyon provided "a continuous panorama of wild and lonely beauty of cliff and forest," diminished only by the sheep-denuded meadows. In Yosemite Valley, he wrote, "feelings of awe at the unspoilable monuments of nature are often marred by . . . the work of unskillful hands upon the foreground of the picture," including fields of stumps, fenced horse pastures, and butchered trees, beneath which piles of branches created a fire hazard, threatening Yosemite "not only for . . . California but for the world of today and of all time to come."[7]

"When I reread it, I am astonished at my own moderation," he wrote Muir, but hoped the press in the East would take up the cry. "Now is the time for your article on the Yosemite Valley, I mean your general descriptive article." He asked Muir to set his own deadline, noting that they needed it three or four months in advance. "I know if you promise with your hand on your left breast pocket, I can depend upon it. Do this and the past will all be forgiven." Then, at the bottom of the page, Johnson handwrote one of the most important things he would ever say to Muir:

Why don't you start an association for preserving California's monuments & natural wonders—or at least Yosemite? It would be a good influence if you guarded carefully the membership. You'd have to face obloquy but you . . . are the one to do it and decent people would help. How timid you Californians are, anyhow![8]

It would take Muir a while to come around to this idea, but in the meantime he did promote California's natural wonders to his younger sister Mary, a University of Wisconsin alumna and talented painter, who was about to move to Nebraska with her husband and children. "Why not come to the glorious climate & country of California instead of the corn & buffalo grass plains swept with blizzards cyclones & sandstorms," he goaded. Muir would not land Mary, but within seven years three of his seven siblings would find their way to Alhambra.

In early December, having read and approved of the *Century*'s Yosemite letters, Muir wrote Johnson: "Yours on Yosemite would be infinitely moderate if addressed to clean & clear-eyed lovers of God's fountain beauty, but to the commercial heathen in his blindness not too moderate at all." He was glad, he told Johnson, "that my awkward word on the subject will not be missed though it makes me feel silly that MacKenzie, turbid with smoke & alcohol, should be able to do so well in an hour what I have been unable to do on a theme I love so well in a whole month." Muir was referring to George MacKenzie, author of an 1888 Yosemite travel guide, under the pseudonym Lewis Stornoway.

Muir promised to take up his article again in a few days but wrung his hands: "I never can tell how anything I begin of a literary kind will end. Sometimes my descriptions are contemptible mean & lean & scrawny, without any color or atmosphere. . . . It may turn out a song, perhaps turn out a sermon." As to Johnson's suggestion that he organize a group to fight for California's natural wonders, Muir politely declined. He would do anything he could "to preserve nature's sayings & doings"; however, he had "no genius for managing societies."[9]

But for Johnson's relentlessness, that might have been that.

On New Year's Day 1890, Muir sent Johnson the map he had requested but reported that the writing was still slow. The weather was unusually hot. Rain ensued and the grippe. Two weeks later, Muir wrote again, saying, "That is a pretty big block of mountains you have indicated for our article," showing just how close their collaboration was in defining what the new Yosemite park might look like. Although he was writing and would do the best he could for their "grand 'Central Park' in the Sierra," he attempted to lower expectations: "To write to order & measure I am about the worst hand you could find."[10]

With the Yosemite letters in the January *Century*, Johnson had kicked the proverbial hornets' nest. In Washington, he had found a firebrand of an ally. Celebrity journalist Kate Field wrote an open appeal to Senator Leland Stanford in her progressive weekly, *Kate Field's Washington*, "to rescue God's noblest work from the hands of vandals," urging him to sponsor a bill in Congress to preserve Yosemite Valley under federal over-sight. If it were "controlled by competent officers of the United States," she argued, "no such condition of nature and man as now disgraces it could endure." The *New York Times* commended her "vigorous protest," adding, "California does not appreciate the grandeur of its possession, or it would allow for its maintenance a sum more adequate than the piti-ful $15,000 a year which is the amount of the present appropriation."

In a mid-February missive, Johnson stumbled upon another bold idea, one that grew out of a previous discussion with Muir. As Johnson mused over politics and their ultimate goal—real change ("I presume you are doing what you can to create public opinion, or at least to influ-ence influential persons in California in regard to the Yosemite")—he asked Muir if he thought it would be possible to reduce the Yosemite Commission to a trio—a forestry expert, an army officer, and a park superintendent—appointed not by the governor but by officials of the University of California. If not, he asked, "What would you say to a bill taking the valley back into government possession on the ground that the original stipulations have not been observed by the state of California?" It was a radical notion, undoing Lincoln's grant to Cali-fornia. He also reiterated the need for a California organization: "It is astonishing to me to note the supineness of California in regard to this matter. I feel certain I could organize one hundred of the best men in New York, within a fortnight, in the interest of the Yosemite Valley." If nothing else, Muir could be the catalyst. "Knowing you as a gentle hermit, I do not expect propagandism from you; but I should think with little effort you could interest some influential people to organize quietly so as to make themselves felt."[11]

"The love of Nature among Californians is desperately moderate; consuming enthusiasm almost wholly unknown," Muir quipped. "Long ago I gave up the floor of Yosemite as a garden and looked only to the rough taluses and inaccessible or hidden benches and recesses of the walls. All the flowers are wall-flowers now." Nevertheless, he held out hope, he told Johnson, that "much may be done by the movement you are making."

He wanted the valley to revert to federal control but feared the response. "How glorious a storm of growls and howls would rend our sunny skies," he imagined, "bursting forth from every paper in the state, at the outrage of the *Century* Editor snatching with unholy hands, etc., the diadem from California's brow!" He added that the *Overland Monthly* editor, Milicent Shinn, had told him that a bill recalling the grant would never pass Congress. As for how much to protect, the more territory the better, including the basins of the high streams flowing into the valley, which would not generate much hostility because they lacked mines and settlements. "Cut off from its branches, Yosemite is only a stump," Muir opined. "However gnarly and picturesque, no tree that is beheaded looks well." He had drawn the proposed boundary line on a map and marked an even greater area that included three groves of big trees, plus Tuolumne Canyon, Tuolumne Meadows, and Hetch Hetchy, which, he noted, "would, of course, meet more opposition." He closed by inviting Johnson to come out for another look: "We would be sure to see some fine avalanches, come on. I'll go if you will, leaving ranch, reservations, Congress bills, *Century* articles and all other terrestrial cares & particles."[12]

In mid-March Governor Waterman lashed out against the criticism of the state's oversight of Yosemite Valley in an interview in the *San Francisco Call* and in a telegram to California congressmen, claiming that "the charge that affairs in the valley are badly managed is false and is the offspring of personal malice, spite, and feeling." He accused Kate Field of vindictiveness because he had once reduced her pay and bizarrely accused Johnson of trying to install his uncle, Frederick Law Olmsted, in a paying position. Johnson and Olmsted were not related, which George MacKenzie pointed out in a lengthy takedown of the governor in the March 23 *New York Times* (and reprinted in the *Bulletin*), calling his accusations "infantile absurdity." According to MacKenzie, Waterman had argued both that the state had fulfilled its duty in funding park upkeep and that the commissioners were doing their best with "very meagre" appropriations. He alleged that Waterman had once boasted about converting the valley floor into a hayfield and that he had seen Waterman driven through a gap in the barbed-wire fences that he now denied even existed.

Johnson replied to Waterman in the *Daily Evening Bulletin*, and Olmsted did so in the *New York Evening Post*. The *Sun* criticized Waterman's "official attack" on Johnson and appealed to California's independent press to protect the valley. "There would seem to be much reason to

fear that the wonderful scenery of the Yosemite may be destroyed," the
Sun stated, "by those to whose supervision it has been committed." As
Johnson prepared to appear before the Public Lands Committees to
argue in favor of Muir's boundaries, he had, as intended, gained the
nation's attention.[13]

As far back as 1881 the farming town of Visalia, in the foothills of the
Sierra Nevada, had convinced a California senator to introduce a bill to
turn the "whole west flank of the Sierra Nevada" into a national park.
The bill went nowhere; however, the town's *Weekly Delta* newspaper had
continued to make the case, covering the region's forest fires, rampant
timbering, and need for conservation—stories and editorials that were now
in the hands of the US secretary of the interior. General William Vandever,
a US congressman representing California's Sixth Congressional District
(from San Diego County to Mono County, more than half the state), had
recently introduced a bill to protect the big trees in the mountains east
of Visalia. Johnson saw an opportunity here for Yosemite.

Muir sent Johnson the long-awaited Yosemite manuscript in April.
"How fares the bill Vandever. I hope you gained all the basin. If you
have, then a thousand thousand trees & flowers will rise up and call
you Blessed besides the other mountain people & the usual 'unborn
generations etc.' In the meantime, for what you have already done, I
send you a reasonable number of Yosemite thanks."[14]

A lot was riding on Muir's story as Johnson planned to use it to
extend the limits proposed by Vandever. On May 14, he asked Muir for
a description of the Tuolumne Canyon, Meadows, and Mount Lyell, "so
that we might advertise . . . the proposed limits of the New National
Park." Muir complied within a week. It "answers the purpose exactly,"
responded Johnson, who submitted an editorial that included part of
Muir's upcoming story about the Yosemite reservation and the Big
Trees to the *Evening Post*. "How much shall we pay you for the Yosemite
material?" Johnson scrawled at the bottom of a letter. To which Muir
responded, "What the Century Co thinks a fair price will be satisfactory to me."

On June 2, Johnson appeared before the Public Lands Committee
to advocate for Muir's limits. He had to battle "the impression that this

was an extension of the present park" and "give reasons why it should be a separate federal park and not part of the state park." He made his points gingerly so as not to offend Congressman Vandever, who was there in support of his speech.[15]

In many ways and many forms—clouds, snow, ice, glaciers, storms, blizzards, falls—water had shaped Muir's world, and he had strived to capture it in words. More than once, water had threatened his life. He had nearly drowned while learning to swim in Fountain Lake, been lured to the brink of disaster by multiple waterfalls, ridden an avalanche down a mountain, and been cocooned in ice. But his fascination for water in extremis had only deepened. One encounter stood out above all the others. The flooding of Yosemite in 1871—during that lonely winter after Emerson's visit—was the most profound display of natural power he had ever experienced, in nature's most marvelous landscape. It was the crescendo of Muir's seminal ten-thousand-word story "The Treasures of the Yosemite."

Even with the photos and artwork he had helped gather and create, it was a daunting task to put the place into context for Easterners, all the way across the continent, let alone to impassion them for its protection. Muir knew he had to transport the reader, and he tackled the job with mighty patience, first describing the resplendent Sierra Nevada from afar, just as he had originally gazed on the range two decades earlier across the central plain, which had been ablaze in golden poppies. It was the play of light, more than the presence of snow on the peaks, that captivated him. Though five hundred miles long and rising in places nearly fifteen thousand feet, the range was smooth and deceptively understated, guarding its greatest features inside, where it was furrowed with mile-deep canyons and sparkling rivers, "mountain streets full of life and light, graded and sculptured by the ancient glaciers," which Muir described in one abundant sentence:

> In many places .... the main canyons widen into spacious valleys or parks of charming beauty, level and flowery and diversified like landscape gardens with meadows and groves and thickets of blooming bushes, while the lofty walls, infinitely varied in form, are fringed

with ferns, flowering plants, shrubs of many species, and tall ever-greens and oaks which find anchorage on a thousand narrow steps and benches, the whole enlivened and made glorious with rejoicing streams that come dancing and foaming over the sunny brows of the cliffs, and through side canyons in falls of every conceivable form, to join the shining river that flows in tranquil beauty down the middle of each one of them.[16]

At last he brought the reader to the seven-mile-long, mile-wide, and nearly mile-deep Yosemite Valley, carved into the granite flank of the range at four thousand feet, a valley where "Nature had gathered her choicest treasures . . . to draw her lovers into close and confiding communion with her." The rocks in its walls glowed with life. Birds, bees, and butterflies stirred its air into music, and the Merced—river of mercy—peacefully glided through it, "reflecting lilies and trees and the onlooking rocks, things frail and fleeting and types of endurance meeting here and blending in countless forms."

The forests surrounding Yosemite were a "tree-lover's paradise," with conifers "surpassing all that have yet been discovered in the forests of the world," where silver firs grew up to two hundred feet tall, and Douglas firs and yellow and sugar pines reached their highest beauty and grandeur, providing air "indescribably spicy and exhilarating." But it was, of course, the majestic sequoias (*Sequoia gigantea*), the "big trees," some twenty-five feet in diameter and pushing three hundred feet tall, that were the conifer kings, and Muir took the opportunity to digress on the two-hundred-mile-long sequoia belt on the west side of the Sierra. Disease resistant, sequoias can live for well over three thousand years, or until destroyed by lightning, fire, or men. These emperors of trees, not found anywhere else in the world, were, Muir believed, surely worth saving. But only the Mariposa Grove, a dozen miles south of Yosemite Valley, had been protected. "Were the importance of our forests at all understood by the people in general," he noted, "even from an economic standpoint their preservation would call forth the most watchful attention of the Government." But far from it. "At present . . . every kind of destruction is moving on with accelerated speed."[17]

Large mills were already threatening the Fresno and Kings River groves. "After the young, manageable trees have been cut, blasted, and sawed, the woods are fired to clear the ground of limbs and refuse," Muir wrote, "and of course the seedlings and saplings, and many of the unmanageable giants, are destroyed, leaving but little more than black, charred monuments." And then, every summer, desolation was wrought by the "incredible numbers of sheep" as they trampled and mowed their way to the mountain pastures. "The shrubs are stripped of leaves as if devoured by locusts, and the woods are burned to improve the pasturage. The entire belt of forests is thus swept by fire."

To Muir, the trees were glorious and essential, but Yosemite Valley was religious: the view "breaks suddenly upon us in all its glory far and wide and deep; a new revelation in landscape affairs that goes far to make the weakest and meanest spectator rich and significant ever-more."

The line was stunning: "a new revelation in landscape affairs that goes far to make the weakest and meanest spectator rich and significant ever-more."

In a fraction of a sentence, in the simplest of terms, Muir had found a way to both raise the landscape to the level of the divine and to save the reader's soul. Yosemite was the cathedral. Royal Arches, El Capitan, and Half Dome its architecture, the falls its holy music. Salvation lay here for those who sought it.

On the switchbacks into the valley, the view constantly evolved. "The eye ranges far up over the green grovy floor between the mighty walls, bits of the river gleaming here and there, while . . . we begin to hear the song of the waters," wrote Muir. Drawn to water like a bee to pollen, he devoted half of his ten thousand words to waterfalls. Arriving on the valley floor, the visitor was lured by Bridalveil, as it "sways and sings in the wind, with gauzy, sun-sifted spray half falling, half floating . . . infinitely gentle and fine; but the hymn it sings tells the solemn power that is hidden beneath the soft clothing it wears." Across the valley, Ribbon Fall—the longest single-drop fall on the continent—leaped "hissing and roaring with force enough to drive a mile of mills, suggesting the 'weeping skies' of cyclones and hurricanes." Farther on, Yosemite Falls, half a mile of gushing water, seemed to pour directly out of the sky. Water made the valley come alive, and it was to water, and the snow, glaciers, and clouds that stored and released it, that Muir would always return.

On December 16, 1871, Muir had gazed up while walking in a Yosemite meadow to see an ominous crimson mushroom cloud forming over Cathedral Rocks. The next morning in the eerie calm, he felt the turbulence in the atmosphere, gray clouds climbing one over the other into the sky. It rained and then began to snow, ten inches covering the ground overnight, and more the next day. Two nights later, rain pounded the snow. The snow line sat only a few hundred feet above, and beyond the pine tops, it snowed. At first, the snow sponged up the water that normally trickled into small tributaries and then flowed into the larger streams. But about midnight the temperature spiked ten degrees, pushing the snow line above the upper basins. Below, warm rain pelted the snow, until it reached its breaking point. Suddenly rainwater and melting snow flowed toward the valley bottom on every slope, heaping, swelling, and plunging in a stupendous flood.

Awakened by the roar, Muir peered out of his cabin at north wall sections that were awash with falls, invaders, strangely out of place. He snatched a piece of bread for breakfast and ran outside. All about him water cascaded—from the sky and every surface—as if he were in a water dream. In every hollow, gorge, and canyon far and near, the landscape had vanished. The swollen, unrecognizable falls were joined by the new, never-before-seen falls. The valley throbbed with an awful, massive, solemn roar of rushing, crashing water. As the world transformed all around him, Muir was both scared and exhilarated. It was as if he were present at the beginning of time and at the end of time all at once—Noah about to board the ark, experiencing the wonder and ecstasy in the ominous, cleansing inundation.

After scanning the scene in awe, Muir set out for the upper meadows, where the valley was widest, to see the walls on both sides and gain broader views. But the meadows were now a lake, dotted with shifting blue islands. Everywhere streams roared like lions across his path, propelling rocks and logs over ground where flowers had recently been growing.

Climbing onto the talus slopes, where the torrents were broken among earthquake boulders, he managed to traverse them, find his way up the valley to Hutchings's Bridge, cross the river, and wade to the middle of the upper meadow. On the south wall between Hutchings's and Sentinel Rock, ten new falls plunged nearly three thousand feet and boomed on the valley floor. More adorned Glacier Point, displaying every imaginable form into which water might be dashed, combed, or woven. Nine more fell between the Three Brothers and Yosemite Falls, ten between Yosemite and Royal Arch Falls, and on Half Dome, eleven. In all, Muir tallied fifty-six new falls in the upper end of the valley. In the distance, more than a hundred silvery threads gleamed. Muir marveled at what he was sure was the most miraculous assembly of falls ever seen.

In the midst of all this, Yosemite Falls could barely be heard. Then in the midafternoon, Muir was startled by a sudden thundering uproar, with booming explosions and heavy gasps. He thought it was an avalanche of rocks, but then he saw that a great flood wave of Yosemite Creek had burst through a logjam, delivering debris carried all the way from Mount Hoffmann, five miles away. Trees, ice, and rubble had crashed down the mountainside, clearing the stream. Now, its onrush, at ten times its fullest springtime volume, could be heard above all, leading the choir of falls, as Muir would have it, in the divine harmony.

For two days and nights the storm displayed its extravagant power, while bird, bear, squirrel, and man hunkered down. The wind, broken into a thousand cascading currents, surged against brows, domes, and battlements, whirling amid the gray clouds, sweeping forward the resulting detritus in ragged trains like glacier moraines. Sometimes half the valley was veiled, leaving here and there some lofty headland cut off from all visible connection, looming alone, dim, spectral, as if belonging to the sky. Muir saw no one and nothing, not even an ouzel.

This was the only time he would experience Yosemite in full flood—clouds, winds, rocks, waters, throbbing together, he felt, in one sublime natural symphony. In his mind, the storm and flood united this region of mountain temples (all deserving to be in one protected park): "The Big Tuolumne Canyon—how the white waters were singing there, and the winds, and how the clouds were marching. In Hetch Hetchy Valley also, and the great Kings River Yosemite, and in all the other canyons and valleys of the Sierra from Shasta to the southernmost fountains of the Kern—five hundred miles of flooded waterfalls chanting together. 'What a psalm was that!'"

CHAPTER 10

Proposed:
Yosemite National Park

The Board of Yosemite Valley and Big Tree Grove Commissioners, headquartered at 26 Montgomery Street in San Francisco,
was not going to take the perceived insult in the August 1890
issue of the *Century* sitting down. In light of the adverse publicity in
Muir's article and the public outcry, as well as nearby fires threatening Yosemite Valley, the outspoken and frequently salty Frank Pixley, head of the Yosemite Commission, found himself in the hot seat
and happy to fight back. "The new growth of timber in the Valley is
becoming a menace to the safety of all property there," he told John
P. Irish's *Daily Alta California*, which toned down his "delightfully
picturesque vocabulary," at times "startling in its close adherence to
the AngloSaxon." Pixley asserted that the growth needed extensive
thinning. "No one but a [strong language here] would ever think to
objecting to it. If it is not cleared out, a big fire will very soon do
great damage there. When I was a Commissioner of the Golden Gate
Park I set out over 400,000 trees, but would anyone, other than a
six-cornered idiot, think it was intended that all those trees should
remain? Of course not. And yet, when recently the Commissioners did
some necessary thinning out of the trees at the Park there was a lot of
flapdoodle talk about 'desecration' and all that. . . . Artists and those

kind of people don't like it, but they haven't any sense, you know; so there is no need to worry about what they say."[1]

As a follow-up, on September 1, Irish sent Muir a sarcastic letter: "My Dear Sir, . . . Will you kindly let me know when you saw hogs roaming at large in the Valley, and whether the ax has been used there to clear fields for the plow, and by whom and on what part of the floor?" He claimed to be seeking facts in order to make up his mind "whether California must confess delinquencies in the management of the grant which should shame her into abdicating of her trust."

If Irish had any argument, it was that the protections afforded to Yosemite by the state and to Yellowstone by the federal government did not amount to much beyond prohibiting private claims to the land. In fact, separating out the land from local jurisdiction sometimes left it more vulnerable to poaching, illegal grazing, outlawry, and timber theft. Federal regulations allowed for little more than expelling rule violators from the park and confiscating their livestock. But Muir and Johnson had faith in the federal government, which was at least disinterested, and could provide troops. The Act of May 7, 1894, would at last bring effective law enforcement to Yellowstone. Meanwhile, Muir believed that federal troops were needed in Yosemite.[2]

In September, Muir published another story in the *Century*: "Features of the Proposed Yosemite National Park." In it he called the upper Tuolumne Valley "the most serenely spacious and . . . delightful summer pleasure park in all the high Sierra." The *Century* had produced a map showing the boundaries for Muir's new national park, and before the story had even run, Johnson was already at work lining up support in the House Committee on Public Lands. A bill was drafted, and Vandever presented it in the House, while Plumb took it up in the Senate. "As we go to press," the *Century* boasted, "the Committee seems disposed to extend the north and south limits east to the Nevada line."

Only fifteen miles from Yosemite Valley and reachable by two trails and a road, Tuolumne Valley would be a highly desirable part of a national park. Its meadows and groves provided congenial campsites with views of snowcapped peaks and access to the Grand Canyon of the Tuolumne, Mono Lake, and Mount Lyell, at 13,114 feet the highest

point in the proposed national park. On the north side of the meadows, Soda Springs provided ice-cold fizzy water. From here, Muir liked
the gentle ascent to the top of the symmetrical reddish-purple Mount
Dana, which was eleven miles away, accessible by mule, and provided
a panoramic view of peaks, glaciers, and desert with briny Lake Mono,
flashing in the sun like a metallic disk, six thousand feet below.

Muir described his 1871 discovery of Lyell's north-facing Lyell Glacier,
the highest, most enduring remnant of the great Tuolumne Glacier, which
had shaped the landscape, and also the largest of the remaining glaciers
in the proposed park. He had hammered stakes in it to measure its movement, which he found to be a little over an inch a day. You could reach
the base of Lyell on horseback by following the meadows along the river.[3]

The Tuolumne Canyon, almost a mile deep in places, extended about
eighteen miles to Hetch Hetchy Valley, a place that Muir said mirrored
Yosemite on a grand scale, including similar rocks, arches, spires, and
domes. But it was the river itself that Muir admired most, "for miles . . .
one wild, exulting, on-rushing mass of snowy purple bloom, spreading
over glacial waves of granite without any definite channel, and through
avalanche taluses, gliding in silver plumes, dashing and foaming through
huge boulder-dams, leaping high into the air in glorious wheel-like
whirls, tossing from side to side, doubling, glinting, singing in glorious
exuberance of mountain energy."

Muir then turned to the case for including Hetch Hetchy, once the
"home and stronghold of the Tuolumne Indians, as Ahwahnee was of the
Grizzlies." Hetch Hetchy was accessible to travelers by a trail off the Big
Oak Flat road, but Muir preferred to rock-hop over the divide directly
from Yosemite Valley to the canyon rim a few miles above Hetch Hetchy.
From there the meadow and its river, thousands of feet below, looked
like a ribbon laced with a silver thread. "The most graceful fall" Muir
had ever seen, the sun-drenched, wind-whipped Tueeulala, plunged a
thousand feet into a "foaming web of cascades among the boulders." It
surpassed even Bridalveil "in peaceful, floating, swaying gracefulness"
and launched Muir into a rumination on the counterintuitive "calm
self-possession" of a stream at the brink:

In coming forward to the edge of the tremendous precipice and taking flight a little hasty eagerness appears, but this is speedily hushed

in divine repose. Now observe the distinctness and delicacy of the various kinds of sun-filled tissue into which the waters are woven. They fly and float and drowse down the face of that grand gray rock in so leisurely and unconfused a manner that you may examine their texture and patterns as you would a piece of embroidery held in the hand. It is a flood of singing air, water, and sunlight woven into cloth that spirits might wear.

Nearby Wapama cascaded over two benches on its descent, like Yosemite Falls, only with much greater volume. No two falls could be more unalike than Wapama and Tueeulala, Muir observed, the one pounding in a shadowy gorge, the other chanting deep, low tones and with no shadows but those of its own pale-gray waters tinted with violet and pink. "One whispers, 'He dwells in peace,'" he wrote. "The other is the thunder of his chariot wheels in power." To Muir, Hetch Hetchy possessed all of the spiritual force of Yosemite and perhaps more, owing to its solemn remoteness.

Muir argued that the bill for the proposed national park surrounding Yosemite Valley should be passed immediately, as timbering and sheep were devastating Yosemite's watershed and the Tuolumne Valley and its watershed. As far back as the summer of 1870, when Joseph LeConte had been in the Tuolumne Meadows with Muir, LeConte had estimated that there were twelve to fifteen thousand sheep grazing, in flocks of up to three thousand head. "The ground is already being gnawed and trampled into a desert condition, and when the region shall be stripped of its forests the ruin will be complete," Muir now wrote. "It is also devoutly to be hoped that the Hetch Hetchy will escape such ravages of man as one sees in Yosemite."[4]

Muir and Johnson were turning up the heat in California, and, encouraged by the impact of Muir's articles, Johnson wanted to go for even more. He thought that Kings Canyon, the more southerly cousin of Yosemite, with many of the oldest sequoias, could also be made a federal park.

After Muir returned from a trip to Alaska, which storms and dense fog had made treacherous, Johnson welcomed him back by sending him marching orders to go to Kings Canyon to work up the boundaries of the potential park.

Four days later, Muir wrote Johnson from the ranch that the grapes were almost ripe and "not a single iceberg or snowbank . . . is in sight." He had learned much during his "nerve trying adventure" in Alaska's icy mountains, which he would try to write up for the *Century*. He would also work on a Kings Canyon piece. "All the world is indebted to you for your work in saving so fine a section of the Sierra from cheap vulgar ruin," he told Johnson. "It would be a fine thing to save the magnificent Kings River region also with the forests about it & in it, though much of it is already in the hands of the lumbermen."

Meanwhile, Irish began an all-out campaign to defend the commission, soliciting letters contradicting Muir's assessment and extracting a clarification from Vandever saying that the *Century* story had nothing to do with his congressional bill to establish a Yosemite National Park. "I can assure you," Vandever avowed, "if . . . it becomes necessary to defend the good name of the State of California or its Board of Yosemite Commissioners, no one will be more ready than myself to perform the duty."

On vacation, Johnson responded to Muir from Long Island: "The combat thickens, John P. Irish being on the warpath." He had just read Irish's editorials in the *Oakland Tribune* and a copy of a letter written by Irish to the editor of the *New York Times*, trashing MacKenzie, Muir, and himself, which he called "one of the funniest pieces of pettifogging" he had ever seen. The letter had been "thrown in the waste basket. . . . Of course, he is furious. You see the trick, to try to make votes by pretending to defend California's sacred honor & reputation, which privately he is besmirching. . . . In the next Congress we shall probably have to face the question of recession of the original grant (unless your legislature does something), and Irish could throw a good deal of dust in the eyes of the average M.C. I hope you'll expose the game in such a way as to defeat his election.

"Tell Mrs. Muir not to let you backslide from the literary life. You have taken your hand off the plow and should not look back." He added, "I wish you could arrange to come East this winter, you and your wife, and pay us a little visit. Burroughs was to have been here this week to visit us, but the wet weather detained him to harvest his grapes. Come & you shall see him & the saucy Mrs. Johnson."⁵

Congressional Act of October 1, 1890

The fall of 1890 was a boon time for the Sierra Nevada. On September 25, President Harrison, who would be hailed as the first great conservationist president, signed the bill creating Sequoia National Park after it passed both chambers of Congress. It contained Mount Whitney, at 14,505 feet, the highest point in the contiguous states, and the Giant Forest, with one of the world's largest trees. In 1886 the Kaweah Colony, a communist logging community, had claimed the area and named the behemoth the Karl Marx Tree. The new national park dispossessed the colony of much of its claimed territory, eventually forcing it to disband, and authorities renamed the tree the General Sherman and supplied a backstory pre-dating the Marx name: On August 7, 1879, the trapper and cattleman James Wolverton, a veteran of General William Tecumseh Sherman's forces, discovered and named the tree after his beloved commander.

Sequoia suddenly became California's first national park. As September wound to a close, Vandever's bill creating Yosemite National Park came up for a vote. It had been modified to include the creation of General Grant National Park, six miles northwest of the new Sequoia National Park, to protect the second-tallest sequoia, the General Grant. Having support from Governor Waterman and the US Department of the Interior and buoyed by Johnson's lobbying, the bill passed the House with no debate and the Senate with little. On the first of October, President Harrison signed the act establishing Muir's proposed Yosemite National Park, thirty-five times the size of Yosemite Valley state park, which it surrounded but did not include. That day, Vandever, in Washington, wired Johnson, "My Yosemite bill passed both houses and approved." Johnson sent the news to Muir, adding, "The Yosemite bill is of course the result of your very outspoken reference to the depredations in that region." The park borders in the bill matched Muir's sketch. This remarkable achievement by Muir and Johnson was almost too good to be true: they had moved a mountain of greed and apathy.

Muir's two articles had demonstrated the everlasting power of the pen, the persuasiveness of insightful observations and passionate beliefs set down on paper. And in the hands of a skillful advocate-editor, that power had been far-reaching. Ever humble, Muir found others to credit:

the California Academy of Sciences, the State University, and even the "soulless" Southern Pacific Railroad, which he otherwise "never counted on for anything good," specifically a Mr. Stow, who had told the state Congress members they "must see that bill . . . went through."

Johnson told Muir that the Senate was also sending a resolution to the interior secretary to investigate malfeasance in the state park, adding, it "has grown out of what I have said about the Yosemite, though I did not think it necessary to push that side of it at the present session." Still, he was trying to advance it in the House before it adjourned.[6]

This was no time for them to rest on their laurels. The fight for Yosemite was far from over. In many ways it had just begun. Miners and stockmen lobbied furiously to regain what they considered theirs and fought for special legislation to carve off pieces of the new park. Railroad and timber interests conspired to gobble up the forests all around it. And then there was the matter of the valley in the heart of the park—arguably the nation's finest natural gem. As long as the state continued to oversee it, Muir and Johnson had to remain vigilant. To Muir, the state was not only not protecting the valley, it was accelerating its demise. Johnson sent letters urging Muir, MacKenzie, the painter Charles Robinson (known as C. D.), and William Armes, an outspoken Berkeley English professor, to engage with the investigating committee, "whoever they may be." Meanwhile Johnson would try to meet with Interior Secretary John Noble to recommend an expert for the commission, namely Frederick Law Olmsted.

The military would take charge of the new reserve, and with the sheep barred, the terrain would recover. As one forestry ranger told Johnson, you could almost follow the boundaries of the park by the edge to which the sheep had devoured the vegetation. It was an environmental victory never to be repeated, at least not with such apparent ease. But they did not know that and so saw every reason to try for more, for Kings Canyon. Less than fifty miles south of Yosemite as the crow flies, in wilder, less spoiled country, and just north of Sequoia National Park, this mile-deep valley among fourteen-thousand-foot peaks was in many respects as impressive as Yosemite Valley and had too long been a victim of the sawyer.[7]

On October 15, Johnson sent Muir a confidential note with a copy of a letter Irish had attempted to publish in the influential weekly

Garden and Forest, edited by Johnson's friend Charles Sargent, a Harvard botanist. "When he dies, it will probably be by falling on his own pen," Johnson said of Irish. "Meanwhile, it might be as well for you to tell me what is the basis of his silly talk about you in the Yosemite," referring to a charge by Irish that Muir was a hypocrite who had profited from timbering in the valley. Then he asked Muir to deliver the Kings Canyon story by December "without fail" to time its appearance with the President's visit to California to open Stanford University. He also asked him to send in his proposed park boundaries on a Land Office map as well as to pay a call on C. D. Robinson in San Francisco to ensure his submission of the art. The sooner he sent the map, the sooner Secretary Noble might halt ingress in the region.

While Johnson's letter was still en route, Muir stole a few minutes from the harvest to write and tell him that he was "up to the scalp in Tokay, Muscat, & Zinfandel, fairly stupid with excess of industry," shipping some two thousand boxes of grapes per day. Muir sometimes had thirty or more workers in the fields, but he was there too, toiling as he had learned to do in his youth, whether planting, pruning, harvesting, or selling. His grapes and pears brought the highest prices. Now, however, he hoped to soon be free for "real work in the wilderness."

He had anticipated some of the concerns expressed in Johnson's letter and had already visited Robinson to see his sketches, though he thought his own were "more telling." If the weather held, he planned to make another run to Kings Canyon before writing the story. "Irish is wild about your success in Yosemite reform," he added.

"I am delighted to hear that your vineyards are prosperous," Johnson responded, on Friday, October 24. "Everybody in New York is eating California grapes." He reiterated that they needed his Kings Canyon story by December. "Put on your seven-league boots and scoot down there, take your rapid-transit pen in hand and finish the thing up; then make Mr. Robinson do his very level best on sketches." Afterward Johnson pressed the Muirs to come East. It would be good for Muir, their causes, and the *Century.* "Your Yosemite articles have made you many new friends in this region." He wanted Muir to speak at various geographical societies, Columbia College, and, appropriately, in Central Park.

Muir wrote back that most of his grapes were in, but Dr. Strentzel, now seventy-six, was unwell, so he had to harvest his father-in-law's too.

He was trying to delegate tasks so that he could leave for Kings Canyon on Monday to gather "fresh facts." As for Irish's scurrilous allegation, he said, "I don't mean to answer him at all. His moral sense seems to have given way & sloughed off in utter ruin & rottenness like a stranded jellyfish trampled & decomposed. To argue with a dead man would be more hopeful labor than with John P."

Nonetheless, Muir explained his work at Hutchings's mill in his early years in Yosemite.

It was true that while Muir was camping in the valley, Hutchings had learned that he was a millwright and asked him to fix his sawmill and to operate it for $90 a month and full board. Muir was in need of both, so he repaired the waterwheel and the machinery and that winter milled several thousand feet of lumber that Hutchings used to build cottages for tourists. "A year or two before I entered the valley a tremendous windstorm blew down a considerable number of the large yellow pines," he explained. These were the trees they had used. He had run the mill for several seasons but never cut down a tree in the valley or knowingly milled any cut down by others. "One of the large mills on Puget Sound cuts more lumber in half a day than I sawed in all these years." Clark, the official guardian of Yosemite, had often visited the mill, admiring its simplicity and praising Muir as a "great genius." "So much for John Muir & his mill being hastily driven out of Yosemite ere he had completed the destruction of its trees," Muir concluded. "But remember this is for you only—none of it to be published. Life is too short for defense of character."[8]

On November 6, Johnson, thinking that Muir was off in Kings Canyon, sent him a message through Louie to also visit the Tulare Big Tree reservation. Secretary Noble wanted to know how best to take care of the recently reserved parks, and his insights would be useful. But Muir had not gone to Kings. At the end of October, his father-in-law had died. Dr. Strentzel's "life's work was all done & well done & closed like a summer day," Muir told Johnson.

But now, as Muir soon wrote, the household was "broken like a house torn asunder and half taken away." Muir was especially moved by the loss felt by Wanda and Helen and called "child love the finest divinest thing on earth." Under the circumstances, he found it impossible to leave the family or the ranch before it got too cold to travel to the high Sierra. He and Louie moved into the Big House to be closer to the aging Mrs. Strentzel, who took over the downstairs east parlor for her bedroom and sitting room, while the Muirs moved in upstairs. It was a permanent change and started a chain reaction.

Despite being away from Wisconsin for so long, Muir had remained close to his siblings through correspondence and was always eager to lend a helpful hand whether spiritually or monetarily. He was in many ways the inspiration and cornerstone of his family. His oldest sister, Maggie, and her husband, John Reid, a farmer, now moved out from Wisconsin and settled into the Muirs' old house, and Reid took over as the ranch foreman. The following year Muir's younger brother and cohort in youthful misadventures, David, would also move to Martinez to work on the ranch, and their second-oldest sister, Sarah, would join them three years later, meaning the first four Muir siblings, those who bore the brunt of their father's harsh servitude on the farm, would eventually reunite in Martinez.

Muir converted a light-filled bedroom with views of the Carquinez Strait and the Suisun Bay into an office, his "scribble den," as the family jokingly referred to it.[9]

CHAPTER 11

A Red-Letter Day

On the night of March 3, 1891, nature unleashed its fury. Gales of rain, sleet, and snow lashed buildings, encased trees, and turned streets into slick scrums of ice and slush, too treacherous for man or beast to travel. It was just the kind of night that Muir reveled in, an opportunity to study frozen water in its many forms—roiling cloud banks, prismatic ice crystals, and intricate snowflakes—the evocation of which he was perhaps unsurpassed at in the English language. But Muir was not the one experiencing it. Johnson was.

It was the penultimate day of the Fifty-First US Congress, which had stretched for the entire first two years of President Harrison's administration and was called by critics the Billion Dollar Congress for its lavish spending and expansion of the federal government, including the increased pensions of Civil War veterans and their survivors. On the slate now among other legislation was a forest reserve bill, a twelve-line amendment to the Sundry Civil Bill drafted by Edward Bowers, an official of the Interior Department, which would allow the president to create forest reserves and scenic regions. Also being considered was a land bill to reverse the Timber Culture Act of 1873, which had inadvertently fostered the amassing of land rights for mining, logging, and future settlement when false homesteaders used it to make fraudulent claims.

The evening was shaping up to be as stormy inside as out. Now a polarizing figure in California, Johnson, in honor of his environmental work, had been named a trustee of the new Red Wood Park in Sonoma

County, a six-hundred-acre stand of coastal redwoods. He had come to Washington, however, on a different quest. For the past eight weeks, he had been in town campaigning for a long-suffering international copyright bill as it careened to its moment of truth on the Senate floor. The commanding editor, who could cast a withering glare through his pince-nez, had stalked the halls of Congress, negotiating delicate compromises and amendments and deftly nurturing alliances. And now, on the last night of the session, the representative of the typographical unions, a faction Johnson had brought around after decades of opposition, was yelling at him, accusing him of betrayal over the reconciliation of an amendment to the House bill that had already passed and threatening to denounce the bill, a certain death blow.[1]

At stake was the chance to end the literary piracy plaguing writers and publishers on both sides of the Atlantic. In the United States, there was no international copyright law, so books written abroad could be published without paying the author. This not only robbed foreign authors, but it also made it more difficult for American authors, who had to be paid royalties, to get published. The act's penalties for infringement of foreign copyrights would place US and foreign authors on equal footing, promoting American literature and, thus, ultimately, the nation's very identity.

A Scot who emigrated to the United States as a boy around the same time as Muir, Andrew Carnegie, steel magnate, philanthropist, and a frequent writer on political and social issues, was an outspoken proponent of copyright protection. Theodore Roosevelt, a member of the US Civil Service Commission, and a writer, was too. It was a cause dear to the *Century*, which had given a platform to Mark Twain and Louisa May Alcott on the issue and had loaned out Johnson to the Copyright League, as treasurer and now secretary, its highest office, requiring half his time.

Muir had also been drafted into the movement. "I have just written to our congressmen, every mother's son of them, on the copyright bill & marvel greatly at my temerity in thus plunging recklessly into this new field of literature," he had told Johnson. It was Muir's first acknowledgment that he had become a direct political advocate, even on matters outside the preservation of nature. "I admire your pluck and perseverance in so worthy a fight as . . . the copyright," he had told Johnson the previous June. And that pluck had rubbed off on him.

He had recently confronted George Fitch, head of the *Bulletin*, on his opposition to copyright. Fitch said "they had not opposed the bill very much—a mean answer," Muir reported to Johnson. "I suppose this raising of the price of literature is what most publishers fear."[2]

Exercising his considerable diplomatic skills, Johnson finally persuaded the typographical unions rep to hold the line. The bill made it out of committee. The Senate voted on it at one in the morning, and it passed, 27–19. After a fifteen-minute waiting period, to allow for any motions to reconsider, it would then return to the House. Massachusetts congressman Henry Cabot Lodge, a Johnson ally "who was of great service to the measure not only in the House but also in the Senate," made sure it was promptly signed by Vice President Levi Morton and then rushed to the House.

At two in the morning, as Johnson sat in the gallery observing, along with publishers Charles Scribner and Bill Appleton, the latter of whom had helped introduce to American readers such great scientists as Darwin, Herbert Spencer (coiner of the term *survival of the fittest*), and glacier expert John Tyndall, the House at last debated the amended copyright bill. To Johnson's great relief, its most cantankerous opponent, Lewis Payson of Illinois, was "asleep on a bench at the back of the chamber, his face covered by a newspaper which rose and fell with his stentorian breathing." The roll call was taken, and during a nerve-racking quarter of an hour in which Payson failed to "awake and rush into the fray," as Johnson feared, the bill passed, 127–77.[3]

Johnson, Scribner, and Appleton cheered their victory, "fairly intoxicated" by the realization that after fifty years of appeals to Congress, "the disgrace of tolerating literary piracy had been wiped from the statute book!"

Or so they thought. The bill still had to move to the Senate for an announcement that it had passed the House. The three went with it to that now sparsely attended chamber, where routine business was being passed by general consent. Suddenly, to their shock, Florida senator Sam Pasco, a London-born Confederate Army veteran, rose and, claiming that the bill had been railroaded through the House, demanded that it be reconsidered. While his motion was pending, the bill, though passed by both houses, could not move to the President for his signature. In the meantime, at five o'clock in the morning, the Senate took a four-hour recess. As Johnson later put it, "The cup of trembling was once more at our lips." Eight years of intense effort on his part weighed in the balance.

Senator Orville Platt, the bill's chief supporter, wrote a whip describing its peril and calling for a nine o'clock vote to defeat the motion. At around six thirty, Johnson, Appleton, and Scribner rushed outside into the still-angry storm to help alert the senators who supported the bill. "No one of us will ever forget the experience of that sleepless night," said Johnson later. "Outside was raging one of the bitterest storms I have ever known." Rain blew in gales, freezing as it fell. They could find no cabs. In any case, "the horses would not have been able to keep their feet upon the frozen and sleety streets." Nonetheless, they delivered every message. The motion to reconsider fell by eight votes, 21–29, and at ten o'clock on the final morning of the session, the international copyright bill moved to the President.

Johnson's work, however, was not yet done. President Harrison, known variously as Little Ben (he was only five foot six) and The Human Iceberg (for his chilly demeanor), had come to the Capitol that morning to sign legislation before the session closed at noon. But Johnson had not toiled so long and so hard to let this historic victory pass without appropriate flair and a personal touch. He had had a pen made from the feather of an American bald eagle in memory of his father, who had prided himself on his ability to make a handsome goose-quill pen and had engendered his son's love of literature and civic engagement. The President had promised to sign the bill with it, if and when the time arrived.

But the pen had been left at the White House. Johnson rushed back out into the wicked maelstrom. He found the President's coachman and delivered instructions for retrieving the pen, along with a dollar tip and the promise of two more if he made it back in time. The coachman raced off over the icy streets.

At a quarter to eleven, President Harrison signed the bill with the eagle quill, putting an end to the notorious era of literary piracy. The achievement would earn Johnson medals of honor from France and Italy and burnish his reputation as a skillful actor on the highest stage of American political life.

That same day Harrison also signed the landmark Forest Reserve Act of 1891, allowing the President to set aside what were then called forest reserves and later became known as national forests. "This masterly stroke," as Johnson would call it, would prove to be an "epoch-making provision": Harrison would use it to protect 13 million acres of forestland. Though the bill lacked any provision for administering the lands, it would later be improved, paving the way for the National Forest System in 1907.

March 4, 1891, Johnson later said, was "a red-letter day in our history."[4]

Riding his copyright victory and still awaiting movement on the stalemated recession of Yosemite Valley, Johnson once again set his sights on a Sierra Nevada prize. "It seems an age since I heard from you or wrote to you, since which wonderful things have happened," he wrote Muir. Secretary Noble had visited the *Century* offices and offered to have the President restrict the claiming of private property in Kings Canyon. Johnson needed Muir's help in providing geographical details, including the location of the headwaters of Kings River, and he wanted Muir's postponed article soon "to pave the way" for making Kings Canyon a public park, which he and Noble agreed that Muir should propose.

Johnson wanted to call the article "A Rival of the Yosemite" and told Muir that if he submitted it soon, it might be as decisive as the Yosemite stories. "I know what nice weather this is to be out of doors," he gently urged, "but of course you will want to write a little also."

Kings Canyon

With the loss of Dr. Strentzel, Muir was now overseeing both farms, and the "leisure for writing" had vanished. After reviewing his notes from previous visits to Kings Canyon, he had decided that he needed to return, as much as anything to get "the scales & burrs of business rubbed off & soaked off in the brush & rocks & winds of that glorious wilderness." His second of three visits to the canyon, in the spring of 1875, had provoked fierce words from his pen. After recovering from his ordeal on Shasta, he had trekked through the southern part of the sequoia range and been incensed at finding five sawmills cleaving the big trees there. He had argued for the preservation of California forests, particularly the big trees, in an article—"God's First Temples. How Shall We Preserve Our Forests?"—in the *Sacramento Daily Record-Union*, hoping to connect with state legislators and convince them it was critical to preserve forests because of their effect on climate, soil, and streams. "Strip off the woods with their underbrush from the mountain flanks, and the whole State, the lowlands as well as the highlands, would gradually change to desert," he wrote. Without trees, heavy rains and snowmelt would turn streams into destructive torrents, washing away topsoil, clogging lower channels, and flooding farms.

Muir decried the forest destruction and urged restrictions to prevent the sawmills from eradicating the "noblest tree-species in the world." Hyde's, on the north fork of the Kaweah, had cut 2 million feet of sequoia lumber the previous season. New mills were devastating the Fresno big trees, while Chas. Converse was about to obliterate a "noble forest" on the Kings River's south fork. After culling what they wanted, the loggers burned the rest, including old trees too enormous to cut and the seedlings and saplings, "cutting off all hopes of a renewal of the forest." While European states were managing their forests, Muir asked if our "loose jointed" government had the will to stop the destruction and called on lawmakers to survey the forests and examine the forces acting on them. With this article, he had launched his life of nature advocacy and activism.[5]

Before setting out again to see how Kings Canyon had fared in the fourteen years since he was last there, Muir waited out the snowy season. At the end of May, he boarded a train in San Francisco. Keith, his preferred traveling companion and illustrator, was battling depression and holed up in his Kearny Street studio with the landscape painter George Inness, the two mutually artistically infatuated and under the influence of the Swedenborgian Church. Getting the two Scots together was always a hit-or-miss thing. "I saw Keith last Saturday," Muir would later tell a mutual friend. "He is doing charming work but is making too much money for mental wealth & is as extravagantly unreasonable unpursuadable & unmanageable generally as ever. So of course he won't go to the wilderness with me."

Muir had somewhat reluctantly asked C. D. Robinson to go in Keith's stead. A tough and conservative critic, Muir had visited Robinson's studio in December and reported to Johnson that his eight large pasteboard sketches for the story were "grand affairs but are all made up of rock showing no level floor." His "lofty sheer-faced cliffs" lacked specificity, and Muir thought they needed at least one illustration with a wider view. Still, Muir was willing to take him along to Kings Canyon in case they needed more illustrations. Robinson would return the favor by committing the cardinal journalistic sin of publishing his own story about the journey—perhaps to pay debts—before Muir submitted his version to the *Century*.

Muir had already sent Johnson a map of his proposed park boundaries. J. P. Moore of Moore & Smith Lumber Company, which owned ten thousand acres of sequoia forest in the Tule River basin, which Muir wanted to include, had told him that he would sell this forest to the government at cost. Johnson forwarded the map to Noble and repeated Moore's offer. Now Muir wanted a chance to assess with his own eyes the damage that Moore & Smith, which had erected a sixty-two-mile flume to the town of Sanger in 1890 and was now floating 3 million feet of lumber a month out of the Kings River headwaters area, had wrought on the forests.[6]

On a previous three-month journey there from Yosemite, Muir had led a group of three men through the sequoia belt to see what lay between the two great canyons. On the divide between the South Fork of the San Joaquin and the North Fork of the Kings River, at ten thousand feet, Muir had left his three exhausted companions to climb Mount Humphreys on his own, skirting glaciers to the summit, just shy of fourteen thousand feet, where he gazed south on rows of crowded peaks above the headwaters of the three forks of the Kings River.

On the ridge above their campsite, Muir and another member of the party scouted the way forward. "The view was truly glorious—peaks, domes, huge ridges, and a maze of canyons in bewildering combinations," Muir wrote, "but terribly forbidding as to way-making." Gazing out in silence, the other man finally sighed and said he was going home. Muir and the other two men crossed the divide into the upper valley of Kings Canyon's North Fork. They descended a side canyon into the main canyon, where live oaks, pines, incense cedars, and tiger lilies surrounded a cascading river and mirror lake, but there was no apparent way forward. After resting awhile, they built their own "rude" trail up the south wall. On the ridge above the Middle Fork, they saw more waves of ridges and mountains. At last they crossed Kings River, passed through stands of sequoias, and entered Kings Canyon. There, in the hazy light of early October, as Muir described, "the ripened leaves, frost-nipped, wrinkled and ready to fall, made gorgeous clouds of color, which burned in the mellow sunshine like the bloom of a rich summer." The deer were migrating to the foothills and the bears feasting on acorns before burrowing in for the winter. It was the Peaceable Kingdom for which Muir was always searching.

Since that memorable expedition, the state's population had boomed by half a million people and its industrial tentacles had spread far and wide. Muir feared what he might find now. On previous visits, he had not seen the valley in flood, but this would be a good year for doing that as cool weather had kept snow on the mountains, "ready to be launched," as he put it, in the kind of natural spectacle that thrilled him. Muir and Robinson set out from Visalia by stagecoach, through miles of wheat fields into the Sierra foothills. At six thousand feet they entered the forest belt. From here, the central plain below looked like an arm of the sea to Muir. "Orange groves and vineyards, fields, towns, and dusty pastures are all submerged and made glorious in the divine light," he observed. "Finer still is the light streaming past us through the aisles of the forest." But then came the devastation. On Mill Creek, "stumps, logs, and the smashed ruins of the trees cumber the ground; the scream of saws is heard." They had reached the Moore & Smith Mills.

Here, Muir discovered, the situation was dire. "At first sight it would seem that these mighty granite temples could be injured but little by anything that man may do," he wrote. But man was superior at nothing if not the destruction of everything—even that which would seem beyond his scale. At the new Kings River Mills, he saw that not only were the massive old pines and firs being "ruthlessly" timbered, but the giant sequoias were targeted in particular. On his previous visit, five mills were cutting big-tree lumber on or near the sequoia belt. Now he found twice as many mills in the area with much more than double the capacity. Anticipating regulation, the loggers were toppling sequoia groves before it was forbidden, clear-cutting everything from saplings—the future—to ancients fifteen feet in diameter. Adding to the shame of it, unlike the coastal redwood, the sequoia made for poor, brittle timber. This wanton logging of the old-growth trees, trees the likes of which had not been seen in his native Scotland, or anywhere else in Great Britain, for half a millennium, roused Muir to indignation:

> Scaffolds are built around the great brown shafts above the swell of the base, and several men armed with long saws and axes gnaw and wedge them down with damnable industry. The logs found to be too large are blasted to manageable dimensions with powder. It seems incredible that Government should have abandoned so much of the forest cover of the mountains to destruction. As well sell the rain-clouds, and the fountain-snow, and the rivers, to be cut up and carried away if that were possible. Surely it is high time that something be done to stop the extension of the present barbarous, indiscriminating method of harvesting the lumber crop.[7]

Moore & Smith was "busily engaged in the work of Sequoia destruction," Muir would later report to Johnson, enclosing a photo of the grim scene. In addition to the ten thousand acres of sequoia lands that Moore had offered to sell to the government, including the thirty-seven-hundred-acre Converse Basin Grove, five miles north of the new General Grant National Park and perhaps the largest and finest stand of sequoias existing, he had told Muir that the company owned sixty thousand more acres of forestland on the Kings, Kaweah, and Tule Rivers. With his dander now up, Muir added, "If the means by which they gained title to so vast a body of land was investigated, they might be induced to part with more still." He was learning the ways of power politics.[8]

Nearly all of the valley's four hundred annual visitors were hunters or anglers. At the mills, Muir hired a "bear-killer guide" named Fox to accompany him and Robinson. After climbing a steep mile from the mill, the thirty-five-mile trail into Kings Canyon passed through General Grant National Park, where, Muir noted, "a few of the giants are now being preserved amid the industrious destruction by ax, saw, and blasting-powder going on around them." After Robinson made a "good drawing" of the famous 267-foot-tall General Grant, which he called "very large and symmetrical," the three men, their horses, and their pack mule climbed to above eight thousand feet and descended the southerly ridge on "a careless crinkled trail" that seemed "well-nigh endless." They had planned to camp at Bearskin Meadow, which

Robinson called "the coldest and most disagreeable halting-place in this region at any time of year" but now "more than usually forbidding in its soggy, wet and cheerless aspect." Since they still had light, they carried on three more miles, stopping at Tornado Meadow around dark.

Early the next morning, they broke camp in a snowstorm, immediately climbing a ridge and then descending to flooded Boulder Creek, which Robinson described as "a raging torrent of snow water some fifty feet wide at the ford." It took them three hours to get the animals across and reloaded. "Had a good trip but a little hard. . . ." Muir told Johnson. "Rain sleet snow & flooded streams slid 2 miles on dead avalanche. Mule with all our goods went down the river but was caught on a grand jam. Robinson growling & blaming the sunspots for all. etc etc etc. But we had a fine rich time for a' that." They picked up two anglers along the way and reached the valley—which was even deeper than the Grand Canyon—late that night.

Although Kings Canyon received nearly double the water flow of Yosemite, its falls were not nearly as impressive. Still, in his forthcoming article, Muir showed in one rhythmic sentence his ability to describe water: "The descent of the Kings River streams is mostly made in the form of cascades, which are outspread in flat plume-like sheets on smooth slopes, or are squeezed in narrow-throated gorges, boiling, seething, in deep swirling pools, pouring from lin to lin, and breaking into ragged, tossing masses of spray and foam in boulder-choked canyons—making marvelous mixtures with the downpouring sunbeams, displaying a thousand forms and colors, and giving forth a great variety of wild mountain melody, which, rolling from side to side against the echoing cliffs, is at length all combined into one smooth, massy sea-like roar."[9]

In the morning the two fishers angled in the eddies of a logjam, landing trout as fast as they tossed flies to them. Then the party set out. Using ropes and log footbridges, they crossed the three streams forming Roaring River, passed through what Fox called the Garden of Eden—the sweet-smelling lupines of Blue Flat—and set up camp in a meadow cabin occupied by a company of wood rats, which, to Muir's delight, munched on the party's provisions, swam in their water bucket, and even skittered across their faces during the night. He also took pleasure in the many birds that made their home in the meadow, as black-headed grosbeaks, Bullock's orioles, and pileated woodpeckers came to play, or to bang their heads, as it were.

The only other people they saw were a mountaineer and his nephew on the boy's first bear hunt, and the two joined their camp. After a few days, the boy shot a black bear "not so big and ferocious a specimen as he could have wished," Muir observed, "but formidable enough for a boy to fight single-handed." The hunters shared bear steaks and bear-oil muffins, pancakes, and bread. They hung strips of bear meat around camp to dry. Although Muir felt he could not refuse the hospitality, he was disturbed by it as well. All the bears—black, brown, and cinnamon—were rapidly disappearing, shot by mountaineers and prospectors for food or poisoned by shepherds. Muir estimated that fewer than five hundred remained in the Kings River area and thought it a shame that animals "so good-natured and so much a part of these shaggy wilds should be exterminated."

Farther in, beneath the range's highest peaks, Muir and Robinson found unspoiled beauty. Many miles up the canyon, they entered Paradise Valley, which roared with waterfalls. It would not be long before this resplendent canyon was opened up to the outside world by a road cutting through the sequoia groves, Muir opined once he got home. While some of these groves had recently been included in the Sequoia and General Grant Parks, he believed all the Kings, Kaweah, and Tule sequoias should be made "one grand national park." In his bold call to action in the *Century*, he implored Congress to "make haste before it is too late to set apart this surpassingly glorious region for the recreation and well-being of humanity."

Muir sent Johnson a map he had drawn of the canyon that "rough as it is . . . has called for much hard work." He had rejected Robinson's name, the White Woman, for the Half Dome–like rock at the head of the valley. Muir thought it looked "no whiter than any other mass of gray granite in the valley" and called it Glacier Monument. Neither was he buying Robinson's Grant Monument, which was "not striking enough for Grant" and too near another Grant monument—the General Grant Tree; Muir dubbed it North Tower. Johnson was pleased with the map, which he agreed was much better than Robinson's. He was sending a copy to Noble and would see if they could get a bill introduced early in the winter session. He reminded Muir to give a comprehensive view of

Kings Canyon in his article, to emphasize its wild beauty and to urge reservation of the region, which on his map they had marked *Limits of the Proposed National Reservation*. "As in the case of the Yosemite, 'the proposed reservation' is only proposed by you and me," Johnson said, "but it will have the same effect of calling public attention to the matter."

Muir was, as usual, anxious about his writing, telling Johnson, "I am bending & stretching at the oar in this Kings River article hard as I can." Nevertheless, on August 15, he delivered the manuscript honed to the requested ten thousand words and only eight months overdue; however, he was still correcting names, heights, and distances to go with the last of the illustrations. He had measured elevations during each of his visits to the valley and was correcting Robinson's overblown guesses. "I fear you will find the article terribly dry & geographical—lean, scrawny, etc.," he wrote Johnson, but he had needed to cover a lot of ground. Something else was bothering him. Robinson was talking too much about their scheme "& even publishing." He told Johnson, "My mother wrote me a month ago that she had been reading what she called an article on Kings R written by R." Three days later, he sent Johnson his final version.[10]

Even while Muir and Johnson were preparing the article, another sequoia tragedy was unfolding in the Kings River area, in an isolated stand a few miles from the General Grant Grove. More than three decades after the Mammoth Tree and the Mother of the Forest were taken by prospectors to be put on display, the 331-foot-tall Mark Twain Tree was being targeted for its size, symmetry, and lack of fire scars. But now it was the world's elite cultural institutions that were requesting ancient trees for their exhibition spaces—and thus tacitly legitimizing the indiscriminate logging as well as showing just how far ahead of their time Muir and his cohorts were in trying to save these irreplaceable trees. Upon request, Moore & Smith had agreed to donate a cross section of the Twain Tree to the American Museum of Natural History in New York City, with the railroad magnate Collis P. Huntington contributing the cost of the labor and transport. To do the job, Moore & Smith had built a twenty-three-foot saw and constructed a landing trench feathered with branches to soften the fall and prevent the massive trunk from shattering. It took the loggers eight days to topple the thirteen-century-old sequoia. They cut a four-foot-thick cross section of its trunk and divided that into a dozen sections around a core, like a pineapple, hauled the pieces out of the mountains in wagons, and loaded them onto a train for the cross-country trip to New York, where they would be reassembled for the exhibit. The next section of the trunk was going all the way to the British Museum in London.

Loggers cutting down the Mark Twain Tree, by C. C. Curtis, ca. 1891.

The remainder of Twain would be reduced to grape stakes and fence posts, leaving only a mighty stump, ninety feet around, as a monument to the trees that once thrived in what became Big Stump Grove, part of the future Kings Canyon National Park. Twain the writer, who was fifty-six, struggling financially, and fighting to stay relevant, was away on an extended tour of Europe. While the situation was ripe for sardonic humor, there is no record of his ever commenting on it.[11]

Muir's story "A Rival of the Yosemite: The Canyon of the South Fork of Kings River" ran in the November issue of the *Century*, leading with an attention-grabber that Johnson quite liked: "In the vast Sierra wilderness far to the south of the Yosemite, there is a yet grander valley of the same kind." It was a provocative statement.

That summer, Johnson had met and bent the ear of Secretary Noble when they both received honorary degrees from Yale, Johnson an MA for the copyright campaign and Noble an LLD for his service as interior secretary. "I have a great deal of faith in that man, and he is thoroughly interested in the protection of public lands," Johnson reported to Muir. Although Johnson had not had time to take up his proposed defense association, he would not let the goal of a united Yosemite National Park die from political inertia. Riding the momentum of the story, he told Muir, "Now if Armes and you would start a petition for the return of the old park to the government, I'll see that the new Congress takes the matter up." Muir sent Johnson two letters about it, and Johnson rushed copies to Noble to consider before his report.[12]

Noble's report to Congress, in mid-December, supported reform in Yosemite and extolled Muir's Kings Canyon article with Robinson's "admirable engravings of the wonderful scenery." He wrote, "These gentlemen as well as the editors of *The Century*, especially Mr. Johnson, have taken a great personal interest in the forest reserves in California, and are worthy of great consideration, both from their experience and intelligence." Noble supported extending Sequoia National Park to encompass the Kings River region, including the Kaweah and Tule sequoia groves.

To take advantage of the momentum, Johnson proposed removing a small section of mining areas, which were "not very parkable," and told Muir he was preparing to go before Congress.

Then came a stunning development on the last page of Johnson's letter. He often dropped significant or breaking news in the margins, but this time the letter was signed for him by an associate, who added in a postscript that Johnson was beset by a "prolonged illness & cannot write again soon."[13]

Johnson's absence would take its toll: though clearly worthy of protection, with backing from the secretary of the interior, Kings Canyon—Muir's "rival of the Yosemite"—would go unpreserved not only for now but for another half century.

CHAPTER 12

The Sierra Club

A s the General Noble Tree fell in the Converse Basin Grove in 1892—a year after Twain's namesake met its demise—the giant sequoia lurched back against its stump in its death throes, as if admonishing the jubilant lumberjacks who had just severed the last fibers of what is believed to be the largest tree ever cut down. The massive, three-thousand-year-old sequoia, named after the sitting secretary of the interior, both until that moment still very much alive, sent the men leaping as it smashed scaffolds and rigging. They fell onto the wildly vibrating stump, some ninety-five feet in circumference—the Chicago Stump, as it would become known—and found themselves balancing on wobbly knees in the midst of their own self-induced earthquake.

They would make a thirty-foot-tall cross section of the tree, cleanly cut at both ends, hollow it out, and then prepare if for transportation to Chicago, where during the upcoming World's Columbian Exposition, it would be erected in the White City, in the rotunda of the Government Building, ringed by benches and outfitted with a spiral staircase.[1]

Now ensconced in the Big House, Muir sought divine order in nature, not in his office. His second-floor study in the front of the house was adorned with Keith paintings—a view of Mount Lyell from sketches made during their 1872 trip to the Upper Tuolumne and a rendering of Yosemite Valley on a cigar-box lid—and was the domestic representation of his expansive mind. No one dared enter and tidy up. The room was so crammed with books, manuscripts, and sketches that it was hard to find a chair to sit in, which is perhaps how Muir, who was easily distracted, wanted it.[2]

The General Noble Tree, named for the Civil War general and secretary of the interior John Noble, was 312 feet tall and 99 feet around. In 1892 the 3,200-year-old tree was cut down for display as the Chicago Centennial Tree at the Chicago World's Fair, leaving in its place what became known as the Chicago Stump, which can still be seen today.

While temporarily without his copilot, Johnson, Muir was by no means rudderless. In fact, this was to be the year that he would cement his environmental legacy. With the battle for the Sierra Nevada being waged on multiple fronts, establishing the environmental defense association that he and particularly Johnson had envisioned was finally on the front burner. The notion of a Sierra support organization had been bandied about since 1886 when Henry Senger, a philologist and professor of German at the University of California, had written Walt Dennison, then Guardian of the Valley, to suggest starting a mountaineering library in Yosemite to serve explorers. Johnson had been encouraging Muir to organize a group to protect the natural beauty of the Sierra Nevada ever since their trip to Yosemite. Now the two notions converged.[3]

Uneasy in the spotlight and not believing himself the man for the job, Muir had at first resisted. Johnson had then asked Theodore Roosevelt's Boone and Crockett Club, formed four years earlier to preserve large game and "promote manly sport with the rifle," to take on the defense of the Western wilderness. But its New York–based leaders had opted to keep their focus east of the Rockies, preferring a separate club for the West, with the two banding together on national issues. Johnson had attempted to launch a Yosemite and Yellowstone Defense Association the previous spring. He had asked Muir to organize a California branch to raise funds and serve as a watchdog. Muir had agreed to do what he could. "But," he warned, "Californians generally care very little about Yosemite & forest parks." He told Johnson that Billy Armes, who had already suggested such an organization, which he called the Sierra Club, would start a branch.

But it was Henry Senger who was doing the legwork in January 1892. He had recruited Warren Olney, a prominent San Francisco attorney and Shiloh veteran, who had moved to California for its celebrated mountains the same year Muir had, and had written Muir. "I am greatly interested in the formation of an Alpine Club," Muir responded, suggesting that Senger also include Armes. "I think with you and Mr. Olney that the time has come" and hope that "we will be able to do something for wildness and make the mountains glad."[4]

They met in Olney's office, at 101 Sansome Street in San Francisco, the First National Bank building, on Saturday, May 28, and based on their discussion, Olney wrote articles of incorporation. The following Saturday, June 4, twenty-seven academics, artists, graduate students, and professionals—mountaineers and environmentalists all—gathered again in Olney's office. Muir had met Olney, who a decade later would serve as mayor of Oakland, in 1889, through their mutual friend Keith. When he knew Muir was coming to visit him in his studio, Keith often sent word to Olney, an avid fisherman and Sierra hiker, so that he could join them for mountain talk. The gatherings grew to include other Muir admirers, all Stanford or University of California professors, including Armes; Senger; John Branner, Stanford's first professor of geology;

and Joseph LeConte, who with ten students (then a quarter of the UC student body) had been guided by Muir in Yosemite in 1870 and who had seconded Muir's theory of the glacial origin of Yosemite Valley.

These charter members created a club to explore, enjoy, and make accessible the mountain regions of the Pacific Coast, to publish information about them, and "to enlist the support and cooperation of the people and the government in preserving the forests and other natural features of the Sierra Nevada Mountains." While it was one of the first mountain clubs for the explicit purpose of guarding against the despoiling of scenic lands, it was not the first mountain club or even the first in the West. The first was the Alpine Club of Williamstown (Massachusetts), begun by a group of outdoors enthusiasts in 1863 for exploring the Berkshires. A decade later, as local wilderness areas dwindled, similar groups, such as the White Mountain Club of Portland (Maine) and the Appalachian Mountain Club (based in Boston and known as the AMC), cropped up to protect hiking, mountaineering, and other wilderness activities. They were among the first conservation clubs in America.[5]

In 1886, *Forest and Stream* editor and Yellowstone activist George Bird Grinnell had helped start the Audubon Society to protect wild birds and their eggs in response to the fashion industry's slaughter of all manner of birds and the eradication of the passenger pigeon. By the following year, the buffalo had been annihilated, tens of millions of them in the most gruesome and wasteful way by industrial hunters primarily selling their hides and heads and leaving their meat to rot on the plains. Sometimes they cut out only their tongues to smoke, pickle, and sell in the East by the barrelful. Elk, grizzly bear, beaver, and many other species prized for hunting were rapidly vanishing as well. That was the impetus for Grinnell and Roosevelt to form the Boone and Crockett Club in 1887 and attempt to influence national legislation for animal preservation, albeit for the purpose of hunting.

The Sierra Club founders assembled in Olney's office once again to elect nine directors for a yearlong term. Olney—who had changed his mind since telling Senger in January that he was unsure about playing an active role—was elected first vice president. Branner was to serve as second vice president, Armes secretary, and Senger corresponding secretary, while Mark Kerr, of the US Geological Survey, would be treasurer.

The only other position to fill was that of president.

Muir, at fifty-four, was still "slender, lithe, and active as an Indian," in the description of Sam Merrill, a young family friend then staying with the Muirs at Alhambra. Though his face was deeply lined from his years of outdoor explorations, he was magnetic and handsome. "His eyes were as clear and blue as California skies; his head well shaped and covered with curly brown hair."

The vote for the president of the Sierra Club went unanimously to John Muir. Johnson, who was not present but would become a charter member, and Senger had each separately encouraged Muir to start such an advocacy group, and both wanted him to lead it. It was more than just Muir's reputation and intellect that united them and the other members in this desire. An environmental organization could have no greater figure at its helm. The evangelical tendencies and deep conviction that had fired his father also burned within Muir—though they were tempered by a more balanced and easier-going nature—making him a natural leader, a philosopher king. In a sense Muir *preached* through nature and through his deep belief that nature would prevail. Until now, he had been waging a lonely war in California against the commercial interests that were exploiting and destroying the forests, rivers, and mountains. Although he had resisted a leadership role, now surrounded by this encouraging and capable band of friends and allies, he accepted the mantle.

"I am sure you will pardon me for being proud of the fact that I was a member of Muir's household when the Sierra Club was born," Merrill later wrote. "Mr. Muir returned from San Francisco and announced to us all at the supper table that the Sierra Club had been organized and that he had been chosen its first president. I had never seen Mr. Muir so animated and happy before."

Olney's office would serve as the club's headquarters for the first year and would be the new epicenter—outside of Muir's cluttered study at the ranch and the editorial offices of the *Century*—of what would become the most demanding and persistent guardian of the environment, one that punched above its weight.[6]

The Sierra Club gained immediate traction. One hundred and eighty-two members joined during its first five months, far outstripping

Armes's prediction of twenty or twenty-five. The club's youngest charter member, Wanda Muir, was eleven. Its oldest was Galen Clark, now
seventy-eight. About a third of the members were college students or
professors; about a sixth, like Muir, were foreign-born. Among those
who signed on were a banjo teacher, a stenographer, a taxidermist, an
Oakland farmwife, the inventor of the cable car, and the founder of
Pasadena's two-year-old New Year's Day Rose Parade. Muir's guide on
Rainier, Philemon Van Trump, would become one of the first members
outside California when he joined the following year. Early members
paid $5 in annual dues (almost $150 today), although students paid
just a dollar.

Enthusiasm ran high. More than five hundred people attended the
club's second general meeting to hear the renowned explorer and US
Geological Survey director John Wesley Powell, who had lost an arm
at Shiloh, speak about his daring voyage through the Grand Canyon in
1869. Powell, whose prophetic warnings against overtaxing the water
capacity of Western lands would go unheeded by Congress, was elected
an honorary member, along with other prominent scientists and environmentalists, including John Tyndall, Secretary Noble, Arctic explorer
A. W. Greely, Mount Whitney namesake Josiah Whitney (his famous
dispute with Muir notwithstanding), Mount King namesake Clarence
King, and Johnson. As president of the Sierra Club, Muir had become,
in a short time, not just a literary and spiritual force for nature, but a
political one.[7]

First Blood

In the two years since Muir and Johnson had successfully petitioned
Congress to reserve fifteen hundred square miles, an area a little larger
than the state of Rhode Island, of mountain wilderness around Yosemite
Valley for a national park, the citizens of the counties from which the
park had been hewn—Mariposa, Tuolumne, Mono, and Fresno—
complained about the lost tax revenue. Along with lumber, mining,
cattle, and sheep interests, they demanded that the park be reduced in
size. In February 1892, California congressman Tony Caminetti had
introduced a bill to shrink it by half, opening up hundreds of mining

claims and exposing meadows and mountainsides to livestock. On November 5, the Sierra Club leaders met and resolved to draft a statement opposing the Caminetti bill and to work for its defeat. This would be the club's first conservation campaign.[8]

During Johnson's illness, he and Muir had been out of touch. "Let me hear a word from you as to the reestablishment of your health & general welfare," Muir wrote in late November. As for himself, he had been "busy & barren," only managing a first draft of the Alaska articles. "The Caminetti bill reducing the area of the Yo. National Park needs watching," he noted. In the meantime, MacKenzie had informed Johnson that the mess in Yosemite was "worse than ever" and sent an *Examiner* opinion piece by the state forester, a position MacKenzie called a "sinecure," occupied by a man who "knows as much about forest management as does a sucking calf," but who was angling to be appointed Guardian of Yosemite.[9]

Alarmed, Johnson, who was gradually recuperating, wrote to Muir and Noble in early December to ask about the status of their bill for the recession of Yosemite Valley. Noble responded that there was no way to advance recession in the current session, unless by an amendment attached to another pending bill. A new bill at such a late date would only anger some and be counterproductive.[10]

Muir was delighted to learn that Johnson was reemerging, but now a serious illness swept through his own house. For more than a week, while Helen and Wanda suffered from an unnamed sickness, Muir stood constant vigil at their bedside, never even taking off his clothes. However, he somehow managed to sign the Sierra Club petition opposing the Caminetti bill on the second day of the new year.

In their letter to the chairman of the House Committee on Agriculture, where the bill was being reviewed, the club "emphatically" protested the reduction of Yosemite National Park, arguing that the problems the park was created to solve would return: "The herds of sheep, which now for two seasons have successfully been kept out of the reservation, would denude the watersheds of their vegetation, the forest fires following in the wake of the herds would destroy the forests and threaten the reservation itself and the timber of priceless value to the prosperity of the State would become the prey of the speculator." The headwaters of the San Joaquin River, used to irrigate the entire San Joaquin Valley, would be compromised as well as the watersheds of the Tuolumne and Merced Rivers, resulting in forest fires that would devastate the sequoia groves. Degradation of the Tuolumne would mar Hetch Hetchy, a rival to Yosemite in "grandeur and uniqueness" and a future chief attraction of the Sierra Nevada.[11]

Unknown to them, that precious water would be coveted by the City of San Francisco, and Hetch Hetchy would face its existential threat not from sheep but from their fellow Californians.

"My dear Mr Johnson," Muir wrote in mid-January 1893, "I was very glad to get your letter of Dec 8th showing you were well again, as good a man as before your dangerous illness or better with all your capacity for work & fight & poetry jubilant & exuberant." He told Johnson that he thought nine-tenths of Californians favored the valley being part of the national park, "which naturally it is." But the other tenth, namely those with a monetary interest in the matter, "will do more fighting in a case of sentiment & scenery" than a thousand mere admirers. "Very few people in California care for scenery to any appreciable extent—to the extent say of subscribing 25 cents each to save Yosemite from being sunk in the sea, El Capitan meadows forests & all—though nominally on the right side."

Nevertheless, the Sierra Club could help, Muir promised. Armes was "a good worker & good fighter." Others had written friends in the legislature and persuaded the *San Francisco Call* to run "some good lively columns." State senator Elliott McAllister, a charter member of the club, would introduce a bill for recession while monitoring the Caminetti bill. Muir enclosed the Yosemite Commission report with the governor's letter to the Senate Public Lands Committee, showing the governor to be "violently opposed to recession." "Caminetti's bill is mainly in the interest of lumbermen & those who own timber claims for sale to lumbermen—Timber claims within the boundaries of the park are very nearly worthless to the owners as they can make no use of them by themselves, not being able to build mills, roads, flumes etc. . . . Anyhow sooner as later we must be successful."[12]

But Muir mostly wanted to turn his attention to his friend Johnson in this first letter of the new year and especially on his recently published poetry: "Your *Century* editorial was capital. And now your poems—it goes without saying that so keen a literary sharp would write nothing silly even in verse, but I never knew before that you were so much a poet." Then as only a true friend and literary peer could do, he dug in, "'The Winter Hour' is a fine manly well-balanced poem but you should not have introduced candlelight as you have in the second line. . . . The 'Hearth song' is lively & goes dancing on like a hillside stream. . . ." He listed a dozen "vivid," "telling," and "fine sturdy poetic lines." "It seems wonderful that such a working, fighting man of affairs as you are should be so much a poet. I'm proud of you—go ahead & pan up more poets gold to brace & cheer & inspire your many already deeply indebted friends." Johnson would respond that of all the letters from poets and favorable reviews, nothing pleased him more than Muir's "cordial approval."

The Sierra Club directors met to strategize. They believed that even if a recession bill passed, which was unlikely, it would be vetoed by the governor, so they decided to concentrate on defeating the Caminetti bill in Congress and establishing a Tulare Park. Johnson saw it differently. "Californians seem at last to be aroused, if not organized, in favor of recession," he wrote Muir in early February. "The most important thing to do is to push the matter to a vote." Then, if it failed, Congress would know that the state legislature had considered the matter and refused to do the right thing. He wanted Muir to send a delegation to Sacramento "to urge the matter on the Legislature."

Meanwhile, Irish was writing "vulgar letters" to Gilder complaining that the *Century* was unfair in not running California governor Markham's report. Johnson thought it "white-washing" and was busy lobbying Noble and the House Public Lands chairman on the Kings Canyon park, which he thought would pass. "I do not easily give up a cause," he told Muir, though doubtless this was not news to Muir. But he did need "ammunition" and asked Muir to keep him informed on the bill's progress.[13]

In New York City, Johnson was not only engaging the *Century* in the cause, he was also working the press—orchestrating favorable stories in the *Post*, *Times*, and *Sun*—while personally writing every member of the Public Lands Committees urging the defeat of the Caminetti bill. On February 21, he wrote Muir, thanking him for sending McAllister's letter about recession. "I do not care three straws on what basis the Yosemite is receded if only it be receded," Johnson replied, incensed by the notion of a two-year wait for public sentiment to be whipped up and the possibility of "another white-washing report" from the Yosemite commissioners.

"If it is not receded at the present session of your Legislature," said Johnson, "I shall have a Congressional investigation set on foot at the extra session, and thus the scandal will be transferred from Sacramento to Washington." Johnson perhaps suspected that Muir was taking his political cues from others less savvy: "As I have said all along, nothing can take the place of the actual introduction of the bill. Nobody can say whether or not he is for or against recession until the bill is introduced." He knew from experience that a campaign was just hot air until votes were to be cast.

While they struggled on the state level, Johnson's faith in Noble paid off on the national level. "Glory halleluiah!" he wrote Muir. "The Secretary of the Interior is carrying out his great measures of forest preservation." Noble had proclaimed three reservations in the Sierras, one along the Grand Canyon, and a million acres around Mount Rainier. Johnson thought they might shoot for the Sierra north of Yosemite National Park next. He added by hand, "Will the Sierra Club take the lead. I am already advocating it—in the April *Century*.

"You of course know that this whole policy has grown out of your three articles printed in *The Century*, which in turn grew out of our talk by the campfire on the upper Tuolumne. Of course I had no idea that Noble was going to do so much, but the suggestion back of all these reservations was your own.

"The art of being a statesman," he concluded, "is to see what is wrong and then go to work to remedy it. Good luck to the Recessionists!"[14]

President Harrison, whose term in office was notable for the admission of six Western states to the union and high tariffs and spending, had not been reelected the previous November, and Johnson now prepared for Grover Cleveland's second regime, which would begin in March, gathering material from Secretary Noble's office to assist in the effort to create forest reserves. While Harrison had been "cordially interested" in the idea, Johnson would later say in an homage to the secretary that it was Noble, departing office along with the President, who was behind the "then well-nigh friendless reform" and thus "officially the pioneer of the conservation movement in this country." Johnson would also comment in his memoirs, "Muir and Noble were the two salient leaders and pioneers of forest conservation, and Noble's torch, like those of most of us, was kindled at the flame of Muir's enthusiasm." Muir and the Sierra Club directors would commend Noble's "glorious forest work."[15]

"With Noble's reservation as a weapon you could succeed, I think," Johnson told Muir, regarding recession. "This is going to [be] a great year for decent things at Washn & it ought to be at Sacramento. But if you cant, you cant."

"Go ahead at Washington," Muir responded. "California, I am convinced, will do nothing about recession for a long time."

Johnson was growing tired of California's indifference and, worse, its malign players, such as Irish, who moreover seemed to be vying for commissioner of public lands. Johnson had written President Cleveland to tell him of his opposition to Irish in the role. And he told Muir, "If good citizens of California care anything about the matter, it is time that they also should protest." Instead, he fumed, they suffer being represented by Irish at their own "peril and disgrace." Maybe the Southern Pacific has the state "under its thumb," he went on. "And if this be the case why speak of California as part of the free republic. 'Who would be free themselves must strike the blow!' Stir up some of the 'timid good' to action. . . . Next winter, if I am alive, there will be a move to repeal the grant of 1864."[16]

Grover Cleveland, the only nonconsecutive two-term president, would spend much of his second term mired in the economic Panic of 1893 and its fallout. Burly and blue-eyed, intense and energetic, Cleveland liked to hunt and fish, drink beer, and go to the races but was otherwise a sober-minded son of an impoverished preacher. Though facing a tumultuous depression and protracted struggles over whether the nation's legal tender should be backed by gold or made of silver, he would manage to address pressing environmental concerns. He chose Hoke Smith, owner of the *Atlanta Journal*, which had supported him for president, to succeed Noble as interior secretary. Smith, an attorney who had made his fortune representing injured railroad workers, would strive to right the land patents of the railroads, improve Indian affairs, and speed the recovery of the still-reeling South. But most urgent to the California conservationists was that he, as soon as possible after taking his seat, reject the "bully, liar, swindler and thief" John P. Irish as head of the Public Land Commission, Muir wrote in a letter to Smith on behalf of the Sierra Club. In this first engagement with Smith, Muir implored him to "walk in the same blessed forest ways as his predecessor"—and to spurn Irish.[17]

"You doubtless know today that our friend Irish has failed to get the Land Commissionership," Johnson crowed to Muir shortly thereafter. And Muir responded, "Your pluck & perseverance for the public good in such matters is immortal & well-nigh divine. Were you not a sadly rare man, the J. P.s of this world would speedily wilt."

At around the same time, the Caminetti bill failed, thanks to Johnson, who had sent the Noble report to the members of both the House and Senate Public Lands Committees and had followed up with a strategically timed telegram from Muir. The recession bill in the California legislature, however, had also failed. Furthermore, the Yosemite Commission had still not hired a reputable landscape architect "to lay out & manage the groves & meadows." But as Muir told Johnson, "our blows have not been altogether without effect." An infamous hog pen and a blight of fences had been demolished. Horses were no longer turned loose to graze in the valley. And the voters would not reelect Caminetti in 1894, putting him out of national office for good.[18]

In the spring of 1893, the World's Columbian Exposition, celebrating the four-hundredth anniversary of Columbus's voyage to the New World and the nation's development since then, opened in Chicago. Having rebounded from the fire witnessed two decades earlier by Johnson, the city was now a colossus of state-of-the-art mills, foundries, machine shops, and iron-and-steel skyscrapers and had muscled out New York, Washington, and St. Louis to host the six-month event. Twenty-six million people now flocked from across the nation and around the globe to the city of a million-plus to experience the dawning of a new age, and a city within the city. The fair's plaster White City was designed by ten US architects, including Chicago's own "father of the skyscraper," Louis Sullivan, whose nonconforming edifice set off a firestorm of opinions. Exhibits displayed new technological feats, and a glimpse of the future. "Chicago asked for the first time whether the American people knew where they were driving," said the great thinker and writer Henry Adams, a descendant of two presidents, who designated the exposition a celebration of the watt, the ampere, and the erg.[19]

As the 1890 census showed, America had changed. "Four centuries from the discovery of America, at the end of a hundred years of life under the Constitution, the frontier has gone," Wisconsin historian Fred Turner lamented in a much-debated address at the fair. The General Noble Tree exhibit was an unwitting symbol of the nation's tragic disregard for its natural wonders. Turner believed that frontier life defined the American character and democracy, which, he said, "came out of the American forest." But the forest, like the "frontier land," was now either claimed or rapidly disappearing.

Muir visited the world's fair that spring. "Some of the buildings would reach all the way across Alhambra Valley & half way up Franklin Canyon [to the west of their ranch] for all I know," he wrote Wanda. But he was unimpressed by "the show of canned peaches, crockery, buggies, stuffed owls and things." They could not compare to an ancient sequoia, like the Noble Tree, or a yosemite (his term for a glacier-carved canyon), and he missed his family. "The whole show is nothing," the adoring father wrote Wanda, now twelve, "to my own two sweet babies."

Still, three days later, before he left Chicago, he told Louie that while Keith's and Hill's paintings on exhibit, four by each, were not their best, he had enjoyed the national art galleries: "There are about eighteen acres of paintings by every nation under the sun, & I wandered & gazed until I was ready to fall down with utter exhaustion." And the buildings and lighting had dazzled him. "For the best architects have done their best in building them while Fred Law Olmstead laid out the grounds. Last night the buildings & terraces & fountains along the canals were illuminated by tens of thousands of electric lights arranged along miles of lines of gables, domes & cornices with glorious effect. It was all fairyland on a colossal scale & would have made the Queen of Sheba & poor Solomon in all their glory feel sick with helpless envy." He was leaving the next day for New York, where Johnson eagerly waited to introduce him—and show him off—to some of the illustrious editors, writers, and scholars in his circle.[20]

Curiously, Muir made no mention in his letter of the General Noble Tree. Perhaps it was too horrific even to acknowledge.

CHAPTER 13

The Preaching of Pine Trees

On Saturday evening, November 23, 1895, when Muir spoke at the Sierra Club's annual public meeting at the Academy of Sciences in San Francisco, he quickly revealed his reluctance to lead the political brawl. He told the packed house, tongue only halfway in cheek, the same thing he had told the directors when they asked him to speak: swaying Congress was "lawyer's work" and "Mr. Olney, our vice president, ought to do it." His own work was in "exploring our grand wilderness" and in calling everybody to come and enjoy its "thousand blessings," not in making speeches and attending society affairs.

But it was Muir that people wanted to hear. The Century Company had published an anthology of his stories, *The Mountains of California*, the previous year, signaling his arrival in the pantheon of American writers. The collection, including two new essays and fourteen stories from his mountain-trekking heyday, addressed nature through the lenses of both science and spirituality. "It rallied and solidified the conservation sentiment of the entire nation," his Pulitzer Prize–winning biographer, Linnie Marsh Wolfe, would write fifty years later, "leading to a new upsurge of determination to preserve the forests."[1]

"This formal, legal, unwild work is out of my line," Muir told the crowd, playing it for laughs, and getting them. "If any harm should come to the woods from my awkward, unskillful handling of the subject this evening, then you must lay the blame where it belongs—lay it on our vice president, sitting at ease there on the front seat, seemingly unconscious of the wrong."

Whether he liked it or not, Muir was now the voice for protecting nature, and for the new activist strain of what today is called conservation but was then known as preservation. His reluctance to speak in a formal setting would prove to be his Achilles' heel and would later leave a gnawing question when it came to one of the biggest environmental battles of all.

Defeated in his efforts to avoid speaking, he had set out to write a concise address, of less than an hour, on the desired topic, "The National Parks and Forest Reservations," but reported that "the subject . . . proved too big." So he had put down his pen and now, trusting to memory, spun an account of his recent six-week ramble in the mountains above Yosemite, up to the headwaters of the Tuolumne and down through the wild canyon to Hetch Hetchy, encountering mounted soldiers, who were "fording roaring, boulder-choked streams, crossing rugged canyons, ever alert and watchful." He was encouraged by the four years of federal oversight. The landscape "broken and wasted" by the sheep on his last visit was now "blooming again as one general garden." Then he swept his audience to the highland glacier meadows:

> I found these blessed flowers blooming again in their places in all the fineness of wildness—three species of gentians, in patches acres in extent, blue as the sky, blending their celestial color with the purple panicles of the grasses, and the daisies and bossy, rosy spikes of the varied species of orthocarpus and bryanthus—nearly every trace of the sad sheep years of repression and destruction having vanished. Blessings on Uncle Sam's bluecoats!

Despite this progress, the national park's status and borders remained precarious. The previous winter, the Sierra Club and friends on both coasts had banded together to defeat a determined attempt to diminish it by half, something Muir now placed in perspective and artfully framed as a fundamental truth and cornerstone of the environmental movement: "The battle we have fought, and are still fighting, for the forests is a part of the eternal conflict between right and wrong, and we cannot expect to see the end of it." It was perhaps the most profound and encompassing sentence ever delivered on the topic. He continued:

> The smallest forest reserve, and the first I ever heard of, was in the Garden of Eden; and though its boundaries were drawn by the Lord, and embraced only one tree, yet even so moderate a reserve as this was attacked. And I doubt not if only one of our grand trees on the Sierra were reserved as an example and type of all that is most noble and glorious in mountain trees, it would not be long before you would find a lumberman and a lawyer at the foot of it, eagerly proving by every law terrestrial and celestial that that tree must come down. So we must count on watching, striving for these trees, and should always be glad to find anything so surely good and noble to strive for.

The valley, he went on, "instead of being most preciously cared for as the finest of all the park gardens . . . looks like a frowzy, neglected backwoods pasture" and needed to be placed under federal supervision. "The welfare of the people in the valleys of California and the welfare of the trees on the mountains are so closely related that the farmers might say that oranges grow on pine trees, and wheat, and grass."

His solution was to bring people to the mountains. "Few are altogether deaf to the preaching of pine trees," he told the crowded hall. "Their sermons on the mountains go to our hearts; and if people in general could be got into the woods, even for once, to hear the trees speak for themselves, all difficulties in the way of forest preservation would vanish."

Finally, as his time at the podium expired, Muir began to cede the stage. "But Professor Dudley has an address for this evening, and I fear I am taking his time."

"I should be very glad to have you continue instead," the gracious professor responded.

At which point Muir took the opportunity to expound on a favorite topic, guarding the new nature reserves. "Mr. Caminetti said last winter that there were seventy-five actual farms included in the Yosemite National Park, whose owners were all praying to have the boundaries so changed as to leave their farms out. But this is not so. On the contrary, there is little or nothing in the park that can properly be called a farm, but only garden patches, small hay meadows, and cattle ranches; and all the owners, as far as I know, are rejoicing in their protection from the sheep scourge.

"The two Sequoia National Parks are also protected by a troop of cavalry; but the grand Sierra Forest Reservation, extending from the south boundary of the Yosemite Park to the Kern River, is not yet protected. Many government notices were nailed on trees along the trails as warnings to trespassers; but as there was no one on the ground to enforce obedience to the rules, cattle and sheep owners have paid little or no attention to them." Muir had it from one who knew that "the troops stationed every summer in the sequoia parks could also effectually guard the great forest reserve at the same time, if only the military authority were extended over it." He hoped it would be done. "But we must remember that after all trespassers are kept off the parks and reservations and running fires prevented, much more will remain to be done. The underbrush and young trees will grow up as they are growing in Yosemite, and unless they are kept under control, the danger from some chance fire, from lightning, if from no other source, will become greater from year to year. The larger trees will then be in danger." Fire was always a problem. "Forest management," he concluded emphatically, "must be put on a rational, permanent scientific basis, as in every other civilized country."[2]

Forestry Commission

In January 1896, Johnson reported to Muir that he had hit upon a solution to achieve one of their goals—the establishment of a National Forest Commission. To avoid a contentious congressional bill, Secretary Smith could invite the National Academy of Sciences to launch a study. Congress would only have to fund it. "By that time," Johnson said, "if anybody wants to fight the appropriation, we shall have a tussle."[3]

Hoke Smith embraced Johnson's idea and charged the Harvard chemist Wolcott Gibbs, president of the National Academy of Sciences, with assembling a group of experts to explore the need for forest reserves and the policies that would be required to manage climate, soil, and water issues and to prevent forest fires. Over the next couple of months, Gibbs, with the advice of Fredrick Law Olmsted, assembled what would be called the National Forest Commission. Gibbs would be an ex officio member, and Muir by his own choice would serve as an unofficial adviser and guide. The botanist Charles Sargent, director of Harvard's Olmsted-designed Arnold Arboretum and an eminent tree expert, would chair the group. Sargent, his reputation as an icy Brahmin notwithstanding, had befriended Muir after Johnson introduced the two on Muir's trip East in 1893, and their friendship would flourish as they served on the commission. It did not hurt that Sargent gushed with praise for Muir's book: "I have never read descriptions of trees that so pictured them to the mind as yours do," he wrote, believing *Mountains* to be a unique work about trees by a writer who was at once a poet, a naturalist, and a keen observer. "Your book is one of the great productions of its kind."[4]

With its scientific gravitas, the commission gave a strong voice on the environment to advocates of a national policy to manage the agricultural and industrial exploitation of the country's natural resources—the long-marginalized amalgam of hunters, landscape gardeners, academics, and visionaries associated with universities and organizations such as the American Forestry Association, the Boone and Crockett Club, and the Sierra Club. Their use of scientific expertise to shape public policy and congressional action would set a new standard. But the political opposition was fierce, and internal strife would divide the commission.[5]

Gibbs chose as the commission's secretary the brash thirty-year-old forestry wunderkind Gifford Pinchot, whom Muir had also met through Johnson in 1893. At a dinner at Pinchot's parents' mansion in New York City, Muir had regaled the party with his story of the dog Stickeen, his lilting Scottish brogue rising to the occasion, and had greatly impressed the young Yale graduate, once chosen as the university's "most handsome" student. The two would keep in touch. An alumnus of France's École Nationale des Eaux et Forêts, Pinchot had implemented European methods of forest management at his family's Pennsylvania estate, Grey Towers, and in his forestry plan for George Vanderbilt's Biltmore, in North Carolina. He had toured the West in the spring of 1891 while working for a timber interest, only to be disappointed by Yosemite Valley. "Can't describe it at all, but wish I had seen it before seeing the Grand Canyon," he wrote in his diary. "Everything is tame after that." Now he was paired with Arnold Hague, of the US Geological Survey,

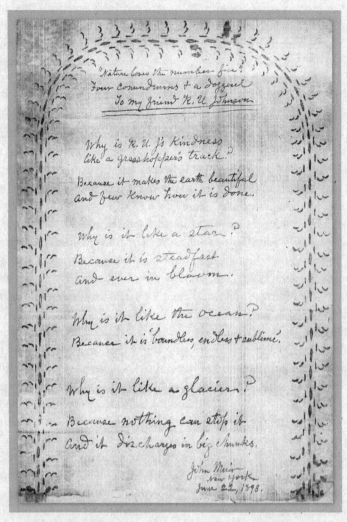

"Nature loves the number five: Four conundrums + a doggerel to my friend R. U. Johnson."
In the summer of 1893 on a trip to the East Coast, Muir was introduced to the
literary and scientific world by Johnson and afterward wrote this appreciation of him.

friends & my influence for good." He was ambivalent partly because he
was chronically bothered by respiratory issues, requiring "icy excursions
rather than exciting ceremonies." Nevertheless, he told Johnson, "I'll
face the fine music & look to you to see me through."[9]

On his way east, however, Muir stopped in Wisconsin to see his mother, Ann, who was eighty-three, and found that she was gravely ill. Ann Muir, a mother of eight, grandmother of many, and long-suffering wife to her dogmatic and domineering husband, who had died in 1885, had been a balm and comfort to her son John in the troubled household and had written him in 1869 after he had reached California that his "description of the fine scenery with which you are surrounded gave me much pleasure." She had proudly followed his writing career. Muir stayed for a week at her bedside and found that she "greatly enjoyed & was comforted" by his presence. He wrote Louie, "We talked over all the old days & the coming changes & I am glad I was brought to her in her hour of need—of loneliness." Since she seemed to be out of immediate danger, Muir left for Cambridge to receive his degree.

Diploma in hand, he went down to New York to visit Burroughs, whom he had met through Johnson. After a quarter century of writing nature poetry and essays, Burroughs was finishing up a book on his close friend Walt Whitman and pondering life on his own Walden-like estate on the Hudson River. Burroughs met Muir at the Hyde Park train depot, rowed him across the river, and took him to Slabsides, his writing cabin in the woods, where he was growing thirty thousand celery plants in a bog that he and his eighteen-year-old son, Julian, had drained. Muir would leave a strong impression on the Harvard undergraduate, who later wrote: "Only among hoboes and the truly great do we ever see such mental poise, such complete triumph over things material." The elder Burroughs was also taken with Muir. "A very interesting man, a little prolix at times," he wrote in his journal. "You must not be in a hurry or have any pressing duty, when you start his stream of talk and adventure. Ask him to tell you his famous dog story (almost equal to *Rab and His Friends*) and you get the whole story of glaciation and etc., thrown in."

They talked about Emerson, swamps, and celery late into the night, and Burroughs ultimately found Muir captivating: "He is a poet and almost a seer," he wrote. "Something ancient and far-away in the look of his eyes. He could not sit down in a corner of the landscape, as Thoreau did; he must have a continent for his playground. He starts off for a walk . . . and walks from Wisconsin to Florida and is not back home in 18 years. In Cal. he starts out one morning for a stroll; his landlady asks him if he will be back to dinner; probably not, he says. He is back in seven days. Walks 100 miles around Mt. Shasta and goes 2½ days without food." Muir should "be put into a book," Burroughs thought, "doubtful if he ever puts himself into one." The next day they hiked in Burroughs's riverside woods, and then Muir set off again. "Probably the truest lover of Nature, as she appears in woods, mountains and glaciers, we have yet had," Burroughs concluded.[10]

Ann Muir died the day after Muir left Burroughs, and he rushed back to Wisconsin for the funeral. Feeling "dull & benumbed" afterward, Muir caught up with the Forest Commission in Chicago in early July. The commission represented a wealth of geographical knowledge, including General Henry Abbot, who had surveyed parts of Oregon in the 1850s, and Yale botanist William Brewer, who had taken part in Whitney's geological survey of California in the 1860s and named Mount Hoffmann, Mount Dana, and Mount Lyell. "We are fairly off & away into the western woods," Muir wrote Johnson, from South Dakota, on Hot Springs stationery, on the fifth. The next day they would go to Deadwood and climb the highest of the Black Hills. "The blackness of which is from a covering of yellow pine. My old Sierra friend. This is its eastern limit. All the Company—Sargent, Brewer, Gen. Abbot & Hague—are good sound fellows & I feel a little like myself once more."[11]

The party arrived in Montana in mid-July. For several weeks they explored forests in Yellowstone, the Rockies, and along the Northern Pacific Railway line, before touring the upper Flathead and Kootenai River basins and then moving on toward Spokane. "We have just come from the famous Yellowstone," Muir wrote Louie on July 15. "The forests & waters hot & cold were in all their glory & we of course enjoyed them unspeakably. . . . Pinchot is out here somewhere but we have not yet found him." Six days later, he reported that they had run across Pinchot on the bank of the Flathead River, "encamped . . . in a bed of Linnea & Pyrola among grand mountain pines, spruces, Thyme & Larches." Muir and Sargent grew even closer in their shared appreciation for trees, and Muir considered Sargent "the only one of the Com. that knew & loved trees as I loved them." That included Pinchot.

In late July, a reporter from the *Morning Oregonian* in Portland interviewed Muir, who though an unofficial member of the commission, was well-known and agreeably outspoken. "The forest must be able to yield a perennial supply of timber, without being destroyed or injuriously affecting the rainfall, thus securing all the benefits of a forest, and at the same time a good supply of timber," Muir said, again revealing his practical side. In his younger years, he had worked in mills and factories, ingeniously retooling machinery and manufacturing lines, before spurning a lucrative industrial career. Muir called the commission's work the precursor to a desperately needed national forestry system. Anticipating their foes, he fired a shot across the bow: "It will be no use for lumbermen or sheepmen to speak of the members as cranks who want to reserve all the forestlands on earth. They have the interests of the country at heart and will advise for what they deem best, without fear or favor, and fully understanding what they are doing."[12]

CHAPTER 14

Only Uncle Sam Can Do That

The forest commissioners' summer of due diligence turned into a fall of vehement debate. Though they did not agree on who should manage the forests or how it should be done, they at last reached a consensus on what exactly to protect. With time running out on Cleveland's administration, the commission rushed a preliminary report to Secretary David Francis, the former Missouri governor who had replaced Hoke Smith as interior secretary, proposing the creation of thirteen reserves in seven Western states. Francis quickly forwarded the proposal to the President, who seized the moment.

Thus, on February 22, George Washington's birthday, less than two weeks before leaving office, Cleveland proclaimed the Washington's Birthday Reserves, protecting more than 21 million acres of woodlands, prioritizing unspoiled watersheds and the long-term use of forests. Combined with the 13 million acres set aside by President Harrison in 1891, the nation's protected forests would now top 34 million acres, an area nearly the size of the state of Illinois. It was a pivotal moment for the country: the unfettered right to claim, strip, and despoil the West for profit—at least when it came to timbering, mining, and grazing—appeared to be a thing of the past.[1]

This pivot did not go unchallenged, however. Spurred on by angry livestock herders and other business interests, congressional delegations from seven Western states lashed out at their East Coast counterparts for butting into Western matters. They appended a rider to the 1897

Sundry Appropriations Act, which was needed to fund the government, eliminating the entire forest reserve system and reopening the timberlands under previous homesteading, timber, and mining acts.

When he heard what they had done, as the *New York Times* later reported, President Cleveland rose indignantly, slammed the table with his fist, and snarled, "Nullify it, will they? Then I'll veto the whole damned Sundry Civil bill!" And he did. Or at least he pocket vetoed it. On March 4, his last day in office, Cleveland left the appropriations bill unsigned, which rescued the reserves, at least temporarily, but meant that as of July the government would have no funding.[2]

That same day, Walter Page, editor of the *Atlantic Monthly*, asked Muir to write a story on the parks and reservations to rally the public. Muir responded that he would if he could find the time. He was busy arguing the issue in the San Francisco newspapers. "I make slow progress, the fight in the west is very bitter. Beds of lies are growing up thicker & taller than the redwood forests & cutting them down seems an endless task."[3]

Opponents of Cleveland's forestry plan demanded that his successor, William McKinley, reverse course. Hailing from Ohio, McKinley, the last president to have fought in the Civil War and the one who would usher in the Progressive Era, transforming the nation in many ways, immediately called Congress into an extra session. Meanwhile, members of the Forest Commission induced their supporters and the media to rouse public opinion for the reserves. With this backing, McKinley stood his ground, or rather Cleveland's. Congress not only struck the rider that would have defeated the forest reserves but, emboldened by forestry advocates, also added new provisions to the sundry bill that would strengthen management of the country's forest reserves for a century to come.

On May 1, Pinchot submitted the Forest Commission's nation-changing final report, recommending the creation of two new national parks—Mount Rainier and Grand Canyon—and significantly more forest reserves in six Western states, along with a system for managing them. On June 4, President McKinley signed into law the Sundry Civil Appropriations Act—known more commonly as the Organic Act—of 1897, which stipulated that the forest reserves were intended to "improve and protect" the forests and their water flow while furnishing the nation with "a continuous supply" of timber. They were to be managed by the secretary of the interior.

The new secretary, Cornelius Bliss, engaged Pinchot as a "confidential forest agent" to put together a plan for their management. Pinchot, happy to return to the Western forests, assembled a small team to travel to the mountains of Idaho, the Pacific Northwest, and the Rockies and spent several months investigating the forests while living off the land. Frequently rising by three thirty in the morning to get a jump on the day, they were shot at, battled rattlesnakes, twice slept in the snow without blankets, and dined on prairie dog and mule-deer antler, the latter roasted like a potato in the campfire. Their most surprising discovery was just how much fire damage had occurred throughout the forests over the centuries. At stops in big cities and small, Pinchot promoted his belief that the forest reserves were "made to be used, not just to look at," generating approval in the press and allies among the business class.[4]

The Forest Commission's work had stoked a still-amorphous conservation movement, with proponents of differing philosophies vying for the upper hand. The politicians and bureaucrats in charge were susceptible to industry pressure and corruption, among them Bliss, who, Johnson told Muir, had allowed Binger Hermann, McKinley's General Land Office commissioner, "to let the Sheep (i.e. the Wolves in Sheep's clothing) into the Oregon & Washington reserves." Hermann would soon become mired in the Oregon land-fraud scandal, in which state officials funneled low-priced public lands slated for settlers to lumber and livestock companies. Johnson warned Muir not to trust Bliss, "a thorough politician," and knew of what he spoke. Bliss's tenure would not survive McKinley's term.[5]

Meanwhile, tensions between Sargent and Pinchot escalated. Muir and Pinchot's relationship suffered as Sargent urged Muir to distance himself from the ambitious Pinchot and his commercial approach. Although Muir shared Pinchot's belief that the forests' resources should be used, while under careful management, and that such a policy was essential for Congress to agree to national forestlands, the two would continue to drift apart.[6]

In July 1897, as a hundred thousand prospectors rushed by ship, boat, and boot through Alaska to the remote Yukon region of northwest Canada to seek their fortunes and wreak havoc on the northern wilderness, Muir, a spry fifty-nine, prepared to return to the snowy north, this time with Sargent. Participants in the Klondike Gold Rush, the largest gold strike in North American history, had to traverse hundreds of miles of perilous river rapids and steep trails in extreme conditions. As with the California Gold Rush, most ended up finding more misery than fortune, while newspaper readers were riveted by their story. Muir and Sargent would be searching for something of more value to them: northern trees—pendulous Canadian hemlock, pagoda-like subalpine fir, and stately Sitka spruce.

Muir's time traveling with the Forest Commission culminated in an ode to the American forest, which ran in the *Atlantic* in August. "I may succeed in hammering & welding some ideas into shape for you, but it will take a long time," he had told Page in April. He had to compel articles "to come in like a cowboy dragging steers with a rope."

However, Page had received the article by mid-May and was thrilled. "We have had nothing in *The Atlantic Monthly* for a long time that it gives me more pleasure to publish, both by reason of the subject and of the writer," he told Muir.[7]

In "The American Forests," Muir hearkened back to his religious roots with a poetic creation myth for the nation's woodlands: "The forests of America, however slighted by man, must have been a great delight to God; for they were the best he ever planted," he began. "The whole continent was a garden, and from the beginning it seemed to be favored above all the other wild parks and gardens of the globe. . . . These forests were composed of about five hundred species of trees, all of them in some way useful to man," and some were "lordly monarchs proclaiming the gospel of beauty like apostles." To Muir's eyes, they were fully alive. Nature fed them, dressed them, loaded them with flowers and fruit. The wind rustled their leaves, exercised their fibers, and pruned them. The snow made them more lovely. He described their beauty in all seasons—and then rang the alarm: "Even the fires of the Indians and the fierce shattering lightning seemed to work together only for good in clearing spots here and there for smooth garden prairies, and openings for sunflowers seeking the light. But when the steel axe

of the white man rang out in the startled air their doom was sealed."
He painted the dystopian scene that followed:

> In the settlement and civilization of the country, bread more than
> timber or beauty was wanted; and in the blindness of hunger, the
> early settlers, claiming Heaven as their guide, regarded God's trees
> as only a larger kind of pernicious weeds. . . . Accordingly, with no
> eye to the future, these pious destroyers waged interminable forest
> wars; chips flew thick and fast; trees in their beauty fell crashing by
> millions, smashed to confusion, and the smoke of their burning has
> been rising to heaven more than two hundred years.

The "bread and money seekers" denuded the Atlantic coast and
devastated the Mississippi River Valley and the vast Great Lakes pine
region. Finally, an "invading horde of destroyers called settlers" crossed
the Rockies to fell and burn "more fiercely than ever," at last reaching
"the wild side of the continent and . . . the great aboriginal forests" of
the Pacific coast. "Clearing has surely now gone far enough," he argued,
swinging back toward hope. "The remnant protected will yield plenty
of timber, a perennial harvest for every right use, without further diminution of its area, and will continue to cover the springs of the rivers
that rise in the mountains and give irrigating waters to the dry valleys
at their feet."[8]

He saw promise in the recent creation of national parks and forest
reservations and in the parks and street and highway plantings in all the
great cities. He believed they showed "the trend of awakening public
opinion." New York's Central Park, once vigorously opposed, was now
praised and renowned, and he believed the same would be true for the
national parks and forest reservations. "There will be a period of indifference on the part of the rich, sleepy with wealth, and of the toiling
millions, sleepy with poverty, most of whom never saw a forest; a period
of screaming protest and objection from the plunderers, who are as
unconscionable and enterprising as Satan. But light is surely coming,
and the friends of destruction will preach and bewail in vain."

Muir's notion of preservation was not without compassion for people.
"The United States government has always been proud of the welcome it
has extended to good men of every nation, seeking freedom and homes

and bread. Let them be welcomed still as nature welcomes them, to the woods as well as to the prairies and plains. They are invited to heaven, and may well be allowed in America. Every place is made better by them. Let them be as free to pick gold and gems from the hills, to cut and hew, dig and plant, for homes and bread, as the birds are to pick berries from the wild bushes, and moss and leaves for nests." The woods would not be diminished or worse off "any more than the sun is diminished in shining."[9]

While Muir notably took this pro-immigrant stance in an anti-immigrant era, he surprisingly rarely acknowledged the country's brutal displacement of Native Americans, whose long stewardship of the land he so admired. His focus was almost wholly trained on the urgent and irrevocable threat that American industry posed to the nation's wilderness. That was his consuming battle.

It was the "mere destroyers . . . tree-killers," he told the *Atlantic* readers, that the government must bring to bay. "For it must be told again and again, and be burningly borne in mind, that just now, while protective measures are being deliberated languidly, destruction and use are speeding on faster and farther every day. The axe and saw are insanely busy, chips are flying thick as snowflakes, and every summer thousands of acres of priceless forests, with their underbrush, soil, springs, climate, scenery, and religion, are vanishing away in clouds of smoke, while except in national parks, not one forest guard is employed." Muir already knew the power of his words, even if they were difficult to put on paper sometimes, and the necessity of repeating his message. His unabashed faith and relentless pursuit of truth would make him a formidable—and to some, a maddening—opponent in future environmental battles.

Muir added with Twain-like wry humor, "Any fool can destroy trees. They cannot run away; and if they could, they would still be destroyed—chased and hunted down as long as fun or a dollar could be got out of their bark hides, branching horns, or magnificent bole backbones." He closed his grand pro-forest essay with a pithy line: "God has cared for these trees, saved them from drought, disease, and avalanches; but he cannot save them from fools—only Uncle Sam can do that."[10]

"The *Atlantic* paper is good & I hear people speak of it," Johnson allowed, while bidding Muir not to "let Page allure you away from your first love." That steady flame, the *Century*, had published an editorial in the September issue titled "The Forest Commission's Great Public Service." In it Johnson said that Cleveland had set a standard for President McKinley, whose administration now had to deal with this "belated and critical problem." The large scale of the reserves, which opponents had balked at—and Johnson believed "posterity will doubtless pronounce . . . blamable moderation"—had been necessary to jar the nation, especially the West, into considering the need to save the forests.[11]

That same month, the *Century* published a story by Muir that Johnson had been waiting a long time for. Dating back to Muir's trip to Alaska in 1880, it was a remarkable tale about a dog and a death-defying adventure in a blizzard on Taylor Bay's Brady Glacier. The "short-legged and bunchy-bodied" dog, Stickeen, named after some members of the Stickeen tribe who viewed the improbable pooch as a "good-luck totem" and "mysterious fountain of wisdom," belonged to Muir's traveling companion Hall Young, a Presbyterian evangelist who would come to be known as the Mushing Parson. Muir was an extraordinary in-person storyteller, and Johnson had enjoyed the harrowing and heartwarming tale on many occasions, once thrice in a single day at different gatherings, but the written version had taken seventeen long years.[12]

"The dog story is at hand and we are correspondingly happy," Johnson enthused. "I have done the story a service by cutting out some of the preliminary material," he told Muir, explaining that his descriptions of Stickeen's "fine qualities" there gave away the surprise. "Remember that this is my story as well as yours," Johnson added. "I know how it is most effective." Still, he had "not dared to add a line."

"I acknowledge your part interest in the pup, as I would never have written the story had you not urged me to do so," replied Muir. "Anyhow be sure to leave the legs of the article long enough to distinctly reach the ground. This Stickeen story easily told has cost me more time & work than anything else I ever wrote." All the same, Johnson was right to be excited; the reward would be Muir's most cherished and enduring tale.[13]

In October, Muir did receive a rival offer for his affections. Page, who in addition to editing the *Atlantic* also served as a literary adviser to the Boston publisher Houghton Mifflin, wrote him a beguiling letter. Burroughs was visiting him and "talks about nothing else so earnestly as about you and your work. He declares in the most emphatic fashion that it will be a misfortune too great to estimate if you do not write up all those bags of notes which you have gathered." Page's offer was simple: "*The Atlantic* wants all the matter that you will write, and . . . Messrs. Houghton, Mifflin & Company," publishers of Emerson, Thoreau, and Burroughs, "wish to bring it out in beautiful and attractive book form." He told Muir to name his terms. "I shall not die satisfied if your bags of notes are not turned into literature," he concluded. His courtship was hard to resist.[14]

By December, when Johnson suggested to Muir that he retain the book rights to his *Atlantic Monthly* articles because the *Century* wanted to be his book publisher, Muir replied that Houghton Mifflin had already acquired the rights to his *Atlantic* stories for two books. "I considered that the *Century* had already got all they were willing to take on Alaska and Forestry," he explained. "If you, my very friend, were the Century Co. all would be plain sailing without rock, cross current, headwind, fog bank." Well, almost. He could not resist coming clean about one more thing: "I'm sorry the title of my last article 'Stickeen' was changed to vulgar caddy adventure with a dog and a glacier—Ever thine John Muir."

Muir's letter "shocked" Johnson, though he leavened his response with a touch of sarcasm: "Last night I got even with you by taking it out on Tesla, who, being a friend of mine, will probably give anything important he has to a rival magazine!" As to the story title, he fired back, "You can write very beautiful articles, but when it comes to a title you cannot hold a candle to a *Century* editor!"[15]

The following year Muir published four stories in the *Atlantic*, including one on Yellowstone and two on Yosemite. After the first, Page wrote him, "The January *Atlantic Monthly* has not long been before the public, but we are hearing all sorts of pleasant things about your paper that constitutes the best part of it." In his piece, "The Wild Parks and Forest Reservations of the West," Muir called these places "the wildest health and pleasure grounds accessible and available to tourists seeking escape from care and dust and early death." The story did the delicate dance that was Muir's literary hallmark: simultaneously painting an unsparing picture of the besieged natural world while proffering optimism and faith in the healing power of nature and man's ability to save it from himself—all with a pleasing poetic flourish.[16]

In just thirty years, Muir had seen California's once-grand Central Valley, "one bed of golden and purple flowers" fifty miles wide and five hundred long, "ploughed and pastured out of existence, gone forever." Sierra forests had been "hacked and trampled," except where guarded by US Cavalry. The Sierra Reserve was sadly neglected. "In the fog of tariff, silver, and annexation politics it is left wholly unguarded" against heedless lumbermen, ravenous hordes of sheep, and shepherds who burned both the seedlings—the forest's future—and "countless thousands of the venerable giants."[17]

Still, Muir's indomitable optimism prevailed: "If every citizen could take one walk through this reserve, there would be no more trouble about its care; for only in darkness does vandalism flourish." And herein lay his solution. Nature needed people as much as people needed nature. It was a symbiotic relationship. Four national parks—Yellowstone, Yosemite, General Grant, and Sequoia—were easily enough reached. Muir beckoned readers to "wander here a whole summer, if you can. Thousands of God's wild blessings will search you and soak you as if you were a sponge, and the big days will go by uncounted."

In 1897 Muir's old friend Galen Clark, who had served two stints as Guardian of the Valley over half a century, finally conceded that a younger man was needed for the job and "retired." Even then, he would stay in Yosemite as a tourist-camp manager and guide while writing books about the place and its former inhabitants. The following spring the Yosemite commissioners asked the Sierra Club to help establish a visitors' center in the state-run park. Together they renovated a cottage and installed a library and an herbarium. They enlisted William Colby, fresh out of law school, as a summer attendant, with the club and the commission splitting his salary. It was a good hire for the Sierra Club. Colby would not only end up serving as Muir's right-hand man, but he would also help lead the club for six decades. In Yosemite State Park, John P. Irish was out, and the Sierra Club was in.[18]

The Scottish-born, Iowa-bred secretary of agriculture Jim Wilson was in office for sixteen years (and is still the longest-serving cabinet member in US history). In all that time perhaps the most momentous decision

Wilson made was offering Gifford Pinchot the job as head of the Forestry Division, then a small and inconsequential unit. At first Pinchot declined the role. But Wilson told him that he understood that the division was "in the Dark Ages," and that Pinchot could direct it as he saw fit. He accepted, and Wilson gave him the simple title Forester, instead of Chief of the Division, which pleased Pinchot, who later quipped that "in Washington chiefs of division were thick as leaves in Vallombrosa. Foresters were not." Pinchot would transform this sleepy division, considered a "bureau of information" by his predecessor, Dr. Bernhard Fernow, who had dispensed guidance on shade trees, ornamental plants, and, according to Pinchot, "the uses of timber after it was cut" but nothing on "applying forest management to American timberlands before they were cut." Taking over his diminutive offices, Pinchot found "clear proof that the Division wasn't thinking about practical Forestry." There were no marking hatchets, the tool with which "the forester marks the trees to cut or leave standing," he noted. "The marking hatchet carries Forestry into the woods," which is exactly what he intended to do.[19]

Under Pinchot, the Division of Forestry (renamed the US Forest Service in 1905) would be a force for commercial conservation. But forest destruction—furthered by the railroads, which had been ceded tens of millions of acres to build out the nation's rail system—accelerated in unprotected places. Not only did the trains burn wood for fuel and spark accidental fires, but the rail companies set fires on purpose to clear land for towns, which in turn created the need for more timber. The railroads also provided wider and wider access to loggers, who diligently stripped the Rockies, the Cascades, the Olympics, and the Sierra Nevada of trees. California, like the Pacific Northwest, was now a lumber source for the entire nation and for export.

As far back as the early postbellum years, before Muir had made his first foray into Yosemite, Michigan timber barons, foreseeing the exhaustion of their own vaunted firs, spruces, and white pines, speculated on California's best timberland; its sugar pines, they thought, would suffice after Michigan's trees were long gone.

By 1899, the Madera Flume and Trading Company, having logged in the vicinity of Yosemite Valley for a quarter of a century, had ingeniously consumed all its forestland—ingeniously because at first much of it had seemed inaccessible. Madera Flume had begun as California

Lumber in 1874, when the Southern Pacific Railroad reached the San Joaquin Valley, providing a way for timber to be hauled to the marketplace. Elsewhere, logs were floated to mills on rivers, but Sierra Nevada streams ebbed and flowed dramatically with the snowmelt, sometimes vanishing altogether. So California Lumber had built a giant flume, a fifty-two-mile V-shaped timber-and-stone colossus, running from its rough-cut mill on Gooseberry Flat to the mill town of Madera ("wood" in Spanish). The flume, which used all the wood the company could mill during the two years of its construction, followed the Fresno River, traversing canyons, streams, and mountainsides and dropping almost a mile along the way. Together with an army of lumberjacks and oxen teams cutting and dragging the trees through the forest, this rustic engineering marvel would devour the forests near Yosemite Valley for half a century.

At the Gooseberry Flat mill, the logs were sorted by size, bundled, and launched into the flume, which dropped steeply down to a station at Salt Springs (today Oakhurst), where wranglers hitched the bundles together in trains. Every six miles timber-herders at herding stations ensured the steady passage of the logs. At the Poison Switch station, they guided the trains through a sharp bend. At French Graveyard, the Hump, and China Store, more bundles were connected. By the time a lumber train reached the finishing mills at Madera, it might stretch several miles. Every day 130,000 board feet floated into Madera to be milled into doors, sashes, or cabinets.[20]

The system was smooth until the vicissitudes of nature or downturns in the economy wreaked havoc. When a devastating drought caused panic in 1877, the lumber stacked up in the yards and California Lumber went bankrupt. It relaunched the next year as Madera Flume and Trading, which managed to survive a lumberyard fire in 1881 and a national depression in the 1890s to continue turning the ancient trees of Yosemite's southwestern border into springy timber.

After two and a half decades, however, the company's forests finally tapped out, and it looked as if Madera Flume's lumbering days were drawing to a close. Then Elmer Cox, of Madera Commercial Bank, which had heavily invested in Madera Flume, paid a visit to Arthur Hill, the mayor of Saginaw, Michigan, who was sitting on a vast tract of timberland next to Madera Flume's now denuded slopes. In May

PART III

THE WATER STEALERS

•

No two streams are alike. I fancy I could discriminate between Merced water and all others. Merced water is one thing, Tuolumne another, Kings River another, while town water, deadened and lost, is nothing—not water at all.

—John Muir, August 1875

124

View of Hetch Hetchy Valley and the Tuolumne River
from the southwest, by Isaiah West Taber, early 1900s.

Presidents: William McKinley, Republican, 1897–1901; Theodore Roosevelt, Republican, 1901–09; William Howard Taft, Republican, 1909–13

Secretaries of the Interior: Ethan Hitchcock, 1899–1907; James R. Garfield, 1907–09

San Francisco Mayors: Washington Bartlett, Democrat, 1883–87; James Phelan, Democrat, 1897–1902; Eugene "Handsome Gene" Schmitz, Union Labor, 1902–07; Edward Taylor, Democrat, 1907–10

San Francisco Watermen: Franklin Lane, city attorney, 1899–1902; Percy Long, city attorney, 1902–06, 1908–16; Carl Grunksy, city engineer; Marsden Manson, city engineer; Michael O'Shaughnessy, city engineer

Allies of Muir and Johnson: Edward Harriman, financier and railroad executive, New York City; Edmund Whitman, Appalachian Mountain Club, Boston; Horace McFarland, president, American Civic Association, Harrisburg, Pennsylvania

Chapter 15

San Francisco's Thirst

It had been fifty years since criminal gangs burned down the chaotic Gold Rush–era town of San Francisco seven times in eighteen months, repeatedly causing millions of dollars of damage. Each time the city rebuilt itself with amazing vigor, but its Achilles' heel was clear: the peninsula—arid and buffeted by fierce winds—was wildly incendiary and severely lacking in sources of fresh water. It also had little firefighting infrastructure. At first water was transported by carts, a laborious system that was inadequate in fighting fires. By 1857 a private business called San Francisco Water Works was bringing water in by flume from Lobos Creek along the Golden Gate shore to pumps that distributed it in the city. Another enterprise, Spring Valley Water Works, dispensed water from a valley that lay on the eastern slope of Nob Hill. At the end of the Civil War, the two merged under the latter name and built an outsize and ruthless statewide water monopoly worthy of the Gilded Age.

Its shareholders included some of the state's wealthiest and most powerful citizens—mining magnate James Ben Ali Haggin and his business partner Lloyd Tevis, banking tycoons Darius Ogden Mills and William Ralston, and railroad millionaires Leland Stanford and Collis P. Huntington—to whom Spring Valley returned 59 percent of its revenues in 1870 and 69 percent in 1875. At first Spring Valley had found its sources on the San Francisco Peninsula, but as its needs grew, the company pursued water south of the city, often under false pretenses or by using eminent domain. Its Swiss engineer channeled the waters of one creek in a redwood flume and designed reservoirs to be built later in the San Andreas Valley and Crystal Springs to take advantage of the hundred thousand acres of seized watershed. When needed, Spring Valley could also draw from the undesirable Lake Merced, which lay in sandy terrain near sea level in the southwest part of San Francisco and was contaminated by proximity to the city's exploding population. Even worse, and eventually condemned, was Lobos Creek, which flowed past two hospitals—one sitting on pits full of its own sewage—and several crowded cemeteries.

In 1877, the city had offered to buy out Spring Valley for a princely $11 million (or $280 million in today's money). Spring Valley balked. Even the changing of California's constitution in 1879 to give the city the right to set its water rates backfired, only fueling corruption, with members of the political machine led by "Blind Boss" Buckley receiving "retainers" to manipulate votes. In 1883, when Mayor Washington Bartlett, elected on his promise to reduce water rates, vetoed an ordinance that would have produced the opposite effect, the supervisors overrode his veto 9–2.[1]

By the turn of the century, the apportioning of water was a serious bone of contention throughout California. Connected by rail to the rest of the nation for three decades (and crisscrossed by cable cars for nearly as long), San Francisco, for one, was growing at a rapid rate, its population spiraling north of three hundred thousand, and its skyline and wealth expanding commensurately. The city already consumed nearly 30 million gallons of Spring Valley's total daily capacity of 35 million gallons and was, by the time of the next census, poised to top half a million people, who would need no less than 40 million gallons a day. In the fall of 1900, Spring Valley grabbed another 10 million gallons a day from Laguna and Calaveras Creeks, sources from the densely cultivated environs of Oakland and Berkeley, which, however, also needed more water.

Finally San Francisco, one of the nation's most notoriously boss-ridden and corrupt cities, was positioning itself to secure its own water source and no longer be bilked by the water tycoons. In 1897, its citizens had elected a reform mayor with a grand vision. Born at the outbreak of the Civil War, James D. Phelan was the wealthy son of a forty-niner. His ambitious father, also James, was a whiskey merchant who had lost his business in the fires and then risen from the ashes to become a real estate, banking, and business tycoon, establishing the First National Gold Bank (later renamed the First National Bank of San Francisco) shortly after the war. The gem in the family crown was the Phelan Building, a six-story triangular masterpiece in the heart of the city's business district, touted as "the finest business structure on the Pacific Coast . . . thoroughly fire and earthquake proof."

After growing up in cloistered privilege, the younger Phelan attended Saint Ignatius College and Hastings College of Law and toured Europe, writing about history and architecture. Back in San Francisco, he thrived as his father's business partner while harboring ambitions for his hometown inspired by London, Paris, and Rome. After inheriting the family fortune in 1892, Phelan expanded it and became one of the city's largest real-estate moguls. Encouraged by *San Francisco Daily Evening Bulletin* editor Fremont Older, Phelan ran for mayor in 1896, campaigning on reform, and won.

The young mayor wasted little time in pursuing his agenda. He immediately threw out eight of the twelve city supervisors on grounds of corruption. Refusing to leave, they occupied City Hall, but Phelan quickly had the police remove them. While a judge later reinstated them, the mayor had made his point. Almost as urgent as the stench of corruption, however, was the stench. In May 1898, Phelan and the supervisors asked civil engineer Carl Grunsky to devise a plan to renovate the city's sewage system. Grunsky looked underground and discovered a jumble of broken and obstructed pipes. Stormwater regularly sent sewage into the streets, and the pipes emptied, unfiltered, at the waterfront anyway. After assessing the situation in detail and projecting the level of demand all the way to the 1960s, Grunsky calculated the cost of repairs and upgrades at $4.6 million.

Phelan also hammered out a charter mandating that the city acquire its own water supply. Despite fierce opposition from the party machine, his "1900 Charter" was adopted by a vote of the citizens. It essentially declared war on Spring Valley, which had long bribed and bullied municipal leaders and smothered competitors—and would not go away without a brawl. The city, meanwhile, had chafed under the private control of its water, disputing the monopoly's rates in court and in the press, and had formed a committee to chart a new course, to gain "absolute control" over its water, like most of the nation's major cities.[2]

Now that Phelan had the power to form a board of public works—thanks to the 1900 Charter—he did so and appointed Grunsky and Marsden Manson to it. They would be his soldiers in the fight, with Manson, a Virginia Military Institute civil engineer with a PhD from the University of California, eventually carrying the load for the city in what would be an epic contest. Their search for a municipal water source went as far as Lake Tahoe. San Francisco needed electricity as well, and Tahoe's water supply could be used to generate hydroelectric power. There was, however, one significant catch. Lake Tahoe was partly in Nevada. Using it would likely mean a lengthy court battle. Surveyors sent to assess the situation in 1900 suggested, instead, a source closer to home: the Sierra Nevada.

The Sierra Nevada search included surveys of two potential reservoir sites on the Tuolumne River in or near Yosemite National Park: Hetch Hetchy, with a watershed of more than four hundred and fifty square miles, and Lake Eleanor, less than a fifth that size. In his detailed report, Grunsky zeroed in on these, believing the city should make use of the Tuolumne near its origin by damming either Lake Eleanor or Hetch Hetchy. According to his estimates, only one was necessary. Grunsky recommended Lake Eleanor, which, together with Spring Valley's sources and Cherry Creek, a small tributary to the west of Hetch Hetchy, could supply the city for the next century.

This was not the first time Lake Eleanor and Hetch Hetchy had been pegged for the job. While collecting water data for needy cities, California's first state engineer, William Hall, had surveyed Eleanor in 1882, the same year an engineer for the town of Sonora, due east of San Francisco, mapped out a Hetch Hetchy water project that would eventually derail over the estimated cost. In 1885, Hall had joined John Wesley Powell's irrigation survey of the West to search for water sources. Hall's assistant mapped out Lake Eleanor but not Hetch Hetchy because, according to Hall, Powell refused to condemn so spectacular a valley to water storage until necessary "in the very distant future." Even though Congress had passed the Yosemite National Park bill, which included

Hetch Hetchy, in 1890, the following year, the Geological Survey again tagged Hetch Hetchy as an ideal place for a dam.[3]

On January 23, 1901, Grunsky told the public works board that the city should immediately secure rights from the Interior Department to build Hetch Hetchy and Lake Eleanor reservoirs to beat out speculators. The only problem: Hetch Hetchy lay within Yosemite National Park, in a place that John Muir and the Sierra Club would certainly defend tooth and nail. On Grunsky's recommendation, Phelan pushed ahead nonetheless, making the request for water rights in February. In 1890, Congress had, while assigning the interior secretary the duty of managing federal land reservations, prohibited the use of lakes and meadows deemed "natural curiosities or wonders" as reservoirs. In response to Phelan's request, however, Congress now passed the Right of Way Act of 1901, allowing grants of right-of-way through public lands to support communications, electrical, and water systems at the interior secretary's discretion.[4]

After settling on the Tuolumne as the city's best option, Grunsky, with the board's approval, set about planning a system to harness it with the same alacrity and foresight he had exhibited in revamping the city's sewers. He surveyed Lake Eleanor and Hetch Hetchy, planned waterworks, and priced out the needed canals, pipelines, and pumps. His detailed report of July 28, 1902, "Tuolumne River Project," convinced the city to file a claim at the Land Office the very next day. But to do so, it had to get creative. As Phelan and others later explained, the Interior Department's regulations did not provide for a municipality to file for a reservoir site—according to the Land Office it had never before been done—so it was filed in Phelan's name. The city's furtive claim would also delay Spring Valley's inevitable counterpunch as well as the wrath of the Sierra Club. A sign nailed to a sturdy young oak tree, at the base of which was an old US Geological Survey benchmark, on the north bank of the Tuolumne above the narrowest part of the Hetch Hetchy gorge, marked Phelan's claim.

In mid-October, Phelan signed rights-of-way applications for two reservoirs, each nearly twelve hundred acres, and filed them in the Stockton Land Office. With this simple act, he ignited a water war that would grip the nation.[5]

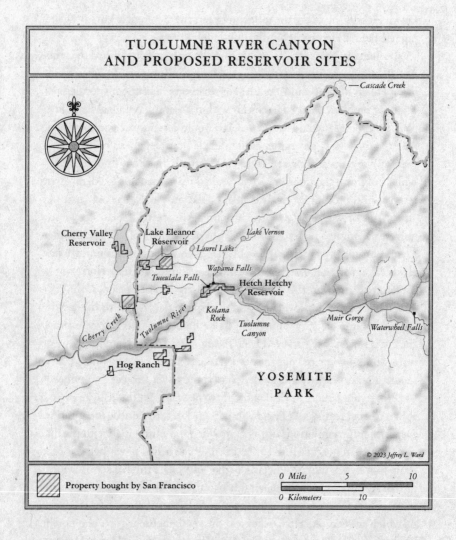

TUOLUMNE RIVER CANYON
AND PROPOSED RESERVOIR SITES

— Cascade Creek

Cherry Valley
Reservoir

Lake Eleanor
Reservoir

Lake Vernon

Laurel Lake

Wapama Falls

Tueeulala Falls

Hetch Hetchy
Reservoir

Kolana
Rock

Cherry Creek

Tuolumne River

Tuolumne
Canyon

Muir Gorge

Waterwheel Falls

Hog Ranch

YOSEMITE
PARK

© 2023 Jeffrey L. Ward

Property bought by San Francisco

0 Miles   5   10

0 Kilometers   10

In the summer of 1901, Muir led the first of what would become annual
Sierra Club "High Trips" to the mountains, providing lessons on the
natural world and campcraft, physical challenge, camaraderie, and communion with nature to the participants, many of whom had never been
to the mountains, expanding his vision for a visited wilderness beyond
anything he could have foreseen. The destination for the first trip was

the Tuolumne River, whose waters were now secretly targeted by San Francisco. All spring Muir had resisted Johnson's invitations to come East to attend meetings of the prestigious National Institute of Arts and Letters, saying he had to continue to "peg away at the Sequoia Parks" and urging Johnson to attend the "Big Tuolumne Meeting" that summer to see the "blessed results of your work in making the Yosemite National Park" and—needling him again for his hard time in the brush—to "once more brave the canyon chaparral." They lived in their own worlds, which intersected primarily in the realm of ideas and the written word.[6]

The High Trips were initiated by Will Colby, now a twenty-six-year-old miners' rights attorney, who had advanced from being summer attendant of the Yosemite visitors' center to secretary of the Sierra Club. While the club's board was ambivalent about his idea, its president was not. Muir, long a proponent of such excursions for the club, warmly encouraged Colby, who convinced a reluctant board to let him try. Shortly thereafter, in the fall of 1900, Colby enlisted a recent arrival in San Francisco, Ed Parsons, a well-traveled Sherwin-Williams salesman and amateur nature photographer, to help him tackle the challenges of planning the trip for the following summer. Parsons, who had climbed with the Mazamas, a Portland-based mountaineering society, would be a steady lieutenant. Ninety-six members signed up for a monthlong trek from Yosemite Valley to Tuolumne Meadows. To prepare, the attendees read Muir's *Mountains of California*.

"As the time draws nigh, I do wish I were with you," Johnson wrote. "I hope that this excursion will stir everybody up to insisting that the government patrol of the Sierra Reserve should be more rigid." Instead of Johnson, Muir was accompanied by Keith, who would later give Colby a painting to thank him for his organizational efforts, Wanda, now twenty and a rising sophomore at Berkeley, and Helen, fifteen. It was the girls' first trip to the mountains.[7]

During the days there were climbs up Mount Dana and Mount Lyell and at night bonfires with singing, storytelling, and lectures by the likes of C. Hart Merriam on biology, Muir on the glacial formation of the Sierra Nevada, and other experts on forestry and the history of Yosemite. But Muir was the focal point of the outing, as the writer Ella

Muir encouraged women, like men, to come to the wilderness.
"Girl graduates, said to be sweet," he wrote, "are not so sweet as girl mountaineers.
Never before have the mountains seen so many young people camping in their
hospitable, life-giving gardens. . . . May their tribe increase until, like Switzerland,
all the mountains echo with their happy voices." Little Joe LeConte captured this
image along the Kings River for the Sierra Club in 1906.

Sexton put it, "guide and apostle" whose "gentle, kindly face, genial
blue eyes, and quaint, quiet observations on present and past conditions
impressed us unforgettably." The trip was considered a great success,
and the next summer's High Trip would double in size.

Among the most successful elements was the addition of women to
what was then largely considered a man's sphere of arduous backcountry hiking and camping. "Nearly all of the women in this party were
Berkeley or Stanford girls," Parsons later recounted, "and their vigor
and endurance were a revelation to all of us. . . . One confirmed mountaineer said that it was the first time he had ever been camping with
women . . . but after this experience he would never go to the mountains
again without the added pleasure of the companionship of women." The
feeling was mutual. Wanda and Helen would enthusiastically return
the following year for the High Trip to Kings Canyon, where Wanda
would report that the college women in camp—sixty undergraduates

and alumnae from twenty different colleges—held a meeting on top of a large granite boulder. "There wasn't one of us that could not comfortably walk twenty miles, or if necessary do anything that has to be done around a camp from cooking a camp meal to packing a mule." Women had proved they belonged in the wilderness and would play a big role in the life of the Sierra Club.[8]

CHAPTER 16

Camping with the President

I n September 1901, six months into his second term, President
William McKinley was shot at point-blank range by an anarchist
in the Temple of Music concert hall at the Pan-American Exposition in Buffalo, New York. He had just given a speech in which he
marveled at the speed and connectedness of modern life and called for
"prosperity, happiness, and peace to all." The glittering exhibition,
lit by means of a recent improvement, an alternating-current power
plant at Niagara Falls, twenty-five miles away, was meant to promote
"commercial well-being and good understanding among the American
Republics." Instead, it cast a pall over the nation, as McKinley hung
on for a week and even looked as if he might survive, until his wound
was beset by gangrene. The President died eight days after being shot,
making him the third president, after Lincoln and Garfield, to be assas-
sinated since the Civil War.

McKinley's vice president, Theodore Roosevelt, an amateur naturalist, writer, rancher, and hunter, who had once aspired to being a
museum director and was at the time in the Adirondacks, where he
had climbed Mount Marcy, New York's tallest peak, rushed to Buffalo
by buckboard and train, reaching the city in twelve hours. At the age
of forty-two, Roosevelt was sworn into the nation's highest office on
September 14, 1901, becoming the youngest president ever. A hero of
the Spanish-American War in Cuba and a former New York governor,
Roosevelt would ramp up the Progressive Era with his Square Deal, a

commitment to busting trusts, protecting consumers, and championing the nation's wilds.

In that regard Houghton Mifflin's release, in the fall of 1901, of Muir's second book, *Our National Parks*, a collection of ten "sketches" from the *Atlantic Monthly*, six of which were about Yosemite, was certainly auspicious. In the book, dedicated to his friend and "defender of our country's forests" Charles Sargent, Muir said he sensed that "tired, nerve-shaken, over-civilized" Americans were turning to nature, "tracing rivers to their sources, getting in touch with the nerves of Mother Earth; jumping from rock to rock, feeling the life of them, learning the songs of them, panting in whole-souled exercise, and rejoicing in deep, long-drawn breaths of pure wildness." They were discovering that "going to the mountains is going home and that wildness is a necessity." The mountains were sources not only of timber and rivers for irrigation, but wellsprings for life itself. He had attempted to show not just their beauty but their "all-embracing usefulness," to stir people to visit them and "get them into their hearts." This alone would ensure "their preservation and right use."[1]

There was continuity in the Department of the Interior, where McKinley's secretary, Ethan Hitchcock, remained in charge under Roosevelt. On January 30, 1903, Hitchcock officially denied former mayor Phelan's applications for water rights in Yosemite. Much of the needed right-of-way was over private land, where the department had no say, he wrote, and the survey used in the maps was not authorized by his department. But primarily Hitchcock, an Alabaman and former ambassador to Russia, had concluded that his duty to preserve scenic beauty prevailed over San Francisco's request for water.

The San Francisco city attorney, Franklin K. Lane, responded to the issues raised by Hitchcock, arguing that the dams would transform Hetch Hetchy into a beautiful lake and ensure that Lake Eleanor would never run dry while regulating water flow below the dams to better serve towns and the agricultural needs of the San Joaquin Valley. "The waters of the winter and spring freshets which flow to the sea unused, often doing great damage," he wrote, ". . . should be impounded in reservoirs for use in the late summer." In April, Lane went to Washington to appeal the decision in person. He argued that the water should be put to the "highest possible use" and that that use was to serve the people of San Francisco.

But in December, Hitchcock ended the discussion. If the Yosemite National Park Act of 1890 required him to preserve the park in a natural state and the Right of Way Act of 1901 authorized him to grant water development for a city's beneficial use, he believed the former act, which designated him as park preserver, took precedence. Phelan and the new mayor, Eugene "Handsome Gene" Schmitz, a dashing musician and orchestra conductor, were not pleased—and not deterred either. Schmitz, notoriously corrupt, simply had to search for a new path forward to reform the city's equally notoriously corrupt water system.[2]

On April 21, 1903, Muir turned sixty-five, and a week later, the nation's greatest nature advocate became a citizen. Muir had thought he was a citizen by virtue of his father's naturalization and had registered to vote in 1896. But when he later applied for a passport and did not have his father's naturalization papers, he found he needed to apply for citizenship himself. He did so at the Contra Costa County Superior Court and was granted his citizenship on April 28. Less than a month after that, he would have the honor of spending three days and nights camping with the twenty-sixth president of his now-officially-adopted country. It came about when their mutual friend C. Hart Merriam suggested that Muir serve as the President's guide in Yosemite during his upcoming whistle-stop tour of the West. Muir, realizing how providential this could prove to be for his beloved mountains, postponed his planned trip across Asia with Sargent. In his last letter of 1901 to Johnson, Muir had told him that he would write the President on forest matters but had no hope for Yosemite recession because the governor strongly opposed it. Now he could make his case to the most powerful man in the nation in person. Roosevelt's support just might make the difference.[3]

Muir would rather have been on his tour with Sargent, searching for exotic plant species in far-flung places, but too much was at stake. Never mind that Roosevelt, when he invited Muir to be his guide in Yosemite, said all he wanted was to be out in the open with Muir and "to drop politics absolutely for four days."

Just back from Italy, Johnson wrote to Muir. He had attended a court ball, three papal functions, and a private presentation to the royal family but confessed he was "glad to be back again in 'God's country.'" He was excited about Muir's upcoming trip with the President. "I know what a great pleasure awaits him in seeing this wonderland under your competent guidance. I hope the President will be impressed with the desirability of the merging of the old Yosemite into our National Park."[4]

Muir and the head of Yosemite Stage & Turnpike's travel office at the Palace Hotel, where Roosevelt would stay while in San Francisco, made plans for mounts, pack animals, gear, provisions, and park rangers to serve as guides. On May 14, 1903, thirteen years after the creation of Yosemite National Park, Muir and Roosevelt, and a party of eight, which included George Pardee, the governor of California, and Ben Wheeler, the president of the University of California, boarded the overnight train from Oakland to Raymond, the nearest rail terminus to the park entrance at the time. Rutherford B. Hayes, the first sitting president to visit the West Coast, had taken a carriage tour of Yosemite in 1880. And though Garfield and Grant both visited Yosemite while not in office, Roosevelt would be the first active president to tour the park in more than two decades.

The train arrived at Raymond at 7:30 a.m. Once a frontier outpost known as Wildcat Station, the town, where Yosemite tourists and supplies for Madera Sugar Pine Lumber were the most frequent off-loads, had an impressive turntable for rotating the locomotive for its return trip. The town was all decked out in bunting and flags and already bustling with a crowd of more than a thousand people. Muir now got a taste of what it was like to be President Roosevelt. As a band blared away, the excited spectators cheered. Then the President, eager for the wilderness and wearing a Norfolk jacket, leather puttees, and a wide-brimmed hat, addressed the crowd from a platform that had been erected in front of a store. As soon as he could, he boarded the eleven-passenger, open-air stage waiting to carry him to the Mariposa Grove of Big Trees. He climbed in front beside the driver, followed by Pardee, Wheeler, and the rest of the official party, including the President's secretary, William Loeb; the secretary of the navy; the surgeon general; and the president of

Columbia University. But a special seat was saved for Muir, just behind Roosevelt, so he could narrate the sights along the way. After what had happened to McKinley, a second stage with Secret Service agents and attendants followed close behind, and they were accompanied by a detachment of thirty US Cavalry on dapple-gray horses.

The coaches traveled eighteen miles to the Ahwahnee Tavern, where they stopped for lunch. Afterward they continued on to Wawona and the Mariposa Grove. Here they were greeted by two photographers: Berkeley professor J. N. "Little Joe" LeConte, Joseph LeConte's son and a future president of the Sierra Club, and Arthur Pillsbury, a stringer for Underwood & Underwood. Pillsbury and LeConte took photos of Roosevelt and Muir in front of the Grizzly Giant with the surgeon general just behind them and the others flanking them. They also took the obligatory tourist shot in the Wawona Tree, through which a tunnel had been cut in 1881 when Yosemite Stage & Turnpike enlarged a fire scar to create a tourist attraction. (The tree, weakened by the tunnel, would fall under a heavy crown of snow in the bitter winter of 1968–69.)[5]

Various promoters had made lavish promises and plans for the President's stay, and more than a thousand people had traveled to Yosemite on diverse invitations and pretenses to see him and hear him speak. But Roosevelt had other ideas. All he wanted to do was rough it with Muir. The valley commissioners, however, had assumed he would be with them and planned events every evening in his honor. With the photos out of the way, Roosevelt took matters into his own hands. He thanked the troops for their services and dismissed them, calling out as they left, "God bless you!" He dispatched the press and photographers and sent the stage with his entourage back to the Wawona Hotel, six miles away, for the gala dinner that evening. He would not be there.

Only a packer named Jackie Alder and park rangers Charlie Leidig and Archie Leonard remained behind with the President and Muir. The two civilian rangers, commissioned in 1899, knew the park better than anybody else; they patrolled its vast slopes and forests during long, lonely winters and guided the troopers stationed there in summers. They set up camp by a cool spring near the Sunset Tree. "Leidig, please don't let anybody disturb me," said the President, who was exhausted from the speeches and glad-handing of his whistle-stop tour. "I'm tired and want rest and sleep." While Roosevelt dozed, Leidig, who was an able cook, fried chicken and steak for supper, which would be served on tin plates beside the campfire.[6]

President Roosevelt with Muir, to his left, and others, standing before the Grizzly Giant in the Mariposa Grove. Roosevelt was eager to abandon such show and escape into the mountains with Muir. Underwood & Underwood, 1903.

Roosevelt and Muir had much to talk about as they ate, including a shared reverence for Emerson. While traveling on the Nile in 1873, the poet had met a young American boy who volunteered to row him ashore. That boy was Teddy Roosevelt. Now thirty years later, he camped with Muir in the same landscape where Muir had once spent time with Emerson. Muir told the story of Emerson's not accepting his invitation to sleep under the stars. "You would have made him perfectly comfortable," Roosevelt commented, "and he ought to have had the experience." After the meal, Roosevelt drank strong black coffee and bedded down near the Sunset Tree, where Alder had laid out a stack of forty wool blankets to serve as the President's bed and covers. "The first night was clear, and we lay down in the darkening aisles of the great Sequoia grove," Roosevelt wrote in his autobiography. "The majestic trunks, beautiful in color and in symmetry, rose round us like the pillars of a mightier cathedral than ever was conceived even by the fervor of the Middle Ages."[7]

The next day, Saturday, May 16, they got up a little after sunrise, broke camp, and mounted up by six thirty. Roosevelt told Leidig to "outskirt and keep away from civilization." Leidig led the group down the trail. Roosevelt's official party had spent the night at the Wawona Hotel. Leidig made sure to avoid it, crossing the river at Greeley's and heading for the remote Empire Meadows Trail. They ate a cold lunch on the ridge east of the meadows. The wind began to blow, and it snowed. Roosevelt could not have asked for a more Muir experience as they each took turns breaking trail through snowdrifts five feet deep while crossing Bridalveil Meadow toward Sentinel Dome. When Roosevelt bogged down, Leidig had to fetch a log to give his horse traction and get him out.

Muir proposed they camp on the ridge behind Sentinel Dome but deferred to Leidig, who wanted to go farther down toward Glacier Point, where they would have access to water and better camping conditions. Roosevelt and Muir sheltered without tents in a fir-fringed meadow, where they cooked their supper—steaks and coffee—over an open fire. It was a far cry from Muir's meals of bread and meat juice. The President, not even knowing how much better he had it, still declared, "Now this is bully!"

After dark Muir, saying, "Watch this," set fire to a large dead pine tree on a ledge and did a Scottish jig around the giant torch. Roosevelt joined in the fun, heartily cheering. It snowed again that night. But around the campfire all was warm, and the two discussed Muir's theory of the glacial formation of Yosemite and traded thoughts on conserving America's forests, Yosemite's in particular, and on the creation of other national parks. These were topics that roused both of them, and Leidig observed that there were moments when "both men wanted to do all the talking." Muir would later note that he "stuffed" Roosevelt "pretty well" on "the timber thieves, and the destructive work of the lumbermen, and other spoilers of the forests."

The two did not always see eye to eye, and Roosevelt would later praise Burroughs (an Easterner and more acquiescent) as "our greatest nature lover and nature writer," placing Muir second. Still, on this night, the seeds of a warm affection between Roosevelt and Muir were planted, and when they woke in the morning blanketed in four or five inches of snow, Roosevelt said, "This is bullier yet! I wouldn't miss this for anything."[8]

The group went to Glacier Point for another scheduled photo session, perhaps with the photographer Arthur Pillsbury although no one now knows for sure, resulting in what would prove to be one of Yosemite's enduring images: Roosevelt and Muir standing together at Overhanging Rock before a panorama of the valley. When they rode on, Roosevelt led the way, followed by Leidig, Leonard, Muir, and Alder. At lunchtime, they reached Little Yosemite Valley—two thousand feet above the main valley—the final plateau before the Merced, having descended twenty miles and fifty-six hundred feet of elevation from Mount Lyell, plunges into Nevada Fall. Here they came face-to-face with a sizable party waiting for the President at the top of the fall. Irritated by the intrusion, Roosevelt asked his crew to keep them away.[9]

In the afternoon, as they approached Yosemite Village, they were taken aback by a crowd and a giant welcome sign hanging from Upper Iron Bridge. A stout line of women gathered in the road to hail the President, who wanted nothing less and whispered to Leidig, "I am very much annoyed, could you do something?"

The mountain man, with a Winchester slung across his saddle and a six-shooter at his side, grinned. "Follow me," he said, then dug in his spurs, causing his mount to rear. The women tumbled back, and as they regrouped on either side, the President made his escape, waving his hat as he went.

But the would-be revelers were far from done. At the Sentinel Bridge, the Guardian of the Valley, the Yosemite commissioners, and the members of the official presidential party greeted the President and escorted him to a small gathering at a local artist's studio. He gave a brief address and announced, "This has been the grandest day of my life! One I shall long remember!" They had organized an elaborate reception and banquet for that evening at the Sentinel Hotel, importing a renowned chef from San Francisco's elite Bohemian Club. The fete was to be capped off by a play of searchlights on Yosemite Falls and an extravagant display of fireworks. Roosevelt dismissed the idea out of hand. When someone recommended he stay for the searchlights, he scoffed, "Nature faking."

President Roosevelt and Muir riding in the valley, with Half Dome in the distance, accompanied by park rangers Archie Leonard and Charles Leidig; left to right: Leonard, Muir, Roosevelt, Leidig.

If the presence of the park commissioners was a nuisance to Roosevelt, it was worse for Muir, who as the Sierra Club president was in a protracted battle with them. Under the pretense of economic progress and Pinchot's "greatest good," these officials, in Muir's opinion, were allowing the insidious destruction of the park they were sworn to protect. He was trying to win the minds of the decision makers—Roosevelt chief among them—with warm ethereal ideas about the wholeness of nature in God's design and the delicate interplay of all its parts. The commissioners were fighting with cold hard dollars. But it was not Muir who now looked sour. Taking in the scene, Roosevelt did not hide his displeasure. Perhaps it had been a stretch of the imagination to think that he was truly out in the wild, but this showy demonstration thoroughly scrubbed even that illusion. All he wanted was to spend another night in the woods with Muir. "We will pitch camp at Bridalveil!" he announced gruffly.[10]

The President and his camping party mounted and started for Bridalveil Meadow, where Muir had suggested they spend their last night. As they left Sentinel Bridge, Roosevelt saw a little girl holding a flag and stopped. Hoisting her up and giving her a kiss, he said, "God bless you, you little angel." Then he set her gently back down next to her mother, waved his party on, and started down the path.

"Charlie, I am hungry as hell," the President told Leidig, when they got to the meadow in the late afternoon. "Cook any damn thing you wish. How long will it take?" Leidig said he would have it ready in thirty minutes. The President lay down on his nest of blankets and snored so loudly that Leidig could hear him over the snapping of the fire. "President Roosevelt, John Muir, and Rangers Leidig and Leonard are encamped at the Bridalveil to-night in a grove of pines and firs," the *New York Times* reported. "Almost within the spray of the beautiful Bridalveil Fall the Chief Executive is resting after one of the most memorable days of his life." Following a dinner of chicken-fried steak, Muir and Roosevelt went out and strolled in the dark meadow. When they returned, they sat around the campfire. Although Leidig reported that the President told stories of, among other things, his lion-hunting trips, he had not yet been lion hunting in Africa, and it is hard to imagine that Roosevelt would have broached that topic with Muir after their discussion the previous night.

As the embers burned lower, Muir explained to Roosevelt that he had an ulterior motive for the trip: He hoped to save Mount Shasta and enlarge Yosemite National Park to include Yosemite Valley and the Mariposa Grove. And he hoped to persuade the President to help him. Exactly what was spoken that evening stayed between them, but Roosevelt later said, "John Muir talked even better than he wrote. His greatest influence was always upon those who were brought into personal contact with him."

Roosevelt would tell one other story about his time with Muir. As they were saying goodbye, Muir remembered that Sargent—Roosevelt would leave out his name, calling him only "a great tree lover and tree expert from the Eastern States who possessed a somewhat crotchety temper"—had written him a letter with a request. Muir, forgetting Sargent's candidness, handed the letter to Roosevelt, saying it would "explain just what I want."

Then Roosevelt would recount what he had read: "'I hear Roosevelt is coming out to see you. He takes a sloppy, unintelligent interest in forests, although he is altogether too much under the influence of that creature Pinchot, and you had better get from him letters to the Czar of Russia and the Emperor of China, so that we may have better opportunity to examine the forests and trees of the Old World.'" Roosevelt had laughed. "John, do you remember exactly the words in which this letter was couched?" he had asked.

"Good gracious! There was something unpleasant about you in it, wasn't there?" Muir had suddenly recalled. "I had forgotten. Give me the letter back." The President did, telling Muir that he "appreciated it far more than if it had not contained the phrases he had forgotten." While Roosevelt could not give Muir and Sargent letters to the two rulers, he promised letters to the appropriate US ambassadors, "which," he said, "would bring about the same result."[11]

In word and deed Roosevelt seemed revived. He wired Hitchcock from Sacramento: "I should like to have an extension of the forest reserves to include the California forest throughout the Mount Shasta region and its extensions. Will you not consult Pinchot about this and have the orders prepared?" On May 19, he sent Muir a transcript of the telegram to Hitchcock. "I trust I need not tell you, my dear sir, how happy were the days in the Yosemite I owed to you, and how greatly I appreciated them," he wrote. "I shall never forget our three camps; the first in the solemn temple of the giant sequoias; the next in the snowstorm among the silver firs near the brink of the cliff; and the third on the floor of the Yosemite, in the open valley, fronting the stupendous rocky mass of El Capitan, with the falls thundering in the distance on either hand."

Back on his whistle-stop tour, Roosevelt made use of freshly inspired elocution in the vein of his new friend Muir, telling Sacramentans:

Lying out at night under the giant sequoias had been like lying in a temple built by no hand of man, a temple grander than any human architect could by any possibility build, and I hope for the preservation of the groves of giant trees simply because it would be a shame to our civilization to let them disappear. They are monuments in themselves. . . . In California I am impressed by how great the state is, but I am even more impressed by the immensely greater greatness that lies in the future, and I ask that your marvelous natural resources be handed on unimpaired to your posterity. We are not building this country of ours for a day. It is to last through the ages.

The President's deeds would be even more impressive. He would sign into existence 5 national parks, 18 national monuments, 55 national bird sanctuaries and wildlife refuges, and 150 national forests. But John Muir wanted one thing more than anything else right now—the recession of the Yosemite grant, to make that special place whole.

Muir was certainly glad he had postponed his trip to spend time with Roosevelt. "Camping with the president was a remarkable experience," Muir told Merriam. "I fairly fell in love with him."[12]

1

John Muir in 1863 at age twenty-five.

2

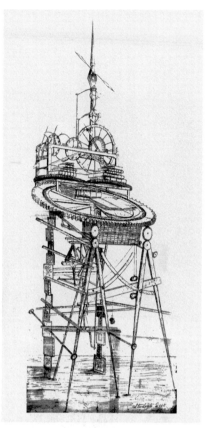

3

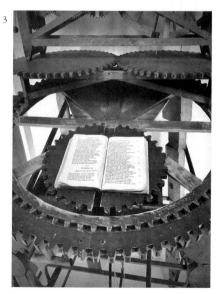

John Muir's drawing for a clock-desk he invented and built out of wood, now on display at the Wisconsin Historical Society at the University of Wisconsin–Madison.

Close-up of Muir's clock-desk. As Muir described in *The Story of My Boyhood and Youth*, at the beginning of each term, he loaded his desk with the books he needed to study. A bed, also of his own invention, set him on his feet in the morning and lit a lamp. After he quickly dressed, "a click was heard and the first book to be studied was pushed up from a rack below the top of the desk, thrown open, and allowed to remain there the number of minutes required. Then the machinery closed the book . . . moved the rack forward and threw up the next in order."

4

The Three Brothers, taken just east of El Capitan, by Carleton Watkins, ca. 1865. "A sharp earthquake shock at 7:30 a.m.," Muir wrote in his journal on January 5, 1873. "Rotary motion tremored the river. . . . A boulder from the second of the Three Brothers fell today."

5

6

Cathedral Rock, by Carleton Watkins, ca. 1861. A group of pinnacles, cliffs, and buttresses, Cathedral Rocks rise over the south side of Yosemite Valley, opposite El Capitan. The three major summits are called Higher, Middle, and Lower Cathedral Rocks. Writing shortly after the Civil War, John Hittell noted that the indigenous people called these formations Poosenachucka, meaning "large acorn cache."

Acorn cache in Yosemite Valley by Charles Pierce, ca. 1901. Black oak acorns, a staple food of the Miwuk, were gathered and stored each fall. Later, the meat would be dried and ground into flour for making mush or flat bread.

8

A Morning Council of the
Miwuk near the Merced River
in Yosemite Valley, June 1872,
by Eadweard Muybridge.

Mirror Lake, a small seasonal lake on Tenaya
Creek between North Dome and Half Dome,
is the last vestige of the glacial lake that filled
Yosemite Valley after the last Ice Age. In spring
and early summer, when filled with snowmelt,
the lake reflects the surrounding rock walls.
Photo by Carleton Watkins, ca. 1860.

Hutchings House with Sentinel Rock in the background. In 1864, James Hutchings, one of Yosemite Valley's first settlers—the publisher of *Hutchings' Illustrated California Magazine* (1856–61) and employer of Muir at his mill—bought the Upper Hotel, built in 1857, and renamed it Hutchings House.

Dr. John Strentzel, considered by some to be the father of California horticulture, at Alhambra, the Strentzels' prosperous fruit ranch, in 1885. Muir had recently brought a giant sequoia sapling back from the mountains in a dampened handkerchief and planted it at an intersection of farm lanes (in the wooden stand to the left of Strentzel). The sequoia eventually towered over the Big House. The 1844 adobe house (back left) was used as a storeroom and worker residence. The Muirs never lived in the adobe house, but their daughter Wanda and her family moved into it in 1906.

Turn-of-the-century glamping near Yosemite Falls. The admission of automobiles to the park in 1913, a move supported by the Sierra Club to provide greater ease of access to visitors, would change the nature of such visits forever.

11

The Big House, built in 1882 by Dr. Strentzel. After he died in 1890, the Muirs moved into the house with Louie's mother, and Muir lived there until his death in 1914.

Wanda, Helen, Louie, and John Muir with their dog Keeny—named for Stickeen, the heroic Alaskan dog that Muir made famous in a story—in front of the Big House, ca. 1905.

New York, January 2, 1902.

The next dinner of the National Institute of Arts and Letters will take place at the Aldine Association, 111 Fifth Avenue, New York, at seven o'clock on the evening of Friday, January 24, 1902, when, by request of the Institute, Mr. Brander Matthews will give an address on "The Art of the Dramatist," to be followed by general discussion of the subject.

The cost to each member, without wine, will be three dollars.

As soon as convenient, will you kindly inform Mr. Johnson, of the dinner committee, whether it is your intention to be present, inclosing check to his order in case of acceptance.

Faithfully yours,

AUGUSTUS THOMAS,
F. HOPKINSON SMITH,
ROBERT UNDERWOOD JOHNSON,
33 East 17th Street, New York,
Committee on Dinner.

[handwritten note:] Martinez Jan 13. Dear Johnson I start this evening for the Canon. Mighty cold I guess but must see it in winter garb. also new fronts you owe John Muir

A round-trip missive: Robert Underwood Johnson inviting Muir to attend a National Institute of Arts and Letters dinner and Muir declining in favor of seeing the canyon in its "winter garb."

Robert Underwood Johnson, associate editor of the *Century Magazine*, at his office on Union Square in New York City.

Richard Watson Gilder. A poet and editor of the *Century Magazine*, Gilder promoted a broad array of social causes, both in print and in many community and arts organizations. So influential was his run at the magazine (1881–1910) that his biographer dubbed the 1880s "The Gilder Age." Theodore Roosevelt remarked, "No worthier American citizen has lived during our time." Photo by Joseph Gessford.

William Keith sought out Muir in Yosemite Valley bearing a letter of introduction from Jeanne Carr, and Muir gleefully took Keith to see many a canvasworthy view. Bound by their love of Burns, banter, and the mountains, the two Scots would laugh, argue, scheme, and camp together for over four decades. Mount Keith, a 13,982-foot peak, was named for Keith in 1896.

John Noble, secretary of the interior (1889–93), by Charles Bell. "We are all heartily in earnest in endeavoring to reserve forest land for the preservation of the water supply," Noble told Johnson. Though Sargent, Cleveland, Roosevelt, and Pinchot were "useful," Johnson wrote, "Muir and Noble were the two salient leaders and pioneers of forest conservation."

Pacheco Pass, by William Keith, 1874, an oil on canvas painting mounted on board. By the time Muir traveled west through the historic pass in the Diablo Range, from the Santa Clara Valley to the Central Valley, in 1868, it had been used by stagecoaches for a decade. In the 1850s, the remote and isolated route had been a favorite of bandits and was often called Robber's Pass.

Mount Shasta from Strawberry Valley, by William Keith, ca. late 1880s, an oil on canvas painting. Despite nearly losing his life on Mount Shasta's summit, Muir always treasured the sight of it. After seeing its snowy peak in the fall of 1874 following a long, tiresome stint in the city, he declared, "All my blood turned to wine, and I have not been weary since!"

A close associate and friend of Muir's in the Sierra Club, William Colby served as a director for forty-nine years and as the club's secretary for all but two years from 1900 to 1946. He instigated and enthusiastically led the club's High Trips for three decades. "A Colby mile," one High Tripper waggishly remarked, "is a mile and a half." This photo shows him on a climb in 1900.

Marion Parsons (center) and other women High Trippers demonstrating some of the many uses of the bandana. Parsons, who became the first female member of the Sierra Club board of directors, assisted Muir in his writing efforts in later years.

Chicago poet Harriet Monroe, who would found *Poetry* magazine in 1912, discovered her love of nature with the Sierra Club in Yosemite National Park.

(*Left and facing page*) Logging in the Converse Basin, where six thousand giant sequoias once grew. All but about a hundred were felled between 1892 and 1918, a fate much lamented by Muir on his several visits to the area. Shown here, a falling sequoia, a stump being blasted apart, and a donkey engine in use, in the early 1900s.

25

26

President Theodore Roosevelt and Chief Forester Gifford Pinchot on the river steamer *Mississippi*, on the Mississippi River, in 1907.

James Phelan, mayor of San Francisco (1897–1902) and US senator from California (1915–21).

Richard Ballinger, secretary of the interior (1909–11), ca. 1909. President Taft's ouster of Interior Secretary James R. Garfield and appointment of Ballinger in his place, followed by lingering scandals and a dispute with the forestry chief Gifford Pinchot, led to a rift in the Republican Party and the return of former president Theodore Roosevelt atop the Bull Moose Party.

As city attorney of San Francisco (1899–1902) and secretary of the interior (1913–20), Franklin Lane had a career that dovetailed neatly with the demise of Hetch Hetchy. In that regard, he was certainly true to himself: "A wilderness, no matter how impressive and beautiful, does not satisfy this soul of mine, (if I have that kind of thing)," Lane wrote in 1917. "It is a challenge to man. It says, 'Master me! Put me to use! Make me something more than I am.'"

San Francisco Examiner cartoon by Oscar Chopin, ca. 1913, gloating over San Francisco's winning campaign to take Hetch Hetchy and mocking the "Nature Lovers" supporting the preservation of the remote valley.

32
33
34

At Christmas 1905, Muir gave his sister Mary an eight-page handmade booklet of pressed and mounted sea mosses from the California coast, including these three.

Freeman included this poster promoting another scheme to bring water to San Francisco in his thorough report. "It may be of interest to compare the facts as found by Mr. Grunsky, and the promoters' claims as set forth in their poster," he wrote, "and note how grossly the promoters exaggerate the storage and yield."

35

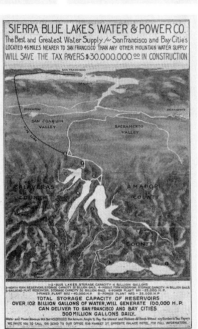

36

A panorama of Hetch Hetchy Valley in 1911, by Matt Ashby Wolfskill.

Muir at his desk in his "scribble den."

Muir with his grandsons John Muir Hanna and Strentzel Hanna, ca. 1910.

Muir and John Burroughs celebrating Burroughs's seventy-fifth birthday, April 3, 1912. The two had traveled together in Alaska on the Harriman Expedition and on a tour of the West in 1909. "Muir will be friendly if you are good listeners," Burroughs told Clara Barrus, his biographer, on the Western tour, "and he is well worth listening to. He is very entertaining, but he sometimes talks when I want to be let alone; at least he did up in Alaska."

40

(*Above*) Johnson, in his office in New York City, where he often wrote Muir and where the American Academy of Arts and Letters was founded. (*Below*) Muir in nature, ca. 1902.

41

CHAPTER 17

Alaska Unites Yosemite

As Harriet Monroe's stagecoach raced over dusty roads and green hills from Merced, where the Santa Fe Railroad had deposited her and a friend, dressed in "mountain clothes"—knee-length skirts, bloomers, and coats, stout knee-high hobnailed boots, and wide-brimmed hats—they felt "most wonderfully free of all conventions and traditions." On the way, they stopped to see the sequoias. "Slowly our eyes measured their girth and height, accepted the mountainous roots, the massive columns, rugged, straight, yet soft-coated as with thick brown furry velvet, against a thousand winters' destructive storms," Monroe wrote. "Gradually our gaze climbed each old trunk . . . to that plume of green away up against the sky; until our imaginations bowed at last to the splendor of this conquest of time and all the elements, to life persistent and triumphant through so many centuries, and still facing the future in the power and beauty of eternal youth."

In June 1904, the Sierra Club returned to Yosemite for its annual High Trip, the second to explore the Tuolumne Canyon. Among the 140 campers, attended by cooks, wranglers, and a host of pack animals, were Frederic Badè—an archaeologist, a professor of Old Testament literature and Semitic languages, and Muir's eventual literary executor and biographer—and Monroe, a Chicago poet who would later found *Poetry* magazine.

Arriving at the camp, in the east end of the valley, Monroe and her friend, each with a single brown canvas bag, limited to fifty pounds, including bedding and clothes for a month, "washed off some of the dust at the river, found friends and food and a place to camp." During a week in the valley, the two were initiated into the ways of the club, "nights in a sleeping-bag, with only tree-tops between us and the stars" and "days of climbing up and down the Valley trails," among their new "free-spirited" friends, who made "light of discomforts." At dawn they bathed in the icy river and "squirmed into our clothes . . . behind any improvised curtain we could rig up out of a cloak or blanket fastened to the trees." They ate from steaming pots and mastered the art of sinking gracefully to the ground without spilling their food. They discovered that the bandanna, the "most indispensable article of camp equipment," could be used as a lunch sack, napkin, apron, nightcap, handkerchief, or washcloth. "We knew literally the emancipation of having 'only one dress to put on,' and the difficulty of keeping that one dress unspotted," she reflected, "and we found it no hardship to wash our washable clothes in the running stream and dry them in the sun and wear them unironed, like Homer's ladies of long ago."[1]

The night before they set out for higher and remoter parts, the group gathered in Camp Curry to dedicate the LeConte Memorial Lodge, which was replacing the club's old Yosemite headquarters. To fund the building of the rough-hewn granite lodge, club members had each pitched in a dollar, while the University of California, Stanford, and the San Francisco business community had all ponied up. LeConte had died in Yosemite on the eve of the first High Trip, and his widow, Caroline, had donated twenty-eight gold nuggets, originally a gift from the admiring students of "Professor Joe" on the couple's golden wedding anniversary. In the absence of Muir, who was on the long-awaited trip with Sargent, Colby presided over the celebration, backed by an American flag draped over the doorway of the lodge. Monroe and Willoughby Rodman, an attorney who would be instrumental in establishing the Los Angeles chapter of the Sierra Club, read poetry.[2]

In the chilly dawn of the Fourth of July, five dozen horses and mules moved the High Trip's camp. As Monroe waited for her companions at the base of Upper Yosemite Fall, "the mighty cataract" seemed to her "like some young Greek god, some athletic nude Achilles, standing there so slim and straight and tall, with his head in the sun and his feet in the clouds." Bivouacked around a bonfire of tree trunks on Porcupine Flat, the campers alternately talked and dozed all night. The next morning a ten-mile tramp brought them to Lake Tenaya, where they frolicked in the cool clear water. On the third day they scrambled through fading snow and frigid streams to Cathedral Lakes at nine thousand feet and then through many miles of forest to Tuolumne Meadows. Finally, exhausted, they reached their twelve-day campsite late in the day and huddled together, shivering, overnight. What followed, according to Monroe, was days of high fellowship with people, mountains, lakes, lofty pines, snowfields, and "sharp difficult summits." They slept on beds of dried grass, ate buckwheat cakes, fresh bread, and mutton—from sheep confiscated by park rangers—and made soda lemonade at "a deliciously cool soda spring" that "bubbled and fizzled out of the red earth."

In small groups they tackled the surrounding thirteen-thousand-footers Dana, Lyell, and Ritter. Monroe's party on Mount Lyell followed a fork of the Tuolumne up to its source in Lyell's glaciers. They camped on the steep slope at the base of the mountain, in a place of "indescribable magnificence—an amphitheater of snowy peaks shutting out the southern stars, the great campfire flaming below us and the lesser fires climbing the slope, while the pearly river slipped away northward into the soft still night." Out in the open, at ten thousand feet, where "dramatic contrasts become the most natural thing in the world," Monroe felt her anxieties melt away:

> To walk over hard snowdrifts under a hot sun, for example; to burn at midday and shiver at night, and soak one's feet in a thousand rills—all without taking cold; to be a barbarian and a communist, a homeless and roofless vagabond, limited to one gown or one suit of clothes; to lose one's last hat-pin or shoe-lacing, and give devout thanks for a bit of string wherewith to tie oneself together; to make one's toilet on a slippery bank, after a brave plunge into an icy river—all these breaches of convention become commonplaces in such a life as this, part of the adventure, a whispering in the ear of nature's secrets.[3]

When the twelve days were up, the entire group broke camp and headed for Hetch Hetchy, at the mouth of the Tuolumne Canyon. After two days on the old Tioga Road, Monroe's party headed down "half-obliterated" trails, so steep that one horse nearly broke a leg. And this was the easy route. Little could she have realized at the time that she would one day read her description of first seeing Hetch Hetchy to a group of US senators who held its fate in their hands: "Suddenly below me—hundreds of feet below—lay the valley, a broad meadow, green as emerald, skirted at the edge with forests and locked in precipitous granite cliffs, mountain high, between which white waterfalls stood erect and slim like dryads. Through this meadow a shining river wandered lazily—we could not see from so far how swift it was—turning back upon its course, tangling itself into *S*'s and *M*'s, as if it were loath to leave so beautiful a place. It looked . . . like that river whose meanderings have been the inspiration of a nation's art, whose pattern you may unravel in your Persian rugs and shawls. This was our Vale of Cashmere."[4]

Ed Parsons, known for his caution on the trail and for being a stickler for the club rules (but also eager to help hikers stretch, cobble, or reinforce their shoes), led a more experienced group directly down through the canyon along the Tuolumne, which near Tuolumne Meadows took on half a dozen streams to form a torrent plunging five thousand feet over thirty miles. In places, noted Badè, the canyon walls rose a mile overhead, and at its narrowest the gorge was a hundred-foot-wide cauldron of churning water. (After his failed attempt to traverse the canyon, Clarence King, the first director of the US Geological Survey, had pronounced it impossible for any "creature without wings.") Where Conness Creek joined the river in chilly cascades, they crossed banks of earthquake talus clad in dense manzanita. Among these "twenty hardiest mountaineers," Monroe noted, "the three women wore knickerbockers or close bloomers—no skirts; and all—men and women alike—carried, slung and strapped over the left shoulder, the slim seven-foot rolls of bedding and provisions . . . while they were tearing through thickets and scrambling up and down vertical rocks and swimming the deep swift river."[5]

That night, scratched and exhausted, they feasted on fire-roasted trout and bedded down under the pines, where, Badè wrote, "the reverberating thunder of the river's batteries, the white glimmer of endless falls far down the canyon, the brilliance of the stars, the flutter and scream of wild creatures terrestrial and aerial, the far-flung shadows of lowering cliffs gliding through every gamut of form under the light of the rising moon" made for an "abysmally grand" night.

In the wildest and deepest part of the canyon the next day, the river hit a downward angle of fifty-five degrees racing with "headlong abandon," hitting depressions and rocketing columns of spray into the air and crashing against giant boulders and ledges in explosions that produced "bombs of spray and fantastic water wheels . . . hurled with titanic energy." The team crawled through miniature forest stands and thickets of azalea teaming with rattlesnakes and signs of mountain lions and bears. Badè caught a diamondback with eleven rattles. He declared the river "stark mad."[6]

By the time the party approached Hetch Hetchy, their clothing and shoes were shredded, and the river, having descended from eighty-five hundred to four thousand feet, slowed, warmed, and loitered in pools among the enormous black oaks. "We had conquered the canyon," Badè crowed, enthusiastically declaring the Tuolumne Canyon one of the world's greatest natural wonders.

Monroe fell in love with Hetch Hetchy while camping beneath the granite dome Kolana, "that bold knight in silver armor who guards this valley as El Capitan does the Yosemite." When it came time to leave, the group hiked to a lumber camp and caught a logging train through a waste of massive pines and cedars, "prone and stripped." "The pain of their degradation was sharp and fresh in each of us like a wound," wrote Monroe, who said she returned to the "frenzy" of city life a changed person. This natural "wonderland" that she had experienced was worth fighting for—so that "all the world and all the ages would follow us."[7]

A week after camping with the President in Yosemite, Muir had set off on his tour with Sargent, starting in Russia, crossing through Siberia and Manchuria to Peking (as Beijing was known at the time), and then on to Japan, Java, and Manila—"to look at trees rocks etc." Muir was untroubled about the Sierra Club, having left it in the capable hands of young Colby, who ran an increasingly well-oiled machine, focusing on legislative issues and community building. In Shanghai, Muir had left Sargent and set out solo for Singapore and India, where he explored cities, temples, and the deodar forests of the Himalayas. An outbreak of cholera prevented him from seeing the celebrated cedars of Lebanon, but he had diverted up the Nile to Aswan, Egypt, and eventually carried on to see the peaks and glaciers of New Zealand. "I began botanical studies over again with all the wildness & enthusiasm of youth," he wrote Johnson, upon his return in May 1904. He had often wished Johnson and Gilder were along. "In less than a month under influence of these Southern Cross wonderlands you would grow back into boyhood."

Diving back into his Yosemite book after his yearlong absence, Muir also pored through the newspapers to keep track of the divisive recession issue as it rose to a head in the state legislature. He was optimistic, writing Johnson, "Your long faithful fight for right management for Yosemite seems now to be nearly won. Everybody now happens to be in favor of recession—the old guardian Galen Clark & even most of the hotel & stage & saddle train owners." Johnson had sent Muir an editorial he had written for the Christmas edition of the *Century* advocating the recession of Yosemite Valley. Ambitiously, he had added a project for the East: the reservation of the tops of the entire Appalachian range. "The top of the Appalachian Range is glorious to think of as a reserve," Muir enthused. "Good luck!"[8]

Colby had drafted the recession bill with the help of the head of the Southern Pacific land department, a former Yosemite commissioner. Colby and Muir wrote the Sierra Club's position on the matter: "The past has demonstrated that the Yosemite Valley is of a national character, and every citizen of the United States is vitally interested in its welfare. Forty years has proven that the State cannot afford to provide a sufficient amount of money to adequately care for Yosemite Valley. . . . But the United States is amply able to do this, and will, if given the opportunity. . . . Few of us even begin to dream of the wealth that will someday be poured into California by the multitudes of travelers who will annually come to enjoy our unparalleled scenic attractions." The club wanted "to hasten that day" and called on the State to do its part "by receding the Yosemite Valley and Mariposa Grove of Big Trees to the National Government." The club hand-delivered its statement, signed by all the directors, to the legislature before the January session. Many politicians claimed that their minds were changed by this document. But the fight only intensified.

In December, the *Examiner* published an article titled "California Must Retain Control of the Yosemite," quoting legislators opposed to recession. Some suspected that the newspaper took this position because its nemesis, the Southern Pacific Railroad, which the paper had long accused of corruption, was said to support recession. The *San Francisco Chronicle* then jumped into the fray, calling out its rival newspaper for claiming that recession was a scheme of politicians while only quoting politicians to support its claim. In every edition from December 19 up to January 9—the day before the legislature was set to vote on the issue—the *Examiner* published a petition against recession to be signed by readers and submitted. Meanwhile the Sierra Club distributed a leaflet to newspapers, politicians, and clubs, and Muir and Colby traveled to Sacramento nine times to meet with legislators.

"Yosemite recession seems promising," Muir wrote Johnson two days after Christmas, "though Hearst's paper here is fighting it with damnable skill & energy." He enclosed "a specimen" of the daily *Examiner* screed.[9]

In early January 1905, with some urging from Colby, Muir wrote Edward Harriman, the president of the Southern Pacific Railroad, to enlist his help in the recession fight. In 1899, Harriman had invited Muir and other scientists and naturalists on an expedition to study the flora and fauna of the Alaska coast. Initially skeptical of Harriman and the merits of the voyage, Muir had eventually joined his friends Merriam and Burroughs on board.

One evening as the scientists assembled on the forecastle to await the dinner bell, Muir heard them talking about "the blessed ministry of wealth, especially in Mr. Harriman's case." He "teasingly interrupted them," he later wrote, "saying, 'I don't think Mr. Harriman is very rich. He has not as much money as I have. I have all I want, and Mr. Harriman has not.'" It had not taken long for Muir's quip to reach Harriman, who sat down beside him after dinner and broached the subject.

"I never cared for money except as power for work," he told Muir. "I was always lucky and my friends and neighbors, observing my luck, brought their money to me to invest, and in this way I have come to handle large sums. What I most enjoy is the power of creation, getting into partnership with nature in doing good, helping to feed man and beast, and making everybody and everything a little better and happier." Muir had found him to be good company, a devoted family man, a peacemaker among the often squabbling scientists, and bold in his efforts to help them accomplish their work.[10]

Now Harriman promptly telegraphed Muir a favorable reply. Johnson also wrote Harriman and got a call from his secretary to say that Harriman had instructed his men to assist them.

On January 10, Muir informed Johnson that the *Examiner* seemed to have let up, "as if played out on its foolish opposition scheme." But it was only the calm before the storm. Muir asked if Johnson could get endorsements from members of Congress or heads of departments, though he did not believe any of the state senators "would be influenced by statements from Congress, the White House or even direct from Heaven." Nevertheless, he thought they might be "bluffed or frightened into decency" and hoped Harriman would "bring railroad influence to bear." The next day, recession bills were introduced in the Assembly and the Senate and were sent to committees. A joint hearing of the two committees was scheduled for the following Wednesday in Sacramento.

Muir went to Sacramento to attend. "I've just returned from the rocky lobby Canyons of the Senate Capitol exploring recession affairs," he told Johnson on January 19. "Found a lot of vicious opposition in the Senate but feel pretty sure we'll win. Perhaps in a week or so the end will be reached." The next morning, the *Examiner* published an article claiming that it had 62,890 signatures on its petition opposing recession, and two days after that the *Chronicle* countered with an interview of Muir favoring recession.

On January 24, the state senators debated the bill in front of a packed gallery. It did not go as Muir had hoped. Senator "Constitutional John" Curtin, known for his oratory skills and ability to use the Constitution to his advantage, launched into a two-hour denunciation of the bill. In 1903, after Governor Pardee had vetoed Curtin's bill to appropriate $150,000 to build a hotel in Yosemite, Curtin had declared that if the state could not afford to build a hotel there, he would likely introduce a bill at the next session to return the valley to the federal government.

But now Curtin, who had also clashed with the Sierra Club over Yosemite's borders, opposed recession. Yellowstone had not received any money for six years, he claimed. (Though Colby had recently told a joint legislative committee, including Curtin, that "Congress gave nearly five hundred thousand dollars to the Yellowstone in two years,

while California hasn't given much more in forty years" to Yosemite.)
"Do you want Yosemite to stand six years without a dollar?" Curtin
asked rhetorically. He was so convincing that the *Examiner* happily ran
the headline "Recession Is Beaten in the Senate" the following day.
But, in fact, the pro-recession forces had managed to postpone the vote
before that could happen. Unimpressed by the arguments, Muir called
it "an all-day dreary fluffy debate." The good news, he told Johnson,
was that their "opponents have fired all their ammunition—mostly
blank sham cartridges & abuse, while our best & heaviest is still in the
locker." While the opposition claimed that they would have won by
three or four votes if the balloting had gone forward, Muir doubted it.
"Next Thursday they will, I guess, be wiser & sadder." On the last day
of January, he returned confidently to Sacramento to continue shepherding the bill, which he believed would soon be voted on in both
houses. Colby would be there too. "Don't you wish you were here to
join us in the booming, reverberating, big cannon fray?" Muir wrote
Johnson before setting out. He hoped this would be "the last battle of
the politicians and domes."

On February 2 the California State Assembly voted on the recession bill. It passed by a significant majority, 46–19. The Senate vote,
however, got postponed. Johnson was "waiting eagerly to hear of the
passage of the Recession bill," as he told Muir. "You are fighting a big
fight and I wish I were in it, but it is altogether best that I have nothing to do with it—at least on the surface." As a "meddling" East Coast
intellectual, he knew he had become a lightning rod on the matter.[11]

Around the time that Yosemite Valley recession was being debated in
Sacramento, Yosemite National Park's outer boundaries and water rights
were on the table in Washington. Both had been long contested. But in
1903, when a lumber company began chopping down trees inside the
park, it became clear that the 1890 borders had been drawn without
meticulous attention to existing deeds. In 1904, beset by claims, the
park commissioners had asked that the borders be reconsidered. Secretary
Hitchcock had appointed former Yellowstone superintendent Hiram
Chittenden and two others to perform this task. As Chittenden traversed
the park that summer, he carried Muir's book *Our National Parks* with

him, and the Chittenden Commission, as it was known, consulted Muir, who, of course, vigorously opposed any shrinking of the park.[12]

The commission ultimately recommended deleting 542 square miles, however, mostly sections that abutted or held private property and were relatively indefensible from invading livestock, miners, and loggers. On the positive side, it called for adding 113 square miles to the north end of the park, almost all of it within the Tuolumne River watershed. Its reasoning, however, was not that the watershed should be kept pure for nature, as Muir would have it, but to protect water rights that might be needed by cities in the future. In the Yosemite Act of February 7, 1905, Congress approved the adjustments, moving the park's western border from Jenkins Hill, about thirteen miles west of what would become the town of El Portal, to a mile east of El Portal. Although public-private land rights issues, including the fact that logging entities still owned prime and prominent tracts within the park's borders, would have to be ironed out later, a planned railroad to the park entrance was able to proceed. Grading would begin in the fall.[13]

There was other big news. On February 20, Hitchcock again denied San Francisco's attempt to grab Lake Eleanor and Hetch Hetchy, saying that it was the "aggregation" of natural scenic features—"beautiful small lakes, like Eleanor, and . . . majestic wonders, like Hetch Hetchy and Yosemite Valley"—that made Yosemite National Park a "wonderland" that Congress "sought by law to preserve for all coming time as nearly as practicable in the condition fashioned by the hand of the Creator—a worthy object of national pride and a source of healthful pleasure and rest." If Congress wanted to set aside reservoir sites there, it could. But he would not.[14]

On February 23, 1905, the recession bill was argued in the California Senate. Muir was there. Senator Curtin again denounced recession on legal and constitutional grounds and called for the people of the state to be given the opportunity to vote on the question. Senator Belshaw, who had proposed the bill, closed the discussion, according to the *San Francisco Chronicle*, "paying his respects to Senator Curtin, whose animus, he declared, was explained by the fact that the member from Tuolumne owned property in the forest reservation surrounding the valley and had discovered that the government would not allow his cattle to trespass on government land."[15]

"I wished you could have heard the oratory of the opposition," Muir reported to Johnson. "Fluffy, nebulous, shrieking, howling, threatening like sandstorms and dust whirlwinds in the desert." The vote would be extremely tight. It was now that Harriman's influence came to bear. While the Southern Pacific Railroad could not take a public stand, its chief counsel, William Herrin, a friend of Keith's and a great admirer of his art, worked with Colby to apply pressure in just the right places. One of their targets was Senator Charles Shortridge, of Santa Clara County, who in January had argued against recession and was, Colby told Herrin, causing trouble. Herrin responded that Shortridge was a man who could be persuaded.

Lo and behold, Shortridge had a change of heart. The *Sacramento Evening Bee* reported that he had received a letter urging him to vote for recession, which had been sent by the San Jose Chamber of Commerce and signed by a dozen prominent people to whom he was in debt. According to the *Bee*, "Shortridge humorously said he would give as graceful an exhibition as possible of a statesman doing a flip-flop." He now, in deference to his constituency, supported recession. In all, nine senators, who had railed against recession in sometimes bombastic speeches on the floor, suddenly changed sides. The vote took place in late February, and although accounts would differ, Colby would recall that it was Shortridge's yea that made the difference. Afterward Muir telegraphed Johnson: "Our long yosemite fight won at last. Bill passed today."[16]

"Sound the loud timbrel! Hurray for you!" Johnson scrawled in reply. "Yosemite is saved, and the Lord must be happier. I have just received your telegram on my return from a public dinner in Philadelphia and am *dee*-lighted! I had begun to lose heart and fear that the machinations of the devilish *Examiner* and its petition might prevail over the sons of Light. I congratulate you with all my heart, my dear Muir, for you have been the heart—the fons et origo—of this movement." He recalled "that night on the upper Tuolumne" sixteen years earlier when they had hatched their "scheme" for a Yosemite National Park and had vowed that if the state did not start to take better care of the old grant, they would have it merged into the new park. "You have been working for this result for many years. It has been a slow victory, but a great one. I rejoice with you, my dear Muir, with all my heart."

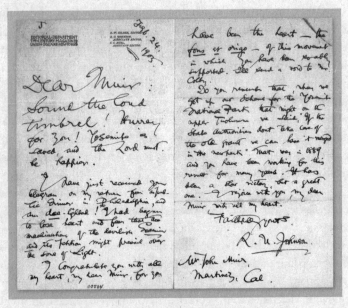

Ecstatic letter from Johnson to Muir celebrating California's
recession of control of Yosemite Valley to the federal government.

That same day, Muir wrote Johnson, singing *his* praises: "I wish I could have seen you last night when you received my news of the Yosemite victory, which for so many years as commanding General you have bravely and incessantly fought for. About two years ago public opinion which had long been on our side began to rise in effective action. On the way to Yosemite both the President and our Governor were won to our side, and since then the movement was like Yosemite avalanches." Still, Muir admitted, the opposition was so fierce that the bill might have been lost in the Senate if not for "the help of Mr. H., though of course his name or his company were never in sight through all the fight."

Muir marveled at his own transformation. "I am now an experienced lobbyist, my political education is complete; have attended legislators making speeches, explaining, exhorting, praying, persuading every mother's son of the legislature, newspapers reporters and everybody else that would listen," he told Johnson. "And now that the fight is finished and my education as a politician and lobbyist is finished I am almost finished myself."

Three days later, Muir sent Johnson a copy of the recession bill. The moment was sinking in. "Hereafter," Muir wrote, "the Yosemite work will be done on your side of the continent and I look to you as leader." And on March 6, he sent Johnson a news clipping showing that the federal government was "already caring for the Valley." He gloated, "Where now is John P. Irish? He has not appeared in the fight at all, but some months before the bill was prepared, he stated . . . that he was in favor of Federal management for Yosemite because the last time that he was there the saloon-keeper was found so ignorant he did not know how to prepare his favorite drink."[17]

Muir had heard rumors that San Francisco wanted to build a 150-foot-tall dam at the mouth of Hetch Hetchy to create a reservoir and that Pinchot had advised the President and the interior secretary that the dam would not detract from the national park. Muir was incredulous. "It would be just the same as saying that flooding Yosemite would do it no harm," he wrote. "This damming of Hetch Hetchy and Lake Eleanor is an old scheme that we had to fight ten or twelve years ago. . . . I hope the Fates will be kind to you and send you all out here this summer. I want to have a long talk with you about the management of the Valley, now that we have at last got it out of the hands of the California politicians."[18]

On the first of May, Johnson sent Muir the essay he had written about him for the influential New York weekly the *Outlook*. In it Johnson recounted the trip where they had conceived the national park and called Muir the "human embodiment of outdoor life" with "one of the most individual and attractive voices I know." He said that he was devoted to getting Muir to convert the "rich store of observation and comparison" in his notebooks into books. As it seemed like an auspicious time to nudge his friend, Johnson did so in the accompanying letter: "Our people are asking . . . about your Yosemite guidebook. How does it come on, and how about the other volumes which you ought to be writing—as I say in my sketch of you—so as to complete the record of your life work?" In late June, he would push again, "it being part of my business in life to lay out your literary work for you."[19]

The Mazamas and the Sierra Club were holding a joint summer outing on Mount Rainier and Mount Hood, on whose summit the Mazamas had been founded in 1894. Johnson had declined several proposals for accounts of the expedition but told Muir he wanted his if he was going. Muir, however, had his hands full. He and Wanda had taken Helen, now nineteen and suffering from respiratory problems, to Sierra Bonita, a ranch owned by friends east of Tucson, Arizona, for the dry air. Wanda had left Berkeley just months before completing her studies to care for Helen. Then Louie, also battling chronic "troubles," developed severe pneumonia.

At the beginning of July, the three returned to Martinez to tend to Louie. "Literary work is now out of sight," Muir told Johnson. "Yesterday when I read your letter to her, she said, 'Give Mr. Johnson my kindest regards, and tell him that had I been able I should have written expressing my thanks for his fine kind article in the *Outlook*.'" Muir called it "good everyway; but in what you say about Yosemite park you are unfair to yourself. This I must try to set right some time when opportunity offers in writing, as I did again and again last winter in speaking about it."

Helen's condition deteriorated, and she had to return to Arizona, accompanied by a teacher. At the end of July, Johnson wrote Muir asking about Louie's health. "Tell her I much appreciated her liking my note about you in the *Outlook*." It arrived just in time. On August 8, Muir wrote back with sad news: "Dear friend Johnson, Mrs. Muir died Sunday morning—funeral tomorrow." Muir's beloved wife was just fifty-eight. She had been, as Helen would later attest, Muir's "perfect helpmate," gladly attending to his work and health and adopting his life interests as her own.

"Let children walk with Nature, let them see the beautiful blendings and communions of death and life," Muir had written many years before on his walk to the Gulf, "and they will learn that death is stingless indeed, and as beautiful as life, and that the grave has no victory, for it never fights. All is divine harmony." And yet the loss of Louie did sting.[20]

Now his life would revolve around his daughters, close friends—many from bonds formed through a mutual love of nature—and environmental work with the Sierra Club. Muir's relationships with his siblings, three of whom now lived at Alhambra, also remained strong. In the months after Louie died, he made for his sister Mary, whom he had, alas, failed to lure to California, a booklet of pressed mosses as a Christmas present. Inside the slim booklet, bound with green ribbon, the exquisitely patterned fronds spoke in subtle yet profound tones of his desire to touch hearts with nature's wonder. Muir's faith in the transformative power of nature would continue to drive him forward—in acts both large and small—at a steady clip, his enchanting optimism undimmed.

CHAPTER 18

The Great 1906 Earthquake Changes Everything

By 1906 San Francisco was a cosmopolitan city of more than four hundred thousand people. Its burgeoning arts scene ranked with those of Chicago and major East Coast cities, and its celebrated Bohemian Club, started by journalists for men who practiced or enjoyed the arts, had already seen more than three decades of performances, revelry, and cloaked influence. Keith was a member. But to the Italian tenor Enrico Caruso, who was reluctantly on tour in the United States, where he found audiences provincial and accommodations subpar, San Francisco was still the Wild West, and he had come suitably armed. Caruso's attitude softened somewhat after Vesuvius erupted on April 5 and earthquakes and lava threatened Naples, where he otherwise would have been. "Maybe it was God's will," he mused, "that I should come this far." Still, at his opening in *Carmen* at the Grand Opera House on Mission Street on April 17, in front of a crowd of three thousand, he wore tucked into his cummerbund a pistol, which he had acquired and learned to use for the trip. After a rousing performance and nine curtain calls, he returned to his suite at the Palace feeling better about things, though this would prove to be unwarranted.

On Wednesday, April 18, at 5:12 a.m., a sudden spasm gripped San Francisco. The ground rocked and bucked for forty-five seconds. Shocking as this was and strangely interminable as it seemed to those thrown out of bed or losing their balance on the predawn streets, it was only the foreshock of the earthquake. After a brief pause—ten or twelve seconds—what would soon be dubbed the Great San Francisco Earthquake began in earnest, testing the Palace Hotel builder's claim that it was "earthquake proof." Windows broke, and the interior took a beating. "Everything in the room was going round and round," Caruso reported. "The chandelier was trying to touch the ceiling, and the chairs were all chasing each other. Crash-crash-crash! It was a terrible scene."

Most of the city was still asleep, but a few policemen, delivery-wagon teamsters, and other early risers were on the streets. Reporter Fred Hewitt, of the *Examiner*, who was out before sunrise that morning, said the pavement pulsated as if it were alive. Horses reared in terror and bolted. The ground undulated like a jump rope—whipping four to five feet per second—and as it repeatedly rose and fell, the surface was lacerated, as if by an invisible knife. Buildings swayed like trees in a storm. The lacerations grew into gaping fissures. After the ornamental dome of the California Hotel crashed through the roof of the fire station, the fire chief fell three stories to his death. Survivors would recall the deafening freight-train roar and the whiteout of acrid dust, as brick facades collapsed into the street and buildings crumbled.[1]

In the city's marshy areas, Gold Rush–era infill of garbage, rubble, dirt, and rocks liquefied, and buildings disintegrated. The four-story Valencia Hotel, on a former marsh in the densely packed working-class South of Market district, sank into a stew of soil and detritus, until only its fourth story, walls crazily askew, remained visible. Despite heroic rescue attempts, thirty of its forty guests were crushed or drowned as broken pipes flooded the soil and muck filled the ruins. Nearby on Market Street, also on marshland, the Greco-Roman columns and masonry facade of the new City Hall, recently completed after decades of corruption and cost overruns, listed and then tumbled to the ground. Building parts rained down on Chinatown's cramped streets, as the ramshackle district's occupants fled to Portsmouth Square.

Although the earthquake lasted less than a minute, it was so powerful that it was felt from Oregon to Los Angeles and east to central Nevada. It occurred along the six-hundred-mile San Andreas Fault with the epicenter offshore, about two miles south of the city. When the Richter scale was created three decades later, the Great San Francisco Earthquake was graded at a magnitude of 7.8 or more, making it one of the three worst ever in the lower forty-eight states. But the rumbling, rending, and tumbling was just the beginning. There would be more than 150 aftershocks, some of them significant, over the next two days—as well as fire.

Dazed people soon filled the streets. Caruso was seen with a towel wrapped around his neck, inexplicably clutching a framed portrait of Theodore Roosevelt, which the President had recently given him. He soon aimed his pistol at a hotel porter, whom he mistakenly thought was trying to steal one of his many wardrobe trunks.

Damaged chimneys, overturned stoves, severed electric wires, and ruptured gas mains caused small fires across the city but no panic at first. Market Street filled with gawkers staring up at San Francisco's most impressive skyscraper, the nineteen-story steel-framed Call Building, housing the offices of the *San Francisco Call* and considered the city's most indestructible building, to see if it would succumb spectacularly, as some predicted, to nature's chest pounding. The *Call* had been the city's leading newspaper for decades, but by 1906 its circulation (sixty-two thousand) had fallen to third best, behind that of the *Examiner* (ninety-eight thousand), and the *Chronicle* (eighty thousand). The Call Building—steel, marble, and granite—the tallest west of the Mississippi when completed in 1898, appeared to be as sturdy as advertised, but the disaster was still unfolding.

Keith was among those flocking toward the fires but for a different reason. He had two thousand paintings and sketches, including sixty large Sierra scenes and a thousand cigar-box panels—like the one Muir kept in his office—much of his life's work, sitting in his Pine Street studio, where he also stored thousands of photographs. He came from Berkeley, where he lived, by train and ferry in the morning, as usual, only this time watching buildings burst into fire from the deck of the ferry. As he tried to make his way to his studio, he was deterred from the attempt to save some of his paintings, many of which he loved so much he had refused to sell them, by a policeman pointing a pistol at his head and commanding him to turn around.[2]

At around eleven that morning flames from the south engulfed the tightly packed buildings of Third Street, catching a hotel on fire. The flames soon leaped from a nearby shoe shop onto the third floor of the Call Building, burning through a suite of offices into the interior corridor, where they were sucked into the elevator shafts and shot on the updraft to the building's signature rooftop dome. There the bolt of fire blew out the windows, launching flames into the sky, before heading back down, exploding the windows floor by floor to feed itself on the fresh air. In two hours the ornate interior of the Call Building was gutted. None of the *Call*'s competitors were spared, as Newspaper Row was ravaged by fire, and the offices of the *Examiner*, the *Chronicle*, and the *Bulletin*, all nearby, soon perished.[3]

The earthquake had fractured or crushed the conduits carrying water into the city and destroyed hundreds of water mains. Firemen attaching hoses to hydrants often found a weak stream that quickly faded to nothing at all. As the flames spread, more and more residents poured into the streets, heading out of town and creating traffic jams and havoc.

Rushing over from his home on Fillmore Street, Mayor Schmitz ensconced himself in the Hall of Justice, since the City Hall was destroyed. On the way, he saw rampant looting and took decisive action, declaring that police officers and federal troops, stationed in the city, were authorized to "kill" anyone engaged in looting or any other crime. He immediately invited many prominent businessmen, politicians, and civic leaders, but none of the members of the Board of Supervisors, to form the Committee of Fifty to help him manage the crisis—even as it was growing worse, much worse. He ordered the gas and electricity to be turned off, meaning the city would go dark, and imposed a nighttime curfew.

PALACE HOTEL.   MONADNOCK BLDG. MUTUAL BANK. CALL BLDG.
            CHRONICLE BLDG.   SHREVE BLDG.

Detail from The Burning City.

The Burning City: San Francisco, 10 am, April 18, 1906. R. J. Walters.

The dozens of individual fires soon combined into three enormous blazes—south of Market Street, north of Market, and in the Hayes Valley, west of the ruined City Hall. As during the destructive fires of the Gold Rush era, high winds were the enemy, spreading the flames with shocking speed. The three blazes soon united in one raging nightmare of a firestorm. With temperatures surpassing twenty-seven hundred degrees Fahrenheit, metal and brick disintegrated while a dense black fog benighted the city.

At Mayor Schmitz's behest, Brigadier General Fred Funston, the five-foot-four, 120-pound commander of the US Army in California, sprang to action, ordering army units at the Presidio and Fort Mason to report to San Francisco police chief Jeremiah Dinan at the Hall of Justice. A navy lieutenant commanding a destroyer sailed with two tugboats to the waterfront. Recognizing that a fast infusion of water was the key to the city's survival, he commandeered more tugboats and directed them to pump seawater to firefighters' hoses while another tug pumped five thousand gallons of fresh water to fire engines desperately fighting the seaside blaze. When these were under control, the lieutenant had his men snake a hose from a tugboat over Telegraph Hill, conveying seawater eleven blocks through the city streets to the area around Montgomery and Jackson Streets (today, Jackson Square) to save what are now some of the city's oldest buildings.

The mighty Palace, however, was not one of them. Well prepared for a fire, with a massive underground reservoir and rooftop water tanks, the hotel was not immediately under threat. Yet while battling the blazes along the waterfront, the fire department siphoned off the hotel's water reserves, leaving it defenseless when the firestorm later came calling. William Ralston's masterpiece was completely consumed.

Meanwhile Funston's troops, directed by Dinan, fanned out into the city to guard vulnerable buildings, restore order, and prevent looting. By forcing thousands to evacuate their homes in an effort to save lives, however, the soldiers often did more harm than good, as many of these people were eager to help save their homes and businesses but were prevented from doing so. With the conflagration growing larger, fire department officials wanted to create firebreaks by dynamiting buildings that were in its path. Funston agreed. Although Schmitz feared destroying property belonging to his supporters, he approved the plan on the condition that it be used as a last resort. But confusion reigned, and Funston began dynamiting aggressively, convinced that it was the only hope for containing the fire. By the second day it was clear this strategy was failing, yet when the dynamite ran low, he pulled the tugboats from fighting the fire and sent them off to get more.

The civilian firefighters and even the soldiers had little experience with explosives, and their efforts actually spread the fire or caused still more horrible results. Although soldiers evacuated Chinatown before dynamiting there, some residents remained behind and, according to one witness, "at least twenty Chinese . . . were blown up." Another witness saw half a dozen people "thrown fifty feet into the air and . . . into the flames." Keith's studio had survived the first day and his friends managed to save twenty-five paintings, but it was finally burned after the dynamiting of the California Market.

Meanwhile, shockingly, arsonists contributed to the fires for insurance claims—as fire damage was covered but earthquake damage was not. In four days, twenty-five thousand buildings and five hundred city blocks across four square miles burned to the ground. More than three thousand people perished, and hundreds of thousands were suddenly homeless. The property damage losses ranged up to $500 million. To this day, it ranks as the second-deadliest natural disaster in US history (after the Galveston hurricane of 1900).

By Saturday, April 21, the fire had burned itself out. A torrential downpour dowsed the final smoldering embers, and shantytowns rose among the ruins, as the homeless queued up for food. Congress provided funds for food, water, medicine, and rebuilding, and other states and countries around the world sent a flood of donations. Having burned down so many times during the Gold Rush era, San Francisco was practiced at rebuilding.[4]

Johnson had been in Italy since January and had witnessed the eruption of Vesuvius—"a grand, if solemn, sight," he told Muir. In June he left Katharine in Florence to recover from an illness (which would take many months) and returned home, only then to learn of San Francisco's devastation. "I hope you do not think me indifferent to your safety in the matter of the earthquake," he wrote Muir. Johnson, knowing that the California postal system was in chaos had immediately written the *Century* office seeking news of Muir. Still, he hoped to hear directly from his friend. "Lordy, what a terrible experience California has been through," he commiserated, and then recalled their first meeting. "Do you remember that the day we met at the Palace Hotel there were two distinct shocks of earthquake? I admire the grit of your people and wish I could have your account of those scenes. It is unbelievable that substantially the whole of the city is gone. How I should like to see you and talk it all over."[5]

Among the less noted casualties of the earthquake was the Memorial Arch on the Stanford campus, which split and crumbled. Part of its grandiose frieze, *Progress of Civilization*—showing Leland and Jane Stanford on horses mapping the Central Pacific's route through the Sierra—crashed to the ground and broke. In a postscript, Johnson smirked, "I'm glad to hear that the Stanford Memorial didn't escape." He did not mention the campus's marble statue of the naturalist, geologist, and Harvard professor Louis Agassiz, who had commended Muir's theories about the glacial formation of Yosemite Valley. The statue fell two stories from the zoology building and pierced a cement walk, burying Agassiz up to his shoulder, legs in the air and a hand extended. "People came running from the quad with such sober faces," one student later recounted, "but when they saw him they couldn't help laughing, and one fellow went up and shook hands with him."[6]

Like Keith, C. D. Robinson lost much of a lifetime of work, thirty years of sketches and paintings. The building where the Sierra Club was founded and its subsequent headquarters were both incinerated. All records, books, memorabilia, and traces of the organization vanished. The club took up temporary headquarters at Berkeley. During the earthquake, Muir had been with Helen, now twenty, among the petrified trees in Adamana, Arizona, where he had built a small adobe house, but Wanda, who was twenty-five and about to marry her beau, Thomas Hanna, had been in Martinez. "I never saw such a smash in my life," she reported. "The whole house has to be rebuilt. What shall I do?" All five chimneys fell and there were fissures in the walls, but the house had survived. Muir would replace the Italian-marble fireplace in the parlor, which was destroyed, with a less ornate Mission-style fireplace. During the repairs, he opened up the two first-floor parlors and the dining room with archways.[7]

"The earthquake did us but little harm, shook down chimneys etc, & some brick buildings in Martinez," Muir told Johnson. "But San Francisco Heavens what desolation!! For strength & beauty only cinder & ashes. . . ." In lieu of working on his writing, Muir had been focusing on forest legislation. "A bill is now before Congress making the first discovered forests 144 square miles in area a National Park. Hope it will pass," he wrote. The resolution accepting Yosemite had passed the House, where Speaker Joe Cannon, an Illinois Republican, was "at last becoming quite friendly." It now needed the approval of the Senate, but, Muir said, South Dakota Republican Alfred Kittredge "to our surprise has been giving us a good deal of trouble." Muir had been monitoring the situation closely and doing what he could to help. "We hope to hear any day that the end of the long, confounded battle has been reached in victory."[8]

This, in fact, occurred the next day.

On June 11, President Roosevelt signed federal legislation making Yosemite Valley and the Mariposa Grove part of Yosemite National Park. The seventeen-year campaign waged by Muir and Johnson together with the Sierra Club—spanning six interior secretaries, five California governors, and the administrations of Cleveland, Harrison, McKinley, and Roosevelt—had at last achieved its goal. All along Muir and Johnson had remained as steadfast as the hills, applying unwavering pressure, and refusing to be denied. Johnson, ever the poet, exclaimed, "Sound the loud timbrel o'er Yosemit-ee! / Jehovah hath triumphed: His forests are free!

"The Sierra Club, which under your leadership bore the brunt of the fight for Recession must be very happy," he continued. "I am sorry to hear that it was burned out and lost all its archives; but it will live in its ashes and do battle for outraged Nature—the Big Trees next, which the misguided will now wish to cut down for the building of the new San Francisco." Johnson closed with editorial advice: "I hope you are not failing to make record of your eventful days. . . . The days come and go and we are all getting older. Look into thy heart and write."

"Yes, my dear Johnson, sound the loud timbrel & let every Yosemite tree & stream rejoice," replied Muir, who had celebrated Wanda's marriage, as well as the Yosemite recession, in June and was back in the "enchanted carboniferous forests" of Arizona. "Getting Congress to accept the Valley brought on, strange to say, a desperate fight both in the House & Senate. Some time I'll tell you all the story. You don't know how accomplished a lobbyist I've become under your guidance. The fight you planned by that famous Tuolumne campfire seventeen years ago is at last fairly gloriously won, every enemy down derry down. Write a good long strong heart-warming letter to Colby. He is the only one of all the club who stood by me in downright effective fighting."⁹

Three weeks after the earthquake and its catastrophic fire, James Phelan wrote of the relief efforts to his uncle George, "Everybody is cheerful and working with the zeal of pioneers in a new land." Amazingly, the Call Building, where the inferno had turned marble surfaces into powder, reopened its lower floors within a month, though its full repairs would take more than a year. The disaster had called the forty-five-year-old former mayor back to leadership both publicly and privately. Considered a rock of stability, Phelan was made president of the San Francisco Relief and Red Cross Funds, and it was to him that President Roosevelt dispatched the $10 million relief check for fire victims. Like the Palace, the Phelan Building—the symbol of James's father's rise and the family's prominence—had turned out not to be "thoroughly fire and earthquake proof." Phelan dynamited its burned-out shell and replaced it with an even-grander building, an eleven-story cement-and-steel skyscraper that this time would be tremor-proof.¹⁰

As San Franciscans set about rebuilding their city, the recriminations surfaced. The culprit, everyone agreed, was the lack of water, and the blame was put on Spring Valley. Politicians claimed that if the water had been controlled by the city, the vast destruction could have been prevented. The city redoubled its efforts to find a freshwater supply. In January, the Board of Supervisors had decided that it was wasting too much time on Hetch Hetchy and had resolved to seek another source. The report of Mayor Schmitz's water committee recognized the prior rights of two irrigation districts to the Tuolumne River and accepted that the national park was off-limits, moving the city away from the Phelan-Grunsky plan and mandating a search for new options. The political boss behind Schmitz, Abe Ruef, had been approached by the president of the Bay Cities Water Company, which controlled water rights in the Blue Lakes region, about a hundred miles north of the city, and had claims on the American and Cosumnes Rivers, with a war chest of a million dollars to buy influence. Bay Cities vouched that the Blue Lakes received far more rainfall than the Tuolumne and that it could, at a lower cost, provide the Bay Area with water for at least ninety years. The threat to Hetch Hetchy seemed to be moot.

But that had been before the fire.

After the disaster, the city formed the Committee on the Reconstruction of San Francisco, which concluded that Spring Valley's water system was inadequate for fire protection and that the city should urgently seek a new fire-protection system. The committee declined to address the water supply, saying this required an extensive engineering review.

With Schmitz on the ropes, and Phelan on the rise, city engineer and Grunsky lieutenant Marsden Manson reversed course and pursued the Phelan-Grunsky solution. He reached out to Pinchot, who had been frustrated by Secretary Hitchcock's refusal to grant the rights. At the same time, Roosevelt was looking for a way to remove Hitchcock, a McKinley man, and replace him with his own guy, James R. Garfield, the son of former president James A. Garfield and a friend of Pinchot's. Replying to Manson, Pinchot confirmed his support of a city water supply from Yosemite that would rival any in the world: "I will stand ready to render any assistance which lies in my power." Six months later—Garfield having replaced Hitchcock in early 1907—Pinchot advised Manson to prepare his case for Garfield, whose attitude, he felt sure, would be "favorable."[11]

CHAPTER 19

Irrefragable Ignorance

K eith, displaying the steadfastness of Muir and other Scotsmen, had wasted little time mourning his lost canvases. "I must paint those two thousand pictures again," he had declared the day after the fire. He plowed back into his work, in a new, smaller studio, on California Street just west of Van Ness Avenue, by all accounts working better and faster than ever before. At the end of June 1907, the *San Francisco Chronicle* reported that the "dean of landscape painters in the West" was painting steadily. Many of the lost paintings, he told the reporter, "I would not have sold for all the gold there is, because I loved them." Then quickly undercutting any self-pity with wry humor, he added, "But it was a glorious fire. It was so big that a man couldn't find fault with it very well. I'm glad they went in a big fire anyway—and then, I can paint plenty more."[1]

Still reeling from the earthquake, San Francisco was also a political mess, with corruption and havoc reigning in its municipal offices. The Schmitz administration, the Board of Supervisors, and several local utilities were charged in a massive corruption scandal. Convicted of extortion and bribery and sentenced to prison, Mayor Schmitz, even from behind bars, refused to resign. His minions barricaded his office, preventing the new acting mayor from moving in. Meanwhile, the new acting mayor, a member of the Board of Supervisors, was in court testifying against the Pacific States Telephone and Telegraph executive who had bribed him and ten other supervisors $5,000 each (about $150,000 in today's money). At a convention to replace Schmitz, the corrupt board was forced to resign en masse, and sixty-eight-year-old Ed Taylor, dean of the Hastings College of Law, emerged as the new mayor. A doctor, lawyer, and poet, Taylor had published a collection of sonnets inspired by Keith's landscapes, which was, mistakenly, taken as a good sign for the city's environmentalists.

With the formulation of environmental policies still in the early, volatile stages on the federal level and nearly nonexistent on the regional and local levels, interpretation of legislation veered sharply from one administration to the next and sometimes even within the same one. To try to resolve the long-standing San Francisco water dispute, US Secretary of the Interior James R. Garfield, a former Ohio attorney and state senator turned Roosevelt adviser and Washington insider, ventured to the West in the summer of 1907. On July 24, despite the President's objections, he held a hearing on what was now being called the San Francisco Hetch Hetchy Project, at the office of the city's newly replenished Board of Supervisors. Forwarding Garfield a letter from Muir, Roosevelt had commented that it seemed unnecessary to decide about Hetch Hetchy now. "Why not allow Lake Eleanor, and stop there?" But Garfield, who was otherwise devoted to Roosevelt, had already set the wheels in motion. As the city had little interest in including the opposition, the meeting went almost unpublicized, though the city itself was well prepared with orators and experts, including both the new mayor and the old pros James Phelan and Marsden Manson. Only a few who opposed the grant had found out about the hearing, and none knew exactly what its purpose was. When Mayor Taylor opened the proceedings, at 8:40 in the evening, neither Muir nor any Sierra Club representative was there.

Garfield promptly tipped his hand, announcing that he thought the matter of a municipal water source of "vital" importance to San Francisco and that the federal government would provide "assistance to you in any way in helping you out of the tremendous difficulties you are facing here at this time." Manson jumped right in, summarizing the recent quest for a water source, which had led to two potential reservoir sites. He presented a relief map, pointing out Hetch Hetchy and Lake

Eleanor. Their drainage area, from the summits of the Sierra Nevada to the San Joaquin Valley, he pointed out, was considered uninhabitable. "No one has lived in this place in the wintertime, except one man, who tried it, and his goat froze to death and he came very near following."

Manson told Garfield that the city's application was based on his pamphlet "Reviewing the Opinions of the Secretaries of Interior and Commerce and Labor," addressed to the President, which had gone via Pinchot to the attorney general, who had confirmed that the matter fell within the interior secretary's purview. "The city now asks you to reconsider the entire case," Manson stated. It only wanted to store extra seasonal or floodwater, which would otherwise go to waste, causing damage as it flowed to the sea, and, in accordance with state laws, to divert the water to the people of San Francisco. The city would not divert waters "now in use" or deprive "one single iota of an industry of one iota of the rights they have."

"The figures presented, as I recall it," Garfield interjected, "show that there is a vast quantity of water," more than enough to supply San Francisco for many years. Manson noted that it was also the only source free of "complicating claims" and provided "the purest water" and, unlike other sites, would remain uninhabited and free of population stress "forever" because it belonged to the federal government. "The reservoir site I hope you will visit," he added somewhat unctuously. "An artist visiting the spot and reproducing it on canvas deliberately painted into the picture a vast lake that the picture would be more attractive, and the converting of this waste tract into a reservoir will enhance the beauties of the park." Perhaps it was better that Muir was not there when Manson called Hetch Hetchy a "waste tract," but Muir also would have encouraged Garfield to see the valley with his own eyes.

P. J. Hazen, a spokesman for the Turlock Irrigation District—the state's first irrigation district, formed in 1887 in the Central Valley to transform the dry prairie into farmland—had heard enough: "Mr. Secretary, I desire to know by what authority these gentlemen represent San Francisco and what is before the secretary now to be heard?" Turlock, which had built the 127-foot-high La Grange Dam on the Tuolumne in 1891, then the highest overpour dam in the country, had not been notified of any application to change the ruling rejecting San Francisco's request for reservoir sites in Yosemite National Park.[2]

What ensued was theater of the absurd. Manson pointed out that the mayor was present, giving them authority enough. Phelan noted that the irrigation districts had telegraphed Washington protesting the proceeding, so clearly they knew about it. "We have not been advised that a hearing would be had at eight thirty tonight, but we are here trying to find out," Hazen calmly insisted.

"The hearing is on the reopening of the case as presented to the Department of the Interior," Garfield snapped.

"The question then before you tonight is as to whether the matter will be reopened!" Hazen insisted.

"It is already reopened," Garfield fired back.

"All that I ask is that whenever that hearing is to be reopened," Hazen continued, doggedly, "we shall be advised of what is presented to you upon that application and that . . . we shall have an opportunity to be heard." Given the circumstances, he said, Turlock was not prepared to present its position.

Neither was the Modesto Irrigation District, whose representative, Mr. Dennett, said he likewise was unaware of any official action to reopen this issue. "This of course is not the time for a discussion of legal questions," he added, "but we believe that under the law we are entitled to the amount of water necessary to the beneficial irrigation of our lands."

Garfield cut in, "Do you claim that you have a right to increased water for irrigation purposes beyond the point or amount covered by your present use?"

The answer was yes, much more. Dennett explained that in the three years since the water had begun to flow into Modesto and Turlock, which had pooled $3 million to build an irrigation system, they had placed 40,000 acres under cultivation. The goal was 250,000. With an annual rainfall of only twelve inches, he pointed out, they irrigated year-round. "Another thing, Mr. Secretary, any estimate as to the claims of San Francisco must be based not upon the average flow of the river, which the city had used; we must take the minimum flow of the river in the lowest year."

As Garfield surprisingly agreed, Phelan interceded, aiming a pointed question at Dennett: "Did your district introduce that bill that was vetoed by the governor?"

Now things grew chippy. The treachery ran deep, it appeared.

"Yes, sir," replied Dennett, "representations had been made to us that a grant would be made to the city with a promise of sufficient water for the districts," and the bill, shaped by unofficial representatives of San Francisco, guaranteed them their water. "Judge of our surprise when, after the bill had been passed by both houses and lay before the governor," Dennett exclaimed, it was opposed by the "coterie of persons in San Francisco who, unofficially representing the city, advised us to submit it."

"Did it not seek, Mr. Dennett, to dedicate all of the stormwaters of the region to the districts?" Phelan pursued.

"No, sir. As nearly as I remember it, the bill was this: there is hereby dedicated and set apart to the irrigation districts . . . such water as may be necessary for the irrigation of the lands in the districts."

Manson probed, "May I ask who were the official representatives of this city who acquiesced in that?"

"Mr. Manson, you yourself made this statement."

"No, sir, I did not. I want to know, sir," Manson roared, "who were the official representatives of this city . . . ?"

"No, sir," Dennett replied calmly, "no official representatives of this city acquiesced in the bill, but the bill was drafted in accordance with suggestions made by *yourself* to representatives of our locality. . . ."

"There will be no difficulty in you people getting together on this proposition," Garfield somehow concluded from this exchange.

Then A. C. Boyle, another Modesto representative, spoke up. "Mr. Secretary, it seems to me, with your sanction to a reopening of the matter, San Francisco should apply to Congress, and if there was anybody there that could speak for the city, I believe I might possibly promise that the opposition that has been developed there"—he turned to Manson and said, "I believe you will admit that it has been pretty effective so far; we have defeated you twice"—"might be wiped out, condition- ally, of course, upon the city applying to Congress for those rights. Let Congress guarantee—Mr. Manson, do I understand that you guarantee us the water we require?"

"By no means, sir," Manson said indignantly, "by no means could the city guarantee what Nature has decreed as the discharge of that river. All the city asks is the privilege of storing the water, the waste flood- water, that last year passed your headgates by the millions of cubic feet, devastated the San Joaquin Valley, and are now flowing in the Pacific Ocean. . . . Right now there is not one single drop of water being stored."

Boyle responded that they had an application in to build reservoirs for that purpose.

"The reservoirs are not built," sniped Manson. "I made the statement that there is no water stored now."

"That is right," said Boyle, refusing to be bullied, "but we are making an application to store these waters for our use."

Since Phelan had beaten everyone else to the punch, Manson had him there. "Prior to that," Manson gloated, "there is one that we have permission to store it for ourselves."

"Which application has been refused," Boyle countered, "so therefore ours is the prior one." Then he grew more sober: "It is a known fact, Mr. Secretary, that when it comes to supplying plant life in opposition to the saving of human life, the laws would demand that the districts let their crops burn up to save the life of one child in San Francisco perishing of thirst. Once San Francisco gets a foothold there, it simply opens up unlimited litigation, and these people have no money to fight San Francisco." They were mostly small farmers, who had mortgaged their homes and bet everything on an irrigation system, he explained. They wanted the matter settled by Congress, "the only people who can guarantee us our rights and guarantee the city's rights so that San Francisco could finance the proposition." Here was the kicker: "We ourselves want these dams built."

"Do I understand the gentleman to say that he wants to build dams in the same place that we want to?!" Manson interjected in disbelief.

"Should not we have to build the dams to store the water? We have an application to store on Lake Eleanor; we have asked the Reclamation Service to build the dam." Here Boyle was referring to the service created by Congress in 1902 to help manage water demands in the West. The idea was to "reclaim," or irrigate, arid lands to sustain the region's booming growth. In its first five years, the soon-to-be-controversial service started thirty projects, dramatically altering the landscape and settlement of the Western states.

Phelan cleared his throat. "Mr. Secretary . . . the application of San Francisco was made in 1902. The secretary decided he had no jurisdiction. Therein was the error; he had jurisdiction, and the application is still before the department; it is revived by this reopening. . . . When the gentleman refers to an act of Congress, he seeks merely to obstruct the application. As for the ability of San Francisco to finance a proposition of this kind . . . there are 475 million dollars' worth of assessable property here that would stand behind bonds issued."

As Phelan was trying to change the subject upon which Boyle felt he was making progress, he cut in, "Has the secretary the right to do anything more than simply to grant the rights? Can he guarantee the supply of water to the districts?" Then he hit home: "If you are willing to go to Congress, I can safely promise that the opposition that has thus far defeated you will be withdrawn. You simply say there is plenty of water for all; that your engineers so tell you. Being an engineer myself, I am fully aware of the weakness of the human nature and know that engineers are liable to make mistakes. In fact, Mr. Grunsky made such a slight mistake that he actually tried to run water uphill."

"On what authority do you state this?" Phelan demanded, taking the bait.

"On the authority of everybody who has seen the ditch water run," replied Boyle to laughter, some stifled and some decidedly not.

It went on like this for two and a half hours. Garfield tried to keep the discussion on track. Manson traded potshots with the district representatives. The city argued that there was enough water for everybody. Contentious as it was, the hearing was not about whether the reservoirs should be built and the water of the Tuolumne commandeered, but about how it should be done and how the interested parties could be sure they got their portion. The Sierra Club's position—and indeed the interest of the majority of Americans—was not even on the table. No Muir. No Johnson.[3]

As the clock ticked toward eleven, Garfield said he would read briefs before deciding, but critically limited their scope: "The question is as to whether or not the department will permit this water to be used by the city if the city wants it. I am very clear in my own mind that . . . the waters of the Sierra reserve cannot be put to any higher or better use. . . . Whether or not the cities will take advantage of such use is a matter the citizens themselves must determine." In this light, he confined the briefs to a discussion of the Tuolumne River. The bottom line: Garfield had already made up his mind about Hetch Hetchy—it was lost.[4]

Muir returned home from a Sierra Club outing to Yosemite to hear the fast-spreading news of Garfield's hearing. "Garfield Reopens the Hetch Hetchy Project" read the headline in the *San Francisco Call*, which characterized the meeting as having "much acrimony" and "considerable suspicion."

San Francisco engineer Russell Dunn, a Spring Valley stockholder and rights holder on the North Fork of the American River, had asserted that at least seven other rivers north of the Tuolumne could provide the needed water at a reasonable cost. Bay Cities Water, whose advocate was the only one at the hearing to expound on the value of Hetch Hetchy as a national park gem, offered an option using the American and Cosumnes Rivers and said the company would submit proof that there was no reason to sacrifice Hetch Hetchy. But it was too little, and too late.

Muir wrote Johnson about the meeting and Garfield's willingness to reopen the issue that his predecessor Hitchcock had assiduously opposed: "We are in for another fight for the Yosemite National Park against the schemers of San Francisco. The damming of the Yosemite itself would not be more destructive to The National Park than this." Only the irrigation districts and the city were present, he told Johnson. "The rights of the nation in the great park were not considered at all. . . . The roof of the Sierra is about 500 miles long, but these schemers for financial reasons seem to think that only the Yosemite portion, used as a National Park, is available to quench the City's thirst & prevent it from being burned up a second time." He was growing weary of it. "To keep thieves & robbers & benevolent grafters out of this greatest of all the American parks has been a constant fight ever since we got it established & it seems to have no end."[5]

Johnson forwarded the letter to Roosevelt while "backing it up strongly" himself. "C. D. Robinson at San Rafael writes us (*The Century*) against invasion of Hetch Hetchy," Johnson told Muir, "but suggesting water be taken from Tuolumne Meadows! Better set him right."[6]

Roosevelt's right-hand man, William Loeb, responded to Johnson, who forwarded an extract to Muir: "The Pres understands that Mr. Pinchot feels very strongly that that scheme is entirely right. The P. has sent copies of your letter together with Muir's to Mr. Pinchot & Sec'y

Garfield for comment." Johnson urged Muir to recommend to Pinchot an alternative and to rally the Sierra Club to support it. In August, Muir and Colby asked club members to protest San Francisco's plans, but even within the club the matter was divisive. Marsden Manson was also a member, and he aggressively lobbied others to support the plan. A line was drawn, and for the most part it pitted those from San Francisco against those living elsewhere. Despite visiting Hetch Hetchy often, Warren Olney, who had been the mayor of Oakland from 1903 to 1905, also believed that the need to crush Spring Valley justified the destruction of Hetch Hetchy and any reduction of the national park.

On August 30, the directors of the Sierra Club met and created a committee—LeConte, Badè, Parsons, and Colby with Muir as chair ex officio—to draft a report on the welfare and improvement of Yosemite National Park, essentially an official statement condemning San Francisco's request to use Hetch Hetchy as a reservoir. Its many reasons were best encapsulated by the line "No greater damage could be done to the great National Park, excepting the damming of Yosemite itself." The minutes of the directors' meeting are terse and do not capture the day's debate. Among the board members present were founder Warren Olney and honorary vice president Gifford Pinchot, who both favored ceding Hetch Hetchy to the city. Muir urged Pinchot to see the valley and offered to accompany him. The two went back nearly fifteen years and had bonded while they did their due diligence on the potential forest reserves.

Although Pinchot entertained the idea, after speaking at the International Irrigation Congress in Sacramento on September 5, he wired Muir, saying he had to return East and did not have time for Hetch Hetchy. Any chance of the two most influential men on the matter spearheading a compromise sparing Hetch Hetchy but still providing for a Tuolumne River reservoir to the west, a solution both at various times would favor, now vanished.[7]

Four days later, Muir wrote President Roosevelt to emphatically express his belief that Yosemite National Park should be left alone, free of "commercialism and marks of man's work other than the roads, hotels etc required to make its wonders and blessings available." Nowhere else was there "so grand and wonderful and useful a block of Nature's mountain handiwork," and Hetch Hetchy was one of its most "sublime and beautiful" features and an important passage to the "magnificent" Tuolumne Meadows, which he deemed "the focus of pleasure travel in the High Sierra." He decried the promoters of the scheme: "However able they may be as capitalists, engineers, lawyers, or even philanthropists, none of the statements they have made descriptive of Hetch Hetchy dammed or undammed are true." He called their proud confidence the result of "irrefragable ignorance."

"Ever since the Park was established it has called for defense," he told the President, rising to a fervor, "and however much it may be invaded or its boundaries shorn, while a single mountain or tree or waterfall is left, the poor stub of a park would still need protection." He then invoked Eden, "the first forest reserve," created by the Lord, guarded by angels, attacked by evildoers. "I pray therefore that the people of California be granted time to be heard before this reservoir question is decided: for I believe that as soon as light is cast upon it, nine tenths or more of even the citizens of San Francisco would be opposed to it."[8]

He enclosed an excerpt from "The Tuolumne Yosemite," an adaptation of a *Century* story that he had published in the *Outlook*. In it he had evoked this "grand landscape garden, one of Nature's rarest and most precious," with lyrical dreaminess:

> Its walls seem to . . . glow with life whether leaning back in repose or standing erect in thoughtful attitudes giving welcome to storms and calms alike. And how softly these mountain rocks are adorned, and how fine and reassuring the company they keep—their brows in the sky, their feet set in groves and gay emerald meadows, a thousand flowers leaning confidingly against their adamantine bosses, while birds bees butterflies help the river and waterfalls to stir all the air into music—things frail and fleeting and types of permanence meeting here and blending as if into this glorious mountain temple Nature had gathered her choicest treasures, whether great or small to draw her lovers into close confiding communion with her.[9]

The President responded as soon as he read the letter: "My dear Mr. Muir, I gather that Garfield and Pinchot are rather favorable to the

Hetch Hetchy plan, but not definitely so." He had sent them Muir's letter and asked for a response and promised to do everything he could to protect Yosemite and the nation's other natural treasures. But coming from a fighting man, his next words seemed tepid: "It is out of the question permanently to protect them unless we have a certain degree of friendliness toward them on the part of the people of the State in which they are situated, and if they are used so as to interfere with the permanent material development of the State instead of helping the permanent material development, the result will be bad." Then he provided Muir with a reality check: "I would not have any difficulty at all if, as you say, nine tenths of the citizens took ground against the Hetch Hetchy project." But so far everyone he knew favored it, putting him in the awkward position of seeming to interfere in the state's growth for a valley few wanted to protect. He closed with kind words: "I wish I could see you in person; and how I do wish I were again with you camping out under those great sequoias or under the silver firs."[10]

Meanwhile, Johnson promised Muir that no snap judgment would be made by Garfield, who would find two letters from Johnson waiting for him upon his return in October. Johnson enclosed an editorial he had written for the October issue but that had been pushed back to November. "If you find anything wrong in it please let me know," he said. He wanted Muir to disseminate it further, after it was published in the *Century*. He asked Muir to send details about the Hetch Hetchy "scheme" so that he would have more ammunition to use: "Make the objections clear. You have only told me the bare fact."[11]

Muir had also written Garfield and would send Johnson copies of the club's resolutions on the "confounded business." Phelan and the San Francisco Board of Supervisors "are at the bottom of the whole black job," Muir wrote. "Manson & Warren Olney (J. P. Irish's partner) are only hired promoters." He asked Johnson to try to get copies of the applications, arguments, and reports on the case from Garfield and signed off, "Faithfully fightingly yours."

The next day Muir spelled out his objections to the scheme for Johnson: (1) Such use would defeat the purpose of creating the park, Hetch Hetchy being one of its primary features, next to Yosemite in beauty and grandeur and visited by thousands. (2) Once dammed, no road or trail could be built around the reservoir without tunneling through rock, so it would hamper access to Tuolumne Meadow, the park's central campground and focal point of leisure travel in the High Sierra. (3) The park is a natural wonderland belonging to all the world and should be preserved in "pure wildness forever." (4) It is Phelan and the San Francisco supervisors, not the citizens in general, who covet it, and not because the water cannot be found elsewhere but because it is cheap.

Manson and Olney were the "noisiest pleaders," Muir complained to Johnson. He called their argument that damming Hetch Hetchy would prevent damage to the lowlands during spring floods "ridiculous" and countered that the flood waters would not be lowered by even half an inch. The idea that the park water was purer and would always stay free of the contaminating influences others would be exposed to was also, he said, false: "On the contrary it is far more liable to contamination from camp sewerage than any other adjacent source." The modest numbers that camped there now would soon be "multiplied ten or a hundred fold by campers and travelers from all the world." He lamented the "monstrous responsibility . . . placed on young Garfield," who had been "submerged beneath reservoirs of lies and lopsided truths. . . . Woe is he and thee and me and all the world's beauty-lovers that such dollar-dotted tangles should approach our sacred Sierra temple, O for a touch of Ithuriel's spear to these eloquent water changers." But, alas, they were being boxed out: "Does it not seem strange to you that the only parties recognized so far in this great question are the Irrigators and Supervisors—What of those of all the world for whom the Park was created?"[12]

On September 23, Muir sent Johnson a copy of the Sierra Club report submitted to Garfield a few days earlier. Pinchot, who had still never seen Hetch Hetchy, had come into the Sierra Club directors' August 30 meeting before its close and listened to the "principal objections discussed." Pinchot's "big mistake," Muir told Johnson, was assuming that Phelan and a few under him spoke for San Francisco. "On the contrary never was a scheme more truly a one-man scheme than this. Not one in a thousand of the citizens of San Francisco . . . care anything about Mr. Phelan's water scheme." But Muir was mistaken in this assessment of public sentiment and the political situation. Although Roosevelt had suggested this, Muir refused to believe it. He regretted that he had not gotten a chance to speak to Pinchot alone to discuss the club's position more fully. In fact, the two would never see each other again and would find themselves on either side of an ever-widening gulf, as they became antagonists in the great environmental debate of their day.[13]

Muir fought back in his inimitable way, networking through nature. In August, he had had a visit from Fred Barber, who worked for a Boston maker and dealer of optics and whom he had met on a Sierra Club outing. The two discussed what apparatus might best suit Muir's botanical studies. After consulting with Bausch & Lomb, Barber had ordered Muir an eyepiece and a hand magnifier. Not only had Muir made a valuable friend for his scientific work, but he had made an ally for his environmental efforts. In late September, he wrote Barber to thank him and broach the subject of Hetch Hetchy. Barber had raised the issue with the president and the forestry counselor of the AMC, who appreciated the Sierra Club's help in "similar undertakings" and were eager to return the favor in this worthy cause. Barber asked Muir to send him a copy of the Sierra Club resolution and promised the AMC would "take some action right away."[14]

In early October, while greed on Wall Street and an attempt to corner the market in United Copper stock were about to trigger a banking collapse known as the Panic of 1907, Keith and his wife, Mary, invited Muir to camp in Hetch Hetchy for three weeks. Muir replied that he would be glad "to take a breath of mountain air" and arranged for a wrangler, horses, a tent, and provisions. Keith was soon reminded of Muir's heedlessness toward culinary refinements. "Muir is a delightful companion to go off with; agreeable, appreciating beauty thoroughly and all that, but I must say he is a mighty poor provider," he later told the *Argonaut*. "Sometimes when I've been away with him for three weeks without any sugar the whole time, I feel that I'll never go on another trip with him—but I generally do, just the same."

The trip, also reported on by the *Call*, was a "delightful one, although very cold." It gave Muir and Keith a chance to refresh their souls and their friendship. The leaves were in color, and the "great godlike rocks" glowed with life, Muir would write in the *Sierra Club Bulletin*. Eager for new subjects, Keith wandered along the riverbank, making dozens of sketches of the scenery, studies for paintings. "In picturesque beauty and charm Hetch Hetchy surpasses even Yosemite," he told Muir. The idea that an artificial lake would enhance the valley was "nonsense," he added, and damming it "nothing short of a crime." Keith's paintings would reveal the valley's rich colors and majestic landscape and—they fervently hoped—open the eyes of Bay Area residents and others to the folly of flooding the place.[15]

CHAPTER 20

Fighting Thieves & Robbers

America was officially smitten with electricity. "The Times Building will be especially illuminated tonight in honor of the birth of 1908," the *New York Times* enthused on New Year's Eve. "The exact moment of the New Year's arrival will be signalized by the dropping of an electrically illuminated ball above the tower." The ball, five feet in diameter and lit by 216 electric lamps, was dropped from the top of a flagpole to the roof of the tower on Times Square with the year flashing "to the four quarters of the town." A new age of glitter and glitz had arrived.[1]

In early January, Muir, now approaching his seventieth birthday, returned to Martinez from the Mojave Desert, where he had taken Helen and a companion, setting out four days before Christmas, for the salubrious dry air. He had built a house for Helen, now a distinguished-looking young woman of twenty-two with wavy dark hair and almond-shaped eyes behind wireless pince-nez, on a ranch near Daggett, California. On the rail line between Los Angeles and Las Vegas, the town was an outpost with reasonable amenities, due to its proximity to silver and borax mines. Helen would have to be there or someplace like it for the next two years while Muir would join her as much as he could. He was devoted to Helen, who since Louie's death had become his typist and first-line critic and who had cooked and kept house for him. "With good sound health," he told her, "so fine & good & great a girl as you are may do anything in this world worth doing." He would be closely involved in her living arrangements and health care with intermittent trips to Martinez and elsewhere to maintain all of his affairs, namely marshaling the Sierra Club. "We must not rest in our H.H. battle until after the Secretary's decision, if then, tho' all my news is favorable so far," he wrote Colby.

To that end, Muir wrote a letter advising several members of Congress that "our great national parks . . . reserved as places of rest and recreation for everybody, are now in danger of being destroyed." The loss of Hetch Hetchy, he told them, would lead to "the exclusion of the people from one half of the entire park and the destruction of many of its most wonderful features." Not only would this be a tragedy, he contended, it would also be a terrible precedent to set for all the national parks. In the name of "all who appreciate the grandeur and majesty of our great mountain parks and who believe that they should be preserved in pure wildness," Muir urged the legislators to reject the city's "unnecessary and destructive" scheme.[2]

Despite this threat to Yosemite National Park and thanks to President Roosevelt, January 1908 was otherwise a banner month for the American landscape. Using the Antiquities Act, passed by Congress in 1906, giving the president the ability to create national monuments to protect significant natural, cultural, and scientific sites on federal lands without congressional approval (and thus avoiding any political and legal wrangling), Roosevelt declared the Grand Canyon a national monument. Prior to this, he had only used the Antiquities Act for smaller monuments, such as the Devils Tower butte in the Black Hills of Wyoming; the Montezuma Castle, a five-story Arizona cliff dwelling of the Sinagua people; and the Northern California volcano Lassen Peak (which in 1914 would roar spectacularly back to life after twenty-seven thousand years of silence). The Grand Canyon, with more than eight hundred thousand acres of mostly unexplored land, was not a small reserve maintained for scientific or historical interest. It was a natural wonder that dwarfed all the other national monuments combined. Two days earlier, Roosevelt had created two other national monuments: Petrified Forest, in Arizona, preserving what Muir deemed "the first grand forests of the world," and Redwood Canyon in California.[3]

The Last Stand

Until the 1800s, the coastal valleys of Northern California were filled with old-growth redwoods, which the indigenous Coast Miwuk people had for thousands of years lived among and tended to, likely using periodic controlled burns to clear out fuel wood and promote growth. They had been forced to move by the advance of missionaries and settlers, and loggers had wiped out most of the redwoods since. But a hard-to-reach stand, just north of San Francisco, had survived. Hearing of plans to cut the trees, dam Redwood Creek, and create a reservoir, William Kent, a real estate and livestock magnate, and his wife, Elizabeth, had swooped in and bought the land, more than six hundred acres, not far from their ranch on the east side of Mount Tamalpais, to prevent the "hideous heedless wickedness," as Kent put it, of those who would "butcher" the redwoods.

When the North Coast Water Company sued to condemn the land it wanted for a reservoir, Kent sent a wire to Gifford Pinchot, a fellow Skull and Bones member who had been two years behind him at Yale, to see if the federal government might intervene to save the last redwood stand on the Marin Peninsula. Kent offered it up as a national forest and was willing to fund policing for two decades, as long as the transfer preempted his being served condemnation papers, which could be within weeks. Pinchot responded that national forest status would not necessarily protect the property the way Kent wanted, but national monument status could. Pinchot maneuvered quickly, coordinating with Secretary Garfield and President Roosevelt. In less than two weeks the deal was done. The Kents would give almost half of the land—294 acres—to the nation to save the trees and only asked that it be named for the man who had inspired them to act, John Muir.[4]

Roosevelt objected to that. "I have a very great admiration for John Muir," he responded. "But after all, my dear sir, this is your gift. I should greatly like to name the monument the Kent Monument if you will permit it." The status-conscious President and conservationist-in-chief may have been trying to undercut the nation's most celebrated "nature lover," as he would soon do at a major environmental conference in Washington, DC. But Kent was not after self-aggrandizement. He insisted the monument be named after Muir.[5]

"This is the finest forest & park thing done in California in many a day, & how it shines amid the mean commercialism & apathy so destructively prevalent these days," a deeply grateful Muir wrote Kent, adding in another letter, "Seeing my name in the tender & deed of the Tamalpais Sequoias was a surprise of the pleasantest kind. . . . You have done me great honor." Asa Gray, with whom Muir had climbed Shasta, had named plants after him, including a daisy that Muir had found in Alaska, and both a Sierra peak and an Alaskan glacier bore his name. "But these aboriginal woods, barring human action, will outlast them all, even the mountain & glacier," he said.

Johnson congratulated Muir in a letter, adding, "If I had my way the whole of the Sierra reservation should be named for you."[6]

At the end of January, Muir, feeling expansive in the flush of his Muir Woods honor, wished the President "another of your great new years," then reflected in a burst of optimism, "When I was walking with Emerson through the giant Sequoias above Wawona he quoted the Scripture, 'There were giants in those days, mighty men of old, men of renown.' Many are beginning to see that there are giants in these days also, by none made more manifest than yourself in the work you have done and are doing joining the oceans, controlling and putting to right our land-ways and water-ways—mountains, forests, deserts, gardens—overcoming all obstacles like a glacier, serene amid the maddest maelstroms, going ahead with the strength of God's simple, unchangeable, foundational righteousness.

"The world is growing better," he continued, "though hard to believe it in the midst of the mad commercial maelstrom now whirling over the country like sand and dust storms on a desert, but these shall pass away—things refuse to be mismanaged long. Good citizens here as everywhere admire you and love you. . . . And though we regret your presidency is drawing near the end we are glad to know that your work will go on and that in reality you will be our President as long as you live.

"I thank you for saving the Tamalpais redwoods," he concluded, now casually—after flattery and gratitude—getting down to his business, "and doubt not you will save our great Yo Park from the commercial money changers. Not a decent citizen of all the country or the world who knows the facts of this Yo affair is in favor of spoiling it."

Three months later, the President responded encouragingly that he was "trying to see if we can not leave the things on the line that you indicate—that is, damming Lake Eleanor and letting San Francisco depend for a generation or so upon that and the Tuolumne tributaries. But of course I must see that San Francisco has an adequate water supply."[7]

On the first of May, Muir and the Sierra Club, running out of patience and perhaps sensing the worst, telegraphed Garfield, "On behalf of People of California and the whole country for whom the Yosemite park was created we request a public rehearing in the Hetch Hetchy matter since San Francisco and irrigationists have had a second hearing." But it was not to be. On May 11, Garfield issued his decision and sent a copy of it to Muir the following day. The news was lengthy and not good, and Pinchot's fingerprints on it were obvious. "It must be remembered that the duty imposed upon the Secretary of the Interior in acting on grants of this kind," Garfield wrote, with a bit of handy and creative self-justification, "prevents him from considering merely the preservation of the park in its natural state, but he must, as well, consider what use will give the greatest benefit to the greatest number," a close paraphrase of Pinchot's favorite slogan.[8]

Garfield went on to parse the words of Congress of February 15, 1901, which, he noted, authorized the interior secretary to permit rights-of-way through the national parks for facilities, dams, and reservoirs to supply water for domestic, public, or other beneficial uses, upon finding it not incompatible with the public interest. "Therefore," he reasoned, "I need only consider the effect of granting the application upon 'the public interest.'" Now he got to the crux of the matter: "The words 'the public interest' should not be confined merely to the public interest in the Yosemite National Park for use as a park only, but rather the broader public interest, which requires these reservoir sites to be utilized for the highest good to the greatest number of people. If Congress had intended to restrict the meaning to the mere interest of the public in the park as such, it surely would have used specific words to show that intent."

Garfield accepted that the city's water supply was "inadequate and unsatisfactory" and that the search for more and better water sources had been pursued by two opposing forces. The water companies had used the long delay in bringing water from the Yosemite Valley to San Francisco to gain control of the other available sources in order to sell them to the city, he noted. The federal government and San Francisco had carefully studied these sources, and both the Hydrographic Branch of the Geological Survey and the city's engineers, after years of investigation, had concluded that the Tuolumne River offered a desirable source.

The water companies fared the worst. Garfield, who was a firm supporter of the President's trust-busting efforts, essentially ignored them as "persons and corporations who have no rights to protect but merely the hope of financial gain if the application of the City is denied." As for the irrigation districts, he saw no conflict. Not only would the city safeguard their rights, it would, while developing its own water supply, help the irrigation districts. He claimed to fully appreciate and sympathize with the arguments of those espousing the national parks for their scenic effects and natural wonders and as health and pleasure resorts, but he was convinced that the public interest would be better served by granting the permit.

"The reservoir will not destroy Hetch Hetchy," he reasoned. "The prime change will be that, instead of a beautiful but somewhat unusable 'meadow' floor, the valley will be a lake of rare beauty." Against that, as he saw it, San Francisco would gain one of the world's purest water supplies and cheap electricity to pump the water and light the city; the Tuolumne and San Joaquin Valleys could access the stored water and the city's excess electrical power to pump water for irrigation; and the public would gain a road, kept by the city, to a remote part of the park. The city had options on private land in the park—some of the finest sites of the settlers—and would buy it and make it available to the public. Finally, the city would patrol its water supply and guard against forest fires. Garfield concluded, "I do not need to pass upon the claim that this is the only practicable and reasonable source of water supply for the City. It is sufficient that after careful and competent study the officials of the City insist that such is the case." He therefore granted the rights to San Francisco, which could now hold a vote and, with a two-thirds majority, choose the Tuolumne River and the two reservoir sites for its water.[9]

The grant came with strings attached, however. While there was no payment to the federal government for land valued at $200 million, the city had to give the nation an equivalent amount of property in or adjacent to the park. It could not develop Hetch Hetchy until its needs exceeded the capacity of the Lake Eleanor reservoir. And the grant's duration was not open-ended: the city had to submit the grant to a vote of its citizens (as its charter required) within two years and, if approved, begin to build the Lake Eleanor dam within three more years. Failing any of this, federal authorities could rescind the grant.

Muir, off promoting the park when Garfield's decision reached Martinez, was appalled when he got word and responded promptly to Garfield: "The more I study your decision . . . the greater seems the mistake you have made in allowing the city to destroy any part of the Park on any pretext whatever." Garfield had relied on Pinchot's "most careful consideration and . . . full accord," but Pinchot had never even seen the Tuolumne Canyon. By ruining Hetch Hetchy, Muir said, Garfield had committed the "grossest waste possible . . . saving with one hand, destroying with the other."

Next Muir rallied the troops. The government had made a "great mistake . . . believing the grossest preposterous misstatements," he wrote Johnson. "However, the Valley will escape damming most likely in our day at least," despite that Pinchot "surrenders everything to politicians & rich schemers." And he told Colby, "The wealthy wicked, the Phelans, Pinchots and their hirelings, will not thrive forever. . . . We may lose this particular fight, but truth and right must prevail at last." San Francisco voters still had to accept the grant, and Congress had to ratify it. That meant there was time for maneuvering and for the political winds to shift.[10]

Just two days after Garfield signed away Hetch Hetchy, the President and Gifford Pinchot hosted a three-day conservation conference at the White House. Under Roosevelt's aegis, Pinchot had risen rapidly and amassed great power. A decade earlier he had reluctantly taken over the feckless Forestry Division of the Agriculture Department, overseeing a staff of ten in a two-room office with an annual budget of less than $30,000. Now he was in charge of fourteen hundred workers with

an appropriation exceeding $3 million (about $90 million today) and
controlled territory four times the size of New England. He had an ego
to match and was a formidable opponent.

Despite the differences between Muir's good friend Sargent and
Pinchot on the National Forest Commission, Muir had bonded with
Pinchot, camping with him beside Lake McDonald, in what would
become Glacier National Park in 1910, while the other commissioners repaired to hotel rooms, and again on the south rim of the Grand
Canyon, where they hugged the campfire on a bitter night and talked
until midnight. In the morning, according to Pinchot, they returned,
like "guilty schoolboys," to assure their companions that they had not
vanished into the abyss. "It was such an evening as I have never had
before or since," Pinchot would say. This relationship helped a fractured commission stay on course. "Muir and I . . . confidently expected
that Mr. Pinchot would be with us in our defense of the purposes for
which the National Park—and in fact all national parks—had been
reserved," Johnson would later write. But Pinchot, who like Johnson
was an honorary vice president of the Sierra Club, was not with them.
"His personal responsibility lies in the fact that Mr. Roosevelt left all
such decisions to him," Johnson later seethed, "for the President said
to me, 'In forestry matters I have put my conscience in the keeping of
Gifford Pinchot.'"[11]

Though Burroughs stood by Roosevelt's side, Muir and the preserva-
tionists were not invited to the conference, including Johnson and others
prominent in forestry before Pinchot's rise, such as Sargent and former
interior secretary Noble, who had launched forest reform and whom
Johnson deemed the pioneer of conservation among officialdom. Muir
had been purposely removed from the invitation list. When Johnson
suggested that Sargent be included, Pinchot replied that there was "no
more room," even though a vast press corps had received invitations.
Pinchot was flexing his muscles and proving that he had a long memory.
Johnson, incensed by his omission from the guest list, decided not to
attend on his press pass, but Richard Gilder, his boss at the *Century*,
ordered him to go.[12]

Prior to the conference, the Sierra Club board of directors had sent the
President and the nation's governors a letter expressing its strong belief
in the "paramount value of scenic beauty among our natural resources":

The moral and physical welfare of a nation is not dependent alone upon bread and water. Comprehending these primary necessities is the deeper need for recreation and that which satisfies also the esthetic sense. . . . Our country has a wealth of natural beauty which is far beyond the power of human hands to create or restore, but not beyond their power to destroy. . . . Preservation is the greatest service that one generation can render to another.[13]

Nature benefited the nation not only physically, morally, and mentally but also economically, the directors argued. In Europe tourism produced half a billion dollars annually. The mountains of the American West offered some of the world's most spectacular and newest "natural pleasure-grounds," attracting tourists, climbers, and lovers of outdoor life from around the globe: "Even from a purely economic point of view it would be extremely unwise to administer our scenic resources in such a way that comparatively private gain results in universal public loss." The directors spoke for the club's members, now more than a thousand, who cared deeply about "every effort to secure to our and coming generations the benefit of our scenic resources."

Once at the conference, Johnson was, of course, ever the professional. He produced a glowing report for the *Century*, despite his personal feelings. Most of the governors were in attendance, along with special guests from universities and scientific and other public bodies. "It is difficult to see how it would be possible to secure a more authoritative, more competent or more national assembly," Johnson wrote. The purpose of the Conference of the Governors of the States was to "consider the waste of our resources of forests, minerals, soil, and water." Considering "the awful momentum of modern life," the President called it "the weightiest problem now before the nation," one that required foresight, which "we are not showing."

The steel magnate Andrew Carnegie, so well-known that he went by only his last name in the article, speaking about iron, told the group that it was "staggering to learn that our once-supposed ample supply of rich ores can hardly outlast the generation now appearing." He was emphatic about forests as well, stating telegraphically: "No forests, no long navigable rivers; no rivers, no cheap transportation. Less soil, less crops; less crops, less commerce, less wealth." James Hill, president of the Great Northern Railway, acknowledged that Americans were the world's most profligate users of natural resources. "The forests of this country, the product of centuries of growth, are fast disappearing." Of coal he said, "We still think nothing of consuming this priceless resource with the greatest possible speed." Another speaker referred to the "insane riot of destruction and waste of our fuel resources." At times, Johnson felt as if he were at a confessional. "Not a single speaker took issue with the alarming facts presented in regard to every field of our natural wealth," he said. Today, the concerns raised seem nothing short of prophetic: "floods, erosion, change of climate, waste of natural gas, and the diminution of seafood." Horace McFarland, a proponent of the architect- and urban-planner-led City Beautiful Movement, which promoted beautification and monumental grandeur in cities, linking it to moral and civic virtue, social harmony, and a higher quality of life, pleaded for the protection of beautiful scenery, a natural asset and form of wealth that should, he urged, be passed to future generations unsullied.

All seemed to feel the peril the nation faced and the need for action. While the governors did not endorse legislation, they found common ground on establishing a White Mountain and Appalachian park, removing the lumber tariff, and creating state forest commissions. They also agreed to meet again. "This conference," Kansas governor Ed Hoch, declared, to much approval, "has cemented the Union as no other influence has ever done before." Indiana governor Frank Hanly deemed it a "milestone in American history." After invoking the Constitution, Washington and Lincoln, and the spirit of working "only for the highest good of all the people," Hill closed the conference loftily: "We may, as a result of the deliberations held and the conclusions reached here today, give new meaning to our future and new luster to the ideal of a republic of living federated states, shape anew the fortunes of this country, and enlarge the borders of hope for all mankind."[14]

Johnson called the conference an "unqualified success" that "realized the most sanguine expectations of its usefulness." Still, he was personally aggrieved. He had formally proposed to Roosevelt two years earlier a "Conference of Governors" in the East to discuss forestry reform. The President had responded that he would talk to Pinchot. The previous September, Johnson had written the President and Pinchot again, providing more details about his idea. But Roosevelt replied that there had to be a local public demand for action, which he did not sense among the states containing the southern Appalachians. Pinchot's assistant responded that a conference to plan for forest preservation in the East would be worth trying, but while working on the Appalachian and White Mountains forest reserve bills, Pinchot and the American Forestry Association had found it difficult to get the governors interested. As Johnson saw it, Pinchot thought the idea was "impracticable."

Yet, as Johnson stood in the White House, having had to use a press pass to practically sneak into the conference that was his brainchild and that some would cite as the formal beginning of the modern conservation movement—and with Pinchot and Roosevelt possibly unaware he was even there—he was stunned when the President, addressing the room with animation, gave credit for the conference to Pinchot, who willingly accepted it. When Johnson confronted Pinchot to ask if he had forgotten the letters he had sent him on the subject, Pinchot replied cavalierly, "Oh, I may have had them in the back of my head."[15]

By the beginning of June, Muir had recovered enough from a bronchial ailment that had kept him housebound to give Johnson, who felt that Roosevelt's and Pinchot's treatment of him was "shabby," a pep talk: He should be proud of inventing the governors' conference, a "most novel & notable affair." Pinchot was "ambitious," willing to "sacrifice anything or anybody," and "distressingly mean" for taking credit for the conference. Muir reassured Johnson that "compensation . . . is sure to come, & we must go ahead fighting." Of all his friends, he said, "none has done so much as you have for the public good in the way of forest preservation & the great parks." Hetch Hetchy was not yet lost. "The preservation of natural beauty" was too often overlooked, "but light must come at last & we must arouse public opinion ere it is too late. Your name will honor my Yosemite book & last long after above squabbles are forgotten."[16]

"Your loyal friendship is one of the comforts of my life," Johnson replied, from the Republican National Convention in Chicago. "I heartily wish you were coming East soon." Then he turned to Muir's Yosemite book: "You ought to make it the aim of your life to finish up what you have to say about the National Park and all that region." At the convention, Roosevelt's endorsement helped his secretary of war, William Howard Taft, gain the presidential nomination. "I can't help but wonder if our opportunist president would have given up the Hetch Hetchy," Johnson wrote by hand in a postscript, "if there had been no Taft delegates to secure in California."

He enclosed the review of the White House conference that he had written for the July issue, which Gilder had sent to Roosevelt to be shown to Pinchot. "The President and his able lieutenant, Mr. Pinchot, head of the Forestry Bureau, are entitled to the greatest credit for working out successfully on a comprehensive plan the idea of a meeting of Governors to consider our failing resources," Johnson had written, certainly under duress. "The President's imaginative grasp of its possibilities and his generalship in arranging it would stamp him a constructive statesman of the first order. . . . We believe its success will be accounted the crowning achievement of his career." Pinchot had responded with a "warm and grateful letter in appreciation of it!" Johnson, still irked, added by hand, "Apparently it doesn't occur to him that any credit is due to my suggestion."[17]

He also sent another editorial, "A High Price to Pay for Water," slated for August, Johnson took a small jab at the White House conference, where despite Horace McFarland's plea, not enough was said of the conservation of one of the nation's chief resources, its "great natural scenery." While Roosevelt, Garfield, and Pinchot's "enlightened . . . forest conservation" had earned them the benefit of the doubt on public lands, the *Century*, early champion of a Yosemite National Park, which brought Hetch Hetchy under protection, found unsatisfactory the reasons given for the administration's extraordinary step of allowing San Francisco to use "one of the most beautiful gorges of the Sierra" as a reservoir. It logically placed the nation's great natural scenery, including Niagara Falls, Yellowstone National Park, and the Grand Canyon, at the service of any neighboring city. Johnson also defended those standing up for the national park—Muir and the members of the Sierra Club and like organizations—who were being branded "sentimentalists" and "poets," saying, "Cant of this sort on the part of people who have not developed beyond the pseudo-'practical' stage is one of the retarding influences of American civilization and brings us back to the materialistic declaration that 'Good is only good to eat.'"[18]

In late September, before setting out for Daggett, Muir wrote a warm letter to Johnson: "I've been crying 'Save the forests' for at least 30 years, but most of the work actually accomplished was done on your suggestions or guidance after 1890." The next point of contention in the Hetch Hetchy battle was, he told his friend, approaching: the supervisors had decided to proceed with the vote to fund their scheme.

The Sierra Club leaders released a hard-hitting flyer against the appropriation—signed by Muir, Badè, Colby, Parsons, and others—saying:

> The law under which the Hetch Hetchy rights were granted by the Secretary of the Interior provides that they "may be REVOKED BY HIM or his successor, in his discretion, and SHALL NOT be held to CONFER ANY RIGHTS, or easement, OR INTEREST in, to, or over any public land, reservation or park." IS THIS THE KIND OF RIGHT THIS CITY WANTS TO SPEND MILLIONS ON?

The flyer pointed out that the city would have to resort to "expensive condemnation proceedings" to get the rights to pump the Lake Eleanor water to the coast; that farther north, where rainfall was heavier, the water was cheaper and unclaimed by irrigation districts; and that to fund the Hetch Hetchy plan, San Francisco would have to float bonds for $75 million. The president of the chamber of commerce preferred to have San Francisco remain "the city with the smallest bonded debt per capita and the lowest percentage of mortgage debt" in the nation. The city had already ordered a saltwater fire-protection system, the flyer pointed out. "This chimerical water project . . . will cost untold millions of dollars and . . . add nothing to the immediate convenience, safety, or strength of the city." The appeal concluded by saying that the promoters of the Hetch Hetchy scheme should have "given exhaustive and careful consideration to every available source" and submitted the best . . .

TO A VOTE SO THAT YOU MIGHT DECIDE FOR YOUR-SELVES WHICH WATER SYSTEM YOU PREFER. . . . The question is put straight up to you, Mr. Voter, and you can not evade it—VOTE AGAINST THE HETCH-HETCHY PROJECT AND BONDS.

Despite Muir's insistence that the average citizen would reject the use of Hetch Hetchy, on November 12, San Francisco voted six to one to accept the grant. An editorial headline in the *Call* read, "In First Open Fight, San Francisco Votes Overwhelmingly for Hetch Hetchy and Against Spring Valley," indicating how the vote was perceived. It was the city versus the water company and no contest; decades of corporate abuse had come home to roost. "The people of San Francisco proclaimed that they want Hetch Hetchy," said the *Call*, "and that they have had enough of Spring Valley's chicanery, bulldozing and more or less legal extortion."[19]

It would be a busy December. San Francisco now had momentum. Roosevelt, by this point a lame duck, was obsessively planning an epic postpresidential African safari. William "Big Bill" Taft, a Yale-educated Ohioan, would not be inaugurated until March, and although he was Roosevelt's handpicked successor, no one knew exactly where he stood on the Hetch Hetchy issue, or whether Garfield and Pinchot, the two most influential advisers on the matter, would survive the transition.

"The 3 or 4 Hetch Hetchy schemers are far from satisfied with the Garfield award," Muir wrote Johnson. "They are going to Congress to make a desperate effort to get what they want, as I knew they would." They wanted "permission to dam H.H. at once. . . . For it is Electric power they want, not water." Six days later, he told Johnson, "I have good hope of winning our park fight in Congress notwithstanding the desperate struggle the schemers are making. . . . We must fight the thieves & robbers now & always."[20]

On December 16, the House Committee on Public Lands held a hearing on Resolution 184, the "so-called Hetch Hetchy resolution." Muir and the Sierra Club went on record with a brief statement, which began: Yosemite National Park was created so that the "scenic features of this great natural wonderland should be preserved in pure wildness for all time for the benefit of the entire nation. Hetch Hetchy Valley is . . . a great and wonderful feature of the park," and a "focus of pleasure travel," a "magnificent campground" crossed by the trails from north and south. Once made more accessible, it would attract travelers from around the world. "If dammed and submerged . . . the high Sierra gateway of the sublime Tuolumne Canyon leading up to the grand central campground of the upper Tuolumne Valley would be completely blocked and closed," which would essentially nullify the law creating the park.

Although Muir was not present, his testimony was introduced through his article "The Endangered Valley" from the January 1909 issue of the *Century*. "As you requested I have shunned controversy," Muir had told Johnson on sending it. "But I trust you will come out strong in an editorial crying Woe to the spoilers of God's best gifts, & all the good citizens of the world will roar Amen." In the article, Muir described Hetch Hetchy's landmarks, including Kolana, "a majestic pyramid" soaring more than two thousand feet, and across from it, Tueeulala Falls, plummeting six hundred feet to a ledge—the most beautiful falls he had ever seen, surpassing even Bridalveil for "airy swaying grace of motion and soothing repose." Nearby but very different, Wapama Falls plunged seventeen hundred feet, roaring and booming in gorge shadows like an avalanche. Though Hetch Hetchy's "walls are less sublime in height than those of Yosemite, its groves, gardens, and broad, spacious meadows are more beautiful and picturesque. It . . . ought to be faithfully guarded."[21]

At the close of the hearing, the matter was referred to a subcommittee to make amendments to the resolution and report back in January.

"It seems incredible that so barbarous a step backward as the destruction of a Yosemite Valley could possibly be taken by Congress," Muir wrote to Johnson two days later, "or that such a question could game a hearing anywhere in Civilization."

He told him, "Go to Washington as often as the grand cause requires & I will bear all the expense." He would have gone himself but was the "prisoner" of a miserable grippe, "the same as nearly ended my life journey last winter." On the last day of the year, he wired Johnson that Badè would be coming to Washington to appear at the committee hearing.

PART IV

A CALIFORNIA WATER WAR

•

Wee, modest, crimson-tippèd flow'r,

Thou's met me in an evil hour;

For I maun crush amang the stoure

    Thy slender stem:

To spare thee now is past my pow'r,

    Thou bonie gem.

—Robert Burns
from *To a Mountain Daisy*

The view from atop Yosemite Lumber Company's incline railroad built to carry logs off the mountainsides above El Portal, near the entrance to Yosemite National Park.

Presidents: William Howard Taft, Republican, 1909–13; Woodrow Wilson, Democrat, 1913–21

Secretaries of the Interior: James R. Garfield, 1907–09; Richard Ballinger, 1909–11; Walter Fisher, 1911–13; Franklin Lane, 1913–20

San Francisco Mayors: Edward Taylor, Democrat, 1907–10; James "Sunny Jim" Rolph, Republican, 1912–31

Congressmen: Representative Halvor Steenerson, Republican, Minnesota; Key Pittman, Democrat, Nevada

Allies of Muir and Johnson: Alden Sampson, New York City attorney, Sierra Club member; Harriet Monroe, poet, Detroit; Henry Osborn, president, American Museum of Natural History, New York City

CHAPTER 21

The Big Stick

On Saturday, January 9, 1909, at a quarter past ten in the morning, House Public Lands Committee chairman Frank Mondell, a Republican of Wyoming, called to order a hearing on Resolution 223, the amended Hetch Hetchy resolution. Mondell, like the rest of the committee members, had been deluged with letters and telegrams about Hetch Hetchy arriving at all hours.

Badè did not show up. He had left Washington suddenly, saying "business calls me away." Instead of testifying, he submitted a six-point argument against the grant on behalf of "a majority of the officers and members of the Sierra Club." It is unknown what important work pulled Badè away in the moment of need, but it is clear that in the end he was sorely missed. As was Muir himself.

In lieu of the learned professor, the club would be represented by Alden Sampson, a New York City attorney and wildlife authority, originally introduced to Muir by Pinchot. Muir had sent telegrams to Pennsylvania congressman John Reynolds, who had been assistant secretary of the interior under Cleveland, and Mondell, a past chair of the Committee on Irrigation of Arid Lands: "The nation relies on you to oppose Hetch Hetchy grant and destructive invasion of national parks. Give the people time to enter their protest."[1]

Muir and the Sierra Club had also helped orchestrate the deluge of protest mail from across the nation. They had teamed up with three Chicago clubs, the Geographical Society, the Playground Association, and the Saturday Walking Club, to produce a "Save the Hetch Hetchy Valley" circular, urging readers to oppose this "gross violation of the people's rights by writing at once" to Mondell and their own congressmen and senators. Back at work the day after Christmas, despite his illness, Muir had sent the circular to friends, asking them to add their voices to the protest.[2]

Mondell and the other members of the committee had received an earful. The geographically diverse and influential group of writers included former interior secretary Noble, *Atlantic Monthly* editor Ellery Sedgwick, the director of the Cleveland YMCA, professors from Johns Hopkins, Princeton, and Berkeley, and members of the AMC, the Mazamas, and the Florida Federation of Women's Clubs.

Thanks in large part to the Sierra Club, it was not just men who had had the opportunity to explore Yosemite. Women were a force among the writers, chief among them Harriet Monroe, whose *Putnam's Monthly* account of the Yosemite High Trip outing in 1904 had showed the power of the park, especially the Tuolumne Canyon, to transform her and her friends: "Difficulties became a stimulus in that mountain air, under those lofty pines," she had written. "The weak grew strong, and the strong became invincible. . . . Young girls tramped over an hundred miles in a week" to Hetch Hetchy Valley, "sparkling below us in the sun, its bright river patterning the green meadows with most intricate windings."[3]

Marion Parsons, Ed Parsons's wife, declared that "the proposed exchange of space in the floor of Hetch Hetchy for Hog Ranch is, to anyone who has seen the two places, absurd, Hog Ranch being without scenic attractions and the Hetch Hetchy one of the most beautiful and enjoyable natural parks." Tallulah LeConte wrote "to protest . . . as long and loud and hard as I can." The city, she said, could "spend a little more of [its] millions and build a dam farther down the river that would serve [its] every purpose and not infringe on Uncle Sam's property." Nevada botanist Laura McDermott asked, "If the rights of one national park are marked with the destructive hand of exploitation, what will be the ultimate fate of all of our country's reserve of wonderland?"

"These great parks and canyon floors are our greatest asset for our claim to a Switzerland in our own country," Martha Walker of Los Angeles asserted. "If we cannot save our best for the whole nation to enjoy, we are doing a great wrong." Florence Keen of Philadelphia wrote, "I see no need of destroying one of our fine national recreation grounds, which are already becoming too few. Once gone they can never be restored, and they are a national asset of which we have no right to deprive future generations."[4]

Edmund Whitman of the AMC, a robust organization of sixteen hundred members in twenty-two states, was the first to argue against the resolution at the hearing, the Sierra Club's Sampson having chosen to go second. In December, the AMC had filed a protest against the Garfield grant. Members, a number of whom had camped in the Tuolumne Canyon, had studied Secretary Hitchcock's 1902 decision, corresponded with Garfield, Pinchot, San Francisco authorities, and hydraulic engineers, and taken pains to inform themselves on the merits of both sides of the matter. They had concluded that Hitchcock had gotten it right the first time, when he judged that there was no "public necessity" compelling him to cede to the city part of the park. In fact, the act of October 1890 required the secretary to preserve its natural wonders in their natural condition.

With a talented roster of members who knew how to lobby and had no divided loyalties, the AMC, founded in 1876 to preserve New Hampshire's White Mountains, was an important ally of the Sierra Club's. It had been involved in land preservation efforts in Massachusetts and the protection of old-growth forests in New Hampshire. It brought perspective, cachet, and unity. As focused as the Sierra Club was on its stewardship of the Sierra Nevada, many of the San Francisco members, having lived for so long under Spring Valley's autocratic rule, were inclined to justify any means necessary to secure a municipally controlled water source.

For that reason, there was a growing rift in the Sierra Club. Its most vocal member at this hearing would not be John Muir or Robert Underwood Johnson but Marsden Manson—for the other side. Fortunately for Muir and Johnson, Whitman, who represented not only the AMC but also "some members of the Sierra Club," was an attorney and a deft speaker. He had spent a month with members of both clubs on a High Trip that traversed Hetch Hetchy and could parse Garfield's decision and the relevant law with the congressmen while entertaining them with anecdotes and wit. While Garfield waited to address the committee, Whitman held the floor for two hours.[5]

When asked if he disputed the right of the secretary of the interior to grant a temporary license or permit the use of Hetch Hetchy for a reservoir, Whitman replied, yes, "and I base that opinion on the opinions that have been rendered to the President to that effect."

"Does not the February statute specifically state that he may grant a reservoir privilege in any of the national parks?" California representative Everis Hayes, a San Jose newspaper publisher, asked. All the arguments would turn on this one point, which would often be interpreted according to the desired outcome.

"It does, subject to the other provisions of that statute," responded Whitman, "and subject to the original statute of 1880, which provided that the secretary should take steps to preserve the natural scenic wonder and curiosities in their original condition."

"But how can you preserve the bottoms . . . in this valley and at the same time use it as a reservoir?" another interlocutor, a Mr. Hammond, asked.

"You cannot," Whitman replied.

When asked if Hetch Hetchy had been "beautified," Whitman responded, "No, sir; it is in its natural condition. I see that in the hearings that have heretofore been had it was spoken of as a 'cattle ranch.' I have never seen any cattle there, and I am told by other people who have been there that there are no cattle. The only way to get cattle in there would be take them up there to the edge of the precipice and push them over." Laughter ensued.

"Did I understand you to say that when you went into the Hetch Hetchy Valley you did so from below," Republican representative Julius Kahn, a San Francisco attorney, asked Whitman, "and in coming back you came though the gorge in the Tuolumne beyond the Hetch Hetchy Valley?"

"I was not vigorous enough to get through that gorge. The gentlemen who did get through had pieces of canvas riveted with copper rivets to the seats of their trousers. I came by way of Hog Ranch." Again, Whitman got the staid group laughing.

John Gaines, a Nashville Democrat and the ranking member of the Public Lands Committee, followed up, "Have any of the men who had their pants fixed in that way come along to testify in this matter?"

"There were some here before the subcommittee the other day."

When asked whether the creation of this reservoir would "destroy the use of the other portions of the park," Whitman responded, "I put it to you, gentlemen, as practical men and assuming you were citizens of San Francisco. What would you say if twenty-three miles above the reservoir there is a large valley visited as I visited it, by nearly two hundred people and fifty animals, staying two or three weeks? There was one unfortunate occurrence there, as I remember, of a young fellow being carried out ill of typhoid fever, and he died on mule back on the journey home. Now the question is, are things of that kind to be allowed to go on in connection with the supply of water for a large city?"

"How about the sides of the valley?" Gaines asked. "Are they penetrable or impenetrable?"

"If I were a fly, I could climb them," Whitman replied, to more chuckling, "but not otherwise."

His testimony closed out on a scatological note. "I want to ask what disposition is made of the excrement and refuse matter?" said Hayes.

"We bathed in the streams. Tin cans were at a premium. The excrement was left around in holes."

"Covered up?" Hayes asked. To which Whitman replied that he thought that "it was generally covered up."

Hayes, who was under the impression that it stayed cold in Hetch Hetchy year-round, then asked, "With the excrement and refuse matter covered and the thermometer at thirty-two degrees, would not that condition destroy all germs that there might be, which otherwise might pollute the water?"[6]

"I will leave that to the committee, that two hundred people, with thirty or forty horses—I do not know whether the horses covered anything. . . ."

At this point the chairman suggested it was time for Whitman to wrap up so that another speaker could be called.

Later, Marsden Manson, who had clearly been waiting for the moment to clear the air, would get in the last word on waste management: "The possible pollution which would come from any quantity of camping in the Tuolumne we believe can be met" because most of it was either "absolutely inaccessible" or "extremely rough" and reachable only a "few months in the year." The pollution from campers would be "extremely small" and "easily corrected." Indeed, he said, "It is now corrected, and

I have been camping with the Sierra Club, of which I am a member. I am very proud of my membership. I have been out with them, and the regulations of the club prescribe that we shall be extremely particular about burying every scrap of camp refuse, and the disposition of fecal matter is very carefully looked after. Deep pits are dug in the sandy soil, and they are filled at the close of camp, and every precaution is taken."

Whitman, having stolen the show, concluded his testimony just before noon: "Gentlemen, . . . this seems to me of so much importance to the country that this committee should not recommend this resolution . . . without further investigation by the new Congress. There is a new administration coming in, and it may take a different view of the matter from the present administration, and I therefore recommend that this matter be postponed until a fresh investigation can be made."

Gaines asked him if President Roosevelt had been to Hetch Hetchy. Whitman said he thought not. "If he had been, he would not have taken the stand he has taken in that."

"If a man of his activity cannot get through there, how can President Taft ever expect to get through it?" Gaines gibed, to guffaws.

Backed up now, the committee had no time to break for lunch. "The secretary of the interior very kindly came here at my invitation this morning," Chairman Mondell said. "Busy man that he is, I regret very much that we have kept him here so long without an opportunity to be heard. If there is no objection, then, the committee will go on with the hearing, and as the secretary of the interior has some other matters to attend to, I expect we had better hear him at this time."

Before he could start, however, a discussion of the volume of letters that the committee members were receiving ensued, leading to an amusing exchange. "I have received one this morning from John Muir," Congressman Reynolds said.

"Who is John Muir?" Gaines asked.

"John Muir is a great naturalist and geologist and a friend of the President," the chairman responded. "He is the man after whom Muir Glacier in Alaska was named."

"Where does he live?" asked Gaines.

"In a little place near San Francisco—Martinez," responded Kahn.

"What is his business?" asked Gaines.

"He is a geologist and scientist," said Kahn.

"A naturalist and explorer," the chairman added. "Now, Mr. Secretary, we regret keeping you."[7]

Secretary Garfield opened with a statement supporting the grant and then answered a barrage of questions. Garfield most certainly knew who Muir was and took issue with him and spoke turgidly about the proceedings and his interpretation of the law: "A great many gentlemen, like Mr. Muir and like Mr. McFarland, and those who have written here, I feel very clear take the wrong view of public interests. They have failed to understand the tremendous importance of the public interest to which I have referred as the domestic use of water. . . . If we look at it from the point of view of those gentlemen, then everything should be made subservient to their single desire to retain the park as it is."

Other than to give his name, which the stenographer spelled incorrectly as "Olden," and his address and to request that Whitman speak first, Alden Sampson had not yet given voice to the Sierra Club at the hearing. He finally spoke up when Garfield asserted that turning Hetch Hetchy into a reservoir for San Francisco would have no impact on the availability of Tuolumne Meadows for camping and exploring the mountains. "May I say just a word in reference to that?" Sampson chimed in. "The practical working would be that it would exclude the public from one-half of the Yosemite National Park." To which Garfield replied tersely, "I think not."

But on this matter, Sampson, who had spent six weeks in and around Hetch Hetchy that summer, was better informed than the interior secretary, and now his words flowed: "But they could not camp on the Tuolumne River, which is the interesting portion of the park. That is the reason why the park was created." And Hayes had implied that the cold weather in Hetch Hetchy would neutralize the germs. "Hetch Hetchy is rather hot. . . . so much so that I left it. There is no frost there in the summer," Sampson said. He also pointed out that Yosemite had had eight thousand visitors the previous summer, an increase of more than 30 percent over the one before, and that looked to be a trend. "There is no earthly reason why the Yosemite should not be surrendered for the use of a city just as much as the Hetch Hetchy, which is almost equal in beauty and in some respects has charms which the Yosemite has not."

Chairman Mondell promptly gave Garfield an out, which he seized, making a swift exit. By the time Mondell finally called on Sampson to make a statement, the reticent spokesman had to be coaxed.

"Is ten or fifteen minutes trespassing on the patience of the committee?" Sampson asked hesitantly. Assured that it was okay, he soon had to admit that he did not, strictly speaking, represent the "corporate body" of the Sierra Club, but a "very large majority of the Sierra Club." Nevertheless, he was a mountain authority who had spent sixteen years as a big-game hunter in the Rockies, and he waxed eloquent on the disputed tract, which he also knew well: "The Tuolumne Valley is one of the most interesting valleys in America. There is a stretch of sixteen miles whose equal I have never seen for certain features of beauty—very extraordinary masses of flowers that give a hue to a whole meadow." He also tried to put to rest the subject of waste and excrement in the watershed: "No intelligent community is going to allow indiscriminate camping along the waters which supply that reservoir. The earth will not be purified by frost; that is out of the question, and they cannot tolerate the presence of campers and refuse of camps and animals on the river immediately above that reservoir."[8]

While disarmingly reluctant, Sampson made his main thrust incisive and clear-eyed: "The citizens of the United States have just as much right to go into the Hetch Hetchy Valley today as they have to come to Washington and see the Capitol. If they are excluded from one-half of the Yosemite National Park, they have been deprived of property which belongs to them, which has been presented to San Francisco. Is it not the proper way to go about this question—I want to say this with all becoming modesty, so far as I am able to accomplish it—is not the intelligent way to find out whether or not other sources of water supply are available before this is presented to that city?"

On the morning of January 12, the Committee on Public Lands resumed its hearing on Resolution 223, albeit without a quorum. The committee was getting impatient. "I wish we could get to . . . a point where we can report or not report it," said Gaines, who now presumably knew who John Muir was. "It is taking up a world of time." Because this session was starting with the testimony of the attorney for Spring Valley Water, however, it was sure to generate sparks. It soon devolved into a sparring match between Spring Valley and San Francisco over whether the city was merely trying to force a sale of the waterworks at a deflated price. "I am asking you gentlemen whether Congress should dismember a national park, one of the beauty spots of the earth . . . to aid San Francisco in a deal with the Spring Valley Water Company," argued the company's attorney, Ed McCutcheon, a law partner of Warren Olney's. "The only purpose and the only effect can be to place San Francisco in a situation where she may say to the Spring Valley Water Company, 'We have you at a disadvantage.'" He implied—almost laughably, since the company had long bilked the city of millions of dollars—that the city was trying to gain the Tuolumne River rights to force Spring Valley into bankruptcy.

To which Gaines retorted, to chuckles, "Do you not think the people have better right to drink God's waters than to smell God's roses?"

"I do not know," McCutcheon responded. "I think those are natural rights each one of which may be enjoyed."[9]

"Which is more necessary?" Gaines posed. "I am looking to the practical part."

"You can get along without many things, but you cannot get along without water," replied McCutcheon, "and I am not so foolish as to stand here and say that this National Park should be preserved at the expense of San Francisco, if San Francisco is solely dependent upon it for a water supply. But that is not the fact." McCutcheon soon brought the discussion around to the issue he wished to hammer home: Why had the San Francisco Board of Supervisors not instituted an eminent domain proceeding to acquire Spring Valley's property? "I will answer that myself, and then you men may answer that, if you please." Chortles rippled through the crowd. The city is afraid to let an impartial tribunal evaluate this property, he stated, "and it comes to you, the representatives in the Congress of the United States, and says, 'Our hands are tied. We are shackled by this monopoly,' which I have said to you cannot be a monopoly in view of the existing rate legislation of California. 'We ask you to give us this *big stick* in order that we may wield it over the Spring Valley company and make it come to our terms.'"

Just who wielded the "big stick" became the next topic of the hearing.

Manson disparaged Spring Valley for its inability to provide quality water, saying it had sources within fifty miles of San Francisco that were subject to the increasing pollution of human activities. On many acres he had found cattle manure so thick that no square yard was uncontaminated, and at an area that was to be bought in Calaveras, he had seen cow carcasses, "with anthrax reported in the region." Later, Manson added that Lobos Creek received the drainage from cemeteries with many thousands of bodies and claimed that Spring Valley's chief engineer "boils and filters" the water coming into his house. He asked McCutcheon if he used water from Spring Valley's pipes in his office or paid for bottled water.

"Do you desire to say to this committee and to the world that the San Francisco water supply is . . . unhealthy?" asked California representative Sylvester Smith, who had introduced the resolution.

"I do not, sir. It is fairly good," responded Manson. "It is better than many municipalities that are getting their supplies under disadvantages."

"You are giving it a pretty hard reputation," said Smith.

"What is the health of San Francisco!" McCutcheon interjected. "What do statistics show the health of San Francisco to be—good or bad?"

"Particularly good," Manson replied, "but it is due to our west winds."

"Yes, I suppose they blow the typhoid germs out of the water," McCutcheon fired back.

"It occurs to me, we ought to eliminate that feature from this discussion," the chairman broke in, "because none of you gentlemen, it seems to me, want to give the city of San Francisco a hard name in that respect."

"Notwithstanding the impurity of the Spring Valley water, you do want to buy that property?" said McCutcheon. He and Smith wanted to see this discussion move to the courts of San Francisco in an eminent domain proceeding that would bog down the city in the courts, keep the debate in a venue where they had sway, and, if needed, at least allow the company to demand a premium price for its property. Manson insisted that he had urged the city to buy Spring Valley. "We earnestly desire to buy it," he would say later in the hearing, and the city was not asking Spring Valley to sacrifice its property. "I will go back to San Francisco, after six years of litigation . . . and go before the people of that city and urge them to purchase the Spring Valley property at a valuation of a million dollars more than was fixed by the court." The court had set a price of $27.5 million, replied McCutcheon. With Manson's premium it would come to $28.5 million (nearly $900 million today).

Manson believed that the city should buy and operate the Spring Valley properties for a decade, as it developed the new sources it now sought, which would inevitably be needed. "The *big stick* that Mr. McCutcheon refers to is now in the hands of the corporation . . . which enjoys the monopoly of that necessity, water supply."

"About the *big stick*," McCutcheon responded. "Are you leaving any big stick in the hands of this corporation when under the laws of the State of California its rates must annually be fixed by the Board of Supervisors of San Francisco and when, if it collects one cent in excess of the rates fixed by that public agency, its works and franchises may be forfeited to the city?"

Gaines asked Manson why the city had not instituted condemnation proceedings. "Is it because for years you have been trying to buy, by contract, these water privileges and the thing has just run along and along and along?"

"It has been an interrupted effort on the part of the city, due to the fact that these administrations are unfortunately subject to political vicissitudes," said Manson, who explained that the "abundant badness" of one city government was "so awful" that beside it the others are "shining examples of virtue and honor."

"We have all had bad city governments," Gaines consoled. "I am not deriding this poor, unfortunate, earthquake-visited city. God knows I want to help her along. . . . In addition to what, we will say, is a bad city government, you have, from year to year, and it seems for thirty years, been trying to buy this by contract. You have gone to them and asked them how much they will take for this property?"

Manson explained that they had been in litigation with Spring Valley for a decade, including a pending case, and they expected more of the same. "We cannot afford to wait," he said. A prolonged drought would "put an absolute stop to the development of the city. . . . We fear the Greeks bearing gifts, when our enemies advise us to a certain course. It is not the first time that condemnation proceedings have been suggested. It is a very dangerous proceeding." Not only had Spring Valley tied up the city in court, Manson pointed out, but it had also sabotaged any attempt by the city to buy its own source, as when it had swooped in and bought the Calaveras site out from under the city and then declined to develop it for three decades. "They are now here trying to keep us from acquiring another system."[10]

"There seems to be no difference of opinion as to the possibility of developing the Spring Valley Water Company's sources of supply," said the chairman, trying to build some consensus as the hearing wound down. Manson asked that the company submit a firm selling price to the city "in dollars and cents."

"Why do you not condemn it?" asked Smith, the political craftsman banging the nail on the head yet again. "Your mind is surcharged with the idea that everything that comes from the Spring Valley Company is full of corruption."

"That is what the Spring Valley Company has been advising us for some time," responded Manson, adding that, as city engineer, "I will never advise them to go and do those things which the Spring Valley attorneys and corporation interests advise."

"You fear the Greeks offering gifts?" McCutcheon said.

"I do."[11]

At which point, after three hours of punches and counterpunches and dogs chasing their own tails, the hearing at last concluded.

CHAPTER 22

We Have Only Begun to Fight

At the beginning of 1909, Muir was in Southern California, staying with friends and "preaching the Tuolumne gospel," as he told Johnson. Although he made no mention of it, the city of Los Angeles was in the middle of its own struggle to procure water. It had recently begun constructing an aqueduct that would drain Owens Valley to the east, igniting decades of conflict with the residents there. Still, he had had a long conversation with Harrison Otis, publisher of the *Los Angeles Times*, and he reported, "all the Pasadena & Los Angeles press is on our side in the H. H. fight. The *Los Angeles Times* is especially influential." He closed with some heartfelt advice: "What a load you are carrying! Don't kill yourself—but watch & pray & strike as you may."[1]

Learning that the Senate Committee on Public Lands was on the verge of sending the Hetch Hetchy resolution to the full Senate, Johnson *had* struck. On February 4, he wrote Muir that he had wired Senator Knute Nelson, of Minnesota, the chairman of the Committee, to protest and respectfully demand a hearing. He had also telegraphed clubs and associations, asking them to protest. He worked into the wee hours of the morning writing to senators, many of whom he knew personally. He believed a hearing was likely and thought they could win on a joint resolution originating in the Senate. He asked Muir to write a letter for the *Century*, the tip of the spear, "calling upon the East to help" and to "keep up the fire of local protest."[2]

At the hearing on February 10, Johnson quickly invoked Muir—in case anyone, à la Representative Gaines, still did not know who he was. "We call him the Grand Old Man of California," he said.

He is known to you, no doubt, as the discoverer of the great Muir Glacier, which bears his name, and is the one man who has been the explorer and describer of the great and magnificent scenery of Yosemite National Park. He knows every foot of it, and no one is entitled even to come into the field of rivalry with Mr. Muir on a question of the natural beauties of California. In that respect I believe him to be the first citizen of California, and the time will come, when he is dead and gone, when California will build him a great monument. Meantime nature has built him a great monument in the Muir Glacier.

On that authority, Johnson went on to state his case, once again praising the Roosevelt administration for its "colossal service" in conserving natural resources. "It is the one thing that five hundred years from now will stand out in the history of this administration," he said, "but I cannot go with the administration to the extent of destroying this valley." He refuted any association with Spring Valley, the brush with which their opponents had attempted to tar them, and then described the "glories of the Park." "Such a treasure ought not to be diverted save for overwhelming reasons and as a last resort," he asserted. "They go to Hetch Hetchy as a first resort."

The senators then questioned Johnson while Phelan and McCutcheon each injected his spin. As Johnson's allotted time wound to a close, he stated forcefully, "Now what I say is, until you have demonstrated that there is not other adequate water supply for San Francisco, you cannot come to us and ask us to dismember a national park, solemnly and unanimously dedicated—I do not believe there was a vote against it in 1890—solemnly dedicated to the people for a specific purpose. In fact, it was dedicated to the whole world. . . . You have no right to ask us to accede to this proposition."[3]

Following Johnson, Henry Gregory of the American Scenic and Historic Preservation Society, invoking Milton, declared, "The glory of our country is not commerce, is not business, is not our national revenue, but the scenery . . . God has given us," a sentiment that perhaps rang hollow given that the society's president was a Tiffany & Co. executive and the honorary president was J. P. Morgan. "In this era of conservation," Gregory concluded, "I lift up my voice in behalf of the preservation of this magnificent scenery."

Whitman "rammed home the unconstitutional argument against Garfield," Johnson reported to Muir, and McFarland spoke of the sanitary issue that would certainly lead to the closure of the watershed. They had saved the best for last. Harriet Monroe took the floor on behalf of the Geographic Society of Chicago and the Saturday Walking Club. "But in a larger sense," she said, "I represent the people of the United States, to whom the Hetch Hetchy Valley has been deeded in perpetuity by Congress, whose children and children's children will have an ever-increasing interest in it." Monroe believed that Yosemite deserved the same support from the legislature as Yellowstone, as she wrote in *Putnam's*:

> In the Yellowstone the Government has spent millions in the construction and care of good roads and trails; and millions must be similarly spent in the Yosemite if its wonders are to be accessible to the people. . . . The Government should say a resolute no to all predatory schemes, however plausible. Its recent weak acquiescence in the plan of the San Francisco Board of Supervisors, who wish to convert the Hetch Hetchy Valley into a reservoir, sets a vicious precedent and should be revoked. . . . And if it is fulfilled, a little garden of paradise, the focal point of many trails and jewel-casket of the upper park, will be destroyed forever.

She dazzled the men before her as she evoked camping in Hetch Hetchy with the eloquence and vision of a poet: "It was a garden of paradise, this valley; a lesser Yosemite, but very different, with an infinitely charming individuality of its own; smaller but more compact, less grand but not less beautiful." No doubt Monroe's hypnotic voice would linger in their heads: "Gentlemen, it rests with you to preserve intact this jewel-casket of the mountains. If you permit it to be flooded, the flowery grasses, the great trees, and the winding pattern of the river will be destroyed forever." She was the only woman to speak at any of the hearings, and the only speaker not to be continually interrupted by the senators. She painted a picture they could see and spoke of a responsibility they could not deny. Her speech was so stirring, Johnson told Muir, that the senators did a rare thing—they applauded her. All in all, Johnson felt the team had made an "admirable impression of defending the public interest." The senators had shaken their hands and effusively congratulated Monroe on her speech.[4]

Later, Johnson would write Muir that he had "the best authority for saying that the joint resolution will not be called up in the House, because of the inaction of the Senate."[5]

Indeed, it was beginning to look as if Monroe had won the day. Not only had her message hit home, but her perception was keen. While listening to the debate in both chambers, she concluded that arguing that the entire watershed would be closed, an idea rejected by Phelan and others, was not a fruitful line of debate. She sent Colby and Parsons a letter advising them to focus on their two best arguments: first, the extraordinary beauty of the valley; and second, the poor precedent of converting part of a national park to private use. She was also shocked that the Sierra Club had not sent anyone from California to speak at the Senate hearing. "No amount of letters and telegrams are a tenth part as impressive as personal appearances and the spoken word."[6]

This lack on the part of the Sierra Club still haunts the history of the proceedings. If Muir himself had testified, would it have made a difference?

A few days after returning to New York City, Johnson spoke to the National California Society of New York at the Waldorf, "on the subject of the dismemberment." During Johnson's speech, Mrs. Grunsky rose and said a certain engineer had told her that it was not necessary to keep the public away from the watershed. Johnson, not knowing who she was, replied that she must be referring to Mr. Grunsky, but on such a subject he "thought it was the sanitary & not the civil engineer who carried weight." The society passed a unanimous resolution opposing the Garfield grant.

On February 19, Johnson told Muir that while he was sure they would win, he expected the Phelan gang to stay and try again. So they needed Congress to revoke the grant or at least appoint a commission. "Perhaps we can get Taft to revoke the grant. Ballinger it is announced is to be Sec'y of the Interior. I'll try to reach him with our documents." Three days later, he told Muir that they needed to press the new administration, and he was meeting with the incoming attorney general the next day. The "Phelan crowd" would try to get to Ballinger, he said, and he wanted Muir to let Ballinger know that they would present him with conclusive arguments for following the precedent of former secretaries Hitchcock and Noble, not Garfield.[7]

In early March, Muir was off in Arizona and the Grand Canyon, camping with Burroughs and a journalist who was documenting the trip for the *Century*. In Washington, William Howard Taft assumed the presidency. He was more conservative, less bullish, more a force of rules and less a force of nature than Roosevelt; they were friends, but their differences on certain issues and their egos would become a nightmare for the Republican Party. Richard Ballinger, a former mayor of Seattle and commissioner of the General Land Office under Roosevelt, replaced Garfield at the Interior Department. Conservationists worried that Taft's environmental protections would not be as staunch as Roosevelt's and that large hydroelectric companies would gobble up resources and control energy prices. Two weeks after the inauguration, Johnson anxiously recalibrated. "I have had no response to my request to know what you and your friends think should be our next move," he wrote Muir in care of Colby since Muir was still away. Lacking that, he advised: "Apply to Secretary Ballinger for a revocation of the grant, and, if that fails (I see the enemy is claiming Ballinger already), institute proceedings to enjoin the Secretary and the Supervisors." They might be able to find a public-spirited lawyer, he said, to take up the cause in the courts in Washington. "If an authority said they had a strong case, it might sway Ballinger, who would fear losing in the courts early in his administration."

Johnson concluded the letter with an air of partisanship followed by a dose of pugnacity: "I've been too busy even to felicitate you on our victory in the Congressional Committees." He urged Muir to send him all the comments of the "S. F. press, libels and all." "If they were in New York, I'd sue the CALL for speaking of me as 'mendacious'—and I'd do it in the public interest."[8]

Muir did not respond until April, as Helen had been hospitalized in Los Angeles with "some sort of typhoid fever," and he had rushed to be with her. At last, he had had a chance to read Johnson's "many good, wise letters" and to meet with Colby and Badè. "We are unanimous," Muir wrote: "(1) In applying to Secretary Ballinger for a revocation of the grant. We do not believe that the enemy has made anything like a conquest of the Secretary, and that the chances for a revocation are good. But if we should fail in this that (2) In accordance with your suggestions, proceedings should be instituted to enjoin the Secretary and the Supervisors on the grounds specified in your letter." He added, "Be assured, My Dear Johnson, that your efforts on behalf of Hetch Hetchy are enthusiastically appreciated by all of us. After you got well you have shown all your old-time indomitable heroism in our big battle so completely won." He then reminded Johnson to send him an accounting of his expenses, which he would "gladly" reimburse.

"Public opinion in our big fight has been constantly growing in our favor," he went on. "I cannot see, even without a revocation of the grant, that they can ever be successful in breaking up our grand Yosemite National Park."[9]

Despite the rising tide of public opinion, however, the turmoil within the Sierra Club itself now drove even Muir to despair. Frustrated and dejected by his inability to lead a united group in this most basic duty to defend the park, he announced that he planned to resign both as president and as a member of the club. It was a momentary loss of confidence. Colby soon convinced him not to do either, assuring him that if he did, the fight for Hetch Hetchy would surely be lost. To alleviate the pressure, Colby suggested that they form a new organization, the Society for the Preservation of National Parks, that would further establish Hetch Hetchy as a national issue with a broad coalition forcefully opposed to the destruction of the park.

Muir agreed and was named president, while Badè was chosen vice president and Colby's wife, Rachel, served as treasurer. The society's advisory council included Johnson, Monroe, Noble, Whitman, McFarland, and Sampson. The organization lived at 402 Mills Building, where Colby, whose law partners represented the city, would pull the strings without being listed as a leader. Nevertheless, he would not pull punches. "Let me assure you that we have only begun to fight," he informed Pinchot with fiery rhetoric, "and we are not going to rest until we have established the principle 'that our National parks shall be held forever inviolate,' and until we have demonstrated to the satisfaction of everyone, including yourself, that the American people stand for that principle."

Meanwhile, Johnson had worked himself to ill health, or so believed Muir, who tried to convince him to join the upcoming Sierra Club outing. "We have a number of good photographers & will take pains to get a big lot of the very best views of the Tuolumne basin," Muir said. "The trip would not cost you any money & might save your life." But Johnson was too busy at work and on the Hetch Hetchy campaign; he did, however, in early September, make time to travel to Beverly, Massachusetts, to visit President Taft.

The Tafts were summering at Dawson Hall, the estate of retired United States Rubber Company president Robert Evans, where Taft's wife, Nellie, hoped the cool breezes of Boston's North Shore would help her recuperate from a stroke (or nervous breakdown, according to some) suffered shortly after Taft's inauguration. The stay had gotten off to a rocky start when souvenir hunters vandalized the cottage that was to be Taft's summer White House. Then it got much worse. As the first couple arrived, they passed a vehicle on the way out carrying Evans, who had been thrown from his horse and would soon die in a Boston hospital. His gracious wife, Maria, soldiered on, enduring the disruptions—including the Secret Service trampling her flower beds—of the Tafts' extended stay. When the walrus-mustached Taft was not golfing or taking automobile excursions, he was holding court. Johnson took the opportunity to suggest that Muir guide the President on his upcoming West Coast swing, just as he had done with Roosevelt. "Tell Muir to join me on my arrival in San Francisco," Taft responded, "and I'll be delighted to have him on the Yosemite trip." Johnson had frankly told Taft that he should revoke the grant, "to set his administration right," and Taft had helped him secure a meeting with Secretary Ballinger.[10]

"Well done for you," Muir wrote Johnson. "These last letters have the ring & vim of your best fighting days. Many thanks for the encouragement they bring to us all on this side of the continent." The invitation to accompany the President in Yosemite had arrived the day before. "A neat job," Muir said. "One of your best. I'm particularly delighted over your Ballinger meeting."

Upon the President's "insistence," Johnson invited Ballinger to lunch at the Century Club and showed him photos of Hetch Hetchy. Ballinger was "astonished at the beauty of the place," Johnson told Muir. "If he is sincere then we have found a sympathetic Secretary." Although Ballinger could not revoke the grant, he could suspend its operation until Congress ruled on it.[11]

On the morning of October 7, 1909, Muir joined President Taft's entourage in San Francisco and traveled with him to Yosemite. "No more competent conductor of a scenic expedition in that region could be had, but Mr. Muir is hopelessly wrong on this most important question," the October 8 *San Francisco Call* declared in its reporting of Taft's visit, referring to Muir's stance on Hetch Hetchy. "In that view Mr. Muir's close attendance on the president is regarded with suspicion." Taft, as Roosevelt had, reveled in the fresh mountain air and Muir's company.

It was a good and timely distraction for Muir, who was mourning the death a month earlier of Edward Harriman. During the two previous summers, Muir and Keith had stayed with the railroad tycoon at his Pelican Lodge on Klamath Lake in Oregon. Harriman had hired a stenographer to help Muir with his writing and had shown his tender side to Keith, who was unwell, by tucking him in bed each night. "O dear! My heart aches over the departure of brave Harriman," Muir had recently written to Johnson. "All through our Yosemite fights since the Recession struggle began to our last one, Hetch Hetchy, he was our steadfast & able friend. None but myself knows how much he accomplished for us."[12]

Muir and the Taft party spent the first night at El Portal, near the entrance to the park, where, unbeknownst to them, the steep verdant mountainsides were about to be denuded by loggers. The next morning they set out for several days of travel by stagecoach and on foot. First they went to Wawona to see the Mariposa Grove, and to drive through the famous Wawona Tree for the requisite photograph.

Like Harriman, Taft would soon fall under Muir's sway. Though the two titans of industry and politics both appreciated Muir's devilish sense of humor, physically they could not have been more different. Harriman was notably diminutive (though Keith described him as having "a Napoleonic head"), while Taft was famously large, six feet tall and

350 pounds. Much was made by the press of his abundant meals, the inability of the horses to carry him, and his perspiration while hiking. As they walked, Taft and Muir engaged in playful banter. Coming down the trail from Glacier Point to the Yosemite floor, Taft pointed to a spot in the valley and told Muir he thought it would make a terrific farm.

President Taft and Muir (both seated in second row of carriage) at the Wawona Tree in Mariposa Grove, October 1909, by Howard Tibbitts.

"Why, this is Nature's cathedral, a place to worship!" Muir retorted.

Taft parried, "Now that would be a fine place for a dam!"

"A dam! Yes, but the man who would dam that would be damning himself!"

But the two also found time to talk seriously. Muir knew that he had hit home when the departing President asked him to meet Secretary

Ballinger in El Portal the next day and supplied him with a letter requesting Ballinger to go with Muir to see Hetch Hetchy, which he did.

Leaving the park, Muir was satisfied that Taft and Ballinger had a good understanding of the "water scheme" and informed Johnson that he had had a "good telling time" with them. Indeed, he had made friends and allies of both men. "Everything looks promising for our side of the fight," he assured Johnson. Colby and the club were working on a new pamphlet "& plan to get at least the Hetch Hetchy part of the Garfield grant revoked & legislation to stop for good the violation of national parks in general." In a follow-up, he told Johnson, "The H. Hetchy sky now seems brighter."[13]

Muir made one more excursion to Yosemite that year, one that contains a note of mystery. He and the Keiths camped for a week in Hetch Hetchy. As Mary Keith casually recorded in her notes of the outing, Muir walked ten miles over a ridge to Lake Eleanor to meet with Mayor Phelan, returning the next day. Sadly for posterity, there is no known account of this seemingly momentous meeting and no suggestion of how it came about.[14]

CHAPTER 23

A Shocking Report

In January 1910, President Taft sacked Pinchot. The outspoken Forest Service chief had accused Secretary Ballinger of corruption and lax environmental oversight in awarding Alaskan coal-mining rights to a partnership that included the Morgans and Guggenheims and then loudly criticized Taft himself as the widely publicized so-called Ballinger Affair unfolded. Roosevelt was not only incensed at the firing of his political ally and confidant but frustrated at Taft's conservation backsliding.

Congress held hearings on the matter, exonerating Ballinger, but the controversy sent shock waves through the Republican Party. With Pinchot fanning the flames and running interference, Roosevelt, fresh from an African safari in the summer of 1910 on which he and his party collected more than ten thousand specimens for the National Museum of Natural History's new building, would not mend fences. Instead, he would form a new Progressive Party (popularly known as the Bull Moose Party) and run against Taft in the 1912 presidential election, ultimately resulting in the first Democratic president of the century. This would in turn have a significant impact on the fate of Hetch Hetchy and Yosemite National Park.

"I'm sorry to see poor Pinchot running amuck after doing so much good hopeful work—from sound conservation going pell-mell to destruction on the wings of crazy inordinate ambition," Muir would later write Johnson, who was now editor of the *Century*. In November

1909, Gilder had died of angina, the same illness that had taken his predecessor, Josiah Holland, and which Johnson would observe was "a particular foe of the literary profession." Although Gilder had been ill, his death came as a surprise as he had been cheerful and industrious, and his colleagues thought he was on the mend.

Several years before, Gilder had called Johnson into his office. "R.U.J.," he had said, "with all the appreciation I had from Dr. Holland, I never had from him any definite assurance that he desired me to succeed to his chair. I wish to tell you now that I have just come from an interview with the trustees, in which I have told them that, in case anything should happen to me, it is my desire that the succession should fall to you." Johnson had worked with Gilder, whose humor, intellect, and goodwill had created an atmosphere of "happiness and comradeship," for thirty-six years. During that time Gilder's focus had shifted from literature and the arts to social causes, though he remained a towering figure in New York City's arts world. Johnson would spend four months responding to the outpouring of condolences.

Gilder, with Johnson by his side, had led what was considered one of the nation's best general periodicals. Their genteel world was giving way to the cynical and pragmatic industrial age, however, and the magazine was facing headwinds. New less expensive publications were siphoning off top writers, and circulation had been slipping for some time. Johnson had his work cut out for him.[1]

Meanwhile, the fissure within the Sierra Club over Hetch Hetchy put the organization in an awkward position. Unable to speak with one voice, it looked weak and conflicted, which played into the hands of San Francisco. Olney, the former mayor of Oakland, had testified to the Senate the previous February that it was likely that Oakland and San Francisco would eventually merge with all the cities around the bay in "one great municipality" with a growing need for water, and thus strongly backed the Hetch Hetchy plan. Any other source would cost the San Francisco taxpayers, already overburdened by the earthquake damages, ten to twenty million dollars more, he argued. The Tuolumne was the only river that had no major water claims to compete with, he maintained, though others disputed it. In 1909, for the first time since the club's founding, Olney had not been reelected one of the club's nine directors in its annual elections.[2]

This was not the first time Olney had been at odds with Muir and others in the Sierra Club. ("Olney the Vice President of the Sierra Club is a friend of John P. Irish!" Muir had written Johnson incredulously in 1893, while also giving Olney an earful about the company he kept.) A poll of the members was taken to determine the club's official position. As outspoken as Olney was, he could not persuade his fellow members, now about a thousand strong. The votes were counted in late January: 589 favored leaving Hetch Hetchy in its natural state and 161 opposed it, meaning that a vast majority—almost 80 percent—of the voting members did not support the city's Hetch Hetchy scheme. Livid, Olney, a founder who had served the club for seventeen years, branded his former friends well-meaning dupes of the greedy and ruthless monopoly Spring Valley and led some fifty members in resigning.[3]

Then things took an unexpected turn, and it looked to be a needless falling-out.

Following his visit to Yosemite with Muir, Taft had instructed George Otis Smith, director of the US Geological Survey, who had visited Hetch Hetchy with Muir and Secretary Ballinger, to conduct a study of Lake Eleanor's water storage capacity. Smith's report called it "amply sufficient to meet the present and prospective needs of the city." In February 1910, Ballinger suspended the department's approval of San Francisco's plan. He told the city it must prove the need (or "show cause") to use Hetch Hetchy as a water source. San Francisco asked for a hearing. Ballinger agreed but told the city to make a broad study of water sources for the Bay Area and to thoroughly evaluate the potential damage to Hetch Hetchy. The momentum had clearly swung back to the nature defenders. Ballinger set the hearing for late May.[4]

As the deadline approached, Manson, who was growing weary of the protracted debate, asked John Freeman, a Rhode Island engineer who had advised Los Angeles on the hydraulics for its aqueduct system, to testify. This would be a pivotal moment in the battle. Freeman was a capable and calculating man with a broad skill set. He had previously served as the chief engineer of the Charles River Dam Commission, which created a lake on the campus of MIT, his alma mater, and he had helped revolutionize the industrial-fire-insurance industry, gaining it a highly favorable tax status. As he coolly wrote in his journal on May 13, 1910, "While in San Francisco, I enlisted under the banner of those who are willing to spoil that 'paradise for campers' on the floor of the Hetch Hetchy, for the benefit of the future water supply of San Francisco." Though he was unable to attend Ballinger's show-cause hearing two weeks later, Freeman arranged for Manson and City Attorney Percy Long to meet with President Taft at the White House.

At the May hearing, Ballinger agreed to extend the deadline to June 1911, giving the city a year to produce the study the department needed to determine the fate of Hetch Hetchy. However, Ballinger would resign three months before that, in the aftermath of the controversy that had already cost Pinchot his job. Meanwhile, Taft appointed the Army Board of Engineers to assess the data for the June hearing.

By January 1911, Freeman, who had visited Hetch Hetchy the previous September and found Manson's efforts wanting, had apparently flipped roles with him and was now in charge, writing Manson brusquely, "I have no evidence that you are prepared to present this matter as fully as the case deserves and probably will require." Freeman was not one to tolerate loose ends.[5]

While those who wanted Yosemite National Park's water were temporarily stymied, those who wanted its timber were forging ahead.

On January 5, Muir, who had recently completed his book *My First Summer in the Sierra* and was working on his Yosemite manuscript, wrote to Oliver Lehmer, the Yosemite Valley Railroad superintendent, to ask for information about the building of the railroad. Although Muir had been collecting material for the book for decades and was, as he told Colby, embarrassed by the amount of notes he had, he did have specifics he wanted to add. "I do not know that I can give you anything for your book as far as the building of the Yosemite Valley Railroad is concerned except what you already know," Lehmer responded four days later, though he did boast that the railroad's traffic of Yosemite tourists passing through El Portal had climbed from four thousand the first year to fifteen thousand in the most recent year.[6]

But at the same time that Lehmer was bringing visitors to Muir's paradise, he was busy plotting destruction at its gates. Although the railroad had ostensibly been built to carry passengers to and from the park, its backers knew that the forests south of Yosemite—teeming with massive pines, spruce, and cedar—were the real jackpot. In 1910, the railroad had partnered with Madera Sugar Pine to form Yosemite Lumber Company and bought ten thousand acres of forest—mostly sugar pines, the tree Muir called the "king of the conifers." These behemoths, which could reach up to 250 feet in height and 10 feet in diameter, grew on the south side of the Merced River, across from El Portal, and were isolated by steep terrain. It was going to take a feat of engineering to harvest them.[7]

The company began to build an "incline" double-track system to the ridge across the river and half a mile above El Portal. The system would use a steam engine, a cable, and the weight of railcars loaded with timber coming down the mountain to pull empty cars to the top. No tedious switchbacks were necessary as the double-track would run straight up the mountain with rollers between the rails to keep the cars aligned. Once the full logging cars arrived in El Portal, the cargo would be transferred to a line running forty-three miles to Merced Falls, where the company's new mills would render millions of board feet of lumber out of the forests bordering—and sometimes even within—Yosemite National Park.

The incline railbed then being graded rose from the riverside at a steep 50 percent grade to a midway switching station, where the loaded cars coming down would pass the empty cars going up. From there, it climbed quickly: a 62 percent grade ran to a trestle crossing a ravine. Beyond the ravine, it got wildly steep—an 80 percent grade for about three hundred feet and 75 percent for the last eight hundred feet to the hoisting station on top. The beauty of the system was that the loaded cars would pull the unloaded ones, making the power needs low. But until then, all the logging machinery, massive cables, and steel for the tracks had to go up the incline. The donkey engine that the company had ordered would be one of the largest on the West Coast. At the top of the mountain, the workers built blacksmith and machine shops, a cookhouse, bunkhouses, and oil and water tanks. The first logging station in the woods would be about two miles from the hoisting station. Four miles of logging road would be built into the forest the first year and could be extended all the way to Wawona, twelve miles away.

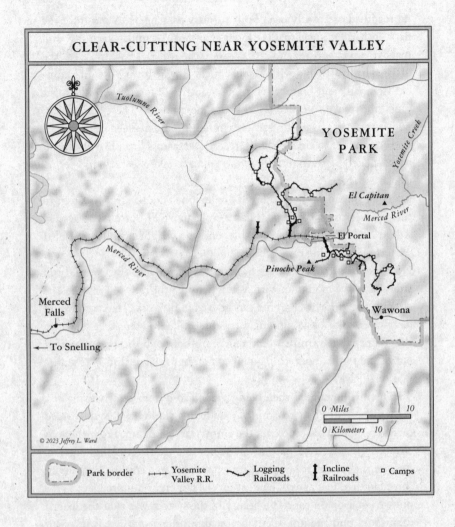

CLEAR-CUTTING NEAR YOSEMITE VALLEY

Tuolumne River

YOSEMITE PARK

Yosemite Creek

El Capitan ▲

Merced River

El Portal

Pinoche Peak ▲

Merced River

Wawona ●

Merced Falls ●

← To Snelling

0 Miles 10

0 Kilometers 10

© 2023 Jeffrey L. Ward

| ⬭ Park border | ┼┼┼ Yosemite Valley R.R. | ∿ Logging Railroads | ⬍ Incline Railroads | ▫ Camps |

The railway would be one of the area's scenic attractions, according to the *Merced County Sun*, visible from the Hotel Del Portal verandas. "The sight of large railroad cars loaded with monster logs being let down from the top of a mount into the canyon," the reporter thought, "should be . . . thrilling." The enterprise, employing eight hundred men, would produce two hundred thousand feet of lumber each day—60 million a year—primarily for the Eastern markets. Yosemite Lumber was also amassing an immense timberland north of the Merced, large enough to feed the mill for half a century. The *Merced Evening Sun* calculated that adding another incline railroad to get to the timber on the north would keep a thousand men felling trees "adjoining Yosemite National park" and a further thousand busy in the mills.

Over fifty years the forests here could produce 3 billion board feet of lumber. It was a dizzying thought, and the *Evening Sun* was eager to run with it. If the company doubled its capacity with the new line, it would make the Yosemite Valley railroad one of the busiest lines on the Pacific coast—by moving not people, but trees.[8]

One man could not fight this, even if he wanted to, and Muir planned to leave it all behind in August 1911 and set out from New York City on a thirty-week, forty-thousand-mile excursion, first and foremost to South America, to fulfill his lifelong dream of following Humboldt's path in the Amazon, the dream that had been thwarted when he caught malaria in the swamps of Florida. It was now or never. Muir had lost his sister Maggie, who lived at Alhambra with her husband, in the spring of 1910, and he had lost Keith a year later, just eight days shy of his own seventy-third birthday. Though he rarely even remembered his exact age, he certainly knew that his days of rambling far and wide were rapidly dwindling.[9]

Before departing on Humboldt's trail, however, Muir had a busy spring and summer ahead of him. He needed to finish his Yosemite manuscript and do some Hetch Hetchy lobbying on the East Coast. He and Johnson arrived in Washington on Thursday, May 4, on "H.H. immortal business," as he wrote Colby the following Monday. They had been extremely productive, including "a long hearty telling talk" with President Taft and three sessions with Taft's new secretary of the interior, Walter Fisher. The two had lunched with the new Democratic House Speaker, Champ Clark, of Missouri, and smoked and discussed Hetch Hetchy with Joe Cannon, the outgoing Republican House Speaker. Muir had seen a lot of senators and representatives, he told Colby, and to top it off made an hour-and-a-half-speech on Hetch Hetchy at a "grand" dinner of the Boone and Crockett Club, headed by none other than Secretary Fisher. "This being the 4th time that I have met Sec.

Fisher he must now know my side of the question fairly well," Muir ventured. "I never imagined I could stand so much dining late hours."

In Boston he visited Sargent and examined the proofs of his memoir *The Story of My Boyhood and Youth*, which Houghton Mifflin was bringing out in 1912. Before a speech at the AMC, he gave an interview to the *Boston Sunday Herald* in which he advocated for a national forest in the White Mountains: "New England has a birth-given right to this breathing spot, and all arguments to the contrary . . . are put forward by thieves and robbers. The ingenious excuses that commercial interests plead for destroying God's handiwork are bewildering, but when you finally see through them, you discover that they are all actuated by greed."

Working himself into a froth, Muir leaped out of his chair, to the reporter's surprise, and onto his proverbial soapbox. "I've been wandering about the mountains and the forests and the streams all my life, and I know something about their beauties, and something too about the irreparable loss they are bound to suffer if commercial enterprises have unrestricted control of them." He clenched his fist as if ready to pummel the nature wreckers. "And what is their loss is the loss of mankind generally, for you cannot measure in dollars and cents the worth to the world of a rarely designed bit of nature." Muir warned the reporter that if he got "really started," he would go on all evening and miss his dinner at the club. But he soon waded back in: "There isn't the slightest hope for preservation when greed makes an entrance into nature's garden spots. We've fought hard to save the Yosemite Valley, the finest mountain park that God ever designed . . . and we've succeeded. It's now the duty of New England to save the White Mountains. If you wait, it's lost; if you don't fight, it's lost.

"While it is true that our forests are worth millions, what of that?" he exclaimed. "Destroy it for its lumber and you have wiped out of existence phenomena that exist nowhere else in this world."[10]

In New York, he spoke about Hetch Hetchy at a dinner at the American Alpine Club, of which he had been made the honorary president. He also picked up an honorary doctorate of letters from Yale "for helping to save Hetch Hetchy," he told Colby. The commencement exercises were "magnificent," he wrote Helen, and "most flattering." He hoped to send her a photo of himself in "academic robes worn . . . in heroic style." In the meantime, he dispatched advice on caring for her young son: "Watch the babe's gums. . . . Have the gums lanced if the pain is great enough to cause restlessness and don't forget care of your dear self."

He had "been tousled and tumbled hither and thither, dinnered, honored, etc., almost out of my wits," he told Colby, but he knew the work was vital. Aligning the environmental groups and friends of their causes was key to their ability to stand up to government and industry forces.[11]

He felt Hetch Hetchy was "comparatively safe," he wrote Colby five weeks after leaving New York, but he warned that "the wicked, whether down or up, are never to be trusted, so we must keep on watching, praying, fighting, overcoming evil with good as we are able." His mistrust was not misplaced.[12]

Wicked or not, John Freeman was pushing forward relentlessly, even as Manson's report lagged behind. Manson proposed an aqueduct with a capacity of 60 million gallons daily. But Freeman, who thought expansively, and strategically, declared that the city's growth would require six times that amount, a volume that would necessitate using the upper Tuolumne, and he wanted to build there immediately. The Garfield grant, however, only allowed for a dam at Hetch Hetchy after the capacity of Lake Eleanor was exhausted, which would prevent a project of the scale Freeman wished to initiate now. This was not the only problem with the Garfield grant, which stipulated that the interior secretary could revoke any permission at any time. Furthermore, it contravened the act creating Yosemite National Park, which prohibited further development within the park boundaries. Instead of seeing these things as an impediment, Freeman began to think bigger.

"I am afraid I am not an entirely subservient counselor," Freeman had told Secretary Fisher and City Attorney Long in April, "for against the wishes of certain of the San Francisco people I have been recommending the policy of opening this case wide-open, wiping all the old agreements off the slate in the belief that something better for the city than the Garfield Permit was obtainable." He gained six more months to figure it out as Fisher agreed to postpone the show-cause hearing until December.

Freeman geared up for a game of hardball. In mid-September, he told Manson to get a copy of the Hetch Hetchy visitors' register with dates, names, and residences. "Show Secretary this, explaining extent of recent advertising and emphasize the benefits of making valley accessible to ten or hundredfold this number, instead of selfish private camping reserve for a few solitude-loving cranks."[13]

Although Freeman was calling the shots, technically Manson was still in charge, and still behind schedule. He again requested and got an extension for the show-cause hearing—this time to March 1912.

By Saturday, December 9, 1911, Yosemite Lumber's staggering incline track from El Portal to the timber belt was nearly finished, but one final hair-raising challenge still had to be surmounted, and the company president, F. M. Fenwick, was there to oversee the critical moment. They now had to hoist the sixty-five-ton donkey engine up the last steep pitch to the top of the mountain. It would be the toughest and most dangerous of all the efforts the workers had made so far.

"This monster engine, apparently clinging to the mountainside like a fly to a pane of glass, was anchored from the top by three steel cables fastened to solid foundations, against which it pulled its slow ascent of this remarkable grade," reported the *Merced Sun*. The donkey engine was being operated by the highly skilled W. W. McNicoll. Signalmen at the anchorage on top and on the slope beside the engine were ready to cue him as he made his way to the top. Fenwick and two dozen workmen were also positioned along the incline. Everything was in place, and everyone knew his role. The anchorage, the cables, and the engine had been tested. The fireman on board the engine with McNicoll built his steam. The signalman on top gave the sign to start. Grasping the lever, the engineer revved his engine.

But just as he did so, the signalman up top saw a cable slip and instantly made the sign to shut off the engine. McNicoll failed to see it. The engine roared and belched clouds of steam as he focused on getting every ounce of energy from it.

The cable began to slip in earnest. The engine, with its sixty-five tons of metal, fire, and boiling water, and the two men inside, slowly ratcheted backward now in a mortal struggle with the slope and gravity. At the last instant the fireman leaped to safety.

"The magnificent iron horse remained on its track, shooting down the 82 percent grade like a bolt of lightning," the *Sun* reported, "until it struck a change in the grade." Then it leaped over two flat cars loaded with railroad steel and crashed onto the mountainside, "demolished among the rocks and trees." Fenwick and the workmen rushed to the wrecked engine, where they found McNicoll's body on one side of the wreckage and his head and left arm, severed by the recoil of the steel cable, on the other.[14]

Yosemite Lumber brought its first trainload of logs off the high ridge above El Portal on the first of August. Loggers transferred the timber to a fifteen-car train to be transported to the Merced Falls mills, each car carrying six thousand board feet. A second train, of twenty-two cars, followed that night. The railroad expected to eventually have sixty logging cars—as soon as they could get them from the manufacturer—and to bring thirty cars of timber down daily.

The building of such a long, steep incline railroad had been watched with keen interest by skeptical lumbermen. McNicoll's gruesome death had seemed to confirm their suspicions, but it was soon forgotten. "Nothing ever before attempted in the way of standard gauge railroads built for logging purposes compares with this," the *Merced County Sun* crowed on August 2. Merced Falls, where Yosemite Lumber's employee cottages boasted electric lights and running water, fast assumed city airs while shops and saloons thrived—and the trees on Yosemite's doorstep fell.[15]

In mid-January 1912, Muir reached South Africa from South America, where he had traveled in the Amazon in pursuit of exotic trees. He headed north to study the baobab trees near Victoria Falls and then to the head of the Nile. On his way to Mombasa, he wrote Johnson, who had also been abroad, "I hope you had a good restful time in Europe & returned rejoicing to your Century work." His own trip, he said, "has been the most fruitful of my life." They would both come back rejuvenated and ready to continue their fight for Hetch Hetchy, now against the regime of San Francisco's newly installed thirtieth mayor, James "Sunny Jim" Rolph, who was beginning a reign of nearly two decades.

Freeman continued to lean on Manson, urging him by telegram to bolster his case. But the dozen years of battling to secure Hetch Hetchy as a water supply had taken its toll on the city engineer, and he had lost his grip on the job. Freeman assumed more responsibilities, agreeing to review and edit certain incoming reports, but in February, Manson, unready for the March hearing, requested yet another extension. Secretary Fisher begrudgingly complied. Even so, Freeman told Manson that he feared his report would be inadequate.

In May, Manson resigned, citing his health, and Mayor Rolph asked Freeman to go to Washington to meet with Fisher and request more time. Four days after Rolph asked him to take charge, Freeman sat down for a rigorous meeting with Fisher, who accused the city of dragging its feet. He gave Freeman until the first of August to submit a study of alternative projects. "I am confident the dates can be met by strenuous work," Freeman reported. He was now in charge.[16]

John R. Freeman (center) with Carl Grunsky (right) and
Michael O'Shaughnessy (left) at Hetch Hetchy, October 6, 1922.

His team transformed a suite in the St. Francis Hotel into their headquarters, adding desks and drafting tables, which were quickly covered with maps, photos, manuscripts, and printer's proofs. They had just under two months to get the job done. Experienced at political warfare, Freeman led his team in reimagining the city's presentation. He knew one thing above all: he needed to think big. "To make an aqueduct 172 miles long into this difficult region commercially successful it must be of a large capacity and planned on a generous scale," the report would openly state. It was no longer 60 million gallons a day for San Francisco; it was 160 million gallons to supply the entire Bay Area and down to San Jose, with a projected need of 400 million gallons a day. Working around the clock, Freeman and his team also recalculated energy-use projections, raising them to two hundred thousand horsepower, an enormous amount for the time. At this scale, the returns on the project looked convincing.

When it came to the art of persuasion, Freeman and his team excelled, especially in using visuals, altering photos to make the proposed new Hetch Hetchy resemble an enticing Norwegian fjord. One photo inserted an imaginary walkway over Wapama Falls to illustrate how charming the path around the sparkling reservoir might be. They were no less creative with numbers: "In its remarkable softness," the report stated, "the Hetch Hetchy water presents an advantage that can be reckoned in dollars and cents in saving in soap"—the citizens would pocket an extra $511,000 each year to be exact—"to say nothing of its greater value for human system[s] or for non-formation of scale in steam boilers."

In July, Freeman presented a four-hundred-page report to Rolph and Long. Its concluding lines were incendiary: "The outlook and the state of the art have moved so fast that the Garfield permit has become practically worthless for the needs of the city. A new permit should be drawn in accordance with the scope of the works." Taking a leaf out of Johnson's playbook, Freeman rallied public support by sending out more than a hundred copies of the massive report to influential people, organizations, and the media across the country. In a cover letter to the president of Harvard, he wrote, "A great deal of dust has been thrown, partly innocently, partly by design, into the eyes of the public on behalf of the nature lovers." Then he headed back to Rhode Island, having earned, in nine months, nearly $50,000—close to $1.5 million today—for his efforts. He had not been overpaid.[17]

Caught off guard, Johnson wrote Muir in shock. "Can you tell me anything about the report just submitted to the secretary of the interior by Consulting Engineer John R. Freeman?" he fairly shouted. "Who is Freeman and what does he stand for?" But Muir, who had returned home in April, via the Suez Canal, Naples, and New York, was busily reacquainting himself with his beloved Sierra Nevada. He had gone off on a High Trip to the Kern River Canyon, southwest of Mount Whitney in Sequoia National Park, where the group joined with a family outing led by Stephen Mather, a borax baron, who had coined the name 20 Mule Team Borax, then turned conservationist and become a Sierra Club stalwart in 1904. Mather would later serve as the first director of the (as-yet-not-conceived) National Park Service.

The Johnsons had recently spent six harrowing weeks nursing their son, Owen, now thirty-one, author of the humorous and well-received Lawrenceville novels and a recent widower, back to health from a bout of typhoid, and Johnson was eager to leave for a vacation in Canada. But first he needed to get the next year's editorial program lined up and wanted stories on the Amazon and Victoria Falls from Muir.

In April the Century Company had published Muir's book *The Yosemite*, which he had dedicated to Johnson, "faithful lover and defender of our glorious forests and originator of the Yosemite of National Park." Marion Parsons, in the June *Sierra Club Bulletin*, called it "the fruit of long experience and loving, earnest, unwearying study," noting that "it is a rare faculty indeed that can make a chapter on geology read like the noblest poetry."

In early August, Johnson heard from Muir, who was finally home. Muir enclosed part of the Freeman report and told Johnson he could not produce the articles in a short window. "Good luck to you on your Canada rest trip," he said. "Don't worry about those hot continents." Being on vacation did not allay Johnson's response. He was "appalled by the enormity of the Freeman document" and wanted anything Muir could send him to counteract it. He closed with a sally: "I am golfing and fishing and resting here—only disturbed by such anxieties about my next year's programme as whether we shall have any articles by John Muir—a former friend of mine!"[18]

That fall, Muir, Colby, and Parsons attended the second annual National Park Conference, at Yosemite, where park superintendents, Interior Department officials, concessioners, and others assembled to discuss park matters. With Secretary Fisher presiding, it was an opportunity for the Sierra Club to make an impression on the man who currently held the fate of Hetch Hetchy in his hands.

Opening the conference on October 14, Fisher launched into a diatribe on the disarray and lack of a central administration of the national parks. The administrative tasks had been dumped on the Interior Department, which Congress had given "no machinery . . . for this purpose," and despite the fact that the parks all had similar transportation, infrastructure, and maintenance issues, each had to beg Congress for its own funding and attention. At the first National Park Conference, in Yellowstone the previous year, there had been unanimous support for a "centralized administration." But in Congress opinions were divided over whether a new bureau should be created or the Interior Department should receive more resources to administer to the parks. Moreover, funding had been scant. The Democrats' drive to decrease appropriations and reduce government "stood in the way," noted Fisher, who was also disappointed by the lack of "vigorous support of some of the gentlemen" in his own party. Still, they had activated "public sentiment," and he was hopeful that Congress would soon take action.

"Before . . . we adjourn this morning," Fisher later announced, "I think we should hear from Mr. John Muir, who, I see, has come in since the meeting convened." It was a show of respect on Muir's home turf.

But Muir abhorred a deadline. "Mr. Secretary, I don't want to start making a speech," he responded. "They will all be hungry before I stop. Isn't this lunchtime?"

"We are going to have a speech from you unless you decline," the secretary insisted. "If you would rather postpone it until some other occasion . . ."

"I think that would be better than to have it just now." Muir did not want to be pressured by time constraints. "A Scotchman can't just touch it and let it go. He has to discourse as they call it and hang on like grim death."

"We will expect to hear from you tomorrow morning when we open the session, if that will meet your convenience. If Congressman Raker is here, we would be glad to have a word from him."

John E. Raker, a lawyer and former judge from Northern California best known as Judge Raker, was a member of the House Public Lands Committee. "There are some matters about which I would like to hear some further discussion," Raker said, steering the discourse to park improvements, transportation, and entrance issues. "While I individually have fairly clear ideas on the subject, at least to myself, I would like to hear some of the discussion from the others first, and while I am not a Scotchman, my people, my class of people, are in the same way: when we get started on a matter we like to run it down . . . like the bulldog at the root, grabbing there and hanging until we pull that one out, then at another one to dig that out, until we get the bad tree down." It was well known in Congress that Raker, who was about to emerge as one of the chief antagonists of Muir and Johnson regarding Hetch Hetchy, was happy to listen to his opponents—in order to later skewer them with their own words.

The following afternoon, Richard Watrous, secretary of the American Civic Association, after discoursing on the association's two-year effort to create a "national park service" and lauding Muir's address, which does not seem to have been recorded, would introduce a statement by unanimous consent: "Resolved: That it is the sense of this conference that there should be created in the Department of the Interior a separate bureau for the conduct of all business pertaining to the national parks and monuments of our country, to be known as the National Park Service."

At the morning session on October 16, Ed Parsons spoke about expanding opportunities for the working class—retail workers and clerks with limited budgets and short vacations. "These parks ought to be open to them," he said. Transportation companies should offer excursion rates and hotel concessioners should provide inexpensive chalets with affordable meals. "Then anyone of meager means could get in here for a weekend or a few days . . . and enjoy this magnificent region."

Colby spoke in favor of admitting automobile traffic to the parks "because we think the automobile adds a great zest to travel and we are primarily interested in the increase of travel to these parks." In Yosemite, in particular, they could come as far as Glacier Point and even into the valley once road turnouts and guard walls in the most dangerous places were built. But Muir would later indicate his lack of enthusiasm for the "puffing machines." "All signs indicate automobile victory," he would say, with resignation, "and doubtless, under certain precautionary restrictions, these useful, progressive, blunt-nosed mechanical beetles will hereafter be allowed to puff their way into all the parks and mingle their gas-breath with the breath of the pines and waterfalls." Still, he thought it would come to "little harm or good."[19]

As a final touch to the conference, Arthur Pillsbury, who had photographed Roosevelt and Muir during their camping trip in 1903 and often photographed Sierra Club outings, presented a groundbreaking film. Disturbed that the parks were mowing meadows for horse fodder and killing wildflowers, he showed a time-lapse recording of the flowers as they grew out of the earth, bent to the sun, and blossomed, with "life struggles so similar to ours." He spoke of the need for parks to protect the flowers before they went extinct, a battle Muir had long been fighting. When Pillsbury presented images from 1895 of meadows full of tall flowers and compared them to more recent ones of empty fields, it convinced many superintendents to better protect their meadows.[20]

In November, while visiting Ed and Marion Parsons in Berkeley, Muir worked on transcribing his Alaska journals. Scrawled four decades earlier from glaciers, canoes, and campsites and having lain fallow since, the journals now came to life as Muir pored over them, spinning tales for the Parsonses and his stenographer. Marion, a friend of Wanda's, who had met Ed on an early High Trip, marveled at both the "fire and enthusiasm" of Muir's narration and the stolid indifference of the stenographer. Not so for the Parsonses: "Household machinery might stop, food grow cold on the table, and the business members of the family miss their morning trains while Mr. Muir pursued . . . his subject to the end," she observed. She was disappointed when Muir had to put the work aside to focus on Hetch Hetchy, but she would later play a vital role in helping him finish his Alaska book.[21]

That same month, the show-cause hearing for the acquisition of reservoir sites, which San Francisco had postponed five times over more than two years, finally took place. The Army Board of Engineers, it turned out, had endorsed the city's proposal, even agreeing that Cherry and Eleanor Creeks did not need to be developed first. But with his term winding down, Secretary Fisher demurred. He concluded the hearing without a decision, stating that there was no clear statutory authority for the secretary of the interior to issue a permit.

The Garfield grant was no more, a cause, it seemed, for great celebration for the defenders of Hetch Hetchy. Ballinger's successor had killed the grant to the city and punted any further action to Congress. In a cruel twist of fate to Muir and Johnson, however, this is exactly what the cunning John Freeman wanted.[22]

CHAPTER 24

The Nature Lovers

I f there was a truce over the holiday season, the gloves quickly
came off again in mid-January 1913, when the *San Francisco Call*
ran an editorial titled "Must San Francisco Pay $30,000,000 for
the Nature Lovers' Whim?" The piece singled out Johnson as being
responsible for the conflict and declared that the Freeman report had put
Hetch Hetchy back in play. The *Call* kept at it in February, mocking
Johnson as "an advocate of boiled water for municipalities" and accusing him of idealism that benefited greedy commercialism, including
the railroads and Spring Valley.[1]

On March 4, Woodrow Wilson, a progressive Democrat and the former
head of Princeton University and governor of New Jersey, having quashed
Taft's hopeless reelection bid and Roosevelt's Bull Moose blitz, was inaugurated as president. Freeman had already arrived in Washington the
day before to begin lobbying Congress for San Francisco. And on that
same day, as if to roll out the red carpet for Freeman, incoming president
Wilson had nominated as his interior secretary Franklin Lane—the city
attorney who had helped Phelan draft a charter requiring San Francisco
to own its own water supply. Horace Albright, an assistant secretary
at the Interior Department (and eventually the second director of the
National Park Service), later said that Lane was appointed specifically
to force the Hetch Hetchy takeover.[2]

Because Fisher had pushed the Hetch Hetchy decision back to Congress, Lane could not reverse Ballinger's show-cause decision and restore the Garfield grant, even if he wanted to. But he could and did lobby senators, finessing concerns over the project, while Percy Long drafted a new Hetch Hetchy bill. It was to be introduced by Judge Raker, whose district included both Hetch Hetchy and the Modesto and Turlock Irrigation Districts—whose representatives had been persuaded (some would say illicitly) that the city's plan was in their interest. Raker had enlisted the support of Representative William Kent, the same William Kent who had given the land for Muir Woods. Most important, Spring Valley was now on board as well.

Freeman and San Francisco's new city engineer, Michael O'Shaughnessy, a former Spring Valley engineer lured by Mayor Rolph into working for the city, lobbied the House Public Lands Committee, which included Kent, whose DC home now became a war room for San Francisco's water team. City Clerk John Dunnigan stayed there while helping draft what became known as the Raker bill, and Phelan, O'Shaughnessy, Long, and others, based at the Willard Hotel, visited often to orchestrate lobbying.[3]

Muir got wind of what was happening and alerted his team, sending an urgent telegram to Henry Osborn: "San Francisco Schemers Making Desperate Efforts to Rush Bill Through Congress. . . . You Know the President and Am Sure You Will Strike Hard."[4]

On the southwestern edge of Yosemite National Park, Yosemite Lumber evolved into a forest-felling colossus. On May 2, 1913, two weeks after the spring cutting season began, Oliver Lehmer, now general manager of the railroad, made a stunning announcement: Yosemite Lumber had acquired twenty thousand more acres of prime timberland. "Operations at El Portal and Merced Falls to be Increased to Gigantic Proportions," the *Merced Evening Sun* announced. The company would begin building new tracks immediately.

Yosemite Lumber had reorganized and raised $5 million from its directors to buy the Bullock Tract, which was on the north side of the Merced across from Yosemite Lumber's original holdings. The tract was considered one of the finest sections of pine timber in the world and was formerly owned by prescient Michigan lumber barons. Yosemite Lumber now became "one of the biggest and most important enterprises on the Pacific coast," boasted the *Evening Sun*. Not only had the company quadrupled its original acreage and timber, but its new holdings abutted government land of a similar size "the stumpage of which can be acquired by the company." The magnitude of the acquisition was staggering. The new holdings contained a potential of more than a billion board feet, and the twenty-thousand-acre government tract another billion—together enough to circle the earth with a foot-wide board nearly fifty times.[5]

Now in the last years of his life, Muir was living in two worlds. Houghton Mifflin had published *The Story of My Boyhood and Youth*, and he was inundated with letters from family, old friends, and new fans. While they were reading about Muir's early life, he was revisiting it. His candid depiction of his boyhood generated much discussion about the Scottish way of raising children. "I think it is often too severe or even cruel," he said in a letter to Mina Merrill, whose family had tended to him when he injured his eye almost half a century earlier in Indianapolis. "And as I hate cruelty I called attention to it in the boyhood book while at the same time pointing out the value of sound religious training with steady work and restraint."

"As we close its cover," Marion Parsons wrote in the *Sierra Club Bulletin*, "the strongest impression that lives with us is of a boy's life, not darkened by long days of toil, but brightened by an inner light that made visible to him the glory and the wonder of the world. . . . Mr. Muir's heart all his life seems to have been 'dancing to a music' most of us never hear."

Muir updated Merrill, whose family had given him so much care and love and had continued to visit him over the years, on his news. "It is now seven years since my beloved wife vanished in the land of the leal," he wrote. But his daughters were both happily married and had children of their own. Wanda, on the ranch in the old adobe, had three "lively" boys, and Helen, in Daggett, two. "I am alone in my library den in the big house on the hill," he told her, and he soon planned to tackle a second volume of his autobiography, carrying him to California. A man celebrated for his love of nature, Muir's love of those close to him was also extraordinary, as Merrill surely knew, and he continued:

> Through all life's wanderings you have held a warm place in my heart, and I have never ceased to thank God for giving me the blessed Merrill family as life-long friends. . . . As the shadows lengthen in Life's afternoon we cling all the more fondly to the friends of our youth. And it is with the warmest gratitude that I recall the kindness of all your family when I was lying in darkness. That Heaven may ever bless you, dear Mina, is the heart prayer of your Affectionate friend, John Muir.[6]

The month of June 1913 brought a stunning turn of events. Though the circumstances were veiled, Johnson, who, during his three-and-a-half-year run, had maintained the integrity of the magazine with an emphasis on "its art, its leadership, its public service, its progressiveness, its alertness, and its tone," had been unable to stem the tide of readership loss. Loath to change the format of the *Century*, he had proposed to the company's trustees maintaining it as it was while producing a new less expensive magazine to take on the competition. The trustees had declined, and Johnson had apparently resigned.

Muir wrote him, "I am greatly surprised to see by the papers that you have resigned the editorship of *The Century*. What does all this mean?" In the same letter, seemingly in shock, he reminded Johnson that they still had much to do for Hetch Hetchy. "I suppose no matter where you are or what your duties may be that you can never cease to be interested in the forest and park work." He said he trusted that whatever had happened would be for the best.[7]

Osborn wrote Muir from New York City on June 18. He had seen Johnson at Columbia's commencement. "It is, as I had feared, that he has practically retired from the great magazine for which he has done so much, apparently to make way for a more commercial or money-making spirit," Osborn reported. "I do not certainly know, but I fear this is the case. It is evidently a severe blow to him, for I could see that Mrs. Johnson (a really devoted wife) tried to keep him off the subject." Osborn said that all who had read *Boyhood* were "delighted," and he was giving it to boys he knew, "because its purpose is so fine under the adventure."

No sooner had Johnson's work crisis struck than came the next exigency, this time regarding Hetch Hetchy. On June 17, Muir, in his official capacity as president of the Society for the Preservation of National Parks, wired Johnson. The steal was on:

HETCH HETCHY SITUATION CRITICAL CITY TRYING RUSH BILL THROUGH CONGRESS. . . . SEND STRONG WIRES LETTERS TO PUBLIC LANDS COMMITTEE HOUSE REQUESTING DELAY TILL REGULAR SESSION STATING WE WERE LED TO BELIEVE NO ACTION TAKEN UNTIL REGULAR SESSION.

Nine days later, Muir asked Johnson, still reeling from the loss of his job, to attend a House Public Lands Committee hearing in progress and to press for a postponement to the next regular session to give the society and the Sierra Club time to swing into high gear again. They sent out twenty thousand leaflets explaining the stakes in Yosemite, including one to each person listed in *Who's Who in America*, and circulated "An Open Letter to the American People," which included a quote from former president Taft, now a Yale law professor (and eighty pounds lighter), saying, "I am with you in the Hetch Hetchy matter."

All of a sudden, the nation was up in arms over the issue, and many senators were caught off guard by the overwhelming response. One of the first matters of discussion when debate opened in the Senate was the unprecedented deluge of public opinion. Utah senator Reed Smoot alone received five thousand letters against damming Hetch Hetchy. Senator Ashurst of Arizona, a supporter of the Raker bill, was shocked and nonplussed at the thousands of letters he had received. Senator Reed of Missouri was perplexed at how the fate of a remote two-square-mile piece of land could throw the nation into "hysteria." In the Interior Department, which was likewise being flooded, Assistant Secretary Albright and several others responded to the mail, attempting to justify Lane's position and forging his signature. Albright, who agreed with Muir, hated this job and would never forget the groundswell of support for the threatened valley.[8]

LET EVERYONE HELP TO SAVE THE FAMOUS HETCH-HETCHY VALLEY
AND
STOP THE COMMERCIAL DESTRUCTION WHICH THREATENS OUR NATIONAL PARKS

To the American Public:

    The famous Hetch-Hetchy Valley, next to Yosemite the most wonderful and important feature of our Yosemite National Park, is again in danger of being destroyed. Year after year attacks have been made on this Park under the guise of development of natural resources. At the last regular session of Congress the most determined attack of all was made by the City of San Francisco to get possession of the Hetch-Hetchy Valley as a reservoir site, thus defrauding ninety millions of people for the sake of saving San Francisco dollars.

    As soon as this scheme became manifest, public-spirited citizens all over the country poured a storm of protest on Congress. Before the session was over, the Park invaders saw that they were defeated and permitted the bill to die without bringing it to a vote, so as to be able to try again.

    The bill has been re-introduced and will be urged at the coming session of Congress, which convenes in December. Let all those who believe that our great national wonderlands should be preserved unmarred as places of rest and recreation for the use of all the people, now enter their protests. Ask Congress to reject this destructive bill, and also urge that the present Park laws be so amended as to put an end to all such assaults on our system of National Parks.

                Faithfully yours,

                John Muir

November, 1909.

Read carefully pp. 20-21 and help to save the Park.

Muir's letter on behalf of the Society for the Preservation of the National Parks, which would be widely reproduced in a circular.

The Sierra Club and its allies had generated media support nationwide. Muir and Johnson tallied the dozens of newspapers backing their efforts, from the *Boston Evening Transcript*, the *New York Times*, and the *Philadelphia Record* in the East, to the *Cleveland Plain Dealer*, the *Indianapolis News*, and the *Louisville Courier-Journal* in the Midwest, to the *Rocky Mountain News* and *Seattle Post-Intelligencer* in the West. In mid-June, Muir wrote a letter on behalf of the Society for the Preservation of National Parks to circulate to newspapers and sent it off to Johnson, who was on the advisory council. Decrying the city's relentless pursuit of Hetch Hetchy, Muir asked editors to run the letter as

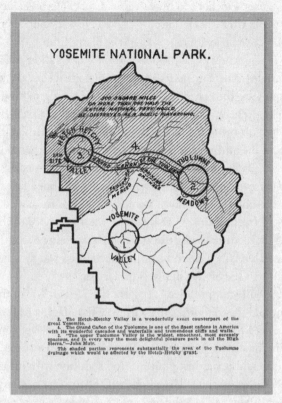

A map from the same circular showing the boundaries of Yosemite National Park
and the impact of a potential Hetch Hetchy dam.

well as editorials and news stories calling on the public to write their congressmen and senators.

Muir, Parsons, Badè, and Colby signed a version of the letter as a petition to Congress, and another version would run in the *New York Times* in July. On June 25, the House Committee on Public Lands began hearings on the bill, which would run off and on through the first week of a sweltering July, so hot and humid that the congressmen and those who appeared before them were permitted to remove their jackets. But San Francisco, sparing no expense to win their coveted source, had sweat to spare. Long, O'Shaughnessy, and Phelan brought in the support of national figures: Pinchot and his successor, Chief Forester Henry Graves, Director of the US Reclamation Service Fred Newell, and Secretary Lane. Edmund Whitman again represented the Sierra Club.[9]

"The fundamental principle of the whole conservation policy is use," Pinchot argued. There is "no reasonable argument against the use of this water supply by the city." Newell, as might be expected, was bullish on the plan. "There is nothing more beautiful than a well-built dam with a reservoir behind it," he categorically stated. Although Phelan, like most of the others, had never seen Hetch Hetchy, that did not stop him from confidently painting a rosy picture. "Constructing a dam at this very narrow gorge . . . we create not a reservoir but a lake," he said, pushing the bounds of reason, "because Mr. Freeman has shown that by planting trees or vines over the dam, the appearance of the dam is entirely lost." Particularly galling was the testimony of San Francisco judge Will Denman, a charter member of the Sierra Club, who emphasized that even the Sierra Club was divided on the issue.

Eugene Sullivan, president of Sierra Blue Lakes Water and Power Company, told the committee that Grunsky and Manson had suppressed the company's report proving that the Mokelumne River could easily fulfill San Francisco's water needs. The congressmen wanted to see it, but Sullivan said it was incomplete. After speaking with his lawyer, he tempered his accusations. Urged on by O'Shaughnessy, Congressman Graham of Illinois called Sullivan "a petty confidence man, whose word was utterly worthless."[10]

"We all send you many thanks for your brave Hetch Hetchy work. In all our fights on park matters you have been and are our mainstay and leader," Muir wrote Johnson at the beginning of July, praising his recent "capital" letters in the *Times* and *Evening Post*. "Send the bills to me," added Muir, who was well-off beyond anything he could have imagined while toiling away in his father's fields but had little use for it. Senator Smoot, the former head of the Public Lands Committee, and California representative Denver Church were both staunch friends, he reassured Johnson. "Be of good cheer. Nothing that we can do on the side of justice can be wholly lost. . . . Be careful of your health these hot days and don't fret, all will turn out for the best in the long run."

But by July 15, Muir was beginning to worry. "This the 23rd year of almost continual battle for preservation of Yosemite National Park, sadly interrupting my natural work," he lamented in a letter to Osborn. "Our enemies now seem to be having most everything their own wicked way working beneath obscuring tariff and bank clouds, spending millions of the peoples' money for selfish ends. Think of three or four ambitious shifty traders and politicians calling themselves 'the City of San Francisco,' bargaining with the United States for half of the Yosemite Park like Yankee horse traders, as if the grandest of all our mountain playgrounds full of God's best gifts, the joy and admiration of the world, were of not more account than any of the long list of tinker tariff articles."[11]

That same day Muir fired off a letter to the editor of the *New York Times*, which was receptive to the preservationist argument. The letter would run on July 21 under the title "Hetch Hetchy Invaders: John Muir Asks That Their Bill Be Not Rushed Through Congress." He had by now crystallized his descriptions and arguments to best rouse the public to action: "The Yosemite National Park is not only the greatest and most wonderful national playground in California, but in some of its features it is without rival in the whole world—its silver fir and sequoia forests, its twin songful rivers, and its twin Yosemites. It belongs to the American people, and in universal interest ranks with the Yellowstone and the Grand Canyon of the Colorado." Recently, he pointed out, "public-spirited citizens all over the country entered their protests" to Congress to thwart San Francisco's "determined attack" on the park. But the city, "ever ready to take advantage of beclouding political changes," was at it again, this time "urging that it should be rushed through as an emergency measure." He called on the people to "aid us in postponing consideration of this destructive bill until the next regular session of Congress."[12]

Johnson sent strong letters to the President, Smoot, Lane, Treasury Secretary William McAdoo, North Dakota senator Asle Gronna, Oklahoma congressman Scott Ferris—who now chaired the House Public Lands Committee—and others, enclosing a July 12 *New York Times* editorial. "The Hetch Hetchy Valley is described by John Muir as a 'wonderfully exact counterpart of the great Yosemite,'" the *Times* had written. "Why should its inspiring cliffs and waterfalls, its groves and flowery, parklike floor, be spoiled by the grabbers of water and power?"

By late July, Muir had further, if not completely, processed Johnson's sudden fall from atop the *Century*. "The longer I brood over the Century Company's behavior toward you the more unthinkably outrageous it appears," he wrote him. "I can't yet venture to say how mad it makes me. But you dear friend have nothing to regret. Though yet young [Johnson had turned sixty in January] you have done a great life work and have all the world with you. . . . I feel sure you will see that all's for the best." Regarding Yosemite, he rattled off some positive responses he had recently received—from Representative James Post of Ohio, "I concur with your views"; from Representative John Esch of Wisconsin, "The objections raised in your protest . . . are conclusive"; and from Senator Miles Poindexter of Washington, "I am heartily in accord with you in this matter. . . . Kindly advise me should it be likely to come up at any time in the Senate."[13]

As for Johnson, he may have been licking his wounds, but he was not idle. On July 24, he sat down to pen a letter to the *New York Times*, in reply to "American Citizen," who had written to ask how to help prevent Hetch Hetchy's destruction.

City representatives had been in Washington for three months lobbying for the "four times defeated" scheme, he pointed out, now presented again in the Raker bill. To shoehorn it into Wilson's emergency summer session, they had, he claimed, concocted a phony crisis based on a water company's ordinary request for citizens to stop wasting water: "If this be an emergency, then heaven help San Francisco, for it would be at least eight years before a drop of water could be obtained from Hetch Hetchy!" The real emergency was the potential forfeit of a natural wonderland that belonged to the American people and should not be given to San Francisco largely to produce commercial power. Muir, the Sierra Club, and the Society for the Preservation of National Parks were fighting the scheme vigorously and, he said, deserved the support of the whole country. "If everyone who reads *The Times* would give ten minutes to the defense of a national park, which belongs in part to him or her—if only by writing the protest on a postal card— Congress could be made to consider the super-commercial value of our great natural treasures, and the fight would be won." It was a clarion call for environmentalists to stand up and be counted.

Johnson claimed that city authorities had concealed from the Army Engineers a report disproving the idea that Hetch Hetchy was the only viable source and replaced it with a bogus one. As he later elaborated in *Collier's*, the city had withheld a report made by its expert, Bartel, showing that the Mokelumne River could provide an ample 432 million gallons a day. "This report apparently gave the death blow to the Tuolumne (Hetch Hetchy) scheme," he wrote. So the city never released it and, instead, rated the river at a much-lower capacity. The Bartel report "was not prepared by an emissary of John Muir and the other 'nature lovers'—a new term of opprobrium for the majority of the American people—but by the city's own expert," with commentary from Marsden Manson, who in 1909, with James Phelan, admitted, "The city could get its supply anywhere along the Sierra by paying for it."

"Why should so important a matter (as important as the leveling of the Falls of Niagara, if such a thing were possible) be determined on such evidence as a covetous city, the chief party in interest, chooses to present to an Army Board?" Johnson asked in the *Times* letter. "In the eyes of the city officials those who are fighting for the people to conserve for them and their descendants the great wonderland which is theirs are 'nature fakers' and 'aesthetic cranks!' Against this philistinism . . . which the rest of the country has outgrown, Mr. Muir summons American citizens to defend their own property, and to prevent the destruction of all that has been gained by the National Park system."[14]

Finally, Johnson hammered Pinchot, who, he said, was "in respect to the uses of great scenery simply a defective . . . like a man without a sense of color or music," adding that he had long been "discredited among conservationists as a man who is greatly swayed by personal prejudices and political exigencies." After Garfield had succeeded Secretary Hitchcock, who had declined "to give the valley over to the wolves," Pinchot had gone out of his way to revive the scheme by recommending to San Francisco that it renew its grant application. "President Roosevelt had grave doubts about the action he afterward took, but Mr. Pinchot prevailed," Johnson asserted. He considered Pinchot a hypocrite, "one who calls upon the country to preserve national property against corporate assault and at the same time revives and supports an assault of exactly this sort."

Johnson was baiting Pinchot. The letter ran on July 27, and the next day Johnson sent it to Muir. "You see . . . that I have opened fire on Pinchot," he wrote. "If he will only reply, we shall get the attention of the country."

"I am not only stirring up others," Johnson told Muir two days later, "but stirring them up to stir up others."[15]

Every Park Will Be Attacked

In August 1913, Muir visited Edward Harriman's widow, Mary, at her ranch on a tributary of the Snake River near Island Park, Idaho. Earlier in the year, she had written Muir that she had read and admired his stories of his youth in the *Atlantic Monthly,* and she had asked his advice on a suitable writer to finish a biography of her husband. Muir had had Houghton Mifflin send a copy of *The Story of My Boyhood and Youth* to her in June with the promise of a properly inscribed volume to come. He had also asked her to do all she could to help defeat the Hetch Hetchy bill, which, he told her, "a few political thieves and robbers are trying to rush thru Congress under the pretense of urgent necessity."

This was undoubtedly a time of reflection for Muir. He missed Harriman, whom he had confided in and whose encouragement (and stenographer) had laid the groundwork for several books, including *My Boyhood and Youth*. In their last days together in Pasadena, Harriman had even tended to Helen, just as he done for Keith. In addition to being a close friend, Harriman had been Muir's one connection to unadulterated power, power that could stop overreaching politicians in their tracks. That was gone, but Mary at least provided him with repose, good company, and warm memories on the ranch, where nature once again fortified him.

Visiting Railroad Ranch was Muir's only escape that summer. "You hardly know how hard the self-denial has been," he would write the

Osborns from Martinez, "to stay here through the blazing summer heat toiling on Hetch Hetchy." He was tired, he told them, but the ten-day visit had "greatly delighted and refreshed" him.[1]

Upon his return from Idaho, Muir had discovered to his dismay that a leaflet he had written and left with Colby and Badè had still not been printed and mailed. "Badè is writing a book about God & Colby is to be absent from the city & Hetch Hetchy for a month," Muir told Johnson.[2]

On Saturday morning, August 30, when the House began to debate the Raker bill, the odds were overwhelmingly in favor of its passage. After two months of hearings, the Public Lands Committee had voted unanimously for approval, and all eleven California Representatives, both Republicans and Democrats, supported it. The question was, who, if anyone, was going to stand up to a unified California?

Representative Eugene Reed, a freshman from New Hampshire in his one and only term, offered an uncompelling start. Overawed by those aligned for the bill, he opposed it primarily, it seemed, because his state's chief forester was against it. Cities in eastern New Hampshire, it appeared, were already asking about water rights in the state's revered White Mountains Forest Reserve, which the foresters dearly wanted to protect. The Raker bill threatened to lower the bar to entry there. When Reed, during his already ham-handed delivery, bungled Johnson's position, thinking him in favor of the bill, he lost credibility with both sides.

Halvor Steenerson, a bespectacled, walrus-mustached Republican from Minnesota, the only other representative slated to speak against the bill, stepped in to clarify that Johnson most definitely opposed it. In fact, just the week before, Steenerson had received a long letter from Johnson, arming him with objections to the bill, and a note exhorting him to speak out: "Unless somebody stands up for the national interest in national parks, they will go to the wolves by default." Steenerson, who had asked to be heard last as he wanted to listen to the arguments for the bill before he spoke, was the opposition's only hope.

Confident of its success after two months of hearings, the committee, nonetheless, laid out a thorough and methodical case for passage of the bill. Its members had strategic roles in the presentation and prepared responses to refute the arguments that had been raised by Muir and Johnson in the circulars and the press. Californians Kent, Kahn, and

Raker all seemed to be bristling for a fight. Kent led off, insouciantly declaring the Raker bill "a higher ideal of conservation than any bill that has come into this House. The ideal conservation is public social use of resources of our country without waste," he elaborated. "We are perfectly certain that the waste [of water] occurs by its nonuse. . . . My ideal of conservation," he said, "would teach that if Niagara Falls could be totally used up in alleviating the burdens of the overworked in sweatshops of New York City, I should be glad to sacrifice that scenic wonder for the welfare of humankind." Before sitting down, he reassured his colleagues: "I can lay claim to being a nature lover myself."

Burton French of Idaho then presented the bill. He seemed to have been put on the defensive by Muir and Johnson and their efforts. Contrary to reports in the newspapers, he argued, the bill had been considered in depth by the committee and was not being railroaded through Congress. He framed the discussion broadly: "California, like other states of the West, must consider carefully and well the question of husbanding the water that falls within its area. Forever, so far as we can now know, the State will need to consider the relative uses of water and determine the question of right use." It was, like Kent's introduction, straight out of Pinchot's playbook. French went on, "The Committee on Public Lands has given its earnest consideration to the merits of the systems proposed, and I believe undoubtedly feels that from an economic standpoint, both for the present and the future, the system that will involve the construction of the Hetch Hetchy Dam is most desirable."

The chairman finally recognized the gentleman from Minnesota for thirty minutes. Steenerson proved a tenacious foe of the bill, a brawler with a velvet glove, a dramatic flair, and a literary bent. "Mr. Chairman, this is not a local question," he began. "If it were, I certainly would not for one moment put my judgment as against the judgment of the California delegation, a delegation that stands deservedly high—as high as any in this House. But the conservation of the natural beauties of mountain scenery is in question, and is one of national importance. All the people of the United States have expressed themselves as in favor of the doctrine of conservation. The people of Minnesota believe in and practice the doctrine of conservation. I could not fairly represent the people of that State unless I raised at least one voice against this bill."

At which point Reed interrupted: "The gentleman will acknowledge that I have spoken against this bill?"

"I think the gentleman said Mr. Muir and Dr. Johnson were in favor of this bill," Steenerson replied.

"I hope the gentleman will not misquote me," said Reed.

"I will not," responded Steenerson. Reed then made another unintelligible attempt to state his position, which Steenerson promptly ignored. He was already being interrupted and challenged by Ferris, the committee chair, whose assignment, it seemed, was to badger him. "This is not a local question," Steenerson emphasized. "If the entire New York delegation should come here unanimously demanding that Niagara Falls be destroyed for the purpose of creating power, would we from the other portions of the United States stand here indifferent? Could we recognize the claim that nobody except the State of New York is interested? This question is exactly analogous."

Steenerson's skewering of the notion that a reservoir might improve the beauty of Hetch Hetchy provided a lighter moment: "Of course, you understand that in a dry time . . . you will have in place of the beautiful floor of the Hetch Hetchy Valley, as described by Mr. Muir, a dirty, muddy pond, with the water drained off to supply San Francisco, and probably some dead fish and frogs in it." There was laughter at this. "Will that be beautiful? And then there will be perhaps large generating works, with rolling wheels and buzzing machinery and transmission wires with a devilish, hissing noise echoing and re-echoing sounds strange and cacophonous." More laughter. "That is what you will offer us in place of the temple of the gods that has been ready for our admiration."

Hailing from Crookston, a rural town in northwest Minnesota, Steenerson railed against the use of federal resources to make big cities more appealing than the country. "Rather would I encourage the people to go to the national parks," he chided his colleagues, "where they can admire nature in its pristine beauty and glory and become imbued with the love of nature." Then he dived in: "It is said this park is hard of access; that only a few hundred people reach it every year; that more will reach it when you have destroyed it. Then they can go in trolley cars and railroad cars; but I would rather have a few see it in its natural glory than in its desecrated form. Perhaps some lone, footsore, weary wanderer may find his way into the valley some day and by means of inspiration of these wonderful surroundings will produce something more valuable than money. Suppose he could write a poem like Burns's 'To a Mountain Daisy'? Why, you could not estimate the value of such a contribution to human thought in its refining effects in dollars and cents. That poem I have read often, but it can never be read too often. The fate of Hetch Hetchy Valley, this beautiful mountain gem, is touchingly like that of the mountain daisy, and when it is gone, I do not believe I shall be the only mourner at its bier." Steenersen entered part of Burns's poem into the record, to remind his colleagues what was at stake.

"Now, you say that is all sentiment; that Mr. Muir and Dr. Johnson are sentimental," Steenersen said, rising to his conclusion. "I grant it, and I am glad of it. You people in California, where woman suffrage prevails, will find out that you have got to pay some respect to sentiment hereafter." Again, laughter. "One reason why I am opposing this bill is that the Woman's Club in Minnesota passed a resolution unanimously in favor of protecting this national park from vandals and desecration. I have great respect for their sentiments. Such sentiments are the foundation of all noble and heroic deeds among men."

The House adjourned, without voting on the bill, until the following Tuesday, September 2.[3]

On September 3, Muir sent Johnson copies of another letter for dispersal and encouraging words: "We all rejoice over the grand rousing work you are doing. . . . The battle signs begin to look favorable." That same day, however, despite Steenerson's gallant effort, the House passed Resolution 7207—the Raker bill—and it was not even close. By a count of 183–43, it authorized the use of Hetch Hetchy and Lake Eleanor as reservoirs for San Francisco. Outraged newspapers around the country called out San Francisco for the theft. The *New York Times,* denouncing the decision, hit on the larger truth: "The only time to set aside National Parks is before the bustling needs of civilization have crept upon them. Legal walls must be built about them for defense, for every park will be attacked. Men and municipalities who wish something for nothing will encroach upon them, if permitted." Hetch Hetchy, "a power project under the guise of providing a water supply for San Francisco," is an "illustration of this universal struggle," the editorial continued. "The politicians of San Francisco . . . have an eye only for utility and utility that flows their way. The chief newspapers and organs of public opinion throughout the country have spoken in opposition to this 'grab.'" The editors called on the Senate to "heed their expression of public sentiment," and failing that, for President Wilson to veto the bill."[4]

Muir and Johnson, firing off overlapping letters and telegrams to each other, redoubled their efforts "to strike hard and very fast," as Muir put it, through the special session. The Sierra Club hurriedly dispatched five hundred illustrated pamphlets to the press and Senate, with a hundred more to Johnson, who barely had time to distribute them before receiving another hundred copies of an updated version. "We will make these leaflets fly in merry flocks," Muir told Johnson. "Expect to rouse Los Angeles region & get women's clubs to speak." They were providing Senator Smoot with all the firepower they could.[5]

On September 25, Muir, in a rare down moment after the Raker bill had been "meanly skulked and railroaded and logrolled through the House," sent Johnson a note of quiet distress. He felt disappointed by his closest lieutenants—Colby and Parsons—in whom he had always had the utmost confidence. "Have just discovered that both Col & P. have carefully concealed all our circulars from California not even sending copies to our Sierra Club members, fearing I suppose the S. F. press. & damage to their business & professions." He understood that careers and families were at stake. "This is natural & perhaps reasonable enough. Mr C's employer is or has been the city's leading lawyer in H. H. affairs. . . . Some of our best Washington friends are kept mum for the sake of family official bread." Muir would never bring this up again. "Of course I'll do what I can without open assistance of our club members who may be dimly on our side." His sign-off, "Ever faithfully Muir," felt a little more weighty than usual.[6]

Five days later, Muir sent Johnson a check for expenses and his "warmest thanks for the long gallant fight for our magnificent parks in which you for the last fifteen years have stood bravely in the front." Muir could see that the battle was winding toward its conclusion, or, at least, its climax, and he assured Johnson, "whatever the outcome of this

Hetch Hetchy struggle all the world is greatly indebted to you." He noted that monetary contributions had not been great, that he, Colby, and Parsons had contributed the lion's share. "This war however must still go on and we must not grow weary in well-doing." He was, in fact, doggedly preparing another circular.[7]

The *New York Times* remained on top of the proceedings, even anticipating them: "The Senate . . . now has a chance to put a spoke in the wheel of the steam roller by which San Francisco's official lobby has heretofore crushed opposition to the Hetch Hetchy bill," the newspaper commented on October 2. It was no wonder that the city had forced it on Congress with "persistence and specious misrepresentation," noted the *Times*, as the bill meant "contracts amounting to $120,000,000, with endless opportunities of 'honest graft.'" "Urged as a measure of humanity," it had been exposed as a "sordid scheme to obtain electric power" that would cost the nation what even Mr. Pinchot admitted was "'one of the great wonders of the world.'"

"The act creating the Yosemite National Park sets forth the importance and duty of reserving these wonders 'in their natural state,'" continued the *Times*, "and the world has a moral right to demand that this purpose shall be adhered to." It again suggested that if Congress were to pass the bill, then the President should look to Grover Cleveland's example—his foresight and his instinct to stand up for the people—when Congress tried to nullify the Washington's Birthday Reserves, which became the National Forests. Wilson should veto it.[8]

On Saturday, October 4, the Senate, exhausted by the debate on tariff reform, which had dragged on for six months, considered the Hetch Hetchy bill. Freeman had appeared as the final witness at the Senate Public Lands Committee's hearing on September 24, artfully guiding the bill through without amendment and setting the stage for a successful floor debate. But now the Senate was depleted, noisy, and fractious. Muir and Johnson were counting on Smoot, but he was not present, nor was California junior senator John Works. Both sent telegrams asking for a postponement of the hearing until they could attend. Works wrote, "Ninety-nine per cent of water users in the irrigation districts are strongly opposed to it and claim that they were betrayed by those who consented to the compromise measure. . . . The bill should not be rushed through at this session under such circumstances."9

Kansas Republican Joe Bristow asked Nevada Democrat Key Pittman, who was in charge of the bill, to allow the senators to recover from the tariff debate before considering it. However, the backers of the bill considered themselves in a position to win now. Pittman, a junior senator who had been coached in his presentation by O'Shaughnessy, refused to postpone, citing the twelve years that San Francisco had already been waiting.

"There is a persistent lobby against the passage of the bill, and I regret to say that that lobby is affecting the minds and the judgment of Members of this body, of people in public life, and of citizens all over the country," Pittman said as he launched into his presentation of the bill. He accused the lobby of causing "thousands and thousands of letters from people throughout this country protesting the passage of this bill" to land on the desks of the Members of Congress and other public officials in Washington. The term "lobby" was a pejorative at the time, and each side hurled it at the other, like a rotten tomato. But, otherwise, Pittman was right. Muir and Johnson had orchestrated a revolutionary campaign, the effectiveness of which Pittman himself was then testifying to on the Congressional Record. In order to fight entrenched interests, it would take the collective voice of the nation. This they had harnessed, and it would prove to be a watershed moment for environmentalism.

When pressed to name the lobby by Idaho senator Bill Borah, who led the fight for the Republicans, Pittman identified Johnson and Whitman. He accused them of "misrepresenting the facts."

He never mentioned Muir. As with the internal struggle at the Sierra Club, Muir's status as a widely beloved writer and personality kept him above the fray. Even during the most heated moments, little of the vitriol would ever be directed at him. That was Johnson's role.

He would, however, invoke Pinchot: "You who are in favor of conservation of the highest type; you who look forward; you who look to Mr. Pinchot as the light of conservation, would you for one moment doubt his sincerity in a matter of this kind? Would you for one moment doubt his judgment in a matter of this kind? And yet Mr. Pinchot states that this is one of the best bills that was ever drafted; that this bill not only aids, not only does more to conserve the national parks, but that it is the highest form of conservation, and places to the best possible use the nature resources of this country."

He also cited Los Angeles: "The city of Los Angeles was granted practically the same privilege in carrying from the eastern slope of the Sierra Nevada Mountain nearly all the water of Owens Valley and depriving many farmers of its use so that it might be put to a higher purpose of supplying the people of Los Angeles and its vicinity with a good domestic supply of water. That act passed through Congress, and that great project has been carried on successfully."[10]

This "privilege," however, would lead to violence in the 1920s and litigation throughout the century.

As the debate went on, exhausted senators lost their focus and began to drift away. When Minnesota's Knute Nelson, a former chair of the committee, finally demanded a quorum call, it failed. The Senate adjourned until the following day. "The Democrats' attempt to railroad the bill through the Senate," the *New-York Tribune* announced, "was blocked, at least temporarily."[11]

Muir had that small victory and something else to celebrate the next morning. In the isolated Big Santa Anita Canyon, the Southern California Section of the Sierra Club, established in 1911, decked its new mountain retreat—Muir Lodge—in bunting for its dedication ceremony. Its namesake, who had many friends in Los Angeles and Pasadena, had contributed $50 toward the construction. Fittingly, a sequoia sapling was planted at a front corner. For the next quarter century, the property would serve as a gathering place and a symbol of the Sierra Club's growing influence.[12]

"The Hetch Hetchy steam roller did not work smoothly on Saturday and therefore on Tuesday it was withdrawn for repairs," the *New York Times* gibed on October 9. The Senate had pushed consideration of the bill to its regular session in December. "The $45,000,000 electric power franchise must wait," said the *Times*. "The plain fact is that mid-Western, Southern and Eastern Senators have been culpably inclined to leave to the determination of some of their Far Western colleagues a measure involving millions upon millions of dollars, grave constitutional questions, revolutionary policies concerning franchises and conservation, and the higher interests of a people proud of our noble scenery. They cannot too promptly set themselves at work to study the question in its broadest and highest aspects: the immense value of great natural wonders, the folly of giving away valuable national resources."

Congressman Kent blamed the setback on a cabal "engineered by misinformed nature lovers and power interests who are working through women's clubs." Women's suffrage was still seven years off, and he considered it a slight on the "nature lovers" to be working with women. Muir, on the other hand, had no such prejudice and relished the support of women. "Doing all we can to bring the influence of women into the fight," he had recently told Johnson.[13]

"I think your plan of battle excellent," Muir told Johnson on October 16. Muir declined to go East himself but promised others would, and added, "We must keep personal letters flying in a countrywide storm thick as snowflakes about the President's head & the Senators." Most important of all, though, he said, "We have to depend on wide-awake enlightened public opinion."

Johnson wrote a letter to the editor of *Collier's*, which ran in the October 25 issue and delivered his most lucid Hetch Hetchy statement, invoking Muir, calling out San Francisco for its greed and manipulation of the facts, and drawing on the words of the late elder Olmsted, who had explained that the grandeur of the park's "superb gorges" lay "in the contrast between sublime, rugged walls and beautiful floor vegetation. . . . To cut down or drown out the underbrush and great trees is to destroy the units by which gradually the mind climbs to a comprehension of the vastness of the whole." Johnson took California to task for its widespread neglect: "Has the State done anything to protect the Calaveras trees, or Mount Lassen, or Mount Shasta, or the Humboldt County redwoods? It is the United States, not California, that has saved her great scenery." He wrote, "There is a great difference between the need of San Francisco for a new water supply and the need to take for that supply a watershed of the Yosemite National Park, involving 500 square miles of magnificent scenery. The array of Influence in support of the bill does not alter the principle involved . . . that except for some reason of supreme necessity these national parks . . . shall lie preserved in their integrity."

He argued that what the city really wanted was an electric power franchise worth some $45 million. "This is a new conflict of commercialism with the interests of the people. Take out of the bill the right to sell electric power, and the city will withdraw the measure at once."[14]

Johnson's letter ran between Heinz spaghetti and Quaker oats ads. Environmentalism was going mainstream. Muir told him it was "capital, the best ever!" The Sierra Club had met to pass resolutions and to work up a "fierce white Hetch Hetchy heat." He followed up the next day complimenting Johnson's latest "first rate—clear sharp telling convincing" circular, and enclosing another check. "Let me know when more is needed. On to victory."

"The Women's Clubs are being stirred in fine order," Muir told Johnson in early November, as the Sierra Club continued to rally this potent force. "Mrs. Emmons Crocker, Chairman Conservation Dept. of the General Federation of Women's Clubs is with us." He asked Johnson to send copies of his circular to her and Mrs. Percy Pennybacker of Austin, Texas, the president, adding, "You are doing gloriously well, dear Johnson."

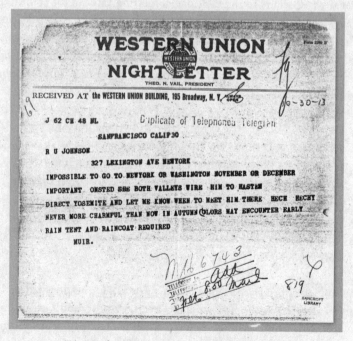

Telegram from Muir to Johnson on October 30, 1913.

Johnson and Osborn were planning a rally of the American Scenic and Historic Preservation Society at the American Museum of Natural History in New York City. Muir was sorry that he could not join them there or in Chicago. Neither could Colby, who had to keep a low profile, Muir told Johnson, though "he is heartily with us" and together with Parsons "furnishes most of needed money." Muir suggested they ask his friend Herbert Gleason, a Sierra Club member and photographer known for his images of Walden Pond, to present a lecture with lantern slides of Hetch Hetchy. He hoped to arrange a similar lecture in Washington. Gleason knew the President's private secretary, and Muir hoped Wilson might be persuaded to attend the lecture and "judge the value of the Valley with his own eyes" via the photographer's powerful images. "We're bound to win, enemy badly frightened," he closed.[15]

On November 15, Muir told Johnson that they had sent out fifteen thousand circulars and would soon have twenty thousand more, new and updated. The heat was on. "You complain I don't promptly reply to your telegrams especially to the Badè one, forgetting I live in the country & Badè is a professor & is delivering his course of lectures. . . . Have devoted all my time to this work for the last 4 months, & only two or three assist with either time or money. But anyhow we are going to win."

Five days later, Muir issued a battle cry to Johnson in a Western Union night letter:

NEVER FOR A MOMENT SINCE THE LONG BATTLE FOR THE INTEGRITY OF OUR PARKS BEGAN HAVE I FEARED DEFEAT AFTER THE PEOPLE WERE AROUSED TO ACTION. FROM ALL THE COUNTRY FAR AND NEAR COME GOOD TIDINGS. THE WOMEN'S CLUBS, ALMOST WITHOUT EXCEPTION, HAVE COME TO OUR HELP. REJOICE, BE OF GOOD CHEER, AND FIGHT TO A TRIUMPHANT FINISH.

On November 15, he wrote Helen, "The H.H. question will probably be decided in the first week of December next, and I still think we will win. Anyhow I'll be relieved when it's settled, for it's killing me. No matter, for I've had a grand life in these divine mountains, and

I may yet do something for those coming after me. Do try to make my load as light as possible by keeping well."[16]

On Friday, November 21, Johnson presided over the rally at the Museum of Natural History, where university professors and other speakers exhorted a raucous crowd to oppose the Raker bill. Whitman blamed the situation on a dispute between the people of San Francisco and a water company. Osborn, just back from Washington, read a letter from former president Taft, who denounced the scheme, saying that for a "reasonable price" San Francisco could find a source of pure water that did not "sacrifice" such "an object of natural beauty . . . as the Hetch Hetchy Valley." The crowd roared in approval, a roar that they hoped would reach Congress.

"We shall have to be strenuous in our endeavors to be successful, as strong influences are against us," Alden Sampson advised them. "It has been said that the Hetch Hetchy . . . is not used to any great extent by tourists and nature lovers and that fewer than three hundred or four hundred persons visit it each year. I know that last year more than thirteen thousand persons admired its beauties. If the bill is passed, it will be a crying disgrace to the people of the United States."

New York was convinced. "Educators Plead for Hetch Hetchy," the *New-York Tribune* declared the next day, "$122,000,000 PLAN IS GRAFT MAGNET." Among the resolutions approved by the audience for the society's platform, the *Tribune* reported, were "Natural franchises must not be given away to municipalities any more than to other corporations" and "Municipal politicians and engineers must not be allowed to destroy the masterpieces of our national scenery."

"Will President Wilson let his name be used as favoring local and very selfish interest against the best opinion of the country?" the *New York Times* asked.

On November 5, 1913, water from the Owens River reached a reservoir in the semi-arid San Fernando Valley, where the city of Los Angeles had long since overtapped its namesake river. William Mulholland, appointed chief engineer of the Bureau of the Los Angeles Aqueduct by the city water commissioners in 1906, had overseen a force of up to

3,900 workers at its peak, digging 164 tunnels to complete the 233-mile aqueduct. His engineering feat was compared to the building of the Panama Canal. At the opening ceremony, the Irish-born engineer preferred to let his enormous accomplishment—one that had taken ruthless methods to bring to fruition and had earned the wrath of farmers in the Owens Valley—do the talking. "There it is," he said as the water arrived. "Take it." Even as its rival to the north, San Francisco, was mired in Congressional hearings, the City of Angels was turning on the taps, poised for record growth.

With the Senate vote set for December 6, the final showdown took place the first week of December. It started with debates on the question of irrigation and the rights of farmers in between the Sierra Nevada and San Francisco. Senator Mark Smith of Arizona, who had practiced law briefly in San Francisco, claimed that those who opposed the Raker bill were "financed by venal, selfish interests . . . forgetting or ignoring the wants and necessities of living men and women." But, in fact, they were barely financed at all, as Muir, Parsons, and Colby could attest. The deep pockets were on the other side. "The San Francisco advocates of the spoliation handsomely maintained at Washington, month after month, quite openly, a very competent and plausible lobbyist," the *New York Times* would rightly claim, "and save for a few hearings and protests they occupied the Washington field most comfortably alone and unopposed."[17]

San Francisco was indeed so well organized and financed that on the morning of Saturday, December 6, the day of the vote, the senators arrived at their chamber to find a sixteen-page "Special Washington Edition" of the *San Francisco Examiner* lying on their desks. The special edition featured an artist's idealized rendering of a dammed Hetch Hetchy, with an idyllic reservoir, a scenic byway etched into the canyon wall, and hotels rising above it. One dubious senator described the bill's supporters as the "most insidious lobby ever assembled in Washington." Bluster and debate carried on through the day. Three minutes before midnight, the Senate voted. As in the House, it was not even close. The measure passed 43–25. Having watched from the gallery, Phelan, Rolph, and O'Shaughnessy repaired to the Willard Hotel. Never mind that they had missed last call, they toasted, fittingly, with glasses of water.

Mayor Rolph and the board of supervisors would treat Pittman to a hero's banquet, with more than a hundred guests, at the Palace Hotel in San Francisco. "Many striking speeches were made felicitating the Nevada senator on his able services in the fight in Washington," the *Carson City Daily Appeal* boasted, "and it was acknowledged that but for the services rendered by Nevada the fight would have been lost."[18]

The bill only needed the signature of President Wilson, and this time Johnson would not be bringing out his eagle quill. The Sunday morning edition of the *Examiner* exclaimed, "San Francisco Wins Hetch Hetchy . . . Battle for Water Rights Comes to Triumphant Finish in United States Senate." While a number of regional newspapers, particularly in the South and West, sided with San Francisco's pragmatic quest for water, many newspapers nationwide condemned the Raker bill. None more powerfully than the *New York Times*. On December 9, it mourned "One National Park Lost," and decried a bill that "converts a beautiful national park into a water tank for the City of San Francisco. . . . When the Congress of the United States approves the municipal sandbagging of a national park in order to save some clamorous city a few dollars, against the protests of the press and people, is it time for real conservationists to ask, What next?"

"Ever since the business of nation-making began, it has been the unwritten law of conquest that people who are too lazy, too indolent, or too parsimonious to defend their heritages will lose them to the hosts that know how to fight and to finance campaigns" the *Times* continued in its biting December 9 postmortem. "The American people have been whipped in the Hetch Hetchy fight. They had the press and enlightened public opinion and all men of public spirit on their side. The lobbyist was too much for them, although at the end the bill was rapidly losing support. If the people had set up a lobby they might have won." It was true that the people would need a corps of professional advocates to take on their well-funded counterparts nationwide. The Sierra Club had entered that realm to stay.[19]

Muir wrote Helen that he was holding out hope the President would veto the bill. "Anyhow I've done my best and am now free to go on with my pen work." He was run down and exhausted. His right lung was infected, and he had a hack that he could not shake.

On December 19, President Wilson did sign the bill, giving San Francisco the right to build the O'Shaughnessy Dam and flood Hetch Hetchy.

Disappointed after so many years of effort, Muir had faith, even now, that right would prevail in the end. As he wrote in his journal, "The people are now aroused. Tidings from far and near show that almost every good man and woman is with us." The loss would only spur the people to greater effort, he was sure.[20]

CHAPTER 26

Immortal Friends

P rior to the start of the new timber season in the spring of 1914, the Yosemite Lumber Company had devoured all the trees in its path right up to the borders of Yosemite National Park. Having recently extended its railroad, it was now prepared to cross into the park, where it owned six thousand acres of woodlands, including centuries-old pines, firs, and cedars. Yosemite Lumber's holdings were not only within the park borders, they were highly visible—along a twelve-mile stretch of the Wawona Road, the main route into the park from the southern San Joaquin Valley and the only road for automobiles between Yosemite Valley and the Mariposa Grove of Big Trees. It was because of its expanse of massive sugar and yellow pines that the road was considered the most scenic in the park.

The automobile—Muir's "puffing machine"—was about to transform the Yosemite experience. In the six years that the train to El Portal had been operating, it had increased tourism manyfold. During that time, Henry Ford had introduced the motor assembly line and started pumping out Model T's. The first cars were allowed in Yosemite in the summer of 1913. Not long after, Ford doubled its daily minimum wage to $5 and implemented an eight-hour workday, meaning more money and more leisure time for workers. It was the dawn of a new era, and Muir was right that there would soon be an urgent need of another "yosemite," Hetch Hetchy, to help manage the throngs of visitors.

Even while Congress and the federal bureaucracy had failed to rescue Hetch Hetchy and the northern reaches of the park, they were working together to fight the potentially catastrophic destruction of scenery in the south. But now it was down to a matter of weeks before Yosemite Lumber would rev its engines and start laying waste to the Yosemite Valley entrance. Once clear-cutting began, it would set the grandeur of the entrance back several centuries.

The Sierra Club, remarkably, now had Judge Raker as an ally, and on February 2, the club's board of directors, with Muir presiding, sent him a telegram in support of the Yosemite National Park Protection bill before the House: "Sierra Club strongly favors exchange of timber lands along Wawona Road in Yosemite National Park for lands of equal value outside of park. We trust that the California delegation in Congress will use every effort to secure the passage of this legislation." In reality, the deal was more complicated than that.

To protect the Wawona Road, as pointed out by the secretary of agriculture, 640 acres of privately owned land in the Sierra and Stanislaus National Forests would need to be transferred to the federal government and included in Yosemite National Park. It would take the cooperation of the Department of the Interior and the Department of Agriculture and an appraisal of the Forest Service—not to mention the concurrence of F. M. Fenwick and the Yosemite Lumber Company—followed by an act of Congress to get it done.

The federal government and national parks advocates, including the Sierra Club, hoped to prevent the destruction of the forest and to eliminate private holdings within the park. This latter goal would prove impossible to achieve by a buyout, however, as Fenwick's evaluation was double that of the government, and the two sides could not come to terms. Nevertheless, a trade was still possible.

In a complex deal swiftly negotiated by Yosemite Lumber and the federal departments, the two sides agreed to exchange 4,560 acres of woodlands. The United States would get the company's highly visible property along the much-traveled entrance to the park and the Mariposa Grove of Big Trees in exchange for 2,040 acres from the Sierra National Forest and 2,520 acres in a less visible part of Yosemite National Park. In the end, the agreement reduced the privately held land within the park by 1,660 acres. It also forbade clear-cutting on the land traded away.

In his assessment of the deal, which he went to great pains to show was fair to both the nation and the company, involving "equal land and timber values," Chief Forester Henry Graves explained that while you could get close to parity, no deal could be exact. The company would have to pay the higher cost of leaving trees for scenic and forestry purposes while logging, as now required. On the other hand, it would profit from the larger trees on the government land. In preventing the cutting of 3,920 acres adjacent to one of the most important and beautiful roads into the park, the government was producing a benefit that "while very great, cannot be measured in dollars and cents."[1]

On the first day of 1914, Muir wrote, "With all my heart dear Johnson I wish you a happy new year and congratulate you on the grand work you have accomplished in the one just closed. . . . As you say the long drawn out battle work for nature's gardens has not been thrown away. The conscience of the whole country has been aroused from sleep; and from outrageous evil compensating good in some form must surely come. And now for new work with the new year. You are still young in years—old only in good deeds—fifteen years younger than your devoted admirer and friend."

In early February, Johnson jokingly told Muir that he was busy trying to scrape together "three meals a day," but it was not far from the truth. Still, he was more concerned for Muir than for himself: "I'm sorry you've been ill, and I can't bear to think of you all alone in that big house when you are not well. This fight has had one happy result for me, my dear Muir. It has brought us even nearer together and revealed to us more clearly the affection we have for each other."[2]

"I beg of you to devote yourself to building up your health so that you may go on with your most important literary work," Johnson wrote in late March. "I hope you will not take too much to heart the apparent victory of the San Franciscans in the Rape of the Hetch Hetchy. I sincerely hope (and with some confidence) that they may yet prevent the valley from going to the dogs." The Hetch Hetchy battle had delayed his post-*Century* rebirth by six months, he said. "But the light is breaking! We are about to realize my dream of an endowed Academy." Johnson had helped establish the American Academy of Arts and Letters in 1904 and had had the pleasure of informing Muir that he had been elected a member in 1909. As secretary of the organization, he had just gained substantial funding and a building site for a home for the academy. "Believe me, dear Muir," he signed off, "with unchanging esteem, affectionately your comrade and friend."[3]

Ed Parsons had taken the Hetch Hetchy loss hard, and his health had suffered. In May, after a short illness, the longtime head of the outings committee died at the age of fifty-three. "The Sierra Club and all his friends have suffered a loss that cannot be measured," wrote Colby, who started a fund to build a stone lodge and club headquarters in Tuolumne Meadows as a memorial to his close friend. "For his unflagging devotion to the lost cause of Hetch Hetchy," wrote Muir, "he paid a heavy price in strength and health as well as in time and money. He will be sadly missed." Parsons's wife, Marion, was elected the Sierra Club's first woman board member, filling her husband's seat. Having been so moved by Muir's readings of his Alaska journal at her kitchen table, Marion now offered to help him with the book.[4]

Muir, who had turned seventy-six in April and now walked with a slight limp that he attributed to his long night on Shasta, did not take part in that summer's Sierra Club outing to the mountains he found so restorative, but he was thus spared a farewell tour of the Tuolumne Canyon and last look at Hetch Hetchy, which undoubtedly would have been painful. Just when he was no longer able to "worship in the high temples of the great Sierra Crown," as he had pressed Emerson to do, however, the poet's granddaughter, Ellen Emerson, came from the East and took part in the Sierra Club journey, seeing what her grandfather, despite being urged on by Muir, had been unable to see, and going where Muir could no longer go. Before braving Muir Gorge on a six-day trek through the Tuolumne Canyon to Hetch Hetchy, she joined the others in hurtling down the slippery chutes at Waterwheel Falls, where Arthur Pillsbury was making moving pictures, capturing, she trusted, their expressions "as they passed from pleased anticipation through frozen horror into delighted relief." She would cherish this outing to Hetch Hetchy. "Impossible to reconcile ourselves," she later lamented, "to the thought of drowning that beautiful meadowland under many fathoms of water."[5]

In Martinez, Muir had what little he needed: a comfortable bed, firewood, his books, and his work. He ate his meals at Wanda's, and with Marion Parsons's help "pegged away" on the Alaska book. He was making up for his long absences by improving the Big House. He had added electric lighting and made a passage from his den into Helen's old bedroom, which he lined with shelves and turned into a library. He had the floors painted and matting laid in the halls.

Despite the sprucing up, books and papers still cluttered Muir's study, like fallen wood in a primordial forest. "Confusion was no word for the state of the manuscripts," observed Parsons, who was both dismayed and amused by his perpetual good spirits amid the chaos. Not only was he working with material from more than thirty years ago—journals that had been consulted to write letters to editors and magazine stories, with up to five versions of some passages—recently he had jumbled two typed copies of the journals, which he kept in a wooden orange crate, while revising sections of both. He scrawled notes on used envelopes and paper bags and in the margins of his voluminous correspondence and mountains of clipped newspaper articles, some preserved by him and some by others. "No scrap of manuscript could ever be destroyed," Parsons noted, and he was constantly finding and reworking rejected material, until she began hiding it "inside a great roll of papers conspicuously tied with red ribbons and labeled in huge capitals 'Copied!'"[6]

Muir often worked from seven in the morning until ten at night, breaking only to read mail and for an hour at lunch and dinner. He applied great "critical scrutiny" to "each sentence, each phrase, each word," Parsons remarked—"not once but twenty times." Writing a book, he told her, was "a long, tiresome, endless job." Along the way he also reveled in the memory of his early explorations, and when he periodically launched into a stirring tale, his face lit up, to Parsons's delight. Slowly but surely, he wrestled the orange crate full of pages and the piles of notes on his desk and tables into a coherent manuscript.

Although they had been together in the same physical space only a handful of times during the four decades of their friendship, Muir missed Johnson. In early August, he wrote him, "Unchangeable immortal friend, I often wish we were fewer miles apart that we might come face to face every day through all the seasons & years. But we meet every day anyhow for you are never out of heart & mind." His Alaska notes were approaching "something like a book," he told Johnson. "Many others are calling for pen work & my years are flying very fast. I wish you could come & spend a year or two with me, tho my house now is only a lonely bachelor place."·

On July 28, 1914, the world was plunged into war with the assassination of Archduke Franz Ferdinand in Sarajevo. In early September, Johnson reported to Muir that the war—or as he put it, "the Kaiser's deviltry"—had postponed his work on the academy endowment, and he was now heavily engaged in protesting against it and raising money for the relief of the Poles, who were caught in the maw of brutal combat between the Germans and the Russians. Meanwhile, the *Century* had fallen into disarray. "They dismissed my successor and tried to sell the magazine but were enjoined and compelled to reorganize," he wrote. "It is a sorry vindication for me!" Johnson asked Muir about the status of the "farmers' protest against the Hetch Hetchy wickedness." Muir responded that it was dead, "like the valley itself in which several hundred men are now doing desolation work." But he quickly moved on: "Your protest against the Kaiser's war work is good & strong. Civilization has not gone very deep as yet, but we are making some slight progress heavenward, &"—he invoked Burns—"'it's coming yet for a' that, that man to man the world o'er shall brothers be and a' that.' . . . The Century Co. made a mortal mistake in letting you go."[7]

On November 18, Johnson, though busy running an academy meeting, wrote Muir: "We hear various rumors here that the Hetch Hetchy grant is to be used only as a club over Spring Valley. I hope this is so and that the vultures may yet abandon their prey. Do make some inquiries." He was sorry that Phelan—riding his Hetch Hetchy victory and his calls to deport Chinese immigrants—had just been elected to the US Senate. "I hoped he'd be snowed under." While Johnson was "nearly used up" by the organizing of the meeting, he was looking forward to the sessions, which would include papers and a concert of compositions by members, as well as something that particularly pleased him, salutations and a paper from an envoy of the French Academy. "Lordy, I wish you were here," he said. "I think of you often and when I get just a little lower down in my purse, I'll come out for a tramp with you."[8]

In early December, Muir wrote what would be his last letter to Johnson, carrying on the conversation in their usual congenial way: "Dear Mr. Johnson, I heard some time ago that a considerable number of men were making beginnings on road work near Hetch Hetchy," and members of the High Trip that passed through the valley in July reported that a few cabins had been built there and a few trees cut, but they had seen "nothing like an earnest beginning of reservoir work." He had heard "hardly a word about Hetch Hetchy" since Phelan had been elected. "Having attained his object he has never a word to say on pure mountain water.

"I would be delighted to have you come out for a California trip next summer," Muir closed. "Come direct to my house. . . . I am, dear old friend, Faithfully yours, John Muir."[9]

Epilogue

After contracting pneumonia while visiting Helen and her family in Daggett for Christmas, Muir died at California Hospital in Los Angeles on Christmas Eve of 1914. He was seventy-six. Some claim that he died of a broken heart because of Hetch Hetchy, but in all probability, given his unwavering faith and optimism, he died still firm in his belief that one day Hetch Hetchy would be set free again, and everything would turn out for the best. He had written what could be a fitting epitaph for himself in his preface to *Our National Parks*, in 1901: "I have done the best I could to show forth the beauty, grandeur, and all-embracing usefulness of our wild mountain forest reservations and parks, with a view to inciting the people to come and enjoy them, and get them into their hearts, that so at length their preservation and right use might be made sure."[1]

Muir's legacy, as the father of our national parks, founder of the Sierra Club, and spiritual leader of the environmental movement, continued to grow after his death. He is now widely hailed as the nation's most influential conservationist. In 1915, in his honor, California created the 210-mile John Muir Trail, from Yosemite Valley to Mount Whitney. In 1976, he was voted the Greatest Californian. Congress declared April 21, 1988, John Muir Day in honor of his 150th birthday, and that same year California designated April 21 as an annual John Muir Day "to observe the importance that an ecologically sound natural environment plays in the quality of life of us all and indeed the future of our existence."

Muir's Sierra Club colleague, literary executor, and biographer Frederic Badè
dedicating the John Muir plaque on the Yosemite Falls trail, 1924.

It should be noted that Muir, who possessed more than a touch of
Scottish misanthropy (for *all* humanity), occasionally used sharp words
and offensive period vernacular. But his writing, often graphic and
descriptive, befitting his engineering and scientific bent, is rarely judg-
mental and toward individuals almost never with preconceived notions
or lack of generosity. In fact, the preponderance of Muir's writing and
work demonstrates that he cared profoundly about all people and held
a special spot for the weak and downtrodden. "We all flow from one
fountain Soul," he told Catharine Merrill in a letter in the summer of
1872. "All are expressions of one Love. God does not appear, & flow out,
only from narrow chinks & round bored wells here & there in favored
races & places, but He flows in grand undivided currents shoreless &
boundless over creeds & forms & all kinds of civilizations & peoples &
beasts, saturating all & fountainizing all." As we face the deepening
environmental crisis of our own age, we can take strength in Muir's
legacy: his steadfast optimism, his deep wisdom, and his relentless
commitment to being a guardian of the valley.[2]

Robert Underwood Johnson continued to be an exemplary and selfless leader, focusing on culture, arts, and war relief. As the permanent secretary of the American Academy of Arts and Letters, he orchestrated a congressional charter in 1916 and opened the organization's headquarters, on the Upper West Side of Manhattan, in 1923. During World War I, Johnson organized the American Poets' Ambulances in Italy, which provided the Italian army with more than a hundred ambulances and dozens of field hospitals, and he was a leader in the Italian War Relief Fund of America. For these efforts, he was decorated by five foreign nations and appointed the US ambassador to Italy in 1920.

Johnson, newly appointed ambassador to Italy, leaving the White House after his interview with President Wilson, in February 1920.

In his memoirs, *Remembered Yesterdays*, published in 1923, Johnson said of his dear friend Muir, "There has been only one John Muir. He was not a 'dreamer,' but a practical man, a faithful citizen, a scientific observer, a writer of enduring power, with vision, poetry, courage in a contest, a heart of gold, and a spirit pure and fine." Johnson believed he was "likely to remain the one historian of the Sierra, which he depicted with the imagination of the seer and the reverence of the worshiper." He acknowledged the John Muir Trail and Muir Woods as fitting tributes but said the nation owed Muir more. "He was the real father of the forest reservation system of America. The Government should create from the great wild Sierra Forest Reserve a National Park, to include the Kings River Canyon, to be called by his name.

"As for the destruction of the Hetch Hetchy Valley," he declared, "California and the Government owe him penance at his tomb."[3]

The battle over Hetch Hetchy Valley is considered the nation's first major environmental controversy. By galvanizing grassroots opposition to the dam, the campaign led by Muir and Johnson created a defining moment in the nation's environmental debate. Thousands of individuals and organizations from across the country petitioned Congress regarding the valley, and a shared love of wilderness was transformed into a sustainable political movement. These petitions essentially gave birth to populist environmental activism. As citizens weighed in with their opinions on the proper use of national parkland and the relationship between local interests and national values, this ultimately benefited the cause of conservation and the protection of our national parks. The loss of Hetch Hetchy raised public awareness about the importance of preserving nature, setting the stage for Congress to pass the National Park Service Act of 1916, which established a new standard of sanctity for the national parks, preventing them from being usurped by local interests and from any further disfigurement. While Muir and Johnson lost the battle for Hetch Hetchy, they belatedly won the war for the national parks, which continue to serve as a model for environmental protection of wilderness around the world today.[4]

The Sierra Club welcomed the National Park Service when it was established in 1916, with Sierra Club member Stephen Mather as its first director and another club member, Horace Albright, as assistant director and later a director. The Sierra Club and the University of California cosponsored lectures in Yosemite Valley that ultimately inspired the National Park Service interpretive programs.[5]

As Muir had noted, "The conscience of the whole country was aroused from sleep." Muir's Sierra Club has grown to nearly 4 million members today. Through the decades, the club has successfully opposed the construction of dams, lobbied Congress to protect millions of acres of wilderness, and fought for cleaner energy.

It took San Francisco two decades to build its dam and 156-mile aqueduct system. The cost of the dam alone was $6,121,000 (nearly $100 million today). Sixty-eight laborers lost their lives during the construction of the system. Considered an engineering marvel, the complex project, overseen by city engineer Mike O'Shaughnessy, included eighty-five miles of tunnels, pumping stations, pipelines, a number of smaller dams, a sixty-eight-mile railroad, hydroelectric generating plants, and electric transmission lines. In 1923, the 385-foot-high concrete arch-gravity O'Shaughnessy Dam was completed, eventually submerging Hetch Hetchy Valley in nearly two hundred feet of water.

In 1930, the city of San Francisco finally acquired Spring Valley Water Company, for $40 million. In 1934, twenty years after Muir's death, thousands of people celebrated as Hetch Hetchy water, at last, crossed the coast ranges and San Francisco Bay and flowed into Crystal Springs Reservoir, formerly owned by Spring Valley and known as the Spring Valley Lakes, in the Santa Cruz Mountains twenty miles south of San Francisco. *Chronicle* writer Royce Brier called it "the wine of triumph in strife with Nature and one of her most closely guarded treasures in the Western land." O'Shaughnessy, chief engineer of the project for twenty-two years, was not there to see it. Two weeks earlier he had died of a heart attack.

The Yosemite Sugar Pine Lumber Company (the final iteration of the Yosemite Lumber Company) closed in 1942. The Yosemite Valley Railroad closed in 1945. Today, Merced Falls is a ghost town.

The Sierra Club has never given up the fight to reclaim Hetch Hetchy. In 1955, it released the film *Two Yosemites*, narrated by club executive director David Brower, contrasting the "ugliness" of the Hetch Hetchy Reservoir with Yosemite Valley. The Reagan administration backed a plan to drain the reservoir in the 1980s but was thwarted by California representatives in Congress. San Francisco mayor and later California senator Dianne Feinstein notoriously said, "All this for an expanded campground? Dumb. It's dumb, dumb, dumb."

"Now is the time to complete a full analysis of the feasibility and many benefits of bringing back the treasure of Hetch Hetchy Valley in Yosemite," wrote Larry Fahn, the president of the Sierra Club, in December 2004. The restoration plan would simply store the same water somewhere downhill from Yosemite National Park. "A fitting tribute to John Muir would be for us to find the wisdom and the will to restore the grandeur of Hetch Hetchy Valley, in the early 21st century, for our families and all future generations."[6]

The battle for conservation must go on endlessly. It is part of the universal warfare between right and wrong.

—John Muir

Acknowledgments

his book was conceived after my mother-in-law won the lottery for a cabin at Yosemite National Park for my father-in-law's seventieth birthday and invited her children and their spouses and kids along to celebrate. On a June afternoon, my wife, Jessica, and I and our daughters reached the Grove of Big Trees clad in shorts and sandals. To our surprise, it began to snow. Thrilled, we scrambled to pile on clothes and then caught snowflakes on our hands and faces, the girls dancing around like wood sprites. The view from Inspiration Point did the rest. A Virginian with Appalachian Mountain roots, I knew that my perception of America had shifted forever, and somehow, profoundly. The stunning view was of a different order of magnitude. I soon discovered that to understand the place one must know John Muir. The adventure had begun. Thank you, Bonnie.

Spouses often get heartfelt "last but not least" offerings in acknowledgments, but in this case that would not be fair. It is a good thing that Jessica was just as moved by Yosemite as I was, and that the place became a part of our mutual DNA, for in addition to the unstinting love and moral support she provided me during the writing of this book, she also poured her own blood, sweat, and tears into the manuscript, reading and editing it, and living it with me, including on subsequent visits to the Sierra Nevada as well as Dunbar, Portage, and Martinez.

A few years back, I was working on another book when Langdon Moss, an aspiring novelist, arrived on my doorstep seeking guidance.

Learning of our mutual admiration for Yosemite and Muir, we struck a deal, and almost overnight, I had a mentee, a researcher, and a new book to write. Many a day we broke bread discussing the relative merits of Thoreau, Emerson, Burroughs, and Muir or parsing the relationships of Muir, Johnson, Roosevelt, and Pinchot. Kudos to Langdon for his research and devotion to this book. Carson Horky later did a stellar job of grabbing the baton and springing forth.

Among the correspondents who provided documents or answers, special thanks to Cathy Deely, great-great-granddaughter of Robert Underwood Johnson; Julia Matisoo of the Moores family; Melinda Pillsbury-Foster, a descendant of Arthur Pillsbury; and Muir experts Bonnie Gisel and Harold Wood, the latter being the webmaster of the Sierra Club John Muir Exhibit and host of the John Muir Global Network (johnmuir.org).

To the many organizations that house the papers and artifacts of John Muir, Robert Underwood Johnson, and others central to this book, my deepest thanks for your heroic efforts to maintain the archives and to retrieve from them: Bill Swaggerty, director of the John Muir Center at the University of the Pacific, who invited me to speak at the 2018 John Muir Symposium, "The Practical Muir," and Mike Wurtz, head of the Holt-Atherton Special Collections and Archives at the University of the Pacific Libraries, provided encouragement and expert assistance. Likewise, Therese Dunn, librarian of the Sierra Club's William E. Colby Memorial Library, and Kylie Chappell, at the Yosemite Conservancy, kindly offered their guidance. To the keepers of the wonderfully designed and not-to-be-missed John Muir Birthplace in Dunbar, Scotland, as well as to the volunteers at the Kern River Valley Historical Society and the Daggett Museum, namely Gene, Nora, and Beth, praise and esteem; your enthusiasm for your communities is inspiring.

Matthew Menke combed the archives at the Tulare Historical Museum, and John Snyder, a curator and William Keith expert at the St. Mary's College Art Museum, generously loaned me the two volumes of Brother Cornelius's Keith biography—for four years. Park rangers Steven and Andy at the John Muir National Historic Site shared their intimate knowledge of Muir's longtime homeplace. Much admiration also to Library of Virginia librarian David Grabarek, who unfailingly brings the hard-to-find sources stashed away in far-flung libraries or the Library of Congress to my doorstep.

To my friends and fellow authors James Campbell, Charles Slack, and Logan Ward, your smart readings of my work, encouragement, and friendship mean even more to me now than they did a quarter century ago when we first started our nonfiction-writing, bourbon-drinking, Scrabble-playing brotherhood. Two other friends, Andy Smith, a teacher and historian, and Bruce Coffey, the creator and director of One School, One Book at Read to Them, read the early manuscript and offered critical suggestions for improving it. Hullie Moore shared his deep enthusiasm and knowledge of Muir with me. Thank you, thank you.

When I first told my agent, Dorian Karchmar, that I was writing about John Muir, she audibly inhaled. A Californian, she had recently been thinking that in this time of climate crisis we needed to hear more about Muir. Dorian held my feet to the fire as I developed a narrative arc around Muir's quest to save Yosemite that avoided veering off (too much) on the myriad tangents of his sprawling life and pursuits. I thank her for that, for her razor-sharp observations, and for her fierce loyalty. My appreciation goes also to her colleague Alex Cane, who read the early manuscript and offered cogent thoughts, and to her assistant, Isabelle Appleton. Dorian's Hollywood counterparts at WME, Elizabeth Wachtel and Sylvia Rabineau, have likewise offered wise counsel.

Having the talent and dedication of the entire Scribner/Simon & Schuster team behind this book is an immeasurable gift. Many thanks to Nan Graham, Scribner's publisher, who supported this project from the very first. Colin Harrison, editor in chief of Scribner, was the ideal coach for this quarterback. Muir and Johnson met and bonded as writer and editor for *Scribner's Monthly* (later the *Century*), which along with *Harper's Magazine*, held sway over the national conversation. Before beginning his distinguished career at Scribner, Colin served as deputy editor at *Harper's*. Like Muir, Colin is a horticulturist (in his spare time raising eighty-five varieties of pears in his orchards), and like Johnson, he has managed to escape the office to dispense sage advice to his writer in remote places of great natural beauty (in Vermont and Provence). Many thanks to Colin and to his able assistant, Emily Polson, who kept the publication of this book, with its old and digitally challenged photos, on the rails through the age of Covid, travel disruptions, and supply chain snafus (with the help of summer intern Vivienne Germain). Annie Craig, Rafael Taveras, and Jason Chappell also helped ensure deadlines were met, while Kyle Kabel and Jaya Miceli made the book look lush and inviting. Mia O'Neill and Lauren Dooley spread the word. Also a special thanks to copyeditor Steve Boldt for his thorough examination of the text and multiple fixes, and to the venerable mapmaker Jeffrey Ward, without whose exquisite work all would be lost.

If I could go back in time, not only would I try to horn in on Muir and Johnson's historic camping trip, but I would also thank the many photographers who hauled their massive gear around Yosemite Valley and whose work, capturing the magnificence of the place and preserving the visual record, now adorns this book, including C. C. Curtis, George Fiske, Joe LeConte, Eadweard Muybridge, Arthur Pillsbury, and Carleton Watkins. And to the brilliant folks at the Cornell University Library who present the nation's essential nineteenth-century periodicals on one easy-to-use and pleasing-to-look-at webpage "Making of America," a site that was a lifesaver during the Covid-19 lockdown, bravo to you and to all your fellow librarians for doing what you do. Your efforts make books likes this one possible.

The finishing touches of *Guardians* were applied at the dining table of the Kings' dear friends Bill and Emily Martin, overlooking Los Angeles, not far from California Hospital, where Muir took his last breath. Thanks for the flawless coffee, the delicious meals, and the nonstop humor, Bill and Emily.

Notes

Where sources have been made obvious in the narrative, they are not repeated in the notes. Unless otherwise noted, all John Muir letters come from the John Muir Papers in the Holt-Atherton Special Collections, University of the Pacific Library.

Abbreviations:

nps.gov: National Park Service website
SC-JME: For Sierra Club citations go to the John Muir Exhibit on the Sierra Club website, which you can access at https://vault.sierraclub .org/john_muir_exhibit/.
UPL: John Muir Papers in the Holt-Atherton Special Collections, University of the Pacific Library

PROLOGUE **The Photo**

1 Russell, 147.
2 Farquhar, 71; Bunnell, 65. On March 28, 1864, California senator John Conness introduced a US Senate bill to grant to California both Yosemite Valley and the Mariposa Grove of Big Trees. In the debate that followed, according to Carl Russell, chief naturalist of the National Park Service, in *One Hundred Years in Yosemite* (1947), Conness entered "the first evidences of national consciousness of park values as we conceive of them today" and "started the long train of legislative acts which have given the United

States the world's greatest and most successful system of national parks."
While the 1864 act, which President Lincoln signed, did not create a
national park, it recognized the importance of natural reservations on
a federal level and gave California the responsibility of preserving and
presenting Yosemite's natural wonders. Mount Conness, a peak above
Tuolumne Meadows, is named for the senator. In 1872, Yellowstone was
part of a territory, not a state, which could have provided its own oversight,
and that is why it received national protection (Jones, 6). Roosevelt was
only the second sitting president to visit the park. Rutherford B. Hayes
took a carriage ride through the valley in 1880, becoming the first sitting
president, albeit a lame duck, to visit.

3 Galen Clark, *Yosemite*, 38–39.

4 These words are Muir's, as retold to Johnson, who recorded them (*Remembered*, 388), while adding that Muir was "so much of a forest pacifist that
he believed that animals would not attack one if they were let alone."
Johnson also said that Muir had "never killed anything in his life," which
was not correct.

5 Lunde, 98–104, 168–69, 172, 189; Muir, *Thousand-Mile Walk*, 69.
Roosevelt was a man of great contradictions. Although as a young bird
enthusiast he had killed and stuffed more than a thousand bird specimens
for his private collection, he had recently made Pelican Island, Florida,
a federal bird reservation and the first national wildlife refuge. On the
way to California, he had visited the site of his first buffalo kill, a seminal
experience for him, but that buffalo had been one of an unfathomable
60 million destroyed in North America in the previous half century, in part
to subdue the Native Americans who depended on them. Then again, he
had made time to see the Yellowstone herd, which had been saved thanks
to him and would help keep the buffalo from going extinct. Roosevelt's
conservation efforts, including his establishment of the influential Boone
and Crockett Club, were largely to preserve animals for hunting.

6 Johnson, *Remembered*, 339; Wolfe, *Son*, 194.

7 LeConte, 29–30.

8 Galen Clark, *Yosemite*, 40–43; Wolfe, *John*, 39–40; and Muir, *Thousand-
Mile Walk*, 61.

CHAPTER 1 **Discovering the Range of Light**

1 Merry, 131–33; Heacox, 11–12.

2 Worster, 38; Braun.

3 Wolfe, *Son*, 32, 97. Muir, though unenthusiastic about going to war,
indicated in a letter to his brother Dan, who went to Canada before him,

that if he had been drafted, he would have gone. "I intend if not drafted to go to Scotland in the spring," he told Dan in a letter of December 20, 1863, before, instead, joining him in Canada. Muir's primary motivation for leaving home was poverty and incompatibility with his domineering father. "If you were here, you would soon wish yourself away again even though there was no war," he told Dan. "You are much better where you are. . . . Father and I cannot agree at all. I could not live at Hickory Hill a single week hardly. My advice is to rest as contentedly as possible where you are." For more on this, see Wood, "Was John."

4 Muir's remarkable mechanical desk, which he designed and carved out of wood, is now on display in the library of the University of Wisconsin. Sympathetic ophthalmia is a rare and little understood reaction in which an injury to one eye causes small clumps of cells to form in the other, usually within two to twelve weeks after the injury. Wolfe, *Son*, 105; letter, Carr to Muir, Mar. 15, 1867, in Gisel, 43; Elder, 378–79; Keeler, "Recollections"; Muir, "Autobiography," pt. 7, 251; Gifford, *John Muir*, photo "John Muir at the age of twenty-five," following 320.

5 Muir's thousand-mile walk across the South took place from September 1 to October 23, 1867, in Kentucky, Tennessee, Georgia, South Carolina, and Florida; Wolfe, *Son*, 110–16.

6 Badè, *Life*, 1:175–78; Wolfe, *Son*, 116; Colwell, 143, 148.

7 Badè, *Life*, 1:178–81; Wolfe, *John*, 23, and *Son*, 117; Muir, "Treasures" and "Ramble," 209–10.

8 Badè, *Life*, 1:182–86.

9 Ibid., 185–89; Sargent, *Galen*, 20; "Galen Clark," nps.gov.

10 Muir, *Thousand-Mile Walk*, 106–16; Badè, *Life*, 1:189–92; Wolfe, *Son*, 117–18, and *John*, 3–4. Note: Here and elsewhere the dialogue is taken from Muir's own writing but may have minor edits. He sometimes presents the same scenes, including dialogue, with slight variations. Badè and Wolfe both say Muir found a place on the dirt floor that first night, curled up in his own blanket, and went to sleep. Muir says in his journal that he slept on the bed-shelf.

11 Wolfe, *John*, 4–5; Badè, *Life*, 1:192.

12 Wolfe, *John*, 22–23; Muir, *Thousand-Mile Walk*, 69.

13 Muir, *My First*, 4–6.

14 Ibid., 36–84, 86, 90.

15 Ibid., 100–104.

16 Ibid., 107–18.

17 Ibid., 118–20; Emerson, *Nature*, 12–13; Muir, "Treasures."

18 Muir, *My First*, 120–21; Elder, 376; Wood, "John Muir Misquoted."

19 "Transcontinental Railroad," History.com, Sept. 11, 2019.

CHAPTER 2 **The Brag About the West**

1 Emerson arrived in Yosemite Valley on May 5, 1871. Gisel, 138; Bosco, cviii; McAleer, 594–601; Thayer, 63, 67–8; Butler "C Book," Wisconsin State Historical Society; Sanborn, 82.

2 Letters, Carr to Muir, May 1 and 16, 1871, in Gisel, 138, 140; Muir, *Wild Muir*, 49. Many years later, in remarks after receiving an honorary MA degree from Harvard, Muir would say that "Emerson, [Louis] Agassiz, [Asa] Gray—these men influenced me more than any others. Yes, the most of my years were spent on the wild side of the continent, invisible, in the forests and mountains. These men were the first to find me and hail me as a brother." Badè, *Life*, vol. 1, ch. 8; Muir, *Our National*, ch. 4.

3 Muir, "Treasures."

4 Letter, Muir to Carr, Apr. 3, and letter, Carr to Muir, May 1, 1871, in Gisel, 135–38; Badè, *Life*, 1:246–52; Wolfe, *Son*, 146–51.

5 Muir, "Ralph Waldo Emerson," SC-JME; McAleer, 597; Russell, 96; Yelverton, preface (by Kate Reed), v, and introduction (by Margaret Sanborn), xxvii, and 5–6. In a Dec. 1, 1871, letter to his brother David, Muir would recommend Yelverton's book *Zanita*: "I helped Mrs Yelverton now Countess Avonmore to write last summer in the valley. I am one of the characters & it contains a good deal of Yosemite scenery."

6 Thayer, 65, 76, 78–79; Gilman, *Journals*, 16:409.

7 Letter, Carr to Muir, May 1, 1871, in Gisel, 138; Thayer, 83; Rusk, 154–55; Wolfe, *Son*, 145–46; Worster, 210; McAleer 601–3.

8 Muir, "Ralph Waldo Emerson," SC-JME; Badè, *Life*, 1:253–55, 247–48; Emerson, *Nature*, 9; letter, Muir to Sarah Muir Galloway, Apr. 5, 1871; Muir's personal edition of *The Prose Works of Ralph Waldo Emerson* (Beinecke Rare Book and Manuscript Library at Yale University), 516.

9 Thayer, 90–91; Badè, *Life*, 1:255–56; Wolfe, *Son*, 140–41, 148, from "Muir's notes"; Muir says he quotes Emerson's "Woodnotes," but no line "Come listen what the pine trees sayeth," so replaced.

10 Galen Clark, *Big Trees*, 31, and *Indians*, xii–xiv; McAleer, 604.

11 Muir, *Our National*, 11–36, 134; Branch, 133; Bosco, cxiii; Wolfe, *Son*, 151; Badè, *Life*, 1:240–41, 252–59; Galen Clark, "Early Days" and *Big Trees*, 62–63, 67, 85; Thayer, 108; Hutchinson, 56–57; "Galen Clark," nps.gov.

12 Brown, 113–14; Hutchinson, 56–57.

13 McAleer, 604–5; "Galen Clark," nps.gov; Thayer; Rusk, 155, letter, Muir to Emerson, July 6, 1871; Emerson, *Journal* (1871), 237–39.

14 Bosco, cxiv; Wolfe, *Son*, 150; Badè, *Life*, 1:255–56; Worster, 210.

15 Letters, Carr to Muir, May 16 and 24, 1871, in Gisel, 140–41; Badè, *Life*, 1:257–58.

CHAPTER 3 **A Ramble in Hetch Hetchy**

1 Gisel, 129; letters, Carr to Muir, May 24, and Muir to Carr, June 22, 1871, in Gisel, 140–42.
2 Author correspondence with Gisel, Apr. 6, 2017.
3 Muir, "Explorations," 142–43; "The Hetch Hetchy Valley," *Sierra Club Bulletin* 1908, 211–20, and revised and reprinted as "Let Everyone Help Save the Famous Hetch Hetchy Valley" pamphlet, Nov. 1909.
4 Muir, "Hetch Hetchy Valley," Mar. 25, 1873; Badè, *Life*, 1:310–12; author correspondence with Gisel, Apr. 6, 2017.
5 Muir, "Explorations," 144; Badè, *Life*, 1:313–16; letter, Muir to Ann Gilrye Muir, Nov. 16, 1871.
6 Letter, Muir to David Muir, Dec. 1, 1871; Russell, ch. 8; Gisel, 13.
7 Badè, *Life*, 1: 313–16.
8 Letter, Muir to Ann Gilrye Muir, Nov. 16, 1871.
9 Muir, "Treasures" and "Yosemite Valley in Flood."

CHAPTER 4 **Johnson Becomes an Editor**

1 Johnson, *Remembered*, 3, 77–78.
2 Ibid., 75–77.
3 Ibid., 23–24, 74, 325–26; Brown, 283–84, 286–87.
4 Johnson, *Remembered*, 81.

CHAPTER 5 **Ice and Fire**

1 Muir, "Salmon Breeding"; Miesse, ch. 21; Muir, "Snow-Storm," "Shasta in Winter," and *Steep*, 29–81. Miller and Morrison, ch. 1: "John Muir and the John Swett Family" by Ruth E. Sutter; "Josiah Whitney," SC-JME.
2 Eichom.
3 White, xxx.
4 Swett, 122.
5 Muir, "Hunting." Muir lived with McChesney and his wife in Oakland for ten months in 1873. Swett would become known as the father of the California public school system.
6 Hartesveldt, ch. 1; Wolfe, *John*, 429.
7 Muir, "Hunting."
8 Lunde, 64–65, 84; Pauly, 1–6.

CHAPTER 6 **Mr. Muir and Mr. Johnson**

1 Muir, "Linnaeus."
2 Letter, Johnson to Muir, Sept. 28, 1877; Muir, "The Humming-Bird," 550.
3 Johnson, *Remembered*, 21, 23, 26–27.
4 Ibid., 31–32, 44, 59–60.
5 Ibid., 589–92.
6 Ibid., 84.
7 "The Strentzel Muir House," nps.gov; Clark and Sargent, xviii. Louisa Wanda Strentzel Muir was born on July 6, 1847, in Honey Grove, Texas: Find a Grave, "Louisa Wanda 'Louie' Strentzel Muir."
8 Lunde, 65–96; Brinkley, 149.
9 Johnson, *Remembered*, 385–86.
10 Ibid., 96–97.
11 Ibid., 209–24. According to Johnson, Mark Twain's publishing company, Charles L. Webster, secretly swooped in and outbid Century for the right to publish the book, even though Grant had told Roswell Smith, "I am glad that you are to publish the book, as I should not have written it if Mr. Johnson had not convinced me that I could" (217).

CHAPTER 7 **Rebirth on Mount Rainier**

1 Arax, 192–93.
2 Today Camp Muir is still the starting point for most summit climbs on Mount Rainier's southeast side. However, the four-mile climb over snowfields to reach Camp Muir from Paradise Valley has claimed lives in thick fog and owing to hidden crevasses. Muir, *Steep*, 265; Wolfe, *John*, 295; White, 155; Molenaar, 61–65.
3 Badè, *Life*, 2:218–19; letter, Muir to David Muir, Aug. 7, 1887; Wolfe, *Son*, 232; Worster, 309.
4 Letters, Muir to Jeanne Carr, Oct. 22, 1887, and Jan. 1888; Gisel, 299.
5 Wolfe, *Son*, 164, 260–61.
6 Tod, "Traveling Companions."
7 Wolfe, *Son*, 238–39.
8 Warner; Wolfe, *Son*, 239, 242–43; White, 151–53.
9 Cornelius, 1:169; Muir, *Steep*, 262–65; Worster, 309; White, 160n12.
10 Molenaar, 65–68; Piper, "Flora"; "Mount Rainier/Gibraltar Ledges," mountaineers.org; White, 159; Gifford, *John Muir*, 902; "Philemon Van Trump," SC-JME.
11 Wolfe, *Son*, 239–42; Muir, *Steep*, 267.
12 Warner; Muir, *Steep*, 267–70; Wolfe, *John*, 296; White, 156–57.

13 *Seattle Times*, May 29, 1938; Muir, *Steep*, 268–69; Warner; Piper, "Narrow Escape." Warner's camera is in the Digital Collections of the University of Washington Libraries, "Arthur Churchill Warner Photographs of Washington State and Alaska, ca. 1884–1945." Many of the original negatives were lost, possibly in the fire of 1889, shortly after they were made.

14 White, 158–59; Pauly and Pauly; Shoop; Letters, Van Trump to Muir, July 8 and 27, 1910, and Louie Muir to Muir, August 9, 1888; "Philemon Van Trump," SC-JME.

CHAPTER 8 Shaken and Stirred

1 Zito.

2 *San Francisco Daily Evening Bulletin*, June 29, 1889.

3 Letter, Johnson to Muir, June 3, 1906; Johnson, *Remembered*, 279–80.

4 Johnson, "Personal" and *Remembered*, 88–91.

5 Wolfe, *Son*, 243–44.

6 Letter, Muir to Louie Muir, June 3, 1889, in Badè, *Life*, 2:235–36; letter, Muir to Carr, Feb. 17, 1889; Johnson, *Remembered*, 280. In the letter to Louie, Muir says they had "a fine glorious ride thru the forest, not much dust," while in *Remembered Yesterdays* Johnson remembers "perilous cliffs and . . . choking clouds of dust," providing a useful reminder of how differently two people might characterize the same event and how different Muir's and Johnson's perspectives were.

7 Johnson, *Remembered*, 280; Clark and Sargent.

8 Wolfe, *Son*, 244; letter, Muir to Louie Muir, June 3, 1889; Worster, 312; Muir, "Yosemite Valley. Beauties."

9 In the twentieth century Olmsted's "Yosemite and the Mariposa Grove: A Preliminary Report, 1865" was at last recognized as one of the most significant philosophical statements of the American conservation movement. *The Evolution of the Conservation Movement, 1850–1920*, American Memory, Library of Congress.

10 Galen Clark, *Yosemite*, 43–44; Johnson, *Remembered*, 289, and "Open Letters: Destructive Tendencies," 478; Hutchings, *In the Heart*, 460; "The Stoneman Hotel, ca. 1890," nps.gov; and letter, Muir to Louie Muir, June 3, 1889. Declared dangerous by the new commission, the Stoneman House would be destroyed by fire a decade later.

11 Letter, Muir to Louie Muir, June 3, 1889; "Galen Clark," nps.gov; *Biennial Report of the Commissioners, 1889–90*.

12 In Greek mythology, the twin giant sons of Poseidon tried to climb to heaven by placing Mount Ossa on Olympus and the Pelion Mountain on Ossa. Letter, Muir to Louie Muir, June 3, 1889; Johnson, *Remembered*, 280–82, 289.

13 Muir, "Snow."

14 Ibid.; Johnson, *Remembered*, 281–84; Yelverton, 7.

15 Johnson, *Remembered*, 283–87, 323–26, 399–400, 593. In "Ramble," 205, Muir recounts the conversation this way: "When we were camped one day at the big Tuolumne Meadows, my friend said, 'Where are all those wonderful flower gardens you write so much about?' And I had to confess—woe's me!—that uncountable sheep had eaten and trampled them out of existence. Then he said, 'Can't something be done to restore and preserve so wonderful a region as this? Surely the people of California are not going to allow these magnificent forests, on which the welfare of the whole State depends, to be destroyed?'"

16 *San Francisco Daily Evening Bulletin*, June 29, 1889.

17 Muir, "Treasures."

18 Wolfe, *Son*, 233, 245; Johnson, *Remembered*, 287.

19 Muir, "Ramble," 207; letter, Johnson to Muir, July 5, 1906; Johnson, *Remembered*, 288.

CHAPTER 9 **Treasures of the Yosemite**

1 Muir, "Yosemite Valley. Beauties"; "Galen Clark," nps.gov.

2 Wolfe, *John*, 283. "Tinkering the Yosemite waterworks would seem about the last branch of industry that even Yankee ingenuity would be likely to undertake," Muir wrote in his journal. "But that men such as the Commissioners should go into the business of improving Yosemite nature, trimming and taming the waterfalls properly to fit them for the summer tourist show, is truly marvelous—American enterprise with a vengeance"; "'The Snow' looks well and reads well," Johnson commented in a letter to Muir on June 22, 1889, jesting: "In what other part of our country could that subject get the prominence the *Bulletin* gives it? A sad comment on your snowless coast." Letter, Muir to Johnson, June 27, 1889.

3 *San Joaquin Valley Argus*, July 27, 1889, 2. Now part of the Sierra National Forest, the Fresno Grove was renamed the Nelder Grove, after its unofficial guardian. The *Los Angeles Times* called Bull Buck "one of the most down-played natural wonders in existence" ("Madera's 'Bull Buck': The Buddha of Big Trees," February 23, 1992). In 2017, the Railroad Fire killed or damaged many of the grove's remaining sequoias. "Nelder Grove—Giant Sequoias," Sierranevadageotourism.org; Muir, *Our National Parks*, ch. 9; Galen Clark, *Big Trees*, 36.

4 Badè, *Life*, 2:221–25; Wolfe, *John*, 28, 344–45; Bruce C. Cooper, "A Brief History of the Palace Hotel of San Francisco," ThePalaceHotel.org;

Muir, *Wild Muir*, 67–68; Muir, "Snakes of Fresno," reprinted in *John Muir Newsletter* 2, no. 2 (April/May 1982), UPL; Calderwood.

5 Letters, Muir to Johnson, July 18, and Johnson to Muir, June 27, 1889.

6 Letters, Muir to Johnson, Sept. 13 and Oct. 29, and Johnson to Muir, Sept. 23, 1889. Hutch was James Hutchings.

7 "Letter from Visitors," *Century*, Jan. 1890, 474–79; Johnson, "Care of the Yosemite Valley" and "Destructive Tendencies."

8 Letter, Johnson to Muir, Nov. 21, 1889.

9 Letters, Muir to Johnson, Dec. 6, and Muir to Mary Muir Hand, Nov. 30, 1889. In 1898, when the US Cavalry protecting Yosemite withdrew because of the Spanish-American War, MacKenzie, a six-foot, brown-haired, blue-eyed self-described newspaperman, would join Yosemite's first civil protection force, one of eleven mounted assistants under two special agents, expelling sheepherders, confiscating illegal firearms, and fighting fires.

10 Letters, Muir to Johnson, Jan. 1 and 13, 1890.

11 *Kate Field's Washington* was published from 1890 to 1895. Scharnhorst, 207–8; *New York Times*, Feb. 14, 1890; Beasley, 1; letter, Johnson to Muir, Feb. 20, 1890.

12 Letter, Muir to Johnson, Mar. 4, 1890. Founded in 1854 in San Francisco, the Mechanics' Institute sponsored an annual exposition featuring inventions, industrial innovation, the arts, and natural resources of the West Coast, promoting immigration to California. *Report of the Twenty-Fourth Industrial Exposition*, 15–16.

13 Letters, Muir to Johnson, Apr. 16 and 19, and Johnson to Muir, Apr. 14, 1890; "The Yosemite," *Sun*, Mar 21, 1890, 4, col. 2–3.

14 Letters, Johnson to Muir, Apr. 14 and 19, and Muir to Johnson, Apr. 16 and 20 and May 8, 1890; Hampton, 142–45.

15 Letters, Johnson to Muir, May 14 (part missing) and 26 and June 3, Muir to Johnson, May 20 and 27 and June 9, 1890.

16 Muir, "Treasures."

17 Ibid., 485–87. The scientific name for giant sequoia that Muir used, *Sequoia gigantea*, was later changed to *Sequoiadendron giganteum*.

18 Ibid.; Muir, "Yosemite Valley in Flood."

CHAPTER 10 **Proposed: Yosemite National Park**

1 "Big Trees in Danger," *Daily Alta California*, Aug. 27, 1889. The bracketed editorial commentary is in the original.

2 Letter, John Irish to Muir, Sept. 1, 1890, Bancroft Library, UC Berkeley; Hampton, 94, 113, 125.

3 Muir, "Features," 656; LeConte, 56, 65. In 2013, the long-shrinking Lyell Glacier was downgraded to an ice field with no discernible movement.

4 Muir, "Features," 663–67; LeConte, 58. Big Oak Flat was a former mining enclave between the Merced and the Tuolumne; the big oak for which it was named was more than ten feet in diameter, but, having been literally undermined, died.

5 Letters, Johnson to Muir, Aug. 28 and Sept. 20, and Muir to Johnson, Sept. 12, 1890, Louie Muir to Johnson, Aug. 27, and Johnson to Louie Muir, Sept. 5, 1890; Hampton, ch. 8; *Biennial Report of the Commissioners, 1889–90*, 8–9.

6 Letters, Johnson to Muir, Sept. 30 and Oct. 3, 1890; Albright and Schenck, 264; Hampton, ch. 8; Norton; Muir, "Ramble," 205; Smith.

7 Johnson, *Remembered*, 288–89; Muir, "Rival"; William R. Jones, ed., preface to 1978 reprint of Muir's Kings Canyon story.

8 Letters, Johnson to Muir, Oct. 15, and Muir to Johnson, Oct. 16 and 24, 1890; Clark and Sargent, 2.

9 Letters, Johnson to Louie Muir, Nov. 6, 1890 (listed as Johnson to *John* Muir on the University of the Pacific website), Johnson to Muir, Nov. 12, 1890; Clark and Sargent, 26.

CHAPTER 11 **A Red-Letter Day**

1 Letter, Johnson to Muir, Dec. 29, 1890; Johnson, *Remembered*, 243, 250, 294. Red Wood Park is now part of Armstrong Redwoods State Natural Reserve. James Armstrong, who logged and ran a sawmill near Guerneville, spared the grove of redwoods and tried to establish a forest reserve in 1891, but the state refused to act. In 1917, the county took control of the property, and it was later made a state park and given reserve status.

2 Johnson, *Remembered*, 241–42; letters, Muir to Johnson, May 27 and June 9, 1890.

3 Johnson, *Remembered*, 255–57; "William H. Appleton," centuryarchives .org.

4 Johnson, *Remembered*, 24, 258–59, 294.

5 Letters, Johnson to Muir, Apr. 30 and May 1, and Muir to Johnson, May 13, 1891; Muir, "God's First Temples."

6 Letters, Muir to Johnson, Nov. 12 and Dec. 12 and 14, 1890, and May 13 and 18, 1891, and Johnson to Muir, May 25, 1891; Lekisch, 103–4; "Hume-Bennett Lumber Company," en.Wikipedia.org.

7 Muir, "Rival," 78–79, 86–90. Sources say Joseph LeConte made the first attempt to climb it in 1898 and failed; first ascent said to be Edward and James Hutchinson in 1904; Muir calls it Humphrey; this would be a major accomplishment.

8 The Converse Basin Grove's six thousand sequoias included some monumental specimens; however, the government would not protect it. Instead, it was logged to near oblivion for decades to come. In 1892, the grove's second-largest tree, the thirty-two-hundred-year-old General Noble Tree, was felled to be exhibited at the 1893 Chicago World's Fair—ironically to prove that such gargantuan trees truly existed, or once existed anyway—making it the largest tree ever cut down and leaving behind the massive "Chicago Stump." Sawed into pieces and reassembled at the expo, the tree was still believed to be a hoax by many viewers. The grove's largest tree, the Boole Tree, was named around 1895 for Frank Boole, general manager of Sanger Lumber Company, which Moore & Smith's Kings River Lumber Company became in 1895. The company leveled the grove but spared the tree that was considered by some to be the largest in the world (though that honor was more often bestowed on the General Grant Tree). The Boole Tree, 113 feet around at the base, has the largest footprint of any living giant sequoia and is the sixth-largest overall. Donald J. McGraw, "The Tree That Crossed a Continent," *California History* 61, no. 2 (Summer 1982); Wendell D. Flint, "To Find the Biggest Tree," Sequoia Natural History Association, 1987; "The Sanger Lumber Company," PacificNG.org.

9 Robinson says it was four miles and three hours from the mills to the Grant Sequoia Park (*Kate Field's Washington*, 318–20). Muir, "Rival," 77–80, 86–88; letter, Muir to Johnson, July 2, 1891; Elisabeth Kwak-Heffernan, "Kings Canyon National Park: USA's Deepest Canyon."

10 Letters, Muir to Johnson, July 14 and Aug. 1, 5, 15, and 18, and Johnson to Muir, Aug. 29, 1891; Muir, "Rival," 90.

11 Hartesveldt, ch. 1; St. George; Powers, 536–40.

12 Muir, "Rival"; letters, Johnson to Muir, July 7 and Nov. 4 and 18, 1891; Johnson, *Remembered*, 293–96.

13 Letter, Johnson to Muir, Nov. 25, 1891; the bracketed word *sidelined* is only semilegible and is a best guess. The signature of the associate is illegible. Even half a century later, Kings Canyon National Park, established in 1940, excluded potential reservoir sites, which were not made off-limits for development until 1965. William R. Jones, former Yosemite National Park chief naturalist, editor's preface to a 1978 reprint of Muir's Kings Canyon story, 288–89.

CHAPTER 12   **The Sierra Club**

1 "General Noble Tree, 1892," SS277143, New York Public Library / Science Source. It wasn't until April 2000, when President Clinton used the Antiquities Act to designate nearly 328,000 acres of Sequoia National Forest the Giant Sequoia National Monument, that the sequoias in the vicinity of the General Noble Tree, now the Chicago Stump, and all of the federally owned giant sequoia groves within Sequoia National Forest, were given permanent protection. The monument is located in two sections divided by Sequoia National Park. US Forest Service website.

2 About 150 of Keith's paintings now reside at St. Mary's College Museum of Art in Moraga, California.

3 Gifford, *John Muir*, 895.

4 Letters, Muir to Johnson, May 13, 1891, and Nov. 28, 1892, and Johnson to Muir, Apr. 24 and May 1, 1891, and Muir to Henry Senger, May 10 and 22, 1892; Jones, 8–9.

5 Keough; Wolfe, *Son*, 254.

6 Jones, 5–9; Punke, 162–66; Lunde, 97; Gifford, *John Muir*, 895–97.

7 Schuknecht; Jones, 11; "Proceedings of the Sierra Club," *Sierra Club Bulletin* 1 (1893–96): 23–24; "Philemon Van Trump," SC-JME.

8 Jones, 12.

9 Letters, Muir to Johnson, Nov. 23, and MacKenzie to Johnson, Oct. 4, 1892.

10 Letter, Noble to Johnson, Dec. 13, 1892.

11 Letter, Muir to Johnson, Jan. 13, 1893; "1893 petition written by John Muir asking the House of Representatives to preserve Yosemite National Park," Digital Public Library of America website.

12 Letter, Muir to Johnson, Jan. 13, 1893. State senator Elliott McAllister was a charter member of the Sierra Club but not a "director," as Muir says in his letter.

13 Letters, Muir to Johnson, Jan. 13 and 23, and Johnson to Muir, Feb. 3 and 10, 1893.

14 Letters, Johnson to Muir, Feb. 21 and Mar. 1, 1893.

15 Here Johnson uses "officially" to mean "among the officials," not some sort of official designation. Johnson, "Noble, Conservationist"; letter, Muir to Johnson, Mar. 21, 1893; Johnson, *Remembered*, 296.

16 Letters, Johnson to Muir, Mar. 9 and 20, and Muir to Johnson, Mar. 14, 1893.

17 Letters, Noble to Johnson, Mar. 2, 1893, and MacKenzie to Johnson, Oct. 4, 1892, and Muir to Johnson, Mar. 21, 1893.

18 Letters, Johnson to Muir, Mar. 23, and Muir to Johnson, Mar. 21 and 29 and Dec. 20, 1893. Irish would be appointed a naval officer of customs

in San Francisco, where he became known simply as "the Colonel." Muir and Johnson had for the most part heard the last of him.

19 Brown, 283–84, 286–87. Not everyone was dazzled. The British writer Rudyard Kipling condemned the city's avarice and savage citizens and hoped to never to see it again. The Italian playwright Giuseppe Giacosa felt the century's dominant characteristic—violence—found its ultimate form there.

20 Letters, Muir to Wanda Muir, May 26, and Muir to Louie Muir, May 29, 1893; Clark and Sargent, 32. Turner, addressing the American Historical Association; Sequoia National Forest website; New York Public Library / Science Source. The Chicago Stump in the Converse Basin Grove of Giant Sequoia National Monument in Fresno County, California, can still be visited today.

CHAPTER 13 The Preaching of Pine Trees

1 Wolfe, Son, 268; Worster, 338–42. Worster (339) calls Wolfe's book "an enduring classic in American nature writing."

2 Muir, "Our National Parks" and "Ramble," 203–8.

3 Letter, Johnson to Muir, Jan. 9, 1896.

4 Wolfe, Son, 269; Worster, 350; letter, Johnson to Muir, Mar. 6, 1896.

5 Williams and Miller, 40.

6 Pinchot, 27; Clayton, 3–10; Brinkley, 340–41; Williams and Miller, 32–34; Char Miller, Gifford Pinchot, 91–93; Steen, Conservation Diaries, 45.

7 Williams and Miller, 32–36; letter, Pinchot Papers, Manuscript Collection, Library of Congress; Drobnicki; Bowers; Hayes, 27–31. Founded by botanists and landscape gardeners in 1875 to promote arboriculture and conserve forests, the American Forestry Association evolved as Pinchot and the Cornell and Yale forestry schools transformed the forestry industry at the turn of the century and professional lumbermen and hardwood users increased their influence in the organization. In 1992, it changed its name to American Forests.

8 Letters, Johnson to Louie Muir, May 1 and 27, 1896.

9 Letter, Muir to Johnson, June 3, 1896.

10 Letters, Muir to Louie Muir, June 28, and Johnson to Muir, July 11, 1896, and Ann Muir to Muir, Nov. 8, 1869; Muir to Johnson, Aug. 5, 1896; Renehan, 184, 205–06; Burroughs, 7–9.

11 Letter, Muir to Johnson, July 5, 1896; Williams and Miller.

12 Williams and Miller; Morning Oregonian, July 26, 1896; letters, Muir to Louie Muir, July 15 and 21, and Muir to Johnson, Aug. 5, 1896.

CHAPTER 14 **Only Uncle Sam Can Do That**

1 Williams and Miller, 38–39.

2 "The Hetch Hetchy Steam Roller," *New York Times*, Oct. 2, 1913.

3 Letters, Page to Muir, Mar. 4, and Muir to Page, Mar. 21, 1897.

4 Williams and Miller, 40, n. 6; Pinchot, 116–17, 123–25, 130; and Steen, *U.S. Forest*, 35.

5 Letters, Johnson to Muir, Aug. 3 and Nov. 16, 1897.

6 Williams and Miller, 39.

7 Letters, Muir to Page, Apr. 16, and Page to Muir, May 27, 1897.

8 Muir, "American Forests," 156–57.

9 At a time of rampant anti-immigration sentiment, Muir's statement reflected a strongly liberal position on this issue.

10 Muir, "American Forests," 156–57.

11 Letter, Johnson to Muir, Aug. 3, 1897; Johnson, *Century*, Sept. 1897, 633–34.

12 Muir, "Adventure with a Dog" and *Stickeen*, 4–5.

13 Letters, Johnson to Muir, July 9, and Muir to Johnson, July 17, 1897.

14 Letter, Page to Muir, Oct. 15, 1897. In 1908, Houghton, Mifflin and Company incorporated and changed its name to Houghton Mifflin Company. This book uses the modern spelling throughout.

15 Letters, Johnson to Muir, Dec. 1 and 14, 1897, and Jan. 4, 1905, and Muir to Johnson, Nov. 16 and Dec. 6, 1897.

16 Letter, Page to Muir, Dec. 30, 1897.

17 Muir, "Wild Parks," 27.

18 "Galen Clark," nps.gov; "Yosemite Conservation Heritage Center," SC-JME. Three bolts in a granite boulder, where riders once tied their horses, still mark the site of Sinning's Cottage, where Old Yosemite Village once stood, now found on the Southside Drive between Sentinel Bridge and the Yosemite Chapel.

19 Pinchot, 131, 135–36, 139. Vallombrosa is a renowned forest outside Florence and home to Italy's tallest tree, a 205-foot Douglas fir, called the Italian Tree King.

20 Linda Gast, "Sugar Pine Lumber Company & Madera Flume Slide Show," *Sierra Sun Times*, Jan. 17, 2016, Goldrushcam.com.

21 Madera Sugar Pine Lumber cut trees for three more decades. By the time the Great Depression struck and the bottom fell out of the timber market, causing the company to go bankrupt, the flume had extracted billions of board feet from the perimeter of Yosemite National Park. Dwight Barnes; "Sugar Pine Company."

Chapter 15 **San Francisco's Thirst**

1 Righter, 36–40; Hudson Bell, "The Early History of Spring Valley Science School," *Fern Hill Times*, Apr. 28, 2018; Grunsky, 22; Lane's "Petition for Review," in *Reports on the Water Supply*, 116–17.

2 Walsh and O'Keefe, 123; Grunsky, 6–7, 100, 117–19; Righter, 44.

3 *San Francisco and the Hetch Hetchy Reservoir: Hearings*, 110; *Reports on the Water Supply*, 149; Righter, 47–49, 52.

4 *Reports on the Water Supply*, 119–20, 143; Righter, 27; "Josiah Whitney," SC-JME; Schneider; Act, Feb. 15, 1901 (31 Stat. at L., 790); "Mr. Phelan's Building," medium.com.

5 In 1903, Phelan said that the personal application was made to avoid the question of whether a municipal corporation could make an original application. In 1908, Interior Secretary James Garfield added that Phelan wanted "to avoid the difficulties which beset a city if it must announce its business intentions to the public before securing options and rights necessary for its project." *Reports on the Water Supply*, 113–14, 120–22, 217–18; Schneider.

6 Letters, Muir to Johnson, Feb. 26 and Apr. 15, 1901.

7 Farquhar, 226; Colby, "Edward Taylor Parsons"; letter, Johnson to Muir, June 19, 1901; Cornelius, 376–79, 597; "Helen Lillian Muir Funk," Find a Grave.

8 Cohen, 20; Hanna, 1; Clark and Sargent, 76–80; Edward Parsons.

Chapter 16 **Camping with the President**

1 The American Presidency Project, presidency.ucsb.edu, "President McKinley's Last Public Utterance"; Muir, *Our National Parks*, ch. 1; Wood, "Was John."

2 Righter, 53–54; Walsh and O'Keefe, 122. *Reports on the Water Supply*, 112–27 and 217–18, says, "This application was considered by the Secretary of the Interior and, on December 22, 1903, rejected on the ground that he did not have the legal power to allow such a right of way within Yosemite National Park."

3 "Theodore Roosevelt," SC-JME.

4 Letter, Johnson to Muir, Apr. 25, 1903.

5 Brinkley, 536–37; "1903—Photographing John Muir and Teddy Roosevelt" and "President Teddy Roosevelt Visits Yosemite—May 15–18, 1903," Arthur C. Pillsbury Foundation website.

6 Russell, ch. 11; Johnston, "Camping Trip"; McAleer, 608; Leidig; Sargent, "Wawona's Yesterdays: First Ranger," Yosemite Online; Brinkley, 538.

7 Curry and Gordon, 250–51; Theodore Roosevelt, "In Yosemite with John Muir," SC-JME.

8 McAleer, 608; Leidig; Wolfe, *Son,* 291–92; Brinkley, 540–46; Curry and Gordon, 251; Muir, *Mountains,* 231.

9 In 1903 the *San Francisco Examiner* hired Pillsbury, a Los Angeles–based photojournalist and Underwood & Underwood stringer, known for documenting the Yukon Gold Rush, to establish a photography department, a position Pillsbury held until 1906. Pillsbury shot many of President Roosevelt's events, including on his Western journey, and produced his own line of postcards, including one of President Roosevelt and his traveling party with Muir in front of the Grizzly Giant. "1903—Photographing John Muir and Teddy Roosevelt," Arthur C. Pillsbury Foundation website.

10 "The President Enjoys Yosemite Valley," *New York Times,* May 18, 1903, 1; Johnson, *Remembered,* 388. Some say it was a hotel chef. Johnson says it was a chef from the Bohemian Club. Wolfe, *Son,* 292–93; "An Artist and His Chocolate," nps.gov; "Christian August Jorgensen (1860–1935)," California Art Research Archive, Bancroft Library; "Chris Jorgensen Artist Home," Yosemite Online.

11 Lunde, 158–61; Leidig; Brinkley, 545–46; Roosevelt, "John Muir."

12 Brinkley, 547; Brands, 293; "100th Anniversary of President Theodore Roosevelt and Naturalist John Muir's Visit at Yosemite National Park," National Park Service press release, May 15, 2003. Letter, Muir to Merriam, Jan. 1, 1904.

CHAPTER 17 **Alaska Unites Yosemite**

1 Monroe, 216–18, 223; Johnson, *Remembered,* 442–43; letter, Muir to Johnson, May 7, 1903.

2 The LeConte Memorial Lodge was moved from Camp Curry to its location across from Housekeeping Camp in 1919 and renamed the Yosemite Conservation Heritage Center in 2016 because of LeConte's racist writings. "History of the Yosemite Conservation Heritage Center," Sierraclub.org.

3 Monroe, 225–26.

4 *Hetch Hetchy Reservoir Site,* 31.

5 Monroe, 226–27.

6 *San Francisco and the Hetch Hetchy Reservoir: Hearings,* 226–31: Badè, "Tuolumne Canyon."

7 *Hetch Hetchy Reservoir Site,* 30–33.

8 Letters, Muir to Johnson, June 18 and July 28, and Johnson to Muir, Sept. 4, Oct. 20 and 26, 1904.

9 Jones, 65, 72; Deverell, 132–33; letter, Muir to Johnson, Dec. 27, 1904.

10 Muir, *Edward Henry Harriman*, unpaginated.

11 Letters, Muir to Johnson, Jan. 10, 19, 26, and 30, and Feb. 2, 22, and 24, and Johnson to Muir, Jan. 17 and Feb. 8, 1905; Jones, 66–71, from *San Francisco Examiner*, Jan. 19, 4, and Jan. 25, 1905, 1–3.

12 Letter, Chittenden to Muir, July 2, 1904.

13 Letter, Muir to Johnson, Mar. 13, 1907; Righter, 27.

14 *Reports on the Water Supply*, 128–32.

15 *San Francisco Chronicle*, Feb. 24, 1905, 1–2.

16 Letter, Muir to Johnson, Feb. 23, 1905; Jones, 71–72; Cornelius, *Keith*, 477–78. In the Senate, the recession bill was approved by an official tally of 21–13. According to Colby, this tally was necessary because of a Senate rule that required passage by a majority of the Senate, not just those members present.

17 Letters, Johnson to Muir and Muir to Johnson, Feb. 24, Muir to Johnson, Feb. 27 and Mar. 6, 1905.

18 Letter, Johnson to Muir, Mar. 8, and Muir to Johnson, Mar. 23, 1905.

19 Letter, Johnson to Muir, May 1, 1905; Johnson, "Personal Impressions," 304–6.

20 Letters, Johnson to Muir, June 27 and July 31, Muir to Johnson, July 4 and 29, Muir to Mr. Hooker, July 3, 1905; Clark and Sargent, 86–87; Shoop; Muir, *Thousand-Mile Walk*, 42

CHAPTER 18 **The Great 1906 Earthquake Changes Everything**

1 Thomas and Witts, 20, 45, 50, 78.

2 Niderost; Key, 228; Cornelius, 1:448–50, 2:131–32.

3 Hobbs, 638; Thomas and Witts, 106–7; Ellen Klages, "Call Building 1906: Burned but Standing," *Argonaut* 4, no. 1 (Summer 1993), foundsf.org.

4 Niderost; Cornelius, 1:449.

5 Letters, Johnson to Muir, June 3 and July 5, 1906.

6 "Earthquake Impacts on Prestige," Stanford University and the 1906 Earthquake website. Agassiz, the statue, suffered only a broken nose and now perches above the entrance to Jordan Hall, alongside Alexander von Humboldt.

7 Clark and Sargent, 87; "Martinez Adobe," nps.gov.

8 Schuknecht; Jones, 79; letter, Muir to Johnson, June 10, 1906; Righter, 58.

9 Letters, Johnson to Muir, July 5, and Muir to Johnson, July 16, 1906.

10 Letter, James D. Phelan to Uncle George, May 8, 1906; Sarah Agudo and Marcin Wichary, "Mr. Phelan's Building," *Urban Explorations*, May 2, 2014, medium.com.

11 Niderost; Righter, 29, 55–60; Badè; Brinkley, 673.

CHAPTER 19 **Irrefragable Ignorance**

1 Cornelius, 1:458, 2:130: *San Francisco News-Letter Wasp*, July 14, 1906, and 2:131–32.
2 The transcript from this meeting comes from *Reports on the Water Supply*, 148–68. The extracts from the transcript have been edited for length and ellipses sometimes omitted. Also, Wolfe, *Son*, 313.
3 *Reports on the Water Supply*, 153–61.
4 *Adjuster Insurance: A Record of Pacific Coast Conditions and . . .* 33 (1906); *Reports on the Water Supply*, 163–68.
5 *San Francisco Call* 102, no. 55 (July 25, 1907), col. 1; letter, Muir to Johnson, July 26, 1907.
6 Letter, Johnson to Muir, Aug. 5, 1907.
7 Letter, Johnson to Muir, Aug. 8, 1907; Jones, 95–96; Clayton, 46–50.
8 Letter, Muir to Roosevelt, Sept. 9, 1907.
9 Ibid.; letter, Muir to Johnson, Sept. 18, 1907.
10 Letter, Roosevelt to Muir, Sept. 16, 1907.
11 Letter, Johnson to Muir, Sept. 12, 1907.
12 Letters, Muir to Johnson, Sept. 18 and 19, 1907.
13 Letter, Johnson to Muir, Sept. 23, 1907; Clayton, 50.
14 Letters, Barber to Muir, Sept. 18 and Oct. 16, 1907.
15 Cornelius 1:475–76; letters, Muir to Keith, Oct. 7, 1907, Muir to Johnson, Nov. 7, 1907, and Muir to Severs, Apr. 27, 1896; Mary Miller, *Argonaut*, Dec. 12, 1908; Muir, "Hetch Hetchy Valley," *Sierra Club Bulletin; San Francisco Call*, Nov. 6, 1907, 6.

CHAPTER 20 **Fighting Thieves & Robbers**

1 "Watch the Times Tower: The Descent of an Electric Ball Will Mark the Arrival of 1908 Tonight," *New York Times*, Dec. 31, 1907.
2 Letters, Muir to Kent, Dec. 21, 1907, Muir to Lukens, Jan. 7, 1908, Muir to Colby, Dec. 21, 1907, and Muir to Helen Muir, Jan. 29, 1909; Shoop.
3 Letters, Muir to Johnson, Oct. 19, Dec. 8 and 15, 1906; Brinkley, 756; Gessner, 146; "Lassen Volcanic Center," USGS website, May 21, 2015.
4 "Muir Woods," nps.gov; Gessner, 143; Clayton, 50–53; Righter, 123; letters, Muir to Roosevelt, Jan. 28, and Muir to Johnson, Mar. 11, 1908.
5 Letter, Roosevelt to Kent, Jan. 22, 1908; Brinkley, 752; letter, Roosevelt to Kent, Jan. 30, 1908.
6 Letters, Muir to Kent, Jan. 14 and Feb. 6, and Johnson to Muir, Jan. 17, 1908.

7 Letters, Muir to Roosevelt, Jan. 28, and Roosevelt to Muir, Apr. 27, 1908.

8 Telegram, Muir to Garfield, May 1, 1908; letter, Garfield to Muir, May 12, 1908.

9 *Reports on the Water Supply*, 217–19; "J. R. Garfield, 84, Son of President," *New York Times*, Mar. 25, 1950.

10 *Reports on the Water Supply*, 219–23; Wolfe, *Son*, 314; Jones, 102; letters, Muir to Garfield, May 1908, and Muir to Johnson, May 14, 1908.

11 Johnson, *Remembered*, 307, 391; Pinchot, 136–39; Clayton, photo section, caption,136; Lukas Keel, "Frenemies John Muir and Gifford Pinchot," *Humanities* 41, no. 1 (Winter 2020).

12 Johnson, *Remembered*, 304–5; Jones, 95; Frederick Palmer, "Pinchot's Fight for the Trees," *Collier's* 40, nos. 2–10 (1907): 271–72. Johnson's letter to the *New York Times* upon the death of John Noble four years later cited Noble's having been "overlooked in sending out the invitations to the great White House conference on conservation" as all the more reason to remember him as "officially the pioneer of the conservation movement in this country."

13 Letter, Sierra Club board of directors (including Muir, Joe LeConte, Colby, Badè, Olney, Parsons, and others) to the President and the Governors of the States Assembled in Conference, May 2, 1908. Johnson, an honorary vice president, did not sign the letter. *Sierra Club Bulletin* 6 (1907–8): 318–19.

14 Johnson, "Patriotism That Counts," 474–76.

15 Johnson, *Remembered*, 302–4.

16 Wolfe, *Son*, 314–15; Johnson, *Remembered*, 305; letters, Johnson to Muir, May 23, and Muir to Johnson, June 2, 1908.

17 Letter, Johnson to Muir, July 1, 1908; Johnson, "Patriotism That Counts," 474–76.

18 *San Francisco and the Hetch Hetchy Reservoir: Hearings*; Johnson, "High Price to Pay for Water," 125–26.

19 Letter, Muir to Johnson, Sept. 25, 1908; *San Francisco Call*, Nov. 13, 1908, 6.

20 Letters, Muir to Johnson, Dec. 1 and 7, 1908.

21 Letter, Muir to Johnson, Oct. 24, 1908; Muir, "Endangered Valley."

22 Letters, Muir to Johnson, Dec. 18, 24, and 30, and telegram, Dec. 31, 1908; *San Francisco and the Hetch Hetchy Reservoir: Hearings*, 118.

CHAPTER 21 **The Big Stick**

1 *San Francisco and the Hetch Hetchy Reservoir: Hearings*, 3–, 5–, 120, 223–31; letter, Badè to Mondell, Jan. 6, 1909; "Mondell, Frank Wheeler," history .house.gov.

2 Letter, Muir to Johnson, Dec. 24, 1908; *San Francisco and the Hetch Hetchy Reservoir: Hearings*, 3, 208–23, 238–39; letter, Muir to Lukens, Dec. 26, 1908.

3 Monroe, 226. Monroe's story ran in *Putnam's* in May, not February, as she thought it would and told congressmen in a letter; she was in the valley in the summer of 1904 and read her poem at the LeConte Lodge dedication, but it is unclear if this is the outing she wrote about in *Putnam's*. According to the Sierra Club website, she was also on a 1909 outing to Tuolumne and Hetch Hetchy.

4 *San Francisco and the Hetch Hetchy Reservoir: Hearings*, 147–49, 153. Among the many perceived injustices in the proposed deal was the exchange of inferior property for park property. San Francisco had bought one parcel that was well situated but unfortunately named Hog Ranch, which became the subject of much derision. Tallulah LeConte was the granddaughter of John LeConte, the first president of the University of California and Joseph LeConte's older brother.

5 Ibid., 5.

6 Ibid., 19–23.

7 Ibid., 55, 24–39.

8 Ibid., 36–37, 44-45; *Hetch Hetchy Reservoir Site*, 15.

9 *San Francisco and the Hetch Hetchy Reservoir: Hearings*, 46, 66, 89–90.

10 Ibid., 94–96, 101–3, 107–9.

11 Ibid., 112–13.

CHAPTER 22 **We Have Only Begun to Fight**

1 Letter, Muir to Johnson, Feb. 7, 1909; "Theodore Lukens House," atlas obscura.com.

2 Letters, Johnson to Muir, Feb. 4 and 12, 1909.

3 *Hetch Hetchy Reservoir Site*, 11, 90–91, 137; letter, Johnson to Muir, Feb. 12, 1909.

4 Letter, Muir to Johnson, Feb. 7, 1909; *Hetch Hetchy Reservoir Site*, 30–33, 90–91, 137; letter, Johnson to Muir, Feb. 12, 1909.

5 Letters, Johnson to Muir, Feb. 22 and 24, 1909.

6 Letter, Monroe to Colby and Parsons, Mar. 2, 1909, in Jones, 103–4.

7 Letters, Johnson to Muir, Feb. 19, 1909, and Johnson to Muir, Feb. 4 and 12, 1909.

8 Not only was Johnson looking forward concerning this battle, he felt that their legacy was at stake. "I am gathering material concerning 'The Pioneers of Conservation' for a future article: Noble, Muir, Powell, Fernow,

Bowers etc. etc. and the *Century*," he reminded Muir. "Somebody must do justice to the men ignored by the Roosevelt Administration."

9 Letter, Muir to Johnson, Apr. 3. 1909.
10 Society for the Preservation of National Parks letter, June 27, 1913; Jones, 97–99; letters, Muir to Johnson, June 29, and Johnson to Muir, Sept. 7, 1909; "Taft Summer White House," https://bevhistsoc.tripod.com/thestory.htm.
11 Letters, Muir to Johnson, Sept. 14, and Johnson to Muir, Sept. 22, 1909.
12 Cornelius, 465–66, 494, 529; letter, Muir to Johnson, Sept. 14, 1909.
13 Wolfe, *Son*, 322–25; letters, Muir to Johnson, Oct. 27 and Nov. 16, 1909; "President Taft at Gateway of Yosemite Park," *Los Angeles Herald*, Oct. 7, 1909; "Taft's Camp Fare Offsets Banquets, *Indianapolis Star*, Oct. 8, 1909, 1; Nilda Rego, "Days Gone By: 1909: John Muir Accompanies President Taft to Yosemite," *Mercury*, May 29, 2014.
14 Cornelius, *Keith*, 477.

Chapter 23 A Shocking Report

1 Letters, Muir to Johnson, Sept. 3 and 8, 1910; Johnson, *Remembered*, 88–93, 132–34; John, ix–xi.
2 Sierra Club website; Cohen, 27.
3 Righter, 67, 69; letter, Muir to Johnson, Mar. 21, 1893.
4 Jackson, 294–96; from Ballinger to mayor and Board of Supervisors, Feb. 25, 1910, Sierra Club website; Wolfe, *Son*, 325.
5 Jackson, 296; Freeman, 297, from letter Freeman to Manson, Jan. 27, 1911; Freeman in Europe, leaving Manson in charge of report but recording ideas about Hetch Hetchy in telegrams and journal entries: Jackson, 296.
6 Letters, Muir to Colby, Jan. 11, and Muir to Johnson, Jan. 26, 1911; www.yosemitevalleyrr.com/prototype/history.
7 "Lumber Mill to Go to Merced Falls," *Merced Evening Sun*, Apr. 1, 1911; "A Big Enterprise," *Mariposa Gazette*, Apr. 8, 1911; "Mill at Merced Falls," *Merced Evening Sun*, July 1, 1911.
8 "Mill to Be Built at Merced Falls," *San Francisco Call*, July 2, 1911, 64, www.newspapers.com/clip/3082030/ow_lehmer_yosemite_railway/; "Road Will Be a Scenic Wonder: Incline from El Portal to Timber Belt Will Negotiate Marvelous Grades for 7000 Feet," *Merced County Sun*, Aug. 11, 1911.
9 Wolfe, *Son*, 328–29.

10 Letter, Muir to Colby, May 8, 1911; *Boston Sunday Herald*, May 21, 1911; Fleck.

11 Colby, "John Muir," 5; Worster, 441; letters, Muir to Colby, May 26 and June 27, 1911; review, Marion Randall Parsons, *Sierra Club Bulletin*, Jan. 1912; Colby, "John Muir"; *Sierra Club Bulletin*, Jan. 1924; letter, Muir to Helen Muir Funk, June 22, 1911. Osborn, who was an acclaimed fossil collector, is now regarded as an innovative museum administrator but a scientist of questionable merit. Later in life he became a supporter of the theory of eugenics, and some have tried to tarnish Muir for being friends with him, but there is no evidence that the two ever exchanged thoughts on the topic. Osborn wrote forewords to the second and fourth editions of Madison Grant's notorious *The Passing of the Great Race*, which was first published in 1916, two years after Muir's death.

12 Letter, Muir to Colby, Sept. 19, 1911.

13 Jackson, 297–98, 304; letter, Freeman to Manson, Sept. 18, 1911.

14 "Accident at El Portal," *Merced County Sun*, Dec. 11, 1911.

15 "Inclined Railroad Is Now Complete," *Merced County Sun*, Aug. 2, 1912.

16 Letter, Muir to Johnson, Feb. 4, 1912; Ray Taylor, 122–23; Jackson, 299.

17 Ray Taylor, 116–17; Jackson, 300–305.

18 Letters, Johnson to Muir, July 26 and Aug. 10, and Muir to Johnson, Aug. 2, 1912; Jackson, 305–6.

19 *Proceedings of the National Park Conference*; "First Automobile Permit Issued 100 Years Ago," Yosemite Ranger Notes, Aug. 23, 2013, nps.gov.

20 Pillsbury, 26; "The Flowers Are Heard—October 16, 1912," Arthur C. Pillsbury Foundation website. Pillsbury made films of many blooming flowers found in Yosemite, which he showed at the studio and used in his lectures at garden clubs and other organizations while promoting preservation across California and the nation.

21 Marion Randall Parsons, "John Muir."

22 Wolfe, *Son*, 363n37; letter, Fisher-Rolf, Mar. 1, 1913, in Jones, 151.

CHAPTER 24 **The Nature Lovers**

1 "Must San Francisco Pay?" *San Francisco Call*, Jan. 14, 1913; Johnson Papers biographical note, New York Public Library; "Underwood Johnson Has Talent for Aiding Dubious Projects," *San Francisco Call*, Feb. 13, 1913.

2 Letter, Muir to Johnson, Mar. 23, 1913; Johnson, *Remembered*, 412.

3 *Congressional Record—House*, 7695–709; Jones, 151; letter, Muir to Johnson, Jan. 18, 1913; Righter, 118; Ray Taylor, 122, 126; Albright and Schenck, 20.

4 Righter, 120–24.

5 "Yosemite Lumber Company Acquires 20,000 Acres of Choice Timber Land," *Merced Evening Sun*, May 2, 1913.

6 Letter, Muir to Mina Merrill, May 31, 1913; *Sierra Club Bulletin* 9, no. 1 (Jan. 1913): 118–19.

7 Letter, Muir to Johnson, June 13, 1913; Johnson, *Remembered*, 134; John, 270.

8 Albright and Schenck, 20; Righter, 112; telegram, Muir to Johnson, June 26, 1913; Mark Alden Branch, "Big Man on Campus," *Yale Alumni Magazine*, Mar./Apr. 2013.

9 Letter, Muir to Johnson, June 15, 1913; Simpson, 168; *Hetch Hetchy Dam Site*, 239.

10 Righter, 121–22.

11 Letters, Muir to Johnson, July 1, and Muir to Osborn, July 15, 1913.

12 *New York Times*, July 21, 1913.

13 Letters, Johnson to Muir, July 22, and Muir to Johnson, July 23, 1913.

14 "The Hetch Hetchy Plan: Robert Underwood Johnson Gives Advice on How to Defeat It," *New York Times*, July 27, 1913 (condensed); *Collier's*, Oct. 25, 1913.

15 Letters, Johnson to Muir, July 28 and 30, 1913.

CHAPTER 25 **Every Park Will Be Attacked**

1 Muir journal, "Island Park," Aug. 1913; letters, Muir to Johnson, Sept. 14, 1909, and Muir to Osborn family, Sept. 13, Muir to Harriman, June 21, and Harriman to Muir, Jan. 1, 1913; Muir eulogy for Edward Harriman, SC-JME.

2 Letter, Muir to Johnson, Sept. 1, 1913.

3 Congressional Record—House, 1913, 3962–4004.

4 "H.R. 7207, the Raker Bill, August 5, 1913," National Archives; letter, Muir to Johnson, Sept. 3, 1913; *New York Times*, Sept. 4, 1913; Simpson, 170.

5 *San Francisco Call*, June 29, 1913; letters, Muir to Johnson, Sept. 1, 11, 12, 14, and 15, 1913.

6 Letters, Muir to Johnson, Sept. 25, and Muir to Osborn family, Sept. 13, 1913.

7 Letters, Muir to Johnson, Sept. 30 and Oct. 16, 1913.

8 "The Hetch Hetchy Steam Roller," *New York Times*, Oct. 2, 1913, 10.

9 Jackson, 98; *New York Times*, Oct. 9, 1913; Righter, 128.

10 Congressional Record—Senate, 1913, 5443–5475.

NOTES TO PAGES 341-357

11 "Republicans Block Hetch Hetchy Scheme," *New-York Tribune*, Oct. 5, 1913, 12.

12 "Muir Lodge, 1913–1938," Sierra Club, Angeles Chapter website.

13 *New York Times*, Oct. 9, 1913; Hayes, 194; letter, Muir to Johnson, Sept. 11, 1913.

14 Letters, Muir to Johnson, Oct. 16, 27, and 28, 1913; "Hetch Hetchy," *Collier's*, Oct. 25, 1913.

15 Letters, Muir to Johnson, Nov. 3, 4, and 10, 1913.

16 Letter, Muir to Johnson, Nov. 15, 1913; telegram, Muir to Johnson, Nov. 20, 1913; Wolfe, *Son*, 340; letter, Muir to Helen Muir Funk, Nov. 15, 1913.

17 *New-York Tribune*, "Educators Plead for Hetch-Hetchy," Nov. 22, 1913, 2; *New York Times*, Nov. 22 and Dec. 4 and 9, 1913; Righter, 129.

18 "San Francisco Wins Hetch Hetchy: Vote 43 to 25," *San Francisco Examiner*, Dec. 7, 1913; Simpson, 174; "Senator Pittman Highly Honored," *Carson City Daily Appeal*, Oct. 8, 1914, 1.

19 *New York Times*, Dec. 9, 1913.

20 Wolfe, *Son*, 341; Wolfe, *John*, 437.

CHAPTER 26 **Immortal Friends**

1 "Yosemite National Park Protection," 63rd Congress, 2d Session, 1–10, 19.

2 Letters, Muir to Johnson, Jan. 1, and Johnson to Muir, Feb. 5, 1914.

3 Letters, Johnson to Muir, Mar. 26 and May 18, 1914; Johnson, *Remembered*, 439–43, 448.

4 Kaufman, 32; Ellen T. Emerson.

5 Marion Randall Parsons, "John Muir"; letters, Muir to Helen Muir Funk, Dec. 3, and Muir to Johnson, Sept. 7, 1914; "The Strentzel/Muir House," nps.gov.

6 Letters, Muir to Johnson, Aug. 4 and Sept. 17, and Johnson to Muir, Sept. 6, 1914.

7 "Phelan Distinguished Son," *San Francisco Call*, Aug. 8, 1930; letter, Johnson to Muir, Nov. 18, 1914.

8 Letter, Muir to Johnson, Dec. 3, 1914.

9 Letter, Muir to Johnson, Dec. 3, 1914.

Epilogue

1 Johnson, *Remembered*, 315; "History," John Muir Institute of the Environment website.

2 Letter, Muir to Catharine Merrill, June 9, 1872.
3 Johnson, *Remembered*, 315–16.
4 "Hetch Hetchy Environmental Debates," National Archives.
5 Sierra Club website.
6 "Our Plan for Restoration," Restore Hetch Hetchy, hetchhetchy.org.

Bibliography

Abbreviations

SC-JME: Sierra Club–John Muir Exhibit. The John Muir Exhibit in "The Vault" on the Sierra Club website.
UPL: University of the Pacific Library. John Muir Papers in the Holt-Atherton Special Collections of the University of the Pacific Library.

Documents

Biennial Report of the Commissioners to Manage Yosemite Valley and the Mariposa Big Tree Grove. For the Years 1889–90. Sacramento: State Office, J. D. Young, Supt. State Printing, 1890.
————. *For the Years 1891–92.* Sacramento: State Office, A. J. Johnston, Supt. State Printing, 1892.
————. *For the Years 1893–94.* Sacramento: State Office, A. J. Johnston, Supt. State Printing, 1894.
Congressional Record—House, vol. 50, part 3, 1913.
Congressional Records—Senate, vol. 50, part 6, 1913.
Hetch Hetchy Dam Site: Hearing Before the Committee on Public Lands, House of Representatives, Sixty-third Congress, First Session on H.R. 6281. A Bill Granting to the City and County of San Francisco Certain Rights of Way in, Over and Through Certain Public Lands, the Yosemite National Park, and Stanislaus National Forest, and Certain Lands in the Yosemite National Park, the Stanislaus National Forest, and the Public Lands in the State of California for Other Purposes. Washington, DC: Government Printing Office, 1913.

Hetch Hetchy Reservoir Site: Hearing Before the Committee on Public Lands, United States Senate on the Joint Resolution (S.R. 123) to Allow the City and County of San Francisco to Exchange Lands for Reservoir Sites in Lake Eleanor and Hetch Hetchy Valleys in Yosemite National Park, and for Other Purposes. Wednesday, February 10, 1909. Washington, DC: Government Printing Office, 1909.

More Light on the Destructive Hetch Hetchy Scheme [pamphlet]. San Francisco: Society for the Preservation of National Parks, Western Branch, 1913.

Proceedings of the National Park Conference Held at the Yosemite National Park, October 14, 15, 16, 1912. Washington, DC: Government Printing Office, 1913. nps.gov.

Report on the Various Projects for the Water Supply of San Francisco, Cal.: Made to the Mayor, the Auditor, and the District Attorney, Constituting the Board of Water Commissioners. George H. Mendell. San Francisco: Spaulding and Barto, Steam Book and Job Printers, 1877.

Reports on the Water Supply of San Francisco, California: 1900 to 1908, Inclusive. C. E. Grunsky and Marsden Manson. San Francisco: Press of Britton and Rey, 1908.

Rodgers, Augustus Frederick. *Report to the Superintendent of the United States Coast Survey, the Honorable C. P. Patterson, on the Question of a Signal or Monument for the Summit of Mount Shasta, California.* May 8, 1875. Found in *Mount Shasta Annotated Bibliography*, ch. 21: "Literature: John Muir."

San Francisco and the Hetch Hetchy Reservoir: Hearings Held Before the Committee on the Public Lands of the House of Representatives, January 9 and 12, 1909, on H. J. Res. 223. Washington, DC: Government Printing Office, 1909. Google Books.

"Yosemite National Park Protection." 63rd Congress, 2d Session, House of Representatives. Mr. Raker, from the Committee on the Public Lands, submitted the following, Report no. 293, to accompany H.R. 12533. Feb. 20, 1914.

Books and Articles

"Accident at El Portal: Donkey Engine Wrecked and the Engineer Killed." *Merced Sun*, Dec. 11, 1911.

Albright, Horace M., and Marian Albright Schenck. *Creating the National Park Service: The Missing Years.* Norman: University of Oklahoma Press, 1999.

Arax, Mark. *The Dreamt Land: Chasing Water and Dust Across California.* New York: Knopf, 2019.

Archer and Bartoy, eds. *Between Dirt and Discussion: Methods, Methodology, and Interpretation in Historical Archaeology.* New York: Springer, 2006.

Badè, William Frederic. *The Life and Letters of John Muir*, vols. 1 and 2. Boston and New York: Houghton Mifflin Company, 1924.

———. "The Tuolumne Canyon." *San Francisco and the Hetch Hetchy Reservoir: Hearing Held Before the Committee on the Public Lands of the House of Representatives, January 9 and 12, 1909 on H. J. Res. 223*, pp. 226–31 (reprint of *Sierra Club Bulletin*, June 1905). Washington, DC: Government Printing Office, 1909.

Barker, Malcolm. *San Francisco Memoirs, 1835–1851: Eyewitness accounts of the birth of a city.* San Francisco: Londonborn Publications, 1994.

Barnes, Dwight. "Lumber Flume Dominated County." www.eclampusvitus .net/DBarnesFlume.html.

Barrus, Clara. "Camping with Burroughs and Muir." Excerpted from *Our Friend John Burroughs.* Boston: Houghton Mifflin, 1914.

Baur, John E. "In the Yosemite with John Muir." *Craftsman* 23 no. 3 (Dec. 1912): 324–35.

———. "A President Visits Los Angeles: Rutherford B. Hayes' Tour of 1880." *Historical Society of Southern California Quarterly* 37, no. 1 (1955): 33–47.

———. "With John o' the Birds and John o' the Mountains." *Century Magazine* 80, no. 4 (Aug. 1910). SC-JME.

Beasley, Maurine. "Kate Field and *Kate Field's Washington*: 1890–1895." *Records of the Columbia Historical Society* (Washington, DC) 49 (1973): 392–404.

Bingaman, John W. *Guardians of the Yosemite.* Desert Printers, 1961.

Bosco, Ronaldo A. "Historical Introduction." In *The Collected Works of Ralph Waldo Emerson, Volume VIII: Letters and Social Aims.* Cambridge, MA: Belknap Press of Harvard University Press, 1875.

Bowers, Edward A. "The Present Condition of the Forests on the Public Lands Source." *Publications of the American Economic Association* 6, no. 3 (May 1891): 57–74.

Branch, Michael B. "'Angel Guiding Gently': The Yosemite Meeting of Ralph Waldo Emerson and John Muir, 1871." *Western American Literature* 32, no. 2 (Summer 1997): 126–49.

Brands, H. W. *The Selected Letters of Theodore Roosevelt.* Lanham, MD: Rowman and Littlefield, 2006.

Braun, Adee. "Looking to Quell Sexual Urges? Consider the Graham Cracker." *Atlantic*, Jan. 15, 2014.

Brechin, Gray A. *Imperial San Francisco: Urban Power, Earthly Ruin.* Berkeley: University of California Press, 2001. Google Books.

Brewer, William Henry. *Up and Down California in 1860–1864: The Journal of William H. Brewer.* Edited by Francis P. Farquhar. New Haven: Yale University Press, 1930.

Brinkley, Douglas. *The Wilderness Warrior: Theodore Roosevelt and the Crusade for America.* New York: Harper Perennial, 2010.

Brown, David S. *The Last American Aristocrat.* New York: Scribner, 2020.

Browne, Janet. "Asa Gray and Charles Darwin: Corresponding Naturalists." *Harvard Papers in Botany* 15, no. 2 (2010): 209–20

Bunnell, Lafayette Houghton. *Discovery of Yosemite and the Indian War of 1851.* New York: Fleming H. Revell, 1892.

Burgess, Jack. "The Yosemite Valley Railroad." www.yosemitevalleyrr.com/prototype/history.

Burroughs, John. John Burroughs Journal, 1896 (May–Sept.). Vassar College Archives and Special Collections.

Butt, Archie. *The Letters of Archie Butt.* New York: Doubleday Page, 1924.

Calderwood, G. W. "John Muir and the Reporter." *Oakland Ledger*, July 1, 1889, 10. UPL. NB: This date cannot be correct since the article about Muir referred to in this story was not written until the night of July 3 and was published on July 4, 1889.

Clark, Galen. *The Big Trees of California: Their History and Characteristics.* Yosemite Valley: Galen Clark, 1907.

———. "Early Days in Yosemite" (originally "A Plea for Yosemite," 1907). Los Angeles: Docter Press, 1964. Yosemite Online.

———. *Indians of the Yosemite Valley and Vicinity.* Yosemite Valley: Galen Clark, 1907.

———. *The Yosemite Valley: Its History, Characteristic Features, and Theories Regarding Its Origin.* Yosemite Valley: Nelson L. Salter, 1910.

Clark, Jean Hanna, and Shirley Sargent, eds. *Dear Papa: Letters Between John Muir and His Daughter Wanda.* Fresno: Panorama West Books, 1985.

Clayton, John. *Natural Rivals: John Muir, Gifford Pinchot, and the Creation of America's Public Lands.* New York: Pegasus Books, 2019.

Clements, Kendrick A. "Politics and the Park: San Francisco's Fight for Hetch Hetchy, 1908–1913." *Pacific Historical Review* 48, no. 2 (1979): 185–215.

Coate, Bill. "Madera Almost Died in Infancy." *Madera Tribune*, May 2, 2017.

Cohen, Michael P. *The History of the Sierra Club: 1892–1970.* San Francisco: Sierra Club Books, 1988.

Colby, William E. "Edward Taylor Parsons Tribute." *Sierra Club Bulletin* 9, no. 4 (Jan. 1915).

———. "John Muir—President of the Sierra Club." *Sierra Club Bulletin*, "John Muir Memorial Number," Jan. 1916.

———. "Reminiscences of William Edward Colby: Oral History Transcript/1953–1954. Interview by Corrine L. Gilb, Bancroft Library, University of California.

Colwell, Mary. *John Muir: The Scotsman Who Saved America's Wild Places*. Oxford, England: Lion Hudson, 2014.

Cornelius, Brother. *Keith: Old Master of California*. vol. 1. New York: G. P. Putnam's Sons, 1942.

———. *Keith: Old Master of California*. vol. 2. Fresno: Academy Library Guild, 1956.

Curry, Timothy J., and Kiernan O. Gordon. "Muir, Roosevelt, and Yosemite National Park as an Emergent Sacred Symbol." *Symbolic Interaction* 40, no. 2 (2017): 247–62.

Deverell, William. *Railroad Crossing: Californians and the Railroad, 1850–1910*. Berkeley: University of California Press, 1996.

Diamant, Rolf, and Ethan Carr. *Olmsted and Yosemite: Civil War, Abolition, and the National Park Idea*. Amherst, MA: Library of American Landscape History, 2022.

Dilsaver, Lary M., and William C. Tweed. *Challenge of the Big Trees*. Three Rivers, CA: Sequoia Natural History Association, 1990.

Drobnicki, John A. "Bowers, Edward Augustus." In *Biographical Dictionary of American and Canadian Naturalists and Environmentalists*, edited by Keir B. Sterling et al., 95–96. Westport, CT: Greenwood Press, 1997.

Ehrlich, Gretel. *John Muir: Nature's Visionary*. Washington, DC: National Geographic Society, 2000.

Eichom, Arthur Francis. *The Mount Shasta Story: Being a Concise History of the Famous California Mountain*. Mount Shasta, CA: Mount Shasta Herald, 1987.

Elder, John C. "John Muir and the Literature of Wilderness." *Massachusetts Review* 22, no. 2 (1981): 375–86.

Ellison, Olaf. "The Mountain Heart's Ease (John Muir)." *Camera Craft* (San Francisco) 1, no. 4 (Aug. 1900): 167–72.

Emerson, Ellen T. "Through the Tuolumne Cañon." *Sierra Club Bulletin* 9, no. 4 (Jan. 1915): 258–60.

Emerson, Ralph Waldo. *Nature*. Boston: James Munroe, 1836.

Farmer, Jared. *Trees in Paradise*. New York: Norton, 2013.

Farquhar, Francis P. *History of the Sierra Nevada*. Berkeley: University of California Press in Collaboration with the Sierra Club, 1965.

Fedarko, Kevin. *The Emerald Mile: The Epic Story of the Fastest Ride in History Through the Heart of the Grand Canyon*. New York: Scribner, 2013.

Fleck, Richard. "A Note on John Muir and the Appalachian Mountain Club." *Appalachia*, n.s., 50, no. 3, #200 (June 15, 1995). SC-JME.

Fox, Stephen. *John Muir and His Legacy: The American Conservation Movement*. Boston: Little, Brown, 1981.

Fraser, Caroline. "In Scotland's Search for Roots, a Push to Restore Wild Lands." *YaleEnvironment360*, Sept. 16, 2010.

Freeman, John Ripley. *On the Proposed Use of a Portion of the Hetch Hetchy, Eleanor and Cherry Valleys—Within and Near to the Boundaries of the Stanislaus U.S. National Forest Reserve and the Yosemite National Park—as Reservoirs for Impounding Tuolumne River Flood Waters and Appurtenant Works for the Water Supply of San Francisco and Neighboring Cities: A Report to James Rolph, Jr., Mayor of San Francisco, and Percy V. Long, City Attorney*. San Francisco: Rincon, 1912.

Gessner, David. *Leave It as It Is: A Journey Through Theodore Roosevelt's American Wilderness*. New York: Simon & Schuster, 2020.

Gifford, Terry, ed. *John Muir: His Life and Letters and Other Writings*. London: Bâton Wicks; and Seattle: Mountaineers, 1996.

———. "John Muir's Literary Science." *Public Domain Review*. Adapted from ch. 3 of Gifford's book *Reconnecting with John Muir: Essays in Post-Pastoral Practice*. Athens: University of Georgia Press, 2006.

Gilman, William H., et al. *The Journals and Miscellaneous Notebooks of Ralph Waldo Emerson*. 16 vols. Cambridge: Harvard University Press, 1960–82.

Gisel, Bonnie Johanna. *Kindred & Related Spirits: The Letters of John Muir and Jeanne C. Carr*. Salt Lake City: University of Utah Press, 2001.

Grunsky, C. E. "Report Upon a System of Sewerage for the City and County of San Francisco." San Francisco: Hinton Printing, 1899. Google Books.

Hampton, Duane H. *How the U.S. Cavalry Saved Our National Parks*. Bloomington: Indiana University Press, 2017 (paperback reprint of 1971 original).

Hanna, Bill. "John Muir Hanna: A Biography." *John Muir Newsletter* (Stockton, CA: University of the Pacific) 17, no. 4 (Fall 2007):1, 4–7.

Hanson, Warren D., Anne Milner, and Franz T. Hansell. *San Francisco Water and Power: A History of the Municipal Water Department & Hetch Hetchy System*. 6th ed. San Francisco: City and County of San Francisco, 2005. OCLC 60658054.

Harrison, Alfred C., et al. *The Comprehensive Keith: The Hundred Year History of the Saint Mary's College Collection of Works by William Keith*. Moraga, CA: Hearst Art Gallery, Saint Mary's College of California, 2011.

Hartesveldt, Richard J., et al. *The Giant Sequoia of the Sierra Nevada*. Washington, DC: National Park Service, US Department of the Interior, 1975.

Hayes, Samuel P. *Conservation and the Gospel of Efficiency: The Progressive Conservation Movement, 1890–1920*. Pittsburgh: University of Pittsburgh Press, 1999. Originally published by Harvard University Press, 1959.

Heacox, Kim. *John Muir and the Ice That Started a Fire*. Guilford, CT: Lyons Press, 2014.

Hickman, Leo. "How a Giant Tree's Death Sparked the Conservation Movement 160 Years Ago." *Guardian*, June 27, 2013.

Hobbs, William Herbert. "The Grand Eruption of Vesuvius in 1906." *The Journal of Geology* 14, no. 7 (Oct.–Nov. 1906).

Huntley, Jen A. *The Making of Yosemite: James Mason Hutchings and the Origin of America's Most Popular National Park.* Lawrence: University Press of Kansas, 2011.

Hutchings, James M. "California for Waterfalls!" *San Francisco Daily California Chronicle*, August 18, 1855.

————. "The Great Yo-Semite Valley." *Hutchings' Illustrated California Magazine*, Oct. 1859.

————. *In the Heart of the Sierras.* Yosemite Valley: Old Cabin; and Oakland: Pacific Press, 1888.

————. *Scenes of Wonder and Curiosity in California.* 2nd ed. San Francisco: J. M. Hutchings, 1862.

Hutchinson, Elizabeth. "They Might Be Giants: Carleton Watkins, Galen Clark, and the Big Tree." *October* (MIT Press) 109 (Summer 2004): 46–63.

Jackson, Donald C. "The Engineer as Lobbyist: John R. Freeman and the Hetch Hetchy Dam (1910–13)." *Environmental History* (University of Chicago Press) 21, no. 2 (Apr. 2016): 288–314. journals.uchicago.edu.

John, Arthur. *The Best Years of the Century: Richard Watson Gilder, Scribner's Monthly and Century Magazine, 1870–1909.* Urbana: University of Illinois Press, 1981.

Johnson, Robert Underwood. "The Care of the Yosemite Valley." *Century*, "Topics of the Time" 39, no. 3 (Jan. 1890): 474–75.

————. "Destructive Tendencies in the Yosemite Valley: Letters from Visitors, III." *Century*, "Open Letters" 39, no. 3 (Jan. 1890): 477–78.

————. "The Forest Commission's Great Public Service." *Century* 54 (May–Oct. 1897).

————. "Hetch Hetchy." *Collier's: The National Weekly* 52, no. 6 (Oct. 25, 1913): 24–25.

————. "A High Price to Pay for Water—Apropos of the Grant of the Hetch Hetchy Valley to San Francisco for a Reservoir." *Century*. Reprinted in *San Francisco and the Hetch Hetchy Reservoir*, 125–26.

————. "Noble, Conservationist." Letter to the editor of the *New York Times*, Mar. 25, 1912. Timesmachine.nytimes.com.

————. "Patriotism That Counts: The Successful Conference at the White House on the Conservation of Our Natural Resources." *Century* 76 (May–Oct. 1908): 474–76.

————. "Personal Impressions of John Muir." *Outlook*, June 3, 1905.

————. *Remembered Yesterdays.* Boston: Little, Brown, 1923.

Johnston, Hank. "A Camping Trip with Roosevelt and Muir." *Yosemite: A Journal for Members of the Yosemite Association* 56, no. 3 (Summer 1994): 2–4. Yosemite Association, Yosemite Online.

————. *Short Line to Paradise: The Story of the Yosemite Valley Railroad.* Rev. 8th ed. Yosemite: Flying Spur Press, 2008.

————. *They Felled the Redwoods: A Saga of Flumes and Rails in the High Sierra.* 3rd ed. Los Angeles: Trans-Anglo Books, 1974.

————. *Thunder in the Mountains: The Life and Times of the Madera Sugar Pine Company.* Rev. ed. Fish Camp, CA, 2006.

————. *The Whistles Blow No More: Railroad Logging in the Sierra Nevada, 1874–1942.* Glendale, CA: Trans-Anglo Books, 1984.

————. *Yosemite's Yesterdays.* Rev. 4th ed. Yosemite: Flying Spur Press, 2014.

Jones, R. Holway. *John Muir and the Sierra Club: The Battle for Yosemite.* San Francisco: The Sierra Club, 1965.

Kaufman, Polly Welts. *National Parks and Woman's Voice: A History.* Updated ed. Albuquerque: University of New Mexico Press, 2006.

Keeler, Charles. "Recollections of John Muir." *Sierra Club Bulletin,* "John Muir Memorial Number" 10, no. 1 (Jan. 1916). SC-JME.

Keith, William. "An Artist's Trip in the Sierra Nevada: Yosemite Valley, July 5th, 1875." *Overland Monthly and Out West Magazine* (San Francisco: John H. Carmany) 15 (1875):198–201.

Keough, James. "Advise and Dissent: Warren Olney and the Club." Sierra Club website. Originally, *Sierra* magazine, Feb./Mar. 1978.

Key, Pierre V. R. *Enrico Caruso: A Biography.* Boston: Little, Brown, 1922.

Kneeland, Samuel. *The Wonders of the Yosemite Valley, and of California.* Boston: A. Moore, 1871.

Lane, Franklin K. "Petition for Review by Hon. Franklin K. Lane, City Attorney, to the Secretary of the Interior." Feb. 24, 1903.

LeConte, Joseph. *A Journal of Ramblings Through the High Sierra.* Yosemite National Park: Yosemite Association, 1994.

Leidig, Charles. "Charlie Leidig's Report of President Roosevelt's Visit in May, 1903." Recorded and filed in the Yosemite Research Library. SC-JME.

Lekisch, Barbara. *Embracing Scenes about Lakes Tahoe & Donner: Painters, Illustrators & Sketch Artists, 1855–1915.* Lafayette, CA: Great West Books, 2003. Google Books.

Lunde, Darrin. *The Naturalist: Theodore Roosevelt, a Lifetime of Exploration, and the Triumph of American Natural History.* New York: Crown, 2016.

MacKenzie, George G. "Destructive Tendencies in the Yosemite Valley. Letter from Visitors." *Century* 39, no. 3 (Jan. 1890): 474–79.

————. "The Yosemite Despoilers: A Reply to Gov. Waterman's Statements." *New York Times*, Mar. 23, 1890.

Mair, Aaron, Chad Hanson, and Mary Ann Nelson. "Who Was John Muir, Really?" *Earth Island Journal*, Aug. 11, 2021.

McAleer, John. *Ralph Waldo Emerson: Days of Encounter.* Boston: Little, Brown, 1984.

Merriam, C. Hart. "To the Memory of John Muir." *Sierra Club Bulletin* 10, no. 2 (Jan. 1917). SC-JME.

Merrill, Samuel. "John Muir and Ralph Waldo Emerson in Yosemite." 1934. In *Voices for the Earth: A Treasury of the Sierra Club Bulletin, 1893–1977,* edited by Ann Gilliam. San Francisco: Sierra Club Books, 1979.

————. "Personal Recollections of John Muir." A campfire talk at Moraine Lake, July 17, 1927. In Gifford, *John Muir,* 892–98.

Merry, Robert W. *A Country of Vast Designs.* New York: Simon and Schuster, 2009.

Miesse, William C. *Mount Shasta: An Annotated Bibliography.* Weed, CA: College of the Siskiyous, 1993.

Miller, Char. *Gifford Pinchot and the Making of Modern Environmentalism.* Washington, DC: Island Press, 2001.

Miller, Sally M., and Daryl Morrison, eds. *John Muir: Family, Friends, and Adventures.* Albuquerque: University of New Mexico Press, 2005.

————. "The Greening of Gifford Pinchot." *Environmental History Review* 13 (Fall 1992): 1–20.

Molenaar, Dee. *The Challenge of Rainier.* Seattle: Mountaineers, 1971.

Monroe, Harriet. "Camping Above the Yosemite: A Summer Outing with the Sierra Club." *Putnam's Monthly* 6 (Apr. 1909–Sept. 1909): 216–27.

Moores, Merrill. "Recollections of John Muir as a Young Man." Manuscript, n.d. UPL.

Muir, John. "An Adventure with a Dog and a Glacier." *Century* 54, no. 5 (Sept. 1897).

————. "The American Forests." *Atlantic Monthly*, Aug. 1897.

————. "Autobiography." Unpublished. UPL.

————. "The Calypso Borealis. Botanical Enthusiasm. From Prof. J. D. Butler." *Boston Recorder* 1 (1866). John Muir Bibliography Resource. UPL. For a later version of this experience, see vol. 1, no. 366: 120–21. See also no. 495.

————. *Edward Henry Harriman.* Garden City, NY: Doubleday, Page, 1911. Yosemite Online.

————. "Edward Taylor Parsons Tribute." *Sierra Club Bulletin* 9, no. 4 (Jan. 1915).

————. "The Endangered Valley—the Hetch Hetchy Valley in the Yosemite National Park." SC-JME.

————. "Explorations in the Great Tuolumne Cañon." *Overland Monthly* 11, no. 2 (Aug. 1873): 139–47.

————. "Features of the Proposed Yosemite National Park." *Century* 40, no. 5 (Sept. 1890).

————. "Forests of the Sierra. The Destruction That Is Being Wrought in the Mountains." *San Francisco Daily Evening Bulletin*, June 29, 1889.

————. "God's First Temples. How Shall We Preserve Our Forests? The Question Considered by John Muir." *Sacramento Daily Record-Union*, Feb. 9, 1876. UPL.

————. "Great Evils Resulting from the Destruction of Forests." *San Francisco Real Estate Circular*, n.d.

————. "The Hetch Hetchy Valley." *Boston Weekly Transcript*, Mar. 25, 1873.

————. "The Hetch Hetchy Valley." *Sierra Club Bulletin* 6, no. 4 (1908): 211–20.

————. "The Humming-Bird of the California Water-Falls." *Scribner's Monthly* 15, no. 4 (Feb. 1, 1878).

————. "Hunting Big Redwoods." *Atlantic*, Sept. 1901.

————. "In the Yo-Semite. Holidays Among the Rocks. Wild Weather—A Picturesque Christmas Dinner—Idyllic Amusements—Poetic Storms—A Paradise of Clouds. Yo-Semite Valley, Jan. 1." *New York Weekly Tribune*, Mar. 13, 1872. UPL.

————. "Journals: July 1867–February 1868." Unpublished. UPL.

————. *Letters to a Friend: Written to Mrs. Ezra S. Carr, 1866–1879.* Boston and New York: Houghton Mifflin, 1915.

————. "Linnaeus (1707–1778)." In *Library of the World's Best Literature*, vol. 16, edited by Charles Dudley Warner. New York: R. S. Peale and J. A. Hill, 1896.

————. "Living Glaciers of California." *Overland Monthly* 9, no. 6 (Dec. 1872): 547–49.

————. *The Mountains of California.* New York: Dorset Press, 1988. Originally published 1894.

————. "Muir on Caminetti's Bill. The Author and Explorer Says Its Passage Would Be Disastrous to the Yosemite." *San Francisco Examiner*, Jan. 15, 1895. UPL.

————. *My First Summer in the Sierra.* Introduction by Gretel Ehrlich. New York: Penguin Books, 1987. Originally published by Houghton Mifflin, 1911.

————. "The National Parks and Forest Reservations." Speech, Proceedings of the Meeting of the Sierra Club Held Nov. 23, 1895. *Sierra Club Bulletin* 7 (1896): 271–84. SC-JME.

————. *Our National Parks.* Boston and New York: Houghton Mifflin, 1901. Reprint, New York: Laglace Classic, 2020.

————. "A Ramble in the Sierra." From an address to the Sierra Club. *Pacific Educational Journal* 12, no. 5 (May 1896): 203–11.

————. "Rescue Forest, Says John Muir. White Mountain Despoilers Are Called Thieves and Rascals by Famous Naturalist. Interest Must Be Fought. Marvels of Yosemite Pictured by Man Who Has Given Life to Studies." (1911). *John Muir: A Reading Bibliography by Kimes.* UPL.

————. "A Rival of the Yosemite: The Cañon of the South Fork of Kings River, California." *Century* 43 (Nov. 1891): 77–97.

————. "Salmon Breeding." *San Francisco Daily Evening Bulletin*, Oct. 29, 1874, 1.

————. "Shasta in Winter." *San Francisco Daily Evening Bulletin*, Dec. 21, 1874, 1.

————. "The Snakes of Fresno. John Muir Says They Will Kill Hogs and Eat Rabbits. Some Queer Experiences of a Geologist in the Hights [*sic*] of the Sierras." Unattributed interview of Muir. *San Francisco Daily Examiner*, July 4, 1889. UPL.

————. "The Snow." *San Francisco Daily Evening Bulletin*, June 22, 1889.

————. "Snow-Storm on Mount Shasta." *Harper's New Monthly Magazine* 55, no. 328 (Sept. 1877): 521–530.

————. *Steep Trails: California, Utah, Nevada, Washington, Oregon, the Grand Canyon.* Boston and New York: Houghton Mifflin, 1928.

————. *Stickeen.* Boston and New York: Houghton Mifflin, 1915.

————. *Studies in the Sierra.* San Francisco: Sierra Club, 1950.

————. *A Thousand-Mile Walk to the Gulf.* Boston and New York: Houghton Mifflin (Riverside Press Cambridge), 1916.

————. "The Treasures of the Yosemite." *Century* 40, no. 4 (Aug. 1890).

————. *The Wilder Muir: The Curious Nature of John Muir.* Yosemite National Park: Yosemite Conservancy, 2017.

————. *The Wild Muir: Twenty-two of John Muir's Greatest Adventures.* Yosemite National Park: Yosemite Conservancy, 1994.

————. "The Wild Parks and Forest Reservations of the West." *Atlantic Monthly*, Jan. 1898, 15–28.

————. "A Wind Storm in the Forests of the Yuba." *Scribner's Monthly* 17, no. 1 (Nov. 1, 1878).

————. "Yosemite Valley. Beauties of the Landscape in Early Summer." *San Francisco Daily Evening Bulletin*, Jun. 21, 1889. UPL.

————. "Yosemite Valley in Flood." *Overland Monthly* 8, no. 4 (Apr. 1872): 347–50. UPL.

Niderost, Eric. "The Great 1906 San Francisco Earthquake and Fire." *American History*, Apr. 2006. Historynet.com.

Norton, Mark. "The Karl Marx Tree: How Southern Pacific Railroad Killed a Socialist Colony in the Name of Creating Yosemite National Park." 48Hills, Aug. 27, 2014. 48hills.org.

Olmsted, Frederick Law. "Yosemite and the Mariposa Grove: A Preliminary Report, 1865." Yosemite Online.

Parsons, Edward T. "The Sierra Club Outing to Tuolumne Meadows." *Sierra Club Bulletin* 4, no. 1 (Jan. 1902): 19–22.

Parsons, Marion Randall. "Book Review: *Travels in Alaska* by John Muir." *Sierra Club Bulletin* 10, no. 1 (Jan. 1916): 121–22.

———. "John Muir and the Alaska Book." *Sierra Club Bulletin*, "John Muir Memorial Number," Jan. 1916.

Pauly, Steve. "The Importance of John Muir's First Public Lecture, Sacramento, 1876." *The John Muir Newsletter*, vol. 9, no. 1 (Winter 1998–99). Stockton: University of the Pacific.

Pauly, Steve, and Patty Pauly. "Louie Strentzel Muir: A Biography." SC-JME.

"Phelan Distinguished Son of City; Mayor of San Francisco Three Terms." *San Francisco Chronicle*, Aug. 8, 1930.

Pillsbury, Arthur C. *Picturing Miracles of Plant and Animal Life*. Philadelphia: J. B. Lippincott, 1937.

Pinchot, Gifford. *Breaking New Ground*. 4th. ed. Washington, DC: Island Press, 1998.

Piper, C. V. "Flora of Mount Rainier." *Mazama* 2 (Apr. 1901): 93–118.

———. "A Narrow Escape." *Mountaineer* 8 (1915): 52–53.

Powers, Ron. *Mark Twain: A Life*. New York: Free Press, 2005.

"President Teddy Roosevelt Visits Yosemite—May 15–18, 1903: A Camping Trip with Roosevelt and Muir." Arthur C. Pillsbury Foundation website.

Punke, Michael. *Last Stand: George Bird Grinnell, the Battle to Save the Buffalo, and the Birth of the New West*. Lincoln: University of Nebraska Press, 2007.

Purdy, Jedediah. *After Nature: A Politics for the Anthropocene*. Cambridge, MA: Harvard University Press, 2015.

———. "Environmentalism's Racist History." *The New Yorker*, Aug. 13, 2015.

Renehan, Edward J. *John Burroughs: An American Naturalist*. Post Mills, VT: Chelsea Green, 1992.

"Republicans Block Hetch Hetchy Scheme." *New York Tribune*, Oct. 5, 1913, 12.

Righter, Robert W. *The Battle over Hetch Hetchy: America's Most Controversial Dam and the Birth of Modern Environmentalism*. New York: Oxford University Press, 2005.

Robinson, Charles D. "The King's River Cañon: The Story of an Artist's Exploring Trip Through It." *Kate Field's Washington* (Washington, DC) 4, no. 20 (Nov. 11, 1891).

Roosevelt, Theodore. *An Autobiography.* 1913. SC-JME.

———. "John Muir: An Appreciation." *Outlook* 109 (Jan. 16, 1915): 27–28.

Rothman, Lily. "Picturing the Wild: How One Photographer Helped Give Birth to the National Park Service." *Time*, n.d. Time.com.

Rothman, Lily, and Liz Ronk. "These 1861 Photographs Helped Save America's Wilderness." Time.com, Aug. 22, 2016.

Rusk, Ralph L. *The Letters of Ralph Waldo Emerson.* vol. 6. New York: Columbia University Press, 1939.

Russell, Carl P. *One Hundred Years in Yosemite: The Story of a Great Park and Its Friends.* Berkeley and Los Angeles: University of California Press, 1947.

Sanborn, Margaret. *Yosemite–Its Discovery, Its Wonders & Its People.* New York: Random House, 1981.

Sargent, Shirley. *Galen Clark: Yosemite Guardian.* Rev. 4th ed. Yosemite: Flying Spur Press, 2001.

———. *Wawona's Yesterdays.* Yosemite: Yosemite Natural History Association, 1961. Yosemite Online.

Scharnhorst, Gary. *Kate Field: The Many Lives of a Nineteenth-Century American Journalist.* Syracuse: Syracuse University Press, 2008.

Schneider, John, curator. *William Keith and the Battle for Hetch Hetchy.* Catalog for art exhibit.

Schuknecht, Catherine. "10 Things You Didn't Know About the Sierra Club's Founding." *Sierra: The Magazine of the Sierra Club*, May 26, 2016.

Shoop, C. Fred. "Wife of John Muir Remarkable Woman: Helen Muir Pens Fine Tribute to Mother." *Pasadena Star-News*, May 22, 1963.

Simpson, John Warfield. *Dam!: Water, Power, Politics, and Preservation in Hetch Hetchy and Yosemite National Park.* New York: Pantheon Books, 2005.

Smith, David A. "Yosemite: The Cavalry Years." n.d. www.militarymuseum.org/YosemiteCavalry.html.

Soulé, Frank, and John H. Gihon and James Nisbet. *The Annals of San Francisco.* New York: D. Appleton & Co., 1855.

Steen, Harold K., ed. *The Conservation Diaries of Gifford Pinchot.* Durham, NC: Forest History Society, 2001.

———. *The U.S. Forest Service: A History, Centennial Edition.* Durham, NC, and Seattle: Forest History Society and University of Washington Press, 2004.

St. George, Zach. "They Seem to Be Immortal: The Expansive, Ongoing Fight to Save the Sequoias." *Guernica*, Apr. 15, 2015.

Strother, French. "Three Days with John Muir." *World's Work* 17, no. 5 (Mar. 1909).

"Sugar Pine Company Pioneer in Industry." *Madera Tribune* 40, no. 2 (May 3, 1927).

Swett, John. "John Muir." *Century* 46, no. 1 (May 1893): 120–23.

Taylor, H. J. "James Mason Hutchings." In *Yosemite Indians and Other Sketches.* 1936. Yosemite Online.

Taylor, Ray W. *Hetch Hetchy: The Story of San Francisco's Struggle to Provide a Water Supply for Her Future Needs.* San Francisco: Ricardo J. Orozco, 1926.

Thayer, James Bradley. *A Western Journey with Mr. Emerson.* Boston: Little, Brown, 1884. Calisphere, University of California.

Thomas, Gordon, and Max Morgan Witts. *The San Francisco Earthquake.* New York: Stein and Day, 1971.

Thomas, Peter, and Donna Thomas, eds. *Anywhere That Is Wild: John Muir's First Walk to Yosemite.* Yosemite National Park: Yosemite Conservancy, 2018.

———. Muir Ramble Route: Walking from San Francisco to Yosemite in the Footsteps of John Muir. Lake Isabella, CA: Poetic Matrix Press, 2010.

Tilton, Eleanor M., and Ralph L. Rusk, eds. *The Letters of Ralph Waldo Emerson.* New York: Columbia University Press, 1939.

Tod, John. "Traveling Companions. How William Keith and John Muir Did Europe Together Without Meeting." *San Francisco Call*, June 13, 1897, 19.

Turner, Frederick Jackson. "The Significance of the Frontier in American History." Paper read at the meeting of the American Historical Association in Chicago, July 12, 1893, during the World Columbian Exposition. Excerpts. National Humanities Center website.

Tweed, William C., and Lary M. Dilsaver. *Challenge of the Big Trees: The Updated History of Sequoia and Kings Canyon National Parks.* Staunton, VA: George F. Thompson, Feb. 20, 2017.

Voices of the People: The Traditionally Associated Tribes of Yosemite National Park. San Francisco: Yosemite Conservancy, 2021.

Walsh, James P., and Timothy J. O'Keefe. *Legacy of a Native Son: James Duval Phelan & Villa Montalvo.* Portales, NM: Forbes Mill Press, 1993.

Warner, Arthur Churchill. "Essay: John Muir's Ascent of Mt. Rainier." Transcription of recording, Dec. 28, 1956. *Mountaineer* 50, no. 1 (1957): 38–45. Website of University of Washington, University Libraries.

White, Graham, ed. *Sacred Summits: John Muir's Greatest Climbs.* Edinburgh: Canongate, 1999.

Williams, Gerald W., and Char Miller. "At the Creation: The National Forest Commission of 1896–97." *Forest History Today* (Spring/Fall 2005): 32–41.

Wolfe, Linnie Marsh, ed. *John of the Mountains: The Unpublished Journals of John Muir.* 2nd ed. Madison: University of Wisconsin Press, 1979.

———. *Son of the Wilderness: The Life of John Muir.* New York: Alfred A. Knopf, 1945.

Wood, Harold W., Jr., "John Muir in Indiana." Apr. 5, 2003. SC-JME.

———. "John Muir Misquoted." SC-JME.

———. "Was John Muir a Draft Dodger?" SC-JME.

Worster, Donald. *A Passion for Nature: The Life of John Muir.* Oxford and New York: Oxford University Press, 2008.

Yelverton, Thérèse. *Zanita: A Tale of the Yo-Semite.* Berkeley, CA: Ten Speed Press, 1991. Originally published New York: Hurd and Houghton, 1872.

"Yosemite Lumber Co. Closes Successful Season in the Hills." *Merced County Sun*, Nov. 14, 1913.

Young, S. Hall. *Alaska Days with John Muir.* New York: Fleming H. Revell, 1915.

Zito, Salena. "The Flood of 1889: The Day Lake Conemaugh Destroyed Johnstown." *Richmond Times-Dispatch*, Apr. 14, 2021.

Image Credits

Interior Credits

190–91 From the *Sierra Club Bulletin,* January 1908; courtesy of Wikimedia
202 Courtesy of the Sierra Club; text source: Wolfe, *John,* 347
210 Courtesy of the Library of Congress
213 Courtesy of Yosemite National Park (UC National Park Service)
228 John Muir Papers, Holt-Atherton Special Collections, University of the Pacific Library. © 1984 Muir-Hanna Trust
236–37 Courtesy of the California Historical Society
276–77 Courtesy of the US National Park Service
301 John Muir Papers, Holt-Atherton Special Collections, University of the Pacific Library. © 1984 Muir-Hanna Trust
314 Courtesy of UC Berkeley, Bancroft Library
326 Courtesy of the Library of Congress
327 Courtesy of the Library of Congress
343 Courtesy of UC Berkeley, Bancroft Library
358 Courtesy of the John Muir National Historic Site (US National Park Service)
359 Courtesy of the Library of Congress

Insert Credits

1 John Muir Papers, Holt-Atherton Special Collections, University of the Pacific Library. © 1984 Muir-Hanna Trust
2 Courtesy of the US National Park Service
3 Author photo
4 Courtesy of the Library of Congress
5 Courtesy of the California Historical Society
6 California Historical Society Collection at the University of Southern California
7 Courtesy of San Joaquin Valley Library System
8 Courtesy of the Library of Congress
9 Courtesy of the US National Park Service
10 Courtesy of the Library of Congress
11 Courtesy of the Library of Congress
12 Courtesy of the John Muir National Historic Site (US National Park Service)
13 Courtesy of the John Muir National Historic Site (US National Park Service)
14 Courtesy of the New York Public Library
15 Courtesy of Wikimedia Commons
16 *Remembered Yesterdays* (Little, Brown and Company, 1923) and the *New York Times* May 3, 1910

17 Courtesy of UC Berkeley, Bancroft Library
18 Courtesy of the Library of Congress; text source: Johnson, *Remembered Yesterdays*, 295–96
19 Courtesy of Saint Mary's College Museum of Art
20 Courtesy of Saint Mary's College Museum of Art; text source: Wolfe, *John*, 189
21 Courtesy of the Library of Congress; text source: Cornelius, *Keith: Old Master of California*, 597
22 Courtesy of UC Berkeley, Bancroft Library
23 Courtesy of the New York Public Library
24 Courtesy of the US National Park Service, SEKI Historic Images
25 Courtesy of the US National Park Service, SEKI Historic Images
26 Courtesy of the US National Park Service, SEKI Historic Images
27 Courtesy of the Library of Congress
28 Courtesy of the Library of Congress
29 Courtesy of the Library of Congress
30 Courtesy of the Library of Congress
31 Courtesy of UC Berkeley, Bancroft Library, M. M. O'Shaughnessy photograph collection
32 Courtesy of the John Muir National Historic Site (US National Park Service)
33 Courtesy of the John Muir National Historic Site (US National Park Service)
34 Courtesy of the John Muir National Historic Site (US National Park Service)
35 The Freeman Report
36 Courtesy of the Library of Congress
37 Courtesy of the UC Berkeley, Bancroft Library
38 John Muir Papers, Holt-Atherton Special Collections, University of the Pacific Library. © 1984 Muir-Hanna Trust
39 Courtesy of the Library of Congress
40 *Remembered Yesterdays*, 134
41 Courtesy of the Library of Congress

Index

Page numbers in *italics* refer to illustrations.

About the Author

Dean King is an award-winning author of ten nonfiction books, including *Skeletons on the Zahara*, *Unbound*, *Patrick O'Brian: A Life Revealed*, and *The Feud*. His writing has appeared in the *Wall Street Journal*, *American Heritage*, *Granta*, *Garden & Gun*, *National Geographic Adventure*, *Outside*, *New York*, and the *New York Times*. He is the chief storyteller in two History Channel documentaries and a producer of its series *Hatfields & McCoys: White Lightning*. An internationally known speaker, King has appeared on NPR's *Talk of the Nation*, ABC's *World News Tonight*, PBS's *American Experience*, BBC Radio, Arte TV France/Germany, and at TEDx.